OXFORD COGNITIVE SCIENCE SERIES

Bayesian Rationality

OXFORD COGNITIVE SCIENCE SERIES

General Editors
MARTIN DAVIES, JAMES HIGGINBOTHAM, PHILIP JOHNSON-LAIRD,
CHRISTOPHER PEACOCKE, AND KIM PLUNKETT

Also published in the series

Concepts: Where Cognitive Science Went Wrong
Jerry A. Fodor

Context and Content
Robert C. Stalnaker

*Mindreading: An Integrated Account of Pretense, Self-awareness and
Understanding Other Minds.*
Shaun Nichols and Stephen Stich

Face and Mind: The Science of Face Perception
Andy Young

Reference and Consciousness
John Campbell

Seeing Reason: Image and Language in Learning to Think
Keith Stenning

Ways of Seeing: The Scope and Limits of Visual Cognition
Pierre Jacob and Marc Jeannerod

If
Jonathon St. B. T. Evans and David E. Over

Bayesian Rationality
The Probabilistic Approach to Human Reasoning

Mike Oaksford
Birkbeck College London

Nick Chater
University College London

UNIVERSITY PRESS

This book has been printed digitally and produced in a standard specification in order to ensure its continuing availability

OXFORD
UNIVERSITY PRESS

Great Clarendon Street, Oxford OX2 6DP

Oxford University Press is a department of the University of Oxford.
It furthers the University's objective of excellence in research, scholarship,
and education by publishing worldwide in

Oxford New York

Auckland Cape Town Dar es Salaam Hong Kong Karachi
Kuala Lumpur Madrid Melbourne Mexico City Nairobi
New Delhi Shanghai Taipei Toronto
With offices in
Argentina Austria Brazil Chile Czech Republic France Greece
Guatemala Hungary Italy Japan South Korea Poland Portugal
Singapore Switzerland Thailand Turkey Ukraine Vietnam

ISBN 978-0-19-852450-2

1005722995

Contents

Preface

This book is the product of twenty years of joint work on the cognitive science of human reasoning that began when we were both post-graduate students at the Centre for Cognitive Science at the University of Edinburgh. The mid-eighties was a tremendously exciting time to be studying cognitive science. Phil Johnson-Laird had recently published his groundbreaking monograph, *Mental models* (Johnson-Laird 1983) which gave a remarkable demonstration of how a single computational framework might encompass reasoning, language understanding and consciousness. At the same time, there was a spectacular flourishing of what became known as connectionism, pioneered by Hinton, Rumelhart, and McClelland. Both seemed to represent quite radical departures from what had been the dominant view in the previous phase of cognitive science research, based on symbolic, logic-based models from artificial intelligence. But it was unclear how, or whether, these new developments could be integrated.

These developments were particularly exciting because prior approaches in cognitive science appeared to have run into the sand. Logic-based approaches to cognition appeared to be viable for mathematical theorem proving and simple formal game playing, but seemed fundamentally ill-suited to representation and reasoning with real-world, common sense knowledge. As students at the Centre for Cognitive Science, this was embodied in the maxim that no PhD student should pursue a project that presupposed a solution to the 'world knowledge' problem. World knowledge appeared to provide a mass of ill-defined, partially contradictory, context-sensitive constraints on human thought and reasoning, but a mass that seemed unmanageable, using the crystalline machinery of logic.

The idea that knowledge consists of multiple 'soft' constraints, however, seemed eminently compatible with connectionist models of memory and cognition. Indeed, Rumelhart, Smolensky, McClelland, and Hinton's (1986) motivation for developing these models was primarily to capture the flexible deployment of the relevant parts of world knowledge that had previously been viewed as organized into symbolic schemata. As Rumelhart observed, 'it was struggling with the concept of a schema and some of its difficulties that led [me] to an exploration of PDP models to begin with' (Rumelhart *et al.* 1986, p. 7). The hope was that initially simple connectionist models based on 'auto-associative' networks might be generalized to deal with the complex 'structured' (i.e. language-like) representations that are required to capture human knowledge. This idea of flexible schemata built on connectionist hardware seemed tantalizingly related to the idea of a mental model as providing the limited set of elements over which human reasoning may proceed, but which may be influenced by the rich texture of background knowledge in memory. As Johnson-Laird (1986, p. 45) once argued, '... the construction of putative counterexamples calls for an active exercise of memory and interpretation rather than formal derivation of one expression from others'.

In retrospect, it seems to us that the problem that cognitive science had run into arose because human reasoning is fundamentally concerned with using knowledge to make plausible conjectures about an uncertain world—and the dominant logical paradigm in cognitive science had little to say about uncertainty or context sensitivity. Connectionism provided a mechanism for dealing with large numbers of probabilistic constraints, and was to some degree based on ideas from probability and information theory, rather than on logic, although this connection was by no means obvious to cognitive scientists at the time (although it was central to the thinking of some of the founders of the connectionist approach, e.g. Ackley *et al.* 1985). Indeed, this trend has continued markedly, to the extent that the current technical literature on connectionism treats these networks as conducting probabilistic reasoning, and views connectionist learning as a type of statistical inference.

One of the early attractions of mental models, suggested by Johnson-Laird (1983), was that the approach was not limited to logical terms and to logical patterns of reasoning, but could smoothly be generalized to deal with relations that seem to introduce uncertainty. For example, not only could mental models represent logical relations such as All A are B, it could naturally represent fuzzy or probabilistic relations such as Most A are B or Few A are B. The intuition that the generalization from purely deductive reasoning to uncertain or context-sensitive everyday reasoning could be achieved was also consonant with contemporary developments in the semantics of natural language. Most notably, Barwise and Perry's (1983) situation semantics attempted to provide a formal account of the context-sensitivity of real human reasoning and of linguistic meaning.[1]

----

[1] It is important to distinguish between uncertainty and context sensitivity, although they are related. Probabilities changes with context, e.g. the probability of encountering a lion in Bloomsbury is lower than encountering one at London Zoo. Moreover, contextual boundaries can themselves be uncertain, a stranger to London might be uncertain whether she is in Bloomsbury or Regent's Park, which should affect the probability she assigns to encountering lions.

Yet from the perspective of high-level cognition, there remained a fundamental missing element—the lack of a theory of inference that could deal with the uncertainty inherent in everyday reasoning. The focus remained steadfastly on logic—to the extent that, as post-graduates, we spent hundreds of hours studying logic and quite literally no time at all studying even the rudiments of probability theory. Indeed, the attitude towards probability theory then current in formal areas of cognitive science was that it was a non-starter as a theory of everyday reasoning. Indeed in our own early critiques of the logicist programme in cognitive science (Oaksford and Chater 1991), we too dismissed the probabilistic approach almost with a wave of the hand. Probabilities were too unconstrained, there were too many of them to keep track of, probabilistic inference would be computationally intractable, and so on.

However, the 1980s also saw a revolution in probabilistic approaches to uncertain reasoning, partly based on a resurgence of the Bayesian approach to probability (e.g. Berger 1985; Bernado and Smith 1994), combined with the use of graphical models, both as representations of complex knowledge structures and as highly efficient parallel computational machines (Lauritzen and Spiegelhalter 1988; Neapolitan 1990; Pearl 1988). These developments have led to a probabilistic revolution in many areas of artificial intelligence (Geman and Geman 1984; Manning and Schütze 1999; Pearl 1988, 2000) that, we believe, should provide a rich theoretical framework for dealing with the cognitive science of human inference.

The acid test, of course, is whether such a probabilistic approach could actually explain the empirical data on human reasoning. The psychology of deductive reasoning has always been beset by a paradoxical mismatch between logic and human behaviour, to the extent that some theorists began to seriously question human rationality (Stein 1996; Stich 1983). But the lesson from artificial intelligence appeared to be that human performance was outstandingly impressive, and logic provided an impoverished toolkit for dealing with the complexities of everyday inference.

We have been developing a probabilistic approach that appears both to mesh with probabilistic ideas in artificial intelligence, and to radically reduce the gap between rational norms and human behaviour. The probabilistic models that we discuss in this book attempt to explain human reasoning behaviour as having a rational basis, in terms of reasoning mechanisms that are adapted to the uncertainty of the everyday world. In these models the numbers representing probabilities are regarded as the products of processes operating over world knowledge. That is, they attempt to incorporate the products of world knowledge in to the reasoning process. We do not believe for a moment that we have solved the world knowledge problem that we were warned against as postgraduates, i.e. how these numbers, or their neural correlates, are arrived at. However, we do believe that probability theory provides the right language to integrate theories of high level reasoning performance with connectionist implementations and ultimately to neural processes in the brain.

The research described in this book has been made possible by many people and institutions. We have received important intellectual input from discussions with, among many others, Nilufa Ali, Alan Allport, John R. Anderson, the late Michael Bacharach, the late Jon Barwise, Isabelle Blanchette, Gordon D. A. Brown, Luciano Buratto, Ruth Byrne, Pat Cheng, Rick Cooper, Robin Cooper, Martin Davies, Peter Dayan, Jonathan Evans, Klaus Fiedler, Gerd Gigerenzer, Geoff Goodwin, David Green, Tom Griffiths, Ulrike Hahn, Ikuko Hattori, Masasi Hattori, Evan Heit, Dennis Hilton, Geoff Hinton, Keith Holyoak, William Jiménez, Phil Johnson-Laird, David Lagnado, Koen Lamberts, Alex Kacelnik, Christoph Klauer, Craig McKenzie, Mike Malloch, Ken Manktelow, Simon Moore, Jonathan Nelson, Steve Newstead, Tom Ormerod, David Over, James McClelland, Nick Perham, Emmanuel Pothos, Martin Redington, Lance Rips, Jerry Seligman, Jo Sellen, David Shanks, Mark Steedman, Keith Stenning, Neil Stewart, Henry Stott, Josh Tenenbaum, Paul Vitányi, J. Mark G. Williams, David Willshaw, and Hiroshi Yama. Thanks also to William Jiménez for his heroic efforts in turning this manuscript into a final form.

On a more personal note, Nick Chater's work has been supported by the University of Edinburgh, Univerity College London, the University of Oxford, and the University of Warwick, as well as by research grants from ESRC, the Leverhulme Trust, the British Academy, the European Community, the Human Frontiers Science Foundation, and Oliver, Wyman and Company. His largest debt is to Louie Fooks, and to our children, Maya and Caitlin Fooks, for making this project, and life in general, meaningful.

Mike Oaksford's work has been supported by the University of Edinburgh, University of Wales, Bangor, the University of Warwick and Cardiff University, as well as by grants from the ESRC, the Leverhulme Trust, the British Academy and the NHS. He would also like to thank his wife Karen, for all her support, love and toleration, and his children, Julia, Joanne, and David for being there.

Chapter 1

Logic and the Western concept of mind

For almost two and a half thousand years, the Western conception of what it is to be a human being has been dominated by the idea that the mind is the seat of reason. That is, humans are, almost by definition, *rational* animals. But, although intuitively compelling, this viewpoint is vacuous unless we know what it means for a person to be rational. From Aristotle to the present day, the project of explaining what rationality means has been the focus of enormous intellectual effort in mathematics, philosophy, and economics. Historically, the dominant idea is that rationality can be explained by comparison to systems of logic, which can serve as ways of distinguishing valid (i.e. rationally justified) from invalid arguments. In this century, this idea has reached an apogee of sophistication. Systems of logic in the traditional sense have been converted into rigorous mathematical theories; and these have provided the foundation for building computational machines for doing logical reasoning. Indeed, modern computation is a physical embodiment of the Western conception of the human mind, converting abstract philosophical speculation into engineering. This is the critical idea behind the cognitive revolution, which re-introduced the mind back into psychological theories in the 1950s. Human thought is seen as a kind of computation; and the brain is therefore seen as a biological computer. Thus, the conception of mind that emerged at the very beginnings of systematic philosophical thought in the Western world has become established as the foundation for modern scientific ideas about the nature of the mind. The classical conception of the mind, as a machine for logical inference in its modern guise in cognitive science, is what we called *logicism* (Oaksford and Chater 1991).

The Western philosophical tradition embodies the view of the mind as rational, and hence logical, from the very outset. Plato viewed formal mathematical reasoning as the only source of genuine knowledge; empirical observations could not lead to knowledge because of the unreliability of the senses. Thus, knowledge can be derived only from proof—a method of providing a chain of reasoning from premises to conclusion, where the links in the chain are self-evident. Thus, for Plato, Euclid's geometry was the paradigm example of well-grounded knowledge, where every step in each geometrical derivation was underwritten by indubitable rules; and reasoning begins from what are taken to be self-evident axioms. But for Plato, the nature of indubitable rules of inference was left implicit—he had no theory of what counts as a 'valid,' and hence certain, link in a chain of reasoning. Aristotle went a considerable way towards tackling this problem in his theory of the syllogism. Syllogisms involve two premises, such as *All women are people; All people are mortal*, from which the conclusion *All women are mortal* can be derived with absolute certainty. As we shall discuss later, Aristotle identified 64 forms of the syllogism. He also developed a systematic, though intuitive, approach to deciding which of these syllogisms had a valid conclusion, and if so, what the nature of this conclusion is. For more than two thousand years, Aristotle's theory of the syllogism almost exhausted logical theory—and indeed, Kant considered all logical questions to have been decisively resolved by Aristotle's account, stating: 'It is remarkable also, that to the present day, it [i.e. logic] has not been able to make one step in advance, so that, to all appearance, it may be considered as completed and perfect.' (Kant 1787/1961, p. 501.) Generations of scholars, from the Greeks to the medieval period, and in some traditions, to the present day, have learned the valid syllogisms by rote as a key part of their education.

Within mathematics, the need for anything more than Aristotle's explicit formulation of logic was not apparent until the eighteenth and nineteenth centuries. What conclusions followed with certainty in a mathematical derivation was regarded as simply self-evident to the intelligent mathematician. But mathematical reasoning itself came into question with the development of puzzles in geometry, previously the paradigm of mathematical certainty. Attempts to prove Euclid's fifth postulate (that parallel lines never meet) from Euclid's first four postulates seemed to end in confusion and failure. Some mathematicians, such as Gauss and Riemann, began to suggest that such a proof was impossible, and therefore that there were perfectly consistent non-Euclidean geometries, in which the fifth postulate does not hold. The resulting crisis led to a profound re-evaluation of the nature of mathematical proof, as itself requiring a mathematical analysis to resolve apparently conflicting intuitions (DeLong 1970).

The attempt to provide a certain foundation for mathematics gave a huge impetus to the development of logic. But a particularly important, and, from the point of view of cognitive science, startlingly prescient, early pioneer of the new logical techniques was Boole. For the first time, he proposed explicit mathematical rules for logical reasoning; and he also extended the scope of logic outside of the syllogism. Intriguingly, Boole's motivations were more psychological than mathematical. His aim was less to resolve problems in the foundations of mathematics than to characterize 'the laws of thought' (Boole 1854/1958), thus embodying the Western conception of mind in a very direct way. With more mathematical goals in mind, Frege further revolutionized Boole's logic, developing 'predicate logic,' which for the first time provided a rigorous mathematical theory of syllogistic reasoning, and much more besides. Frege's logicist programme of providing a rigorous foundation for mathematics was followed by Russell and Whitehead, who attempted to reduce mathematics to logic. A related, but distinct, viewpoint was pioneered by Hilbert, who viewed mathematics as a process of explicit symbol manipulation, where the rules of symbol manipulation were defined without any reference to what the symbols were about.[1]

This 'formalist' tradition provided the foundations of the branch of logic called proof theory. This is concerned with rigorous specifications of the rules of proofs in terms of formal operations on symbols, which later underpinned the development of digital computers, as well as providing a core hypothesis about the operation of the human mind (e.g. Fodor and Pylyshyn 1988; Newell and Simon 1976). These developments in formal logic fed directly into developments in philosophy. Frege and Russell began to apply the formal systems that they had devised for understanding mathematical argument to informal philosophical argument, framed in natural language. This was the beginning of the enterprise of formal semantics—specifying precisely the meaning of sentences in terms of their underlying logical form.[2]

The view that philosophy should proceed by a careful logical analysis of natural language provides the dominant philosophical tradition of the twentieth century: analytic philosophy (we return to some of these issues in Chapter 3). Indeed, one outgrowth of this viewpoint, logical positivism, took it that, unless natural language claims and arguments could be reframed in rigorous logical terms, such claims and arguments could be rejected as quite literally non-sense (e.g. Ayer 1936; see Sahotra 1996a). Despite the attractions of this austere viewpoint, this logical positivist viewpoint ultimately proved to be unworkable—for example, it proved too austere to allow the meaningfulness of the philosophical claims of which it was composed; and more generally, it proved essentially impossible to provide a convincing rendition of just about any informal everyday argument, in logical terms (Sahotra 1996b).

....

[1] This is not strictly true of Hilbert himself, who distinguished clearly between 'contentful' finite mathematics, and other parts of the subject whose terms were to be construed differently.

[2] And in terms of the referential relations between atomic sentences and the world.

From the point of view of the thesis of this book, logical positivism, as a philosophical programme, seems closely analogous to the logicist conception of human cognition that we shall discuss extensively below. According to the logicist viewpoint, informal human reasoning can be reconstructed in logical terms; and the mind is a logical reasoning machine. The failure of the logical positive programme thus bodes ill for logicist theories of cognition— i.e. the view that the logical reasoning is a, or perhaps the, core building block of cognition. We shall suggest that logic is simply not an appropriate foundation for understanding informal, everyday thought, whether one is concerned with providing a justification for knowledge (the key project in philosophy), or a descriptive account of mental processes (the key project in cognitive science).

Logic in psychology

Within psychology and cognitive science, a logicist conception of the mind was adopted wholeheartedly by early cognitive theorists such as Piaget (e.g. Inhelder and Piaget 1955). Piaget viewed the pinnacle of cognitive development as attaining the 'formal operational' stage, where the mind is capable of reasoning according to a particular formal system of logic: propositional logic. The process of cognitive development is seen as a series of stages of enrichment of the logical apparatus of the child, enabling increasingly abstract reasoning, which is less tied to the specific sensory-motor environment. The early foundations of cognitive science and artificial intelligence involved attempting to realize logical systems practically, by building computer programs that can explicitly derive logical proofs. Tasks such as mathematical reasoning and problem solving were then viewed as exercises in logic, as in Newell and Simon's *Logic theorist* and *General problem solver* (Newell *et al.* 1958; Newell and Simon 1972). Moreover, Chomsky's (1957, 1965) revolutionary work in linguistics showed how the syntactic structure of language could be represented in a deductive logical system, from which all, and only, the grammatical sentences of the language could be generated. Although the implications of this viewpoint for the mental representation of language in the brain have remained contentious, a natural interpretation is that the language processing system involves a logical component, which animates these abstract linguistic rules to construct syntactic structures for specific sentences during language comprehension and production (e.g. Shieber *et al.* 1995). Moreover, in the psychology of adult reasoning, this logical conception of mind was again used as the foundation for explaining human thought. Thus, human reasoning was assumed to be logical and hence rational; and apparently irrational performance was explained away in terms of errors of comprehension. For example, Henle stated: 'I have never found errors which could unambiguously be attributed to faulty reasoning.' (Henle 1978, p. xviii.)

Simultaneous with the construction of the logicist programme in cognition, there were some discordant and puzzling observations. Specifically, researchers such as Wason, who attempted to verify the Piagetian view of the adult mind as a perfect logic engine, found that people appeared surprisingly and systematically illogical in some experiments. Given the dissonance between these results and the emerging logicist paradigm in cognitive science, these results were largely set aside by mainstream cognitive theorists, perhaps to be returned to once the logicist approach had reached a more developed state. But the general form that an account of apparent irrationality might take was that all illogical performance resulted from misunderstandings and from the faulty way in which the mind might sometimes apply logical rules; but the central notion that thought is based on logical reasoning was to be retained. This fundamental commitment to logic as a foundation for thought is embodied in contemporary reasoning theory in two of the main theoretical accounts of human reasoning (see Chapter 4). The *mental logic* view (Braine 1978; Rips 1983, 1993) assumes that human reasoning involves logical calculation over symbolic representations, using systems of proof that are very similar to those developed by Hilbert in mathematics, and used in computer programs for theorem-proving in artificial intelligence and computer science. The *mental models* view (Johnson-Laird 1983; Johnson-Laird and Byrne 1991) takes its starting point as the denial of the assumption that reasoning involves formal operations over logical formulae, and instead assumes that people reason over concrete representations of situations, or 'models', in which the formulae are true. This provides a different method of proof (for discussion see Oaksford and Chater 1991), but one that can achieve logical performance by an indirect route. Although mental logic and mental models both give logic a central role in human reasoning, they explain apparent irrationalities in different ways. For example, mental logics may explain errors in terms of the accessibility of different rules, whereas mental models theory explains errors in terms of limitations in how mental models are constructed and checked, and how many models must be considered. Moreover, both pick up the standard strategy for reconciling logical thinking with apparently irrational performance due to Henle: logical errors emerge from people misinterpreting the premises (i.e. adopting a logical form other than that intended by the experimenter).

This logicist reaction to data appearing to show that people are not always rational, seems entirely reasonable. Every new theory in science could be immediately refuted if the mere existence of data apparently inconsistent with the theory were assumed to falsify it decisively. For example, Newton's theory of gravitation was inconsistent with the known perturbations in the orbit of Uranus for 150 years, until the discovery of Neptune reconciled theory and observation. However, puzzling data can turn into crucial anomalies that end in the rejection of an entire programme of research. Thus, consider another puzzle for Newtonian theory, the 'perihelion of Mercury' (Putnam 1974). Just as with the orbit of Uranus, the Newtonian explanation of this phenomenon required postulating another celestial body influencing Mercury's orbit, just as Neptune was found to influence the orbit of Uranus. But whereas Newtonian calculations predicted the existence of Neptune, which was subsequently observed, similar calculations for the putative celestial body influencing Mercury indicated that it should be visible, although no such body could be observed. Consequently, maintaining the Newtonian explanation required somehow allowing the presence of a very heavy but invisible body, which was implausible. By contrast, in the twentieth century it became clear that this puzzle could be explained by switching to a non-Euclidean theory of space, provided by Einstein's General Theory of Relativity—in retrospect, the orbit of Uranus was a mere puzzle, but the orbit of Mercury was a crucial anomaly.

The difference between a mere puzzle and a falsifying anomaly, according to Kuhn (1962), is that a puzzle is data that can only be explained by the present theory in an implausible way; but this turns into an anomaly where an alternative theory provides a more plausible explanation. Thus, science is viewed as fundamentally comparative and competitive—the theory that wins out is that which provides the most plausible explanation of the available data and, in particular, certain critical anomalies (for a deep analysis of these issues, see Lakatos 1970). In this light, what are we to make of Wason's early discoveries of apparent human illogicality?

The first question to address is: how plausible is the style of explanation offered by logicist accounts of reasoning for reasoning errors?[3]

One cause for concern is that in some reasoning tasks, the overwhelming bulk of people's responses may, in some way or another, be illogical. Hence, in explaining actual reasoning performance, the logical component that is presumed to underpin human thinking appears to be doing surprisingly little work. A further

---

[3] As we discuss more fully later, it is important to distinguish different senses of giving an 'account' of reasoning. Normative, philosophical accounts are not concerned with an account of how humans reason. As we will see, there is debate in the literature over how far such normative accounts also function as a part of accounts of how humans reason, which is the primary topic of this book.

cause for concern is that people find it surprisingly difficult to conform to the rules of logical reasoning, even when given extensive courses of instruction in how to do so (Cheng *et al.* 1986), as anyone struggling to learn a logical or a computer-programming language will be fully aware. These factors severely stretch the credibility of considering logic as the very core of human thinking. We will extensively consider this point in relation to specific reasoning tasks in Chapters 5 to 7.

The second, and crucial, question is: Can an alternative, more plausible, explanation of these puzzling aspects of human reasoning be provided? A radical suggestion, which we develop in this book, is that the Western conception of the mind as a logical system is flawed at the very outset. Logicism emerged in Plato in rejecting the uncertainties of the real world, and focusing on the mathematical realm, where certain knowledge can be obtained. The discipline of mathematical logic later developed as a means of formalizing mathematical reasoning—attempting to provide a rigorous and certain account of mathematical proof. However, the human mind is primarily concerned with practical action in the face of a profoundly complex and uncertain world; it is presumably not primarily concerned with reasoning about certain and eternal mathematical truths (Barwise and Perry 1983). Accounts of reasoning that apply only to the latter, and which are able only to underwrite infallible inferences, may be entirely inappropriate to explaining how people categorize, understand, reason about, and make decisions in their everyday environment. Moreover, analysing language in terms of logical forms may itself be misguided, if the function of language is to communicate information, ideas, and arguments about the uncertain world with which people must cope. With these thoughts in mind, it might seem less surprising that people's reasoning frequently does not conform to the laws of logic, because logical ability may not of course be much use for a cognitive system concerned with practical action rather than mathematical reflection.

From a probabilistic point of view

What kind of theory might be more suited to explaining practical action in an uncertain world? In this book, we will consider that cognition should be understood in terms of probability theory, the calculus of *un*certain reasoning, rather than in terms of logic, the calculus of certain reasoning. The logical mind should be replaced by the probabilistic mind. The view that thought should be understood in terms of probability has a parallel and equally long and distinguished pedigree to the idea that reasoning is based on logic. Plato insisted that the only kind of knowledge worth having is certain knowledge—and to the extent that our acquaintance with the complex world of everyday life is uncertain, we must admit to having no genuine knowledge of it. Aristotle, by contrast, took a more pragmatic line, because he was interested not only in mathematical and philosophical reasoning, but also with the scientific description and analysis of the everyday world, and with practical affairs and human action. An often quoted passage from *The Nicomachean Ethics* (1995, 1094b, 24–25) notes that 'it is the mark of an educated man to look for precision in each class of things just so far as the nature of the subject admits: it is evidently equally foolish to accept probable reasoning from a mathematician and to demand from a rhetorician demonstrative reasoning'. But, just as Aristotle had no rigorous theory of logic, he had no theory of probable reasoning either.

The programme of developing a mathematical theory of probable reasoning began in the latter half of the seventeenth century. The meaning of the term 'probability' has always, from the beginning, been loaded with two related but distinct interpretations (Hacking 1975).

The first motivation for developing a theory of probability was the attempt to provide a theory of successful gambling (Gigerenzer *et al.* 1989). Gambling typically uses devices specifically designed to produce random outcomes, such as coins, dice, roulette wheels, and shuffled decks of cards. The discrete character of the different possible outcomes suggests interpreting probabilities in terms of the frequencies at which different outcomes occur, over the long term. So, according to this 'frequentist' interpretation of probability (von Mises 1939), to say that the probability of a four in throwing a fair dice is one in six is to say that, in the long run, the frequency of fours will be about 1/6 of the total number of throws.

The second motivation for developing a theory of probability is more closely connected to Aristotle's comment on the rhetorician. The goal in rhetoric, in its traditional, rather than pejorative, sense, is to provide reasoned arguments why people should hold certain opinions, in areas where certain knowledge is impossible. Thus, in medical diagnosis or in deciding court cases by jury, a range of pieces of evidence, e.g. a patient's symptoms or a witness's testimony, must somehow be combined to give some degree of belief that a disease is present or that the defendant is guilty. From this view, probability is interpreted subjectively, in terms of a person's degree of belief or strength of opinion. Indeed, the very word 'probability', which initially referred to the degree to which a statement was supported by the evidence at hand, embodied this interpretation—that is, probability originally signified rational degree of belief (Gigerenzer *et al.* 1989). Jakob Bernoulli explicitly endorsed this interpretation when he entitled his definitive book *Ars conjectandi*, or the *Art of conjecture* (Bernoulli 1713). This 'subjectivist' conception ran through the eighteenth and into the nineteenth centuries (Daston 1988), frequently without clear distinctions being drawn between probability theory as a model of actual thought (or more usually, the thought of 'rational', rather than common, people; Hacking 1990) or as a set of normative canons prescribing how uncertain reasoning should be conducted. In a sense, then, early probability theory itself was viewed as a model of mind. Indeed, intriguingly, Boole, the great pioneer of mathematical logic, also gave a prominent role for probability in *The laws of thought*—thus, adopting a rather sophisticated compromise between the probabilistic and logicist views in one of the earliest pre-cursors of the computational view of mind.

As the distinction between normative and descriptive models of thought became more firmly established, probability theory was primarily seen as having normative force, as characterizing rationality; whether or not people actually follow such normative dictates was seen as a secondary question. Indeed, there is a parallel with the development of logic here. To the degree that logic was viewed as aimed at providing a rigorous foundation for mathematics, rather than as capturing principles of human thought, it became important to distinguish logical reasoning from human intuitions about reasoning— because a principal objective of the development of a mathematical theory of logical reasoning was to help adjudicate mathematical or philosophical disputes in which human intuitions clash. That is, a mathematical theory of logic might provide an independent court of appeal, in the face of the frailty of human thought. Similarly, as probability became mathematicized, its purpose was increasingly to adjudicate puzzles and disputes that exceed informal human reasoning abilities. Hence, both logic and probability were increasingly seen as rather distant from actual human reasoning, although providing a standard against such reasoning might fairly be judged.

The distinction between the frequentist and subjectivist conceptions of probability was not always clear to early probability theorists. Arguments based on a frequentist point of view were mixed in with discussions that could only make sense from a subjectivist standpoint. But the confusion is perhaps understandable, given that these different interpretations of probability seem to be closely related. For example, a gambler's decisions must be determined by their degrees of belief in the various outcomes that the randomization device might produce—and somehow these degrees of belief should be connected to the long-term frequencies of these outcomes. Similarly, the degree of belief that a certain patient has a particular disease, should somehow be systematically related to the frequency of these symptoms being simultaneously present with the disease. This fundamental ambiguity in the interpretation of probability has been the centre for philosophical controversy until the present, but mathematically both interpretations suggest the same rules of probabilistic reasoning (Hacking 1975, 1990). Indeed, the modern accepted formal system for probabilistic reasoning, developed by Kolmogorov, is used indiscriminately by adherents of frequentism and subjectivism alike.

While mathematically neutral, the distinction between frequentist and subjective interpretations of probability is crucial in the *application* of probability. For the frequentist, the probability calculus can only be applied where frequencies can be obtained—e.g. for events such as throwing a die or choosing a card that can be repeated indefinitely many times. Probability is therefore simply not defined in relation to unrepeated events, such as the probability that Oswald shot Kennedy. There is no universe of events of Kennedy shootings, in which we can count the number of times that Oswald was the culprit and the number of times that Kennedy was shot by somebody else. However, for the subjectivist, this intuitively natural way of speaking about probabilities of single events does not betray some informal usage that should be treated as distinct from the proper and justifiable treatment of the technical notion of probability. Instead, the subjective views probability as fundamentally concerned with degrees of belief, given certain bodies of evidence, where those beliefs may be about any proposition whatever. Similarly, for the frequentist, it is simply incoherent to ask: what is the probability that a scientific theory is true, given some set of data? Analogously, it is incoherent to ask, what is the probability that the object in the distance is a horse, given some perceptual evidence? But for the subjectivist, these questions are perfectly sensible—and the probability calculus promises to help show how evidence from scientific observation or perceptual data can be used in determining the relevant degrees of belief in various scientific hypotheses, or the identity of the object in the distance. Thus, it is necessarily the subjectivist interpretation of probability that is in play in the extensive literature on probabilistic theories of the confirmation of scientific theories (e.g. Earman 1992; Horwich 1982; Howson and Urbach 1993) and probabilistic theories of the perception (e.g. Knill and Richards 1996), or the brain (Rao *et al.* 2002).

It is worth pausing for a moment, to consider terminology. In the philosophical literature on the interpretation of probability, the view that probabilities express degrees of belief, developed in various forms by Cox (1946 1961), di Finetti (1937 1972), Keynes (1921), Savage (1954), Ramsey (1931), and others, is typically known as the *subjectivist* viewpoint. But in the scientific community, and in much mainstream philosophy of science, this viewpoint is generally known as the *Bayesian* viewpoint. The terminology is rooted in the fact that subjectivists frequently invoke Bayes' theorem, an elementary theorem of probability that will loom large in this book—but it is crucial to keep in mind that Bayes' theorem, as a theorem of probability, is of course accepted by subjectivists and frequentists alike. In this book, we shall use the terms *subjectivist* and *Bayesian* interchangeably.

We have seen that, to the extent that probability theory is used as a framework for understanding human reasoning, as a rival to formal logic, it must be interpreted subjectively, as a theory about degrees of belief. This immediately raises the issue of what, if anything, degrees of belief *mean* from a psychological point of view. It seems highly implausible that people can specify with any accuracy the probabilities that they assign to given beliefs. But if this is so, how are we to measure what people's degrees of belief are? Indeed, how are we even to make sense of what it means for people to have such 'implicit' degrees of belief?

One immediately appealing approach to attempting to tease out people's degrees of belief is by looking at the choices that they make. This at least provides a way of obtaining some indication of what a person's subjective probabilities are. Suppose, for example, that I am offered £5 if I correctly guess which horse wins the race. If I then choose Dobbin rather than Red Rum, then this presumably indicates that my subjective probability that Dobbin will win is greater than my subjective probability that Red Rum will win (with the assumption that I would prefer to win, rather than not to win, the £5). A more general approach along these lines involves comparing different 'lotteries' with different probabilities and different 'prizes' associated with each outcome. This approach promises to spell out exactly how much more probable I think it is that Dobbin will win than Red Rum will win by considering the difference in the prizes that I will accept for the two horses. The rough idea is that the *odds* that I will accept on a horse (in the sense of the term used by bookmakers), reveals my subjective probabilities concerning the outcomes (Ramsey 1931).

There are a variety of reasons why this viewpoint is open to challenge. One line of attack concerns the interaction of utilities and probabilities—perhaps winning £10 is only slightly more valuable to me than winning £2. In this case, I should tend to bet on the favourite rather than an outsider. A typical tack to deal with this is to argue that people do not really make decisions (gamble) in order to maximize money, but in order to maximize expected utility; and hence the Ramsey-style argument should ideally be applied when the value of the possible outcomes is measured in 'utils' rather than monetary value. Of course, there is, in practice, no independent way of determining the amount of utility that a person associates with an outcome, aside from the very choice behaviour that we use to determine their probabilities. In short, probabilities and utilities must be fitted *simultaneously* to people's choices between options (including their choices between gambles). An important result is that if we know an agent's preferences between all possible relevant gambles, we can simultaneously infer their utilities and subjective probabilities (in the case of utility, this cannot be done uniquely but is well-defined up to unimportant additive and multiplicative constants) (Savage 1954). But the question remains: How reliable are the results of this simultaneous fit? How confident can we be that the resulting probabilities (and, for that matter, the utilities) really do reflect the degrees of belief (or the degree of value) that a person holds? Without some independent means of assessing utility, there seems no way of answering this question.

One line of thought is that we should abandon the question as unanswerable. The 'revealed preference' (Samuelson 1937) viewpoint that has become standard in theories of individual rationality in economics, adopts this position. Indeed, a popular way of expressing this view is to say that imputing particular probabilities or utilities to a person is not really to make a claim about their internal psychological make-up at all. Rather it is just to specify a model of their behaviour that gives a convenient summary of their dispositions to choose between particular options, such as gambles. A similar viewpoint is current in the rational explanation of animal behaviour (e.g. McFarland and Houston 1981; Stephens and Krebs 1986). For example, by choosing to forage at patch A rather than patch B, an animal may be viewed as implicitly 'revealing' that it assigns a higher subjective probability to finding a substantial food supply at patch A. But theorists of animal behaviour are not led to the view that any such probability is represented in the animal's cognitive system.

Is this 'instrumentalist' viewpoint appropriate for the analysis of the human cognitive system from a psychological point of view? Or should we assume that probabilities associated with beliefs can somehow be explicated in terms of mental representations; and perhaps that these representations might be measured directly, given suitable empirical cunning or perhaps even suitably powerful brain-scanning technology? We shall leave the question of the status of subjective probabilities open for the moment, and return to the issue when we have seen, later in this book, how psychological explanations based in a probabilistic framework actually work in practice.

Our recent discussion, concerning the rationality of decisions on how to act, raises a different strand of thought on rationality, from that we have been considering so far: one according to which the rationality of an agent is assessed in terms of what it *does* rather than what it *knows*. From the standpoint of economics or, more generally, the programme of rational choice theory (Arrow *et al.* 1996; Elster 1986) that is now widely used throughout the social sciences and the study of animal behaviour, rationality is assessed against the quality of decisions about action. Although one of the motivations for the probabilistic approach that we advocate here is that it provides an appropriate basis for deciding how to act in a complex and uncertain world, we will not primarily address the vast literature on rational choice and action. We shall focus instead on the traditional territory of the psychology of human reasoning—understanding how people reason, in order to gain knowledge, rather than how they decide (although in Chapter 6, on the deontic selection task, we shall make a brief detour into a rational-choice type model of a particular reasoning task, in which the reasoner is given specific goals, and hence implicitly, utilities, to achieve).

A few comments are in order about the wider literature concerning rational choice, however. First, rational choice theory is deeply enmeshed with questions of probability and utility, as we have discussed—and hence in this literature, probability, rather than logic, has always been centre-stage. Second, in a parallel with the discovery of results in the psychology of reasoning that have led researchers to doubt people's ability at logic, there has been a much larger empirical research programme in the psychology of decision-making that has led researchers to doubt people's ability to follow the norms of rational choice theory (e.g. Colman 2003; Gigerenzer and Todd 1999; Gigerenzer 2002; Goldstein and Hogarth 1997; Kahneman et al. 1982; Kahneman and Tversky 1979 2000; Stewart et al. 2006). This might appear to lead to the conclusion that a probabilistic view of mind is in no better shape that a logicist view of mind—perhaps people are no better at reasoning about probability than they are about logic.

We believe, however, that this conclusion is not warranted. Certainly, it is true that people's ability to deal with verbally (or, in the case of probabilities, numerically) specified reasoning problems, concerning both logic and probability, is extremely limited and subject to error. After all, the development of logic and probability as formal, mathematical theories, were the result of huge intellectual effort—neither sprang naturally forth, fully formed from the human mind. The key question for cognitive science is, however, what is the appropriate rational framework for modelling people's reasoning about the everyday world?[4]

---

[4] One might want to distinguish at this point between slow reflective reasoning and rapid intuitive reasoning, and to indicate which it is that we want to give an account. As we will see as we begin to explore the psychology of reasoning, this distinction is not as clear cut as it may seem—most researchers are of the view that a bit of both goes in any piece of reasoning.

That is, the question is: to what extent can such reasoning be reconstructed in logical, or probabilistic, terms?

This puts some distance between empirical results from verbal reasoning studies, whether about logic or probability, and theories of cognition, in two ways. The first is that, even if the mind were a probabilistic or logical calculating engine, it is by no means necessary that it will be possible to engage that engine's reasoning abilities with verbally stated probabilistic or logical puzzles, which it is presumably not adapted to handle. This point is no deeper than the trivial observation that, although the early visual processes in the retina may be appropriately viewed as computing elaborate convolutions and decorrelations of the retinal image, this does not mean that we can thereby readily solve problems concerning convolution or decorrelation, when stated in mathematical terms. Mathematics problems, even if precisely analogous to the kinds of problem that the brain routinely solves in, say, perception and motor control, are simply presented in the wrong format for any specialized neural machinery to be applied.

The second way in which empirical results on verbal problems may be distanced from theoretical claims concerning logicist or probabilistic views of the mind, is that the latter claims may be viewed not as claims about the computational machinery of the mind or brain at all—but rather as specifying the appropriate 'rational analysis' (Anderson 1990, 1991a; Oaksford and Chater 1998) in terms of which we should understand the problems that the cognitive system solves. We shall outline and expand on the concept of rational analysis in Chapter 2, and this concept will be central to the development of concrete theories in the psychology of reasoning in Chapters 5 to 7 of this book. In a nutshell, the idea is this: to understand cognitive processes requires analysis at (at least) two very different levels: first, we need an analysis of *what* problem the cognitive system is solving, and what a good solution to this problem looks like; and, second, we need an analysis of the specific mental processes and representations that are used to solve the problem in practice.

We can ask about the role of normative theories, such as logic and probability theory, at both of these levels. That is, we can ask how far the problems that human reasoning addresses can appropriately be reconstructed in terms of probability or logic; and we can ask to what extent the machinery of the cognitive system can be viewed as implementing probabilistic or logical calculations. We suspect that the first question is the place to start—and that the psychology of reasoning has traditionally answered it incorrectly, with problematic results. We will argue, in Chapter 3, that real-world reasoning can almost never be reconstructed in logical terms—instead, as we suggest in Chapter 4, most human reasoning can be more appropriately reconstructed in a probabilistic framework. So the key conclusion from Chapters 1 to 4 of this book will be that the psychology of reasoning needs to shift from the assumption that the reasoning problems that people solve in everyday life should be viewed as logical reasoning problems, to the view that the world confronts us with problems of probabilistic reasoning. But if these arguments are to produce a fundamental shift in the empirical project of studying human reasoning, this means that we must provide an alternative framework for understanding human reasoning—which is not based on logical ideas (as are the mental logic and mental models accounts), but are instead based on probability. The goal of the second half of the book is to indicate how such a probabilistic alternative can be constructed. We provide a probabilistic rational analysis of the three most important tasks in the psychology of 'deductive' reasoning: conditional inference; the Wason selection task; and syllogistic reasoning. We argue that the probabilistic account provides a much better fit with the empirical data than existing viewpoints.

Now what about the second level of analysis? To what extent can the mind or brain be viewed as a probabilistic (or for that matter, logical) calculating engine? This is not the primary focus in this book—but it is nonetheless a fundamental question for cognitive science. We suspect that, in general, the probabilistic problems faced by the cognitive system are simply too complex to be solved directly, by probabilistic calculation. Instead, we suspect that the cognitive system has developed relatively computationally 'cheap' methods for reaching solutions that are 'good enough' probabilistic solutions to be acceptable. In particular, where, in this book, we propose a specific processing theory (in our account of syllogistic reasoning), this account consists of a set of simple, but surprisingly effective, heuristics—heuristics that, however, lead to errors, which we argue are evident in the empirical data. Moreover, in related work in the topic of rational choice and decision-making, which we do not consider in this book, we have similarly proposed models that solve probabilistic/ decision-making problems, but do so using relatively cheap, and hence approximate, methods (Chater *et al.* 2003; Stewart *et al.* 2005).

To the degree that algorithmic models can be formulated, it might be thought that our first level of analysis, concerning the appropriate rational analysis of the problems faced by the cognitive system, is simply redundant. But this is not the case—the rational analysis explains *why* the particular algorithms used by the cognitive system are appropriate. That is, without a characterization of what problem the cognitive system solves, we cannot even ask, let alone answer, the question of why the algorithm has a particular form, or how effectively it works. And, moreover, it may be that a good deal of empirical data about human reasoning (and indeed, human cognition more generally) can be understood as arising from the structure of the problem itself—i.e. the nature of the problem drives any reasonable algorithmic solution to have particular properties, which may be evident in the data. This idea is a core motivation for the rational analysis approach (Anderson 1990, 1991a): we shall see that most data on human reasoning, particularly on conditional inference and in Wason's selection task, can be understood purely at the rational level—i.e. without formulating an algorithmic theory of any kind.

Wider implications

We have traced two viewpoints of the basis of people's ability to carry out 'deductive' reasoning tasks, one based on logic and the other on probability. We have set out the claims for which we shall argue: that probability, rather than logic, provides an appropriate framework for providing a rational analysis of human reasoning; and we shall suggest, further, that this undercuts existing logic-based theories of reasoning. While our focus will be primarily on human reasoning, both in the real world and the laboratory, it is worth stressing that the implications of the debate between the two approaches has ramifications that go far beyond the psychology of deductive reasoning.

This work has direct relevance to any area of cognition that is viewed as involving inference, from social judgement, to perception, categorization and learning (e.g. Cheng 1997; Cheng and Novick 1992; Fiedler 2000; Fiedler et al. 2000; Griffiths and Tenenbaum, 2005; Knill and Richards 1996; Pothos and Chater 2002; Tenenbaum 1999; Tenenbaum and Griffiths 2001).

The debate concerning the fundamental framework for understanding high-level reasoning is potentially relevant across the gamut of research on clinical disorders, to the extent that these may be explicable in terms of disorders of reasoning (e.g. Beck et al. 1979) and across the gamut of applied psychological research concerned with the practical reasoning performance from military leaders to health care professionals (Dixon 1976; Gigerenzer 2002).

There are close connections, as we have already indicated, between the issues addressed in this book and cognate issues in other disciplines—especially in economics and the study of animal behaviour. This is the point of connection between the work in this book, which focuses on inference and knowledge; and rational choice theories of human decision-making. It is also of significance to research domains, such as the study of belief revision and knowledge representation in artificial intelligence (Pearl 1988; Stephens and Krebes 1986), and theory change in the philosophy of science (Howson and Urbach 1993), in which a principal goal is to model human argument and reasoning (even where a further goal may be to improve upon such reasoning).

The issues we raise in the context of high-level cognition arise, equally, at the neural level (e.g. Rao *et al.* 2002; Rieke *et al.* 1997). Here the fundamental question is: to what extent can aspects of neural processes be viewed as probabilistic calculating engines (or, perhaps, as engines performing cheap approximations to probabilistic calculations)? The study of human reasoning has, of course, fundamental implications for the nature of human rationality, and for foundational philosophical issues concerning related notions, such as justification and knowledge (Bovens and Hartman 2003). Moreover, the nature of human reasoning is of direct relevance to our view of ourselves and each other—and it directly interconnects with questions concerning the status of our everyday 'folk psychological' explanations of behaviour (Sellars 1956; Stich 1983).

Despite this range of potential implications, the main focus of the core of this book will be, as we have indicated, relatively narrow. The empirical psychological tradition on which we focus in this book has concentrated on logic, and has involved constructing reasoning tasks that are intended to assess the degree to which people can reason logically. This research goal is built into the title of the field the 'psychology of deductive reasoning'. We have seen that this field of research has revealed that people's reasoning often appears to be wildly at variance with logical rationality. But this seems to threaten the very idea that people are rational animals at all—and thus to undercut the very starting point of more than two millennia of research effort into understanding human rationality. By attempting to rethink the psychological study of human deductive reasoning, and hence resolving this apparent paradox, we aim to provide an insight into broader issues concerning the nature both of rationality and of the mind.

Chapter 2

Rationality and rational analysis

One of the central goals of this book is to show how empirical data on human reasoning can be reconciled with the notion that people are rational. This raises two questions: first, the general theoretical question of how the concept of rationality relates to human behaviour; and, second, the methodological question of how to develop 'rational' explanations of behaviour. The answer to the first question will provide a starting point for tackling the second—for which we advocate John Anderson's (1990) methodology of rational analysis.

To get the discussion started, we first consider what it *means* to be rational. Immediately reflection suggests that the task is a difficult one, because the notion of rationality appears in a wide variety of contexts, and is used in a wide variety of apparently rather loosely related senses. For example, in clinical psychology, as well as in the law, rationality enters immediately, to the extent that we attempt to draw a boundary between sanity and madness, or to determine when people are not to be held responsible for their actions. In economics and, increasingly, other areas of social science, human behaviour is explained as the outcome of 'rational choice' (Becker 1976, 1991; Elster 1986). This approach to human behaviour, which we alluded to in the previous chapter, involves assuming that rationality is spelled out in terms of beliefs and desires (with associated probabilities and utilities). The idea is that people's behaviour can be explained as rationally justified, in relation to these postulated degrees of beliefs and levels of desire. But rationality assumptions go much deeper still—such assumptions seem to lie at the heart of the folk psychological style of explanation in which we describe each other's minds and behaviour (Fodor 1987; Sellars 1956). Assumptions of rationality also appear equally essential to interpret each others utterances and to understand texts (Davidson 1984a; Quine 1960). So rationality, in an intuitive sense, appears to be at the heart of the explanation of human behaviour, whether from the perspective of social science or of everyday life. Let us call this *everyday* rationality: rationality concerned with people's beliefs and actions in specific circumstances.

In this informal, everyday sense, most of us, most of the time, are remarkably rational. In daily life, of course, we tend to focus on occasions when reasoning or decision-making breaks down. But our failures of reasoning are only salient because they occur against the background of rational thought and behaviour. The rationality of this thought and behaviour is achieved with such little apparent effort that we are inclined to take it for granted—to view it as emerging from plain common sense, where such common sense must be a simple thing indeed. People may not think of themselves as exhibiting high levels of rationality—instead, we think of people as 'intelligent', performing 'appropriate' actions, being 'reasonable' or making 'sensible' decisions. But these labels refer to human abilities to make the right decisions or to say or think the right thing in complex, real-world situations—in short they are labels for everyday rationality.

Indeed, so much do we tend to take the rationality of common-sense thought for granted, that the immense subtlety and sophistication of common-sense reasoning has only been discovered in the latter part of the twentieth century. This discovery emerged from the project of attempting to formalize everyday knowledge and reasoning in artificial intelligence, where initially high hopes that common-sense knowledge could readily be formalized, were replaced by increasing desperation at the impossible difficulty of the project. Indeed, the project of formalizing common-sense has been brought to an effective standstill (e.g. McDermott 1987) in the face of a nest of difficulties, sometimes grouped under the heading of the 'frame problem' (see Pylyshyn 1987). Two related difficulties are worth highlighting. First, that it does not seem possible to break down the knowledge underlying common-sense into manageable chunks (whether schemas, scripts, or frames; Minsky 1977; Schank and Abelson 1977), which can be understood separately. Instead, each aspect of common-sense knowledge appears inextricably entangled with the rest (e.g. Fodor 1983), so that it seems difficult or even impossible to represent common-sense knowledge in an incremental fashion. Alongside this difficulty stand deep problems in understanding how the plethora of partial constraints embodied in any incomplete and inconsistent knowledge-base can be used to make reliable inferences. This problem is particularly difficult because common-sense inferences are typically defeasible—that is, the addition of new information can overturn a current conclusion. This appears to imply that the entire knowledge-base must somehow be accessed, if a conclusion is to be asserted, because otherwise that conclusion may be overturned by some other piece of knowledge. We have discussed these complex issues in detail elsewhere (Oaksford and Chater 1991, 1995b, 1998a). But in the present context what is important is the upshot of the discussion: that everyday, common-sense reasoning is remarkably, but mysteriously, successful in dealing with an immensely complex and changeable world and that no artificial computational system can begin to approach the level of human performance. This is the root of the theoretical starting point of this book: that most people, most of the time, are remarkably rational; and hence that the principal challenge in the psychology of reasoning is to understand how such impressive levels of rationality are achieved.

But in addition to this informal, everyday sense of rationality, concerning people's ability to think and act in the real world, the concept of rationality also has another root, linked not to human behaviour, but to mathematical theories of good reasoning, such as logic and probability. According to these calculi, rationality is defined, in the first instance, in terms of conformity with specific formal principles, rather than in terms of successful behaviour in the everyday world.

The two sides of rationality raise the fundamental question of how they relate to each other: how are the general principles of formal rationality related to specific examples of rational thought and action described by everyday rationality? This question, in various guises, has been widely discussed— in this chapter, we shall outline a particular conception of the relation between these two notions, focusing on a particular style of explanation in the behavioural sciences, *rational analysis* (Anderson 1990). We will argue that rational analysis provides a good characterization of how the concept of rationality is used in explanations in psychology, economics, and animal behaviour, and provides an account of the relationship between everyday and formal rationality, which has implications for both. Moreover, this view of rationality leads to a re-evaluation of the implications of data from psychological experiments that appear to undermine human rationality. As we shall argue in detail in Chapters 5, 6, and 7, the experimental evidence demands a change concerning which formal account defines the normative standard in experimental tasks.

The discussion in this chapter falls into two parts. First, we discuss formal and everyday rationality, and various possible relationships between them. Second, we outline how the programme of rational analysis, which is the framework of the research in this book, leads to a new conception of how formal and everyday rationality are related.

Relations between formal and everyday rationality

Formal rationality concerns formal principles of good reasoning—the mathematical laws of logic, probability, or decision theory. At an intuitive level, these principles seem distant from the domain of everyday rationality—how people think and act in daily life. Rarely, in daily life, do we accuse one another of violating the laws of logic or probability theory, or praise each other for obeying them. Moreover, when people are given reasoning problems that explicitly require use of these formal principles, their performance appears to be remarkably poor as we have mentioned. People appear to persistently fall for logical blunders (Evans *et al.* 1993), probabilistic fallacies (e.g. Tversky and Kahneman 1974) and to make inconsistent decisions (Kahneman *et al.* 1982; Tversky and Kahneman 1986). Indeed, the concepts of logic, probability, and the like do not appear to mesh naturally with our everyday reasoning strategies: these notions took centuries of intense intellectual effort to construct, and present a tough challenge for each generation of students.

We therefore face a stark contrast: the astonishing fluency and success of everyday reasoning and decision-making, exhibiting remarkable levels of everyday rationality; and our faltering and confused grasp of the principles of formal rationality. What are we to conclude from this contrast? Let us briefly consider, in caricature, some of the most important possibilities, which have been influential in the literature in philosophy, psychology, and the behavioural sciences.

The primacy of everyday rationality

This viewpoint takes everyday rationality as fundamental, and dismisses the apparent mismatch between human reasoning and the formal principles of logic and probability theory as so much the worse for these formal theories.

This standpoint appears to gain credence from historical considerations—formal rational theories, such as probability and logic, emerged as attempts to systematize human rational intuitions, rooted in everyday contexts. But the resulting theories appear to go beyond, and even clash with, human rational intuitions—at least if empirical data that appears to reveal 'blunders' in human reasoning is taken at face value.

To the extent that such clashes occur, the advocates of the primacy of everyday rationality argue that the formal theories should be rejected as inadequate systematizations of human rational intuitions, rather than condemning the intuitions under study as incoherent. It might, of course, be granted that a certain measure of tension may be allowed between the goal of constructing a satisfyingly concise formalization of intuitions, and the goal of capturing every last intuition successfully, rather as, in linguistic theory, complex centre-embedded constructions are held to be grammatical (e.g. 'the fish the man the dog bit ate swam'), even though most people would reject them as ill-formed gibberish. But the dissonance between formal rationality and everyday reasoning appears to be much more profound than this. As we have argued, fluent and effective reasoning in everyday situations runs alongside halting and flawed performance on the most elementary formal reasoning problems.

The primacy of everyday rationality is implicit in an important challenge to decision theory by the mathematician Allais (1953). Allais outlines his famous 'paradox', which shows a sharp divergence between people's rational intuitions and the dictates of decision theory. One version of the paradox is as follows. Consider the following pair of lotteries, each involving 100 tickets. Which would you prefer to play?

A.	B.
10 tickets worth $1,000,000	1 ticket worth $5,000,000
90 tickets worth $0	8 tickets worth $1,000,000
	91 tickets worth $0.

Now consider which you would prefer to play of lotteries C and D:

C.	D.
100 tickets worth $1,000,000	1 ticket worth $5,000,000
	98 tickets worth $1,000,000
	1 tickets worth $0.

Most of us prefer lottery B to lottery A—the slight reduction in the probability of becoming a millionaire is offset by the possibility of the really large prize. But most of us also prefer lottery C to lottery D—we do not think it is worth losing what would otherwise be a certain $1,000,000, just for the possibility of winning $5,000,000. This *combination* of responses, although intuitively appealing, is inconsistent with decision theory, as we shall see. Decision theory assumes that people should choose whichever alternative has the maximum expected utility. Denote the utility associated with a sum of $X by U($X). Then the preference for lottery B over A means that:

$$10/100.U(\$1,000,000) + 90/100.U(\$0) < 1/100.U(\$5,000,000) +$$
$$8/100.U(\$1,000,000) + 91/100.U(\$0) \quad (2.1)$$

and, subtracting 90/100.U($0) from each side:

$$10/100.U(\$1,000,000) < 1/100.U(\$5,000,000) +$$
$$8/100.U(\$1,000,000) + 1/100.U(\$0) \quad (2.2)$$

But the preference for lottery C over D means that:

$$100.U(\$1,000,000) > 1/100.U(\$5,000,000) +$$
$$98/100.U(\$1,000,000) + 1/100.U(\$0) \quad (2.3)$$

and, subtracting 90/100.U($1,000,000) from each side:

$$10/100.U(\$1,000,000) > 1/100.U(\$5,000,000) +$$
$$8/100.U(\$1,000,000) + 1/100.U(\$0) \quad (2.4)$$

But (2.2) and (2.4) are in contradiction.

Allais's paradox is very powerful—the appeal of the choices that decision theory rules out is considerable. Indeed, rather than condemning people's intuitions as incorrect, Allais argues that the paradox undermines the normative status of decision theory—that is, Allais argues that everyday rational intuitions take precedence over the dictates of a formal calculus. Moreover, accounting for the psychological basis of Allais' paradox has become a central objective of descriptive theories of choice, in psychology and economics (e.g. Birnbaum 2004).

Another example arises in Cohen's (1981) discussion of the psychology of reasoning literature. Following similar arguments of Goodman (1954), Cohen argues that a normative or formal theory is 'acceptable ... only so far as it accords, at crucial points with the evidence of untutored intuition' (Cohen 1981, p. 317). That is, a formal theory of reasoning is acceptable only in so far as it accords with everyday reasoning. Cohen uses the following example to demonstrate the primacy of everyday inference. According to standard propositional logic, the inference from (2.5) to (2.6) is valid:

> If John's automobile is a Mini, John is poor, and   (2.5)
> if Johns's automobile is a Rolls, John is rich.
> Either, if John's automobile is a Mini, John is rich, or   (2.6)
> if Johns's automobile is a Rolls, John is poor.

Clearly, however, this violates intuition. Most people would agree with (2.5) as at least highly plausible; but would reject (2.6) as absurd. A fortiori, they would not accept that (2.5) implies (2.6) (otherwise they would have to judge (2.6) to be at least as plausible as (2.5)). Consequently, Cohen argues that standard logic simply does not apply to the reasoning that is in evidence in people's intuitions about (2.5) and (2.6). Like Allais, Cohen argues that rather than condemn people's intuitions as irrational, this mismatch reveals the inadequacy of propositional logic as a rational standard. That is, everyday intuitions have primacy over formal theories.

This viewpoint is not without problems. For example, how can rationality be assessed? If formal rationality is viewed as basic, then the degree to which people behave rationally can be assessed by comparing performance against the canons of the relevant normative theory. But if everyday rationality is viewed as basic, assessing rationality appears to be down to intuition. There is a danger here of losing any normative force to the notion of rationality—if rationality is merely conformity to each others predominant intuitions, then being rational is like a musician being in tune. On this view, rationality has no absolute significance; all that matters is that we reason harmoniously with our fellows. But there is a strong intuition that rationality is not like this at all—that there is some absolute sense in which some reasoning or decision-making is good, and other reasoning and decision-making is bad. So, by rejecting a formal theory of rationality, there is the danger that the normative aspect of rationality is left unexplained.

One way to re-introduce the normative element is to define a procedure that derives normative principles from human intuitions. Cohen appealed to the notion of reflective equilibrium (Goodman 1954; Rawls 1971), where inferential principles and actual inferential judgements are iteratively bought into a 'best fit' until further judgements do not lead to any further changes of principle (narrow reflective equilibrium). Alternatively, background knowledge may also figure in the process, such that not only actual judgements but also how they relate to other beliefs are taken into account (wide reflective equilibrium). These approaches have, however, been subject to much criticism (e.g. Stich and Nisbett 1980; Thagard 1988). For example, there is no guarantee that an individual (or indeed a set of experts) in equilibrium will have accepted a set of *rational* principles, by any independent standard of rationality. For example, the equilbrium point could, for example, leave the individual content in the idea that the Gambler's fallacy that an event is more likely if it has not occurred recently is a sound principle of reasoning.

Thagard (1988) proposes that instead of reflective equilibrium, developing inferential principles involves progress towards an *optimal* system. This involves proposing principles based on practical judgements and background theories, and measuring these against criteria for optimality. The criteria Thagard specifies are:

(1) *robustness*: principles should be empirically adequate;

(2) *accommodation*: given relevant background knowledge, deviations from these principles can be explained; and

(3) *efficacy*: given relevant background knowledge, inferential goals are satisfied.

Thagard's (1988) concerns were very general: to account for the development of scientific inference. From our current focus on the relationship between everyday and formal rationality, however, Thagard's proposals seem to fall down because the criteria he specifies still seem to leave open the possibility of inconsistency, i.e. it seems possible that a system could fulfill (1) to (3) but contain mutually contradictory principles. The point about formalization is of course that it provides a way of ruling out this possibility and hence is why a tight relationship between formality and normativity has been assumed since Euclid and Aristotle. From our perspective, accounts like reflective equilibrium and Thagard's account, which attempts to drive a wedge between formality and normativity, may not be required. We argue that many of the mismatches observed between human inferential performance and formal theories are a product of using the wrong formal theory to guide expectations about how people should behave.

An alternative normative grounding for rationality seems intuitively appealing: good everyday reasoning and decision-making should lead to *successful action*. For example, from an evolutionary perspective, we might define success as inclusive fitness, and argue that behaviour is rational to the degree that it tends to increase inclusive fitness. But now the notion of rationality appears to collapse into a more general notion of adaptiveness. There seems to be no particular difference in status between cognitive strategies that lead to successful behaviour, and digestive processes that lead to successful metabolic activity. Both increase inclusive fitness; but intuitively we want to say that the first is concerned with rationality, while the second is not. More generally, defining rationality in terms of outcomes runs the risk of blurring what appears to be a crucial distinction—between minds, which may be more or less rational, and stomachs, that are not in the business of rationality at all.

The primacy of formal rationality

Arguments for the primacy of formal rationality take a different starting point. This viewpoint is standard in mathematics, statistics, operations research, and the 'decision sciences' (e.g. Kleindorfer *et al.* 1993). The idea is that everyday reasoning is fallible, and that it must be corrected by following the dictates of formal theories of rationality.

The immediate problem for advocates of the primacy of formal rationality concerns the *justification* of formal calculi of reasoning: why should the principles of some calculus be viewed as principles of good reasoning, so that they may be allowed to overturn our intuitions about what is rational? Such justifications typically assume some general, and apparently incontrovertible, cognitive goal; or seemingly undeniable axioms about how thought or behaviour should proceed. They then use these apparently innocuous assumptions and aim to argue that thought or decision-making must obey specific mathematical principles.

Consider, for example, the 'Dutch book' argument for the rationality of the probability calculus as a theory of uncertain reasoning (de Finetti 1937; Ramsey 1931; Skyrms 1977). Suppose that we assume that people will accept a 'fair' bet: that is, a bet where the expected financial gain is 0, according to their assessment of the probabilities of the various outcomes. Thus, for example, if a person believes that there is a probability of one in three that it will rain tomorrow, then they will be happy to accept a bet according to which they win two dollars if it does rain tomorrow, but they lose one dollar if it does not.

Now, it is possible to prove that, if a person's assignment of probabilities to different possible outcomes violates the laws of probability theory in any way whatever, then it is possible to offer them a combination of different bets, such that they will happily accept each individual bet as fair, in the above sense, but where *whatever the outcome* they are certain to lose money. Such a combination of bets—where one side is certain to lose—is known as a Dutch book; and it seems incontrovertible that accepting a bet that you are certain to lose must violate rationality. Thus, if violating the laws of probability theory leads to accepting Dutch books, which seems clearly irrational, then obeying the laws of probability theory seems to be a condition of rationality.

The Dutch book theorem might appear to have a fundamental weakness— that it requires that a person willingly accepts arbitrary fair bets. But, in reality of course, this might not be so—many people will, in such circumstances, be risk averse and choose not to accept such bets. But the same argument applies even if the person does not bet at all. Now the inconsistency concerns a hypothetical— the person believes that *if* the bet were accepted, it would be fair (and that, a win, as well as a loss, is possible). But in reality, the bet is guaranteed to result in a loss—the person's belief that the bet is fair is guaranteed to be wrong. Thus, even if we never actually bet, but simply aim to avoid endorsing statements that are guaranteed to be false, we should follow the laws of probability.

We have considered the Dutch-book justification of probability theory in some detail to make it clear that justifications of formal theories of rationality can have considerable force.[1]

Rather than attempting to simultaneously satisfy what may be a myriad of possibly conflicting intuitions about good and bad reasoning, formal theories of reasoning can be viewed, instead, as founded on simple and intuitively clear cut principles, such as that accepting bets that you are certain to lose is irrational. Similar justifications can be given for the rationality of the axioms of utility theory and decision theory (Cox 1961; Savage 1954; von Neumann and Morgenstern 1944). Moreover, the same general approach can be used as a justification for logic, if avoiding inconsistency is taken as axiomatic. Thus, there may have been good reasons for accepting formal theories of rationality, even

---

[1] Dutch-book arguments remain, however, controversial—e.g. there are, however, a range of alternative justifications, based on theories of preferences (Savage 1954), scoring rules (Lindley 1982), and derivation from minimal axioms (Cox 1961; Good 1950; Lucas 1970). Although each argument can be challenged individually, the fact that so many different lines of argument converge on the very same laws of probability has been taken as powerful evidence for the view that degrees of belief can be interpreted as probabilities (for discussion see: Earman 1992; Howson and Urbach 1993).

if, much of the time, human intuitions and behaviour strongly violates their recommendations.

If formal rationality is primary, what are we to make of the fact that, in explicit tests at least, people seem to be such poor probabilists and logicians? One line would be to accept that human reasoning is badly flawed. Thus, the heuristics and biases programme (Kahneman and Tversky 1973; Kahneman *et al.* 1982), which charted systematic errors in human probabilistic reasoning and decision-making under uncertainty, can be viewed as exemplifying this position (see Gigerenzer and Goldstein 1996), as can Evans' (1982, 1989) heuristic approach to reasoning. Another line follows the spirit of Chomsky's (1965) distinction between linguistic competence and performance—the idea is that the people's reasoning competence accords with formal principles, but in practice, performance limitations (e.g. limitations of time, memory, and language comprehension) lead to persistently imperfect performance, when people are given a reasoning task.

Reliance on a competence/performance distinction, whether implicitly or explicitly, has been very influential in the psychology of reasoning. In Chapter 1, we noted that two of the leading theoretical frameworks for modelling human reasoning, mental logic (Braine 1978; Rips 1994) and mental models (Johnson-Laird 1983; Johnson-Laird and Byrne 1991) rely on a distinction between reasoning competence and performance. Both these frameworks assume that classical logic provides the appropriate competence theory for deductive reasoning—they differ only over how the dictates of this competence theory are implemented in mental processes. Thus, according to both theories, logically errors in people's actual reasoning behaviour are explained in terms of 'performance' factors.

Mental logic assumes that human-reasoning algorithms correspond to proof-theoretic operations (specifically, in the framework of natural deduction, e.g. Rips 1994). This viewpoint is also embodied in the vast programme of research in artificial intelligence, especially in the 1970s and 1980s, which attempted to axiomatize aspects of human knowledge, and views reasoning as a logical inference (e.g. McCarthy 1980; McDermott 1982; McDermott and Doyle 1980; Reiter 1980, 1985). Moreover, in the philosophy of cognitive science, it has been controversially suggested that this viewpoint is basic to the computational approach to mind: the fundamental claim of cognitive science, according to this viewpoint, is that 'cognition is proof theory' (Fodor and Pylyshyn 1988; see also Chater and Oaksford 1990).

Mental models concurs that logical inference provides the computational-level theory for reasoning, but provides an alternative method of proof. Instead of standard proof theoretic rules, this view uses a 'semantic' method of proof. Such methods involve search for models (in the logical sense)—a semantic proof that A does not imply B, might involve finding a model in which A and B both hold. Mental models theory uses a similar idea, although the notion of model in play is rather different from the logic notion. How can this approach show that A does imply B? The mental models account assumes that the cognitive system attempts to construct a model in which A is true and B is false; if this attempt fails, then it is assumed that no counter-example exists, and that the inference is valid (this is similar to 'negation as failure' in logic programming; Clark 1978).

Mental logic and mental models assume that formal principles of rationality—specifically classical logic—(at least partly) define the standards of good reasoning. They explain the non-logical nature of people's actual reasoning behaviour in terms of performance factors, such as memory and processing limitations.

Nonetheless, despite its popularity, the view that formal rationality has priority in defining what good reasoning is, and that actual reasoning is systematically flawed with respect to this formal standard, suffers a fundamental difficulty. If formal rationality is the key to everyday rationality, and if people are manifestly poor at *following* the principles of formal rationality (whatever their 'competence' with respect to these rules), even in simplified reasoning tasks, then the spectacular success of everyday reasoning in the face of an immensely complex world seems entirely baffling.

Everyday and formal rationality are completely separate

Recently, a number of theorists have suggested what is effectively a hybrid of the two approaches outlined above. They argue that formal rationality and everyday rationality are entirely separate enterprises. For example, Evans and Over (1997, p. 2) distinguish between two notions of rationality:

Rationality$_1$: Thinking, speaking, reasoning, making a decision, or acting in a way that is generally reliable and efficient for achieving one's goals.

Rationality$_2$: Thinking, speaking, reasoning, making a decision, or acting when one has a reason for what one does sanctioned by a normative theory.

They argue that 'people are largely rational in the sense of achieving their goals (rationality$_1$) but have only a limited ability to reason or act for good reasons sanctioned by a normative theory (rationality$_2$)' (Evans and Over 1997, p. 1). If this is right, then achieving one's goals can be achieved without following a formal normative theory—i.e. without there being a *justification* for the actions, decisions, or thoughts that lead to success: rationality$_1$ does not require rationality$_2$. That is, Evans and Over seem committed to the view that thoughts, actions, or decisions that cannot be normatively justified can, nonetheless, consistently lead to practical success.

But this hybrid view does not tackle the fundamental problem we outlined for the first view sketched above. It does not answer the question: *why* do the cognitive processes underlying everyday rationality consistently work? If everyday rationality is somehow based on formal rationality, then this question can be answered, at least in general terms. The principles of formal rationality are provably principles of good inference and decision-making; and the cognitive system is rational in everyday contexts to the degree that it approximates the dictates of these principles. But if everyday and formal rationality are pressumed to be unrelated, then this explanation is not available. Unless some alternative explanation of the basis of everyday rationality can be provided, the success of the cognitive system is again left entirely unexplained.

Everyday rationality is based on formal rationality: an empirical approach

We seem to be at an impasse. The success of everyday rationality in guiding our thoughts and actions must somehow be explained; and it seems that there are no obvious alternative explanations, aside from arguing that everyday rationality is somehow based on formal reasoning principles, for which good justifications can be given. But the experimental evidence appears to show that people do not follow the principles of formal rationality.

There is, however, a way out of this impasse: essentially, this is to reject the idea that rationality is a monolithic notion that can be defined a priori, and compared with human performance. Instead, we treat the problem of explaining everyday rationality as an empirical problem of explaining why people's cognitive processes are successful in achieving their goals, given the constraints imposed by their environment. Formal rational theories are used in the development of these empirical explanations for the success of cognitive processes—but which formal principles are appropriate, and how they should be applied, is not decided a priori; but in the light of the empirical usefulness of the explanation of the cognitive process under consideration.

According to this viewpoint, the apparent mismatch between normative theories and reasoning behaviour suggests that the wrong normative theories may have been chosen; or that the normative theories may have been misapplied. Instead, the empirical approach to the grounding of rationality aims to 'do the best' for human everyday reasoning strategies—by searching for a rational characterization of how people actually reason. There is an analogy here with rationality assumptions in language interpretation (Davidson 1984; Quine 1960). We aim to interpret people's language so that it makes sense; this is Davidson's (1984a) *principle of charity*. Similarly, the empirical approach to rationality aims to interpret people's reasoning behaviour so that their reasoning makes sense.

Crucially, then, the formal standards of rationality appropriate for explaining some particular cognitive processes or aspect of behaviour are not prior to, but are rather developed as part of, the explanation of empirical data. Of course, this is not to say that, in some sense, formal rationality may be prior to, and separate from, empirical data. The development of formal principles of logic, probability theory, decision theory, and the like may proceed independently of attempting to explain people's reasoning behaviour. But which element of this portfolio of rational principles should be used to define a normative standard for particular cognitive processes or tasks, and how the relevant principles should be applied, is constrained by the empirical human reasoning data to be explained.

It might seem that this approach is flawed from the outset. Surely, any behaviour can be viewed as rational from *some* point of view. That is, by cooking up a suitably bizarre set of assumptions about the problem that a person thinks they are solving, surely their rationality can always be respected; and this suggests the complete vacuity of the approach. But this objection ignores the fact that the goal of explanation here is to provide an empirical account of data on human reasoning. Hence, such explanations must not be merely possible, but also simple, consistent with other knowledge, independently plausible, and so on. In short, such explanations are to be judged in the light of the normal canons of scientific reasoning (Howson and Urbach 1993). Thus, rational explanations of cognition and behaviour can be treated as on a par with other scientific explanations of empirical phenomena.

This empirical view of rational explanation is attractive, to the extent that it builds in an explanation of the success of everyday rationality. It does this by attempting to recruit formal rational principles to explain why cognitive processes are successful. But how can this empirical approach to rational explanation be conducted in practice? And can plausible rational explanations of human behaviour be found? The next two sections of this chapter answer these questions. First, we outline a methodology for the rational explanation of empirical data—*rational analysis*. We also illustrate a range of ways in which this approach is used, in psychology, and the social and biological sciences. In Chapters 5–7, we will use rational analysis to re-evaluate the psychological data, which has appeared to show human reasoning performance to be hopelessly flawed, and argue that, when appropriate rational theories are applied, reasoning performance may, on the contrary, be rational.

The programme of rational analysis

The project of providing a rational analysis for some aspect of thought or behaviour has been described by the cognitive psychologist John Anderson (e.g. Anderson 1990, 1991a). This methodology provides a framework for explaining the link between principles of formal rationality and the practical success of everyday rationality not just in psychology, but throughout the study of behaviour. This approach involves six steps:

1. Specify precisely the goals of the cognitive system.
2. Develop a formal model of the environment to which the system is adapted.
3. Make minimal assumptions about computational limitations.
4. Derive the optimal behaviour function given 1–3 above. (This requires formal analysis using rational norms, such as probability theory and decision theory.)
5. Examine the empirical evidence to see whether the predictions of the behaviour function are confirmed.
6. Repeat, iteratively refining the theory.

According to this viewpoint, formal rational principles relate to explaining everyday rationality, because they specify the optimal way in which the goals of the cognitive system can be attained in a particular environment, subject to 'minimal' computational limitations. The assumption is that the cognitive system exhibits everyday rationality—i.e. successful thought and action in the everyday world, to the extent that it approximates the optimal solution specified by rational analysis.

The framework of rational analysis aptly fits the methodology in many areas of economics and animal behaviour, where the behaviour of people or animals is viewed as optimizing some goal, such as money, utility, inclusive fitness, food intake, or the like. But Anderson (1990, 1991a) was concerned to extend this approach not just to the behaviour of whole agents, but to structure and performance of particular cognitive processes of which agents are composed. Anderson's programme has led to a flurry of research in cognitive psychology (for an overview of recent research see: Oaksford and Chater 1998a), from areas as diverse as categorization (Anderson 1991b; Anderson and Matessa 1998; Lamberts and Chong 1998), memory (Anderson and Milson 1989; Anderson and Schooler 1991; Schooler and Anderson 1997), searching computer menus (Young 1998), and natural language parsing (Chater *et al.* 1998). This research has shown that a great many empirical generalizations about cognition can be viewed as arising from the rational adaptation of the cognitive system to the problems and constraints that it faces. We shall argue below that the cognitive processes involved in reasoning can also be explained in this way.

The three inputs to the calculations using formal rational principles, goals, environment, and computational constraints, each raise important issues regarding the connection between formal rational principles and everyday rationality. We discuss these in turn, and in doing so, illustrate rational analysis in action in psychology, animal behaviour, and economics.

The importance of goals

Everyday thought and action are focused on achieving goals relevant to the agent. Formal principles of rationality can help specify *how* these goals are achieved, but not, of course, what those goals are. The simplest cases are economic in spirit. For example, consider a consumer, wondering which washing machine to buy. Goals are coded in terms of the subjective 'utilities' associated with objects or events for this particular consumer. Each washing machine is associated with some utility (high utilities for the effective, attractive, or low-energy washing machines, for example); and money is also associated with utility. Simple decision theory will specify which choice of machine maximizes subjective utility. Thus goals enter very directly; people with different goals (here, different utilities) will be assigned different 'rational' choices. Suppose instead that the consumer is wondering whether to take out a service agreement on the washing machine. Now the negative utility associated with the cost of the agreement must be balanced with the positive utility of saving possible repair costs. But what are the possible repairs; how likely, and how expensive, is each type? Decision theory again recommends a choice, given utilities associated with each outcome, and subjective probabilities concerning the likelihood of each outcome.

But not all goals may have the form of subjective utilities. In evolutionary contexts, the goal of inclusive fitness might be more appropriate (Dawkins 1977); in the context of foraging behaviour in animals, amount of food intake or nutrition gained might be the right goal (Stephens and Krebs 1986). Moreover, in some cognitive contexts, the goal of thought or action may be disinterested curiosity, rather than the attempt to achieve some particular outcome. Thus, from exploratory behaviour in children and animals to the pursuit of basic science, a vast range of human activity appears to be concerned with finding out information, rather than achieving particular goals. Of course, having this information may ultimately prove important for achieving goals; and this virtue may at some level explain the origin of the disinterested search for knowledge (just as the prospect of unexpected applications may partially explain the willingness of the state to fund fundamental research).

Nonetheless, disinterested inquiry is conducted without any particular goal in mind. In such contexts, gaining, storing, or retrieving *information*, rather than maximizing utility, may be the appropriate specification of cognitive goals. If this is the goal, then information theory and probability theory may the appropriate formal normative tools, rather than decision theory.

This aspect of rational analysis is at variance with Evans and Over's distinction between two forms of rationality, mentioned above. They argue that 'people are largely rational in the sense of achieving their goals (rationality$_1$) but have only a limited ability to reason or act for good reasons sanctioned by a normative theory (rationality$_2$)' (Evans and Over 1997, p. 1). But the approach of rational analysis attempts to explain *why* people exhibit the everyday rationality involved in achieving their goals by assuming that their actions approximate what would be sanctioned by a formal normative theory. Thus, formal rationality helps *explain* everyday rationality, rather than being completely separate from it.

To sum up: everyday rationality is concerned with goals (even if the goal is just to 'find things out'); knowing which formal theory of rationality to apply, and applying formal theories to explaining specific aspects of everyday cognition, requires an account of the nature of these goals.

The role of the environment

Everyday rationality is concerned with achieving particular goals, in a particular *environment*. Moreover, everyday rationality requires thought and action to be adapted (whether through genes or through learning) to the constraints of this environment. The success of everyday rationality is, crucially, success relative to a specific environment—to understand that success requires modelling the structure of that environment. This requires using principles of formal rationality to specify the optimal way in which the agent's goals can be achieved in that environment (Anderson's step 4) and showing that the cognitive system approximates this optimal solution.

In psychology, this strategy is familiar from perception, where a key part of understanding the computational problem solved by the visual system involves describing the structure of the visual environment (Marr 1982). Only then can optimal models for visual processing of that environment be defined. Indeed, Marr (1982) explicitly allies this level of explanation with Gibson's 'ecological' approach to perception, where the primary focus is on environmental structure.

Similarly, in zoology, environmental idealizations of resource depletion and replenishment of food stocks, patch distribution and time of day are crucial to determining optimal foraging strategies (Gallistel 1990; McFarland and Houston 1981; Stephens and Krebs 1986).

Equally, in economics, idealizations of the 'environment' are crucial to determining rational economic behaviour (McCloskey 1985). In micro-economics, modelling the environment (e.g. game-theoretically) involves capturing the relation between each actor and the environment of other actors. In macro-economics, explanations using rational expectations theory (Muth 1961) begin from a formal model of the environment, as a set of equations governing macro-economic variables.

This aspect of rational analysis contrasts with the view that the concerns of formal rationality are inherently disconnected from environmental constraints. For example, Gigerenzer and Goldstein (1996) propose that 'the minds of living systems should be understood relative to the environment in which they evolved *rather than* to the tenets of classical [i.e. formal] rationality...' (p. 651) (emphasis added). Instead, rational analysis aims to explain *why* agents succeed in their environment by understanding the structure of that environment, and using formal principles of rationality to understand what thought or action will succeed in that environment.

Computational limitations

In rational analysis, deriving the optimal behaviour function (Anderson's step 4) is frequently very complex. Models based on optimizing, whether in psychology, animal behaviour or economics, need not, and typically do not, assume that agents are able to find the perfectly optimal solutions to the problems that they face. Quite often, perfect optimization is impossible even in principle, because the calculations involved in finding a perfect optimum are frequently computationally intractable (Simon 1955, 1956) and, moreover, much crucial information is typically not available. Indeed, formal rational theories in which the optimization calculations are made, including probability theory, decision theory, and logic, are typically computationally intractable for complex problems (Cherniak 1986; Garey and Johnson 1979; Good 1971; Paris 1992; Reiner 1995). Intractability results imply that no computer algorithm could perform the relevant calculations given the severe time and memory limitations of a 'fast and frugal' cognitive system. The agent must still act, even in the absence of the ability to derive the optimal solution (Gigerenzer and Goldstein 1996; Simon 1956). Thus it might appear that there is an immediate contradiction between the limitations of the cognitive system and the intractability of rational explanations.

There is no contradiction, however, because the optimal behaviour function is an explanatory tool, not part of an agent's cognitive equipment. Using an analogy from Marr (1982), the theory of aerodynamics is a crucial component of explaining why birds can fly. But clearly birds know nothing about

aerodynamics, and the computational intractability of aerodynamic calculations does not in any way prevent birds from flying. Similarly, people do not
need to calculate their optimal behaviour functions in order to behave adap-
tively. They simply have to use successful algorithms; they do not have to be
able to make the calculations that would show that these algorithms are
successful. Indeed, it may be that many of the algorithms that the cognitive
system uses may be very crude 'fast and frugal' heuristics (Gigerenzer and
Goldstein 1996), which generally approximate the optimal solution in the
environments that an agent normally encounters. In this context, the optimal
solutions will provide a great deal of insight into why the agent behaves as it
does. However, an account of the algorithms that the agent uses will also be
required to provide a full explanation of their behaviour (e.g. Anderson 1993;
Oaksford and Chater 1995b).

This viewpoint is standard in rational explanations across a broad range
of disciplines. Economists do not assume that people make complex game-
theoretic or macro-economic calculations (Harsanyi and Selten 1988); zoolo-
gists do not assume that animals calculate how to forage optimally (e.g.
McFarland and Houston 1981); and, in psychology, rational analyses of, for
example, memory, do not assume that the cognitive system calculates the optimal forgetting function with respect to the costs of retrieval and storage
(Anderson and Schooler 1991). Such behaviour may be built in by evolution
or be acquired via a long process of learning—but it need not require on-line
computation of the optimal solution.

In some contexts, however, some on-line computations may be required.
Specifically, if behaviour is highly flexible with respect to environmental variation, then calculation is required to determine the correct behaviour, and *this*
calculation may be intractable. Thus the two leading theories of perceptual
organization assume that the cognitive system seeks to optimize on-line either
the *simplicity* (e.g. Leeuwenberg and Boselie 1988) or *likelihood* (von
Helmholtz 1910; see Pomerantz and Kubovy 1987) of the organization of the
stimulus array. These calculations are recognized to be computationally
intractable (see: Chater 1996). This fact does not invalidate these theories, but
it does entail that they can only be approximated in terms of cognitive algorithms. Within the literature on perceptual organization, there is considerable
debate concerning the nature of such approximations, and which perceptual
phenomena can be explained in terms of optimization, and which result from
the particular approximations that the perceptual system adopts (Van der
Helm and Leeuwenberg 1996).

It is important to note also that, even where a general cognitive goal is
intractable, a more specific cognitive goal relevant to achieving the general

goal may be tractable. For example, the general goal of moving a piece in chess is to maximize the chance of winning. However, this optimization problem is known to be completely intractable because the search space is so large. But optimizing local goals, such as controlling the middle of the board, weakening the opponent's king, and so on, may be tractable. Indeed, most examples of optimality-based explanations, whether in psychology, animal behaviour, or economics, are defined over a local goal, which is assumed to be relevant to some more global aims of the agent. For example, evolutionary theory suggests that animal behaviour should be adapted so as to increase an animal's inclusive fitness, but specific explanations of animals' foraging behaviour assume narrower goals. Thus, an animal may be assumed to forage so as to maximize food intake, on the assumption that this local goal is generally relevant to the global goal of maximizing inclusive fitness. Similarly, the explanations concerning cognitive processes discussed in rational analysis in cognitive psychology concern local cognitive goals such as maximizing the amount of useful information remembered, maximizing predictive accuracy, or acting so as to gain as much information as possible. All of these local goals are assumed to be relevant to more general goals, such as maximizing expected utility (from an economic perspective) or maximizing inclusive fitness (from a biological perspective). At any level, it is possible that optimization is intractable; but it is also possible that by focusing on more limited goals, evolution or learning may have provided the cognitive system with mechanisms that can optimize or nearly optimize some more local, but relevant, quantity.

The observation that the local goals may be optimized as surrogates for the larger aims of the cognitive system raises another important question about providing rational models of cognition. The fact that a model involves optimizing *something* does not mean that the model is a *rational* model. Optimality is not the same as rationality. It is crucial that the local goal that is optimized must be relevant to some larger goal of the agent. Thus, it seems *reasonable* that animals may attempt to optimize the amount of food they obtain, or that the categories used by the cognitive system are optimized to lead to the best predictions. This is because, for example, optimizing the amount of food obtained is likely to enhance inclusive fitness, in a way that, for example, maximizing the amount of energy consumed in the search process would not. Therefore, determining whether some behaviour is rational or not depends on more than just being able to provide an account in terms of optimization. Rationality requires not just optimizing something but optimizing something reasonable. As a definition of rationality, this is clearly circular. But by viewing rationality in terms of optimization, general conceptions of what are reasonable cognitive goals can be turned into specific and detailed models of cognition. Thus, the programme of rational analysis, while not answering the ultimate question of what rationality is, nonetheless provides the basis for a concrete and potentially fruitful line of empirical research.

This flexibility of what may be viewed as rational, in building a rational model, may appear to raise a fundamental problem for the entire rational analysis programme. To pick up an example we have already mentioned, it may be that our stomachs are well adapted to digesting the food in our environmental niche. Indeed they may even prove to be optimally efficient in this respect. However, we would not therefore describe the human stomach as rational, because stomachs presumably cannot usefully be viewed as information-processing devices, which approximate, to any degree, the dictates of normative theories of formal rationality. Stomachs may be well or poorly adapted to their function (digestion), but they have no beliefs, desires, or knowledge, and make no decisions or inferences. Thus, their behaviour cannot be given a rational analysis and hence they cannot be related to the optimal performance provided by theories of formal rationality. Hence the question of the stomach's rationality does not arise.

In this section, we have seen that rational analysis provides a mode of explaining behaviour that clarifies the relationship between the stuff of everyday rationality—reasoning with particular goals, in a specific environment, with specific computational constraints, and apparently abstract principles of formal rationality in probability theory, decision theory, or logic. Formal rational principles spell out the optimal solution for the information-processing problem that the agent faces. The assumption is that a well-adapted agent will approximate this solution to some degree.

Later, we shall see how the rational analysis approach can lead to specific accounts of the three key areas of the psychology of deductive reasoning: conditional reasoning (Chapter 5), Wason's selection task (Chapter 6), and syllogistic reasoning (Chapter 7). In the present chapter, we have set out an empirical programme for investigating the rationality of any particular human behaviour. But to carry out this programme in practice requires choosing a particular framework for developing rational analyses of reasoning.

One key clue that probability theory, rather than logic, will provide more appropriate rational analyses, is the nature of everyday reasoning. Perhaps our theories of laboratory tasks should be inspired by our theories of human everyday reasoning, on the assumption that the cognitive system is adapted to reasoning in the everyday world rather than to reasoning in the laboratory.

This suggests that it would be useful to consider the degree to which real-world reasoning can be modelled using logic. If it can, then we would be confident that people's underlying logical competence must be quite impressive and that their apparently dismal laboratory performance must somehow be explicable in terms of the impoverished or unrealistic nature of the tasks, just as the visual system is subject to a wide range of perceptual illusions using impoverished stimuli (Cohen 1981). If, on the other hand, everyday reasoning does not involve logical reasoning to any substantial degree, then the possibility must be admitted that people are genuinely poor at logical reasoning— because this is not the kind of reasoning to which the cognitive system is adapted. It also raises the further possibility that people might tackle supposedly 'logical' reasoning tasks by co-opting non-logical reasoning strategies that they use in everyday life. This would lead to the paradoxical conclusion that 'logical' reasoning tasks may not be treated as logical tasks by experimental participants at all.

In the next chapter we address the question of the nature of everyday reasoning head-on. The traditional assumption, in both philosophy and psychology, has been that logic is at the core of everyday reasoning; but we shall suggest research in a range of disciplines suggests that, on the contrary, human everyday reasoning is fundamentally uncertain.

Chapter 3

Reasoning in the real world: how much deduction is there?

The topic of this book is what has traditionally been termed the psychology of *deductive* reasoning. Deductive reasoning has been studied extensively in the laboratory—but to what extent does deduction arise outside the laboratory, in daily life? In an intuitive, everyday sense of the term 'deduction', the question has little bite because deduction is often used as synonomous with sound reasoning of any description. It is this intuitive sense of the term that is in play when we think of Sherlock Holmes' celebrated powers of 'deduction'—referring to his facility with (rather subtle and convoluted) pieces of reasoning about the everyday world. But, in the context of the psychology of reasoning, as in logic and linguistics, deduction has a specific technical meaning.

A conclusion follows *deductively* from a set of premises when the conclusion *must* be true, if the premises are true. Arguments for which this holds are *deductively valid*. The force of the *must* is not merely a matter of practical possibility—it expresses a logical necessity. Thus, although in the world we happen to live in, it is reasonable to conclude with a high degree of certainty from the premise 'Icarus falls into the sea' to the conclusion 'Icarus gets wet', this argument is not deductively valid. This is because there are logically possible worlds in which, for example, people falling into the sea are kept dry by a powerful force which repels water. For an argument to be deductively valid, the conclusion must be true in all logically possible states of affairs, so long as the premises are true. From the point of view of psychology, the concept of 'logically possible states of affairs' and related notions may sound rather difficult to pin down definitively. This impression is entirely correct. Indeed, there is considerable philosophical controversy concerning whether it is possible to derive coherent notions of logical possibility and logical necessity at all (e.g. Lewis 1973; Quine 1960).

One important feature of deductive reasoning is that it is truth-preserving. If we start with a true set of premises, then any conclusions that deductively follow from those premises must also be true. That is, deductive inference is certain: if the premises hold, then the conclusion holds with complete certainty.

To put it another way: if the premises hold, then the conclusion holds, independent of any other information whatever. This means that, if a conclusion follows deductively from a set of premises, then it must also follow deductively from that set of premises conjoined with any set of additional premises. That is, nothing can overturn a deductive inference. This property is known as 'monotonicity'—the intuition being that adding a premise can never lead to the deletion of a conclusion. Our inference about Icarus is not deductively valid, and is hence non-monotonic. This is because if we were to learn, to our astonishment, the additional premise concerning the hitherto unknown repulsive force then the conclusion no longer follows—learning new information overturns an old conclusion. By contrast, a classical logical inference such as:

> all people are mortal;
> Socrates is a person;
> Socrates is mortal;

is deductively valid. This is because, whatever else we may learn about people, human mortality, Socrates, or, indeed, whatever other facts we learn at all, the conclusion still follows. (At least on the standard logical analysis of the meanings of these phrases. As we will discuss in Chapter 4, the logical interpretation of the meanings of natural language sentences can themselves be challenged, and cannot be taken as axiomatic. Hence, the question of which natural language arguments are deductively valid is, similarly, a matter for debate, rather than a priori decision. Indeed, the probabilistic interpretation of the conditional, and of the quantifiers, that we describe below, has important implications for which inferences are, and are not, deductively valid.)

Deductive reasoning is, of course, much in evidence in mathematics. For example, suppose that the commutativity of addition (that is, $x + y = y + x$, for all x and y) can be deduced from some axiomatic formulation of arithmetic. It therefore follows that commutativity holds, *whatever* further axioms are added. Deductive reasoning is, of course, common throughout mathematics. Indeed, the fundamental driving force behind the development of modern logic was the attempt to formalize mathematical reasoning, initiated by Frege, Russell, Whitehead, and others.

Other modes of reasoning, which are not deductively valid, are 'non-monotonic'—adding premises can lead to conclusions being withdrawn. An important example is 'induction', in which general laws or regularities are inferred from particular observations. At any time, it is possible that a new observation may conflict with the regularity and undermine it. For example, a new observation of a non-black raven logically undermines the inductive inference that *all ravens are black* based on the observation of numerous black ravens. Thus, adding a new premise (a new observation) can remove the conclusion, and hence induction is non-monotonic. Another example is abduction, which typically involves inferring causes from their effects. For example, in a detective mystery, a particular set of clues might, for example, suggest that the butler is the murderer. But a new and decisive clue (e.g. the chauffer's bloodstained shirt) might overturn this conclusion. Thus abduction too is non-monotonic, and hence not deductive. In everyday reasoning, uncertain reasoning is clearly very prevalent. This raises the question of how much deductive reasoning occurs in daily life.

It is typically assumed that deduction plays at least a partial role in almost every other aspect of cognition (Johnson-Laird and Byrne 1991; Macnamara and Reyes 1994; Rips 1994). For example, Johnson-Laird and Byrne (1991, pp. 2–3) argue for the centrality of deduction:

> ... because of its intrinsic importance: it plays a crucial role in many tasks. You need to make deductions in order to formulate plans and to evaluate actions; to determine the consequences of assumptions and hypotheses; to interpret and formulate instructions, rules and general principles; to pursue arguments and negotiations; to weigh evidence and to assess data; to decide between competing theories; and to solve problems.

Thus, the idea that a deductive competence theory is central to human cognition both has a long pedigree and is widely held by many leading figures in the psychology of reasoning.

In this chapter, we argue against this tradition in the psychology of reasoning. We claim that almost no everyday human reasoning can be characterized deductively, or has any significant deductive component. Although many theorists have argued that deduction is at the core of cognition, we argue that it is at the periphery. However, we begin by clarifying what we mean by the claim that human reasoning involves deduction by introducing Marr's levels of description of a computational process.

Deduction, reasoning, and Marr

The claim that human reasoning involves deduction can be understood in a number of different ways. We can understand these different interpretations in terms of two of Marr's (1982) three levels of computational explanation.

Marr's highest level of analysis is the *computational* level where 'the performance of the device is characterized as a mapping from one kind of information to another, the abstract properties of this mapping are defined precisely, and its appropriateness and adequacy for the task at hand are demonstrated' (Marr 1982, p. 24). Marr uses the example of a cash register. The theory of arithmetic provides the computational-level analysis of this device and its appropriateness is demonstrated by showing that our intuitive constraints on the operation of a cash register map directly onto this mathematical theory (Marr 1982, p. 22). In the case of human reasoning, psychologists have typically assumed that deductive logic plays the role that arithmetic plays for the cash register, i.e. logic characterizes the inferences people draw. Whether or not this is true is clearly an empirical question, just as it is an empirical question whether or not a particular piece of machinery functions as a cash register.

Marr's *algorithmic* level describes how to compute the function specified at the computational level. This level also involves specifying the representations that the algorithm manipulates in computing the function. Thus in the case of the cash register, using Arabic numerals as the representations involves using the standard rules 'about adding the least significant digits first and "carrying" the sum if it exceeds 9' (Marr 1982, p. 22) as an algorithm. Although the choice of algorithm is constrained by the choice of representation, it is not uniquely constrained—there may be several ways of computing a certain function using the same representation. It could be the case that deduction provides a crucial component at the algorithmic level. In computer science, this idea is embodied in theorem provers, which are computational systems for proving logical theorems. Theorem provers can be used to reason about the everyday world, given axioms embodying everyday knowledge. They have also been used to construct general programming languages, such as PROLOG (Clocksin and Mellish 1984).

Hypotheses about deductive reasoning at the computational and algorithmic levels have been prevalent within the psychology of deductive reasoning. Many theorists argue for deduction at both levels. For example, Inhelder and Piaget (1955, p. 305) go as far as to say that human 'reasoning is nothing more than the propositional calculus itself'. For Piaget, attainment of the formal operational stage in cognitive development is, by definition, revealed in the ability to show logical reasoning behaviour. Thus, logic is viewed as an appropriate computational-level description of mature human behaviour. But, moreover, the quotation above reveals that the mechanism that achieves this performance is itself logic. This view is still widely advocated in current psychology of reasoning, by advocates of 'mental logic' (Braine 1978; Braine and O'Brien 1991; Henle 1962; Lea *et al.* 1990; O'Brien *et al.* 1994; Politzer and Braine 1991; Rips 1983, 1994; for a collection on these issues, see Macnamara and Reyes 1994). For example, Rips (1994, p. viii) argues for what he calls the Deduction System Hypothesis, that logical 'principles ... are central to cognition because they underlie many other cognitive abilities... [and] that the mental life of every human embodies certain deduction principles'.

Although the claim that logic has a role at the computational and algorithmic levels are often held together, they are clearly independent. It is possible that while logic characterizes the behaviour of a device at the computational level, the algorithms that produce the behaviour are not themselves logical. This viewpoint is explicitly advocated in the psychology of reasoning by Macnamara, who also places deductive logic at the centre of human cognition, but articulates this thesis more guardedly (Macnamara 1986, p. 22):

> A logic that is true to intuition in a certain area constitutes a competence theory [in Chomsky's (1965) sense] for the corresponding area for cognitive psychology.

As Marr (1982) notes, 'competence theory' is simply another way of talking about a computational level account. Mental model theory (Johnson-Laird 1983; Johnson-Laird and Byrne 1991) explicitly takes the view that logic is part of the computational-level theory of reasoning. But mental model theory is typically viewed as not involving logical inference at the algorithmic level. Instead mental model theory assumes that deductive reasoning involves the construction and manipulation of mental models.

The converse position is also possible. The algorithms underlying thought might follow deductive logic, but the behaviour resulting from those algorithms might be best characterized in non-deductive terms. For example, a theorem prover could implement list-handling operations or arithmetic. Therefore, the computational-level characterization of what the program is doing will involve descriptions of list manipulation or arithmetical calculation, rather than logical proof. Within the psychology of reasoning, this viewpoint has not been explicitly advocated, as far as we know. However, it is reasonable to interpret influential theorists in the foundations of cognitive science, such as Fodor, as advocating this position. Thus, Fodor and Pylyshyn (1988, pp. 29–30) argue that, 'It would not be unreasonable to describe Classical Cognitive Science as an extended attempt to apply the methods of proof theory to the modeling of thought', and they proceed strongly to defend this position. Because proof theory is the mechanism by which deductive inferences are made, this amounts to the claim that cognition is deductive at the algorithmic level. But Fodor (1983) also argues extensively that almost all aspects of thought are 'non-demonstrative', that is, non-deductive, in character (and we shall outline some of these arguments below). Therefore, Fodor seems to reject deduction as a computational-level theory of reasoning, but embraces logic as an algorithmic theory.

In this book, we shall focus primarily on whether deductive logic provides an appropriate *computational*-level description of human reasoning, rather than dealing with the algorithmic level. As we have seen, the assumption that deduction does provide a computational-level description for much human inference is shared by many contemporary researchers on reasoning, including advocates of mental logics and mental models. Of course, no theorist would propose that deductive logic could provide a computational-level theory of all aspects of human reasoning, such as reasoning under uncertainty (Tversky and Kahneman 1974), decision-making (Baron 2000; Tversky and Kahneman 1986), abductive (Gluck and Bower 1988), and inductive (Gorman and Gorman 1984; Wason 1960) reasoning. Instead, deductive logic is assumed to provide a computational level account of an important class of human reasoning.

We now consider various possible arguments or sources of evidence for the role of deduction in human thought. We begin with two possibilities that, while superficially attractive—and instructive about the problems involved—prove not to be decisive.

How much deduction is there? Two easy answers

We consider two methods of investigating the question of how much everyday reasoning is deductive at the computational level, which initially appear to provide decisive answers to our question. First, the collection and analysis of corpora of everyday arguments promises to reveal the statistical prevalence of deductive reasoning directly. Second, a priori considerations from computer science appear to decide the question, before any empirical investigation is carried out: specifically, any computational process whatever can be viewed as deductive. In this section, we show that neither of these considerations can decide the question. In the next section, we show that when these sources of evidence are viewed from a more sophisticated perspective, the question can be genuinely addressed. The two sources of evidence provide two criteria of adequacy on theories of reasoning, from epistemology and artificial intelligence, neither of which can be met by a cognitive science of reasoning using deduction as its computational-level theory.

Looking at everyday argument

This strategy involves collecting and analysing corpora of everyday natural language arguments and deciding what fraction of them are deductively valid. If deduction is prevalent in everyday verbal argument, it is also likely to be prevalent in everyday verbal reasoning; at least, if we make the reasonable assumption that what people say is closely related to what they think.

The problem is that whether or not a natural language argument is deductive cannot be straightforwardly ascertained by purely logical analysis. Consider, for example, the argument:

> Birds fly.
> Tweety is a bird.
> Therefore, Tweety flies.

One way of assessing the validity of this argument is to translate it into a logical formalism, such as the predicate calculus, as follows:

$$\forall x(Bird(x) \Rightarrow Flys(x))$$
$$Bird(Tweety)$$
$$\therefore Flys(Tweety).$$

According to the logical properties of the predicate calculus, this is a deductively valid argument: in logical terms, there is no model in which the premises are true, but the conclusion is false. But this only means that the original argument is deductively valid if the *translation* from natural language into the logical language is accepted as capturing the 'logical form' of their natural language statements (Haack 1978). In practice, this step is frequently highly controversial. For example, even the logical terms, 'not' ($\neg$), 'and' ($\wedge$), and 'or' ($\vee$) are notoriously distant relatives of their natural language counterparts (e.g. Hodges 1977; Horn 1989; Lemmon 1965). The relation between the universal quantifier ($\forall$) and the existential quantifier ($\exists$) and the terms 'all' and 'some' in natural language is even more complex (Barwise and Cooper 1981). This is particularly true when, as in our example sentence 'birds fly', the quantification is not explicit. Should this sentence be treated as meaning that *all* birds fly? Or is a better interpretation that it means that *most* birds fly, that *normal* birds fly (McCarthy 1980), or perhaps that it is reasonable to assume that a bird flies unless there is reason to believe the contrary (Reiter 1980, 1985)? On any of these latter interpretations, the conclusion of the above inference does not follow deductively—Tweety may be one of the exceptional non-flying birds. Therefore, whether or not a natural language argument is deductive depends on how the premises and conclusions are translated into logic and this translation is a highly controversial matter.

Moreover, both philosophers (e.g. Davidson 1984a; Quine 1960) and psychologists (Smedslund 1970) have pointed out that there is a circularity in the relationship between studying reasoning and studying the meaning of what people say. That is, which translation of a natural language statement is correct depends on how people *reason* with that statement. For example, is the statement rejected as soon as a counter-example is found? Will a person wager an arbitrarily large sum of money against the possibility that the premises are true but the conclusion false? The logical form of a statement is intended to capture the patterns of reasoning in which it figures; and hence the nature of reasoning with the statement constrains the choice of translation. But, of course, discovering how people reason with a statement is a question in the psychology of reasoning. So psychologists cannot look to a purely logical analysis of natural language arguments as a neutral way of assessing how much deduction people do, because the appropriateness of any particular logical analysis itself depends on how people reason. We shall pursue the question of the interpretation of natural language arguments, and whether some arguments are appropriately interpreted in terms of deductive logic at all, in Chapter 4.

For now, we conclude only that the fact that logical analysis of natural language arguments itself depends on psychological considerations, rules out the obvious methodological strategy of collecting and analysing a corpus of everyday arguments.

An answer from computer science?

So our first approach to get an easy answer to the question 'how much deductive is there?'—to look directly at corpora of everyday arguments is not conclusive—because there is no neutral and uncontroversial way of deciding whether a natural language argument is deductive or not. But perhaps there is another easy way to answer the question of the prevalence and importance of deductive reasoning in cognition, which does not depend on empirical considerations at all. This argument, although often encountered in conversation, is rare in the literature—perhaps because, as we shall see, it does not stand up to analysis.

The argument is as follows. Cognitive science is built on the assumption that cognition is computation. And there are deep results in computer science that suggest that all computations can be viewed as deductive, i.e. logical, inferences.

To spell the argument out in more detail, let us start by introducing the celebrated, but extremely simple, class of computer—the Turing machine. A Turing machine consists of two components. The first component is a linear 'tape' consisting of squares that may contain the symbols '0' or '1' or may be left blank. The tape can be extended indefinitely in both directions, and hence there can be infinitely many different patterns of 0s and 1s on the tape. The second component is a 'control box', consisting of a finite number of states, which operates upon the tape. At any time, the control box is located over a particular square of the Turing machine's tape. The control box has a small number of possible actions. It can read the symbol on the tape over which it is currently located; and it can replace the current symbol with a different symbol, and the current state of the control box may be replaced by one of the finite number of other possible states. It can also move left or right along the tape, one square at a time, or it can halt, at which point the computation is terminated. Which actions the control box performs, is determined by two factors: the current state of the machine, and the symbol on the square of the tape over which it is located.

A Turing machine can be viewed as a computer in the following way. The input to the computation is encoded as the string of 1s and 0s, which comprise the initial state of the tape. The nature of the control box (that is, which symbols and states lead to which actions and changes of state) determines how this input is modified by the operation of the control box. The control box might, for example, leave the initial input intact, delete it entirely and replace it with a completely different string of 1s and 0s, or more interestingly perform some useful manipulation of the input which may involve many steps. This resulting string encodes the output of the computation. A control box can therefore be associated with a mapping from inputs to outputs, defining the computation that it performs. According to the Church–Turing thesis (Boolos and Jeffrey 1980), if a computation can be performed by any physical device whatever, then there is a Turing machine that can perform that calculation. The class of Turing machines is, therefore, universal. Indeed, any class of machine above a very moderate level of complexity is universal—though crucially the equivalence between machines only holds when time and memory limitations are ignored.

So far, we have assumed that cognition is computation, and all computation can be captured by a Turing machine. Now we can make the crucial connection with logic. It is straightforward to formalize the operation of a Turing machine in logical terms. The premises simply describe the initial state of the machine and a set of conditionals, which explain the behaviour of the machine when it has a specific current input under the control box and is in a specific state. By carrying out deductive, logical inference, we can now perfectly model the subsequent behaviour of the machine.

It is tempting to conclude that all computation can be formalized as deductive, logical inference. And if we maintain the central tenet of cognitive science that cognition is a kind of computation, it follows that cognition can be viewed as deductive logical inference. Hence deduction appears to be the centre of cognition in general and, therefore, the psychology of reasoning in particular.

It would therefore appear that the question of how much deduction there is in human cognition is decided the moment we adopt the assumption that cognition is computation. Any behaviour that can be explained in computational terms must automatically have a logical interpretation at both the algorithmic and the computational level. Consequently, it appears that *all* cognitive processes are thereby deductive. However, there is clearly something seriously wrong with this line of argument. If it is accepted, then any cognitive task is necessarily a logical task. This would mean that arithmetic, reading, probabilistic reasoning, motor control, perceptual processing, syntactic analysis, and so on, are all examples of logical reasoning. Furthermore, this means that all mundane computations, such as spreadsheets, word processing, solving differential equations, doing actuarial calculations, all have deductive logic as their computational-level theory. But this is close to a *reductio ad absurdum* of this line of reasoning. The point of computational-level theory is that it describes both the purpose of the computation, and the objects and relations it is *about*. Thus, a computational-level theory of a cash-register must involve numbers and numerical operations; a computational-level theory of syntactic analysis must deal with words, phrases and sentences of natural languages, and so on. However, the objects involved in providing the overarching logical analyses outlined above involve states and possible state transitions of a Turing machine, or mathematical objects in abstract function spaces. A logical description in terms of these objects provides a computational-level description of a sort, but at such an abstract level of specification that it says nothing about the *point* of the computation. At this level of description, it is not possible to discriminate a computational process that carries out actuarial calculations from one that does word processing or produces natural language utterances. The whole point of Marr's (1982) computational-level analysis is to make exactly these distinctions, to which these highly abstract analyses are insensitive.

In the case of human reasoning, it is crucial that a computational-level theory views human reasoning as about the objects and relations in the everyday world. The claim that an inference from 'Birds fly' and 'Tweety is a bird' to 'Tweety flies' is (or is not) deductive, only makes sense where we interpret these statements as referring to birds, flying, and Tweety, not to states of a computational device, or to objects in an abstract function space.

Therefore, the apparently decisive a priori arguments from computer science turn out to be entirely beside the point in determining whether or not human inference should be understood deductively. The results from computer science only apply to a level of analysis so abstract as to be of no practical value in constructing computational- or algorithmic-level theories of human reasoning.

How much deduction is there? Lines of evidence

We now turn to two arguments that are related to the empirical and computational arguments we looked at in the last section but which correspond to more sophisticated research strategies. First, unless we are to give up the claim that human reasoning has any rational justification, then a deductive account of how people *should* reason about the world must be viable. That is, deduction must be central to our theories of epistemology, which define the very standards of rationality against which we measure actual human reasoning performance (Brown 1988). Second, any psychological theory must be computationally viable. Therefore, if deduction is the foundation of human thought, then it must be possible to design and successfully implement artificial intelligence systems that reason about the real world using deduction.

We argue that the claim that human reasoning is based on deduction at the computational level fails on both counts. It represents an epistemologically outmoded tradition that has not proved viable in artificial intelligence.

Epistemological adequacy

In this section our argument is in three parts. First, we argue that the view that deduction is the foundation for reasoning about the world reflects an outmoded epistemological tradition. Second, we consider what aspects of reasoning might be deductive and conclude that the obvious candidates turn out to be non-deductive in character. Finally, we briefly consider, and reject, a possible defence of the centrality of deduction in cognitive science, which seeks to exploit the fact that epistemology considers how we *should* reason, whereas cognitive science is concerned with how people actually *do* reason.

Could deduction be the foundation for thought?

Euclid provided the first systematic exploration of deductive reasoning (Coolidge 1940). Beginning with definitions, and apparently self-evident axioms, he showed how purely deductive argument could establish a large class of geometrical truths. The Euclidean method has proved to be enormously fecund, not just in geometry, but throughout mathematics.

But mathematical reasoning does not seem, superficially, to have much in common with everyday thought. In particular, mathematics appears to be about establishing certainties concerning abstract objects (for discussion see: Putnam and Benacerraf 1983). In contrast, everyday thought appears to be about making the best sense possible of an ill-defined, concrete external world, in which certainty is rarely, if ever, encountered (Barwise and Perry 1983). Can deduction extend beyond the mathematical realm, and provide a route to knowledge concerning the external world? This question is crucial for the psychology of reasoning, for it concerns the scope that human deductive reasoning might have. It is also a central question in the history of epistemology (Russell 1946).

Euclid's astonishing successes in geometry, and the absence of any comparably impressive achievements using other reasoning methods, suggested that deductive reasoning could also provide a foundation for knowledge of the external world. From Plato to Kant, an influential line of philosophers has attempted to establish non-mathematical knowledge using deductive argument. Attempts to model scientific enquiry on Euclid's deductive model had a profound influence on Greek and medieval science (Russell 1946). Spinoza even went as far as using the Euclidean method in his *Ethics*, with definitions, axioms and 'proofs'. It would not be unreasonable to suggest, then, that psychologists of reasoning have simply taken over a preoccupation with deduction that has been evident more widely in Western thought since Plato.

However, more recently, the view that science derives knowledge of the world by deduction from self-evident foundations has fallen into disrepute (Lakatos 1970, 1977; Popper 1935/1959). Contrary to the Euclidean picture, science appears to proceed by plausible conjecture on the basis of observation, not by deductively certain inference. For example, Bacon explicitly advocated alternative inferential methods for what he called inductive reasoning (Urbach 1987). In the twentieth century, it has become increasingly accepted that people derive knowledge of the world by different means from knowledge of mathematics (for example, see: Russell 1919). The non-deductive origin of scientific knowledge is a common thread linking diverse views in modern philosophy of science, for example (Glymour 1980; Howson and Urbach 1993; Kuhn 1962; Lakatos 1970; Putnam 1974; Thagard 1988; Toulmin 1961; van Frassen 1980). In epistemology more generally there is agreement that knowledge of the world does not have a deductive basis (see: Goldman 1986; Lehrer 1990; Pollock 1986; Thagard 1988).

The deductive picture has, however, remained influential as a standard against which philosophers may assess other knowledge-gathering methods. In particular, scepticism concerning knowledge of the world, from Descartes onwards, has its roots in the distance between the certainty that deduction can assure, and the lack of certainty that non-deductive empirical methods of inquiry provide (Burnyeat 1983). That no one has met the sceptical challenge to provide a certain grounding for knowledge reinforces our thesis that science does not obtain knowledge by deductive means.

So, it seems that we have two paradigms of thought: mathematical knowledge, where deductive inference appears to be of primary importance; and empirical, scientific knowledge, in which deductive inference plays at most a secondary role. Both within epistemology and in psychology, there is agreement that we should view human thought as generally analogous to scientific, rather than mathematical, enquiry (Fodor 1983). For example, many philosophers advocate the view that common sense and science are parts of the same general project of understanding the world, differing only by degree of systematicity and rigour (e.g. Goodman 1951; Quine 1960, 1990). Developmental psychologists frequently view the child as a 'naïve scientist' (Carey 1988; Karmiloff-Smith 1988); accounts of causal reasoning in adults also use the naïve-scientist metaphor (Jaspars *et al.* 1983; Kelley 1967); psychologists view learning from experience in any domain as involving inductive inference (Holland *et al.* 1986), and so on.

Perhaps surprisingly, one of the strongest advocates of the logic-based view of thought, Fodor (see: Fodor and Pylyshyn 1988), has put an important and persuasive case for the non-deductive character of thought. He notes that the perceptual system attempts to infer the causes in the external world of the inputs to the sensory receptors, and that such reasoning is an instance of inference to the best explanation (Harman 1965). This pattern of inference, like induction, is uncontroversially non-monotonic. From a distance, the perceptual system may misclassify sensory input as being generated by a horse. However, on moving closer it may be apparent that it is actually generated by a cow. The addition of new information overturns the original conclusion—additional information indicating that another explanation is better, overturns what was previously the best explanation. Thus, perception involves non-monotonic, and hence non-deductive, reasoning. Moreover, Fodor argues that what he calls 'central' cognitive processes, of belief revision and common-sense thought, face a problem analogous to scientific inference. For reasons similar to those we have outlined above, Fodor believes that scientific inference is non-monotonic and that it is not deductively formalizable. He therefore concludes that central cognitive processes will likewise be non-deductive in character.

To sum up so far: there is a long tradition in epistemology, initially inspired by Euclidean geometry, which attempts to provide deductive foundations for non-mathematical knowledge. According to this model, it seems quite reasonable to postulate that deduction is the foundation of human thought. However, the rise of science has involved plausible, but uncertain, inferences that do not fit this deductive pattern. Furthermore, human cognition is related to empirical, non-deductive, enquiry, rather than deductive, mathematical enquiry. So the view that deduction provides the foundation for human thought may be unworkable, a vestige of an outmoded epistemological tradition.

What aspects of thought might be deductive?

The conclusion that deduction is not the foundation for thought does not, of course, imply that no thought is deductive. From the point of view of the psychology of reasoning, the study of deduction may still be of wide significance to psychology, if some substantial and important aspects of human reasoning are deductive. Indeed, many psychologists of reasoning appear, at least in some passages, to advocate this relatively modest position. Johnson-Laird and Byrne (1991), who advocate a central role for deduction, nonetheless concede that much human reasoning is not deductive in character. For example, they point out that even Sherlock Holmes, whose 'powers of deduction' are legendary, does not really solve problems deductively at all. Johnson-Laird and Byrne note that Holmes' inferences are plausible conjectures, which although ubiquitous in everyday life are not the consequences of deductively valid arguments.

Pursuing the analogy with science, it is interesting that, although philosophers of science have generally abandoned the view that scientific inference might be deductive, some continue to advocate the view that certain aspects of science involve deductive inference. Roughly, the view is that, although forming theories does not involve deductive inference, deduction is crucially involved in prediction, explanation, and theory testing. Most notably, the hypothetico-deductive account of prediction and hypothesis testing (Popper 1935/1959), and the deductive-nomological view of scientific explanation and prediction (Hempel 1965), advocate this view. If this view is right, we can conjecture that deduction plays an analogous role in everyday human thought. Thus perhaps, deduction does have an important, if not exclusive, role in human cognition.

However, deductive views of science provide little support for the deductively inclined psychologist of reasoning. Contrary to the views of Hempel and Popper, recent philosophy of science has suggested that prediction, explanation, and hypothesis testing in science are not really deductive in character. Taking prediction as an example, according to the deductive view, a prediction is a deductive consequence of a theory or a hypothesis together with some initial conditions. So, according to Hempel's view we have the following picture:

$$T \wedge I \models P \tag{3.1}$$

where T denotes the theory, I the initial conditions, P the prediction, and '$\models$' the relation of deductive entailment (i.e. (3.1) states that T and I logically entail P). For example, Newton's laws (T) together with information (I) about the state of the system at time, t_0, deductively imply particular trajectories (P) for the planets at subsequent times $t > t_0$. However, as critics have pointed out (Duhem 1914/1954; Lakatos 1970, 1977; Putnam 1974; Quine 1953), this conclusion only follows *all other things being equal*. Real physical systems are not causally sealed off from external forces; they are open systems.

Consequently there are limitless possible intervening forces and factors, i.e. 'auxiliary hypotheses' (Putnam 1974), that could intervene to make the prediction fail—unexpected frictional, electromagnetic, or as yet undiscovered forces, changes in physical constants in different parts of space/time, and so on.

The non-deductive character of scientific prediction becomes clear when the prediction does not fit with observation. If the prediction followed deductively from the theory, then the theory would automatically be falsified. However, in practice, the theory may be fine, because auxiliary hypotheses, such as those noted above, may be the cause of the mismatch between prediction and observation. Putnam (1974) notes, for example, that Newton's Laws are entirely compatible with square orbits, given appropriate additional forces

One possible defence for the deductive view is to argue that the predictions can be derived deductively, but only when the auxiliary hypotheses are added to the set of premises. This suggestion involves modifying the entailment in (3.1) as follows:

$$T \wedge I \wedge AH_1 \wedge AH_2 \wedge \ldots AH_i \ldots \wedge AH_n \mid = P. \tag{3.2}$$

If the prediction turns out to be false, then the scientist may reject either the theory under test, the specification of the initial conditions, or one of these auxiliary hypotheses, rather than the theory under test.

But is this strategy really viable? We noted above that science, and for that matter everyday reasoning, is concerned with causally open systems, where there are indefinitely many unexpected external factors. This means that an infinite number of auxiliary hypotheses are required to determine, with certainty, that a particular prediction holds—each hypothesis being concerned with one of the indefinitely many factors that might impact the open system under consideration. Thus, at whatever level of detail the inference (3.2) is spelled out—i.e. however many and however detailed, the auxiliary hypotheses that are added—the conclusion will still not follow deductively. There will always be further factors that, if known, could serve to undermine the conclusion. These considerations suggest that scientific reasoning cannot be reconstructed in deductive form (Quine 1953; Putnam 1974).

We have considered prediction in science at length because precisely analogous considerations arise in attempting to model common-sense reasoning in deductive terms (e.g. Schiffer 1987), as we shall see in the discussion of default rules in artificial intelligence below.

We have so far argued that deduction is not appropriate for formalizing predictive and explanatory reasoning: that is, the derivation of empirical predictions about the world does not proceed by deductive inference. The final position we consider is that deductive reasoning leads not to empirical predictions, but to conceptual or analytic truths. For example, perhaps it follows deductively from what it is to be a bachelor, that bachelors must be male. Kant's programme for establishing the properties of space, causality, and the like, pursued this line: the idea was that these properties are not really properties of the external world, but conceptual necessities of human thought (Scruton 1982). Perhaps this kind of inference is deductive.

Modern epistemology suggests that it is not, however, because the distinction between conceptual and empirical claims cannot be maintained. For example, Quine (1953) has forcefully argued that there is no non-circular way to characterize the distinction between analytic, conceptual truths and synthetic, empirical truths. According to contemporary epistemology, all statements are revisable in the light of experience—none are purely conceptual truths derived by deductive argument alone (although for an opposing point of view, see: Katz 1990). Furthermore, the development of mathematics and physics since Kant has shown that 'conceptual necessity' is unexpectedly flexible. For example, Kant took the Euclidean character of space to be conceptually necessary, but modern science has shown that space is in fact non-Euclidean (Putnam 1962/1975). Hence, what appears to be conceptual knowledge, which might potentially be the result of deduction, may be empirical, and so not derived by deduction. In sum, epistemological considerations suggest that deduction is not central to human thought in either making empirical predictions, or in establishing conceptual truths.

From the first part of the epistemological argument above, we concluded that deduction cannot be the primary means of acquiring knowledge of the world. In the second part, we have searched for a substantial residual role for deductive reasoning, and failed to find one. From an epistemological point of view, one might suspect that deduction plays only a small role in human reasoning.

We have shown that deduction does not provide an adequate epistemology. If deduction is never or rarely *justified*, then it seems unlikely to provide a useful design principle for intelligent systems, whether human or artifical.

A possible defence?

Epistemology and the philosophy of science are concerned with how people *should* reason, rather than how they *do* reason: it is *normative* rather than descriptive. This appears to leave open the possibility that the epistemological arguments described above may be accepted, but that they imply only that people *should not* use deduction in everyday life. This seems not to preclude the possibility that people actually *do* reason deductively about the everyday world. But this defence fails for a number of reasons.

First, notice that epistemological considerations show that interesting conclusions never (or almost never) follow deductively from known premises about the real world. This means that, if people do reason deductively about the real world, then the conclusions that they will be able to draw will be entirely uninteresting: they will not support induction of general rules, allow predictions about, or explanations of, the everyday world, or even reveal conceptual 'analytic' truths. The arguments from contemporary epistemology above show that reasoning deductively about the world would not yield conclusions of any interest, despite a long philosophical tradition to the contrary. Therefore, it would seem bizarre, to say the least, to suppose that that deduction is central to human thought, even though we have no reason to believe that the results of deduction would be useful.

Second, it is clear that people *do* predict, explain, and find regularities in the scientific and everyday worlds, and use this knowledge as a basis for decisions and action. These abilities are of fundamental cognitive significance. So suppose that one insists, in some desperation, that much everyday reasoning is perversely based on deduction, and one admits that this deductive reasoning reaches no useful conclusions about the real world. Then one would still have to grant that reasoning that *does* lead to substantial and interesting conclusions about the everyday world is not based on deduction. But given that these concessions must be granted, deductive reasoning is clearly marginal, rather than central, to cognition, which is the conclusion for which we are arguing.

Third, the attempt to drive a wedge between how people *should* reason and how they *do* reason is not persuasive in this context, because the epistemological arguments that we discussed above are themselves derived from the actual practice of scientific reasoning. The tendency to make inductive leaps with no deductive justification, the Quine–Duhem thesis, the failure to automatically reject hypotheses when their predictions are disconfirmed, and so on, are not merely abstract methodological recommendations. They are manifest in the history of science (e.g. Kuhn 1962). Indeed, in the philosophy of science, and contemporary epistemology more generally, the constraints between accounts of how people *should* and *do* reason are so tight that many philosophers have argued that they cannot be separated (Kornblith 1994; Quine 1969; Thagard 1988).

A final defence might be that people do derive interesting conclusions about the world (e.g. prediction, explanation, and the like), that they use deduction to do this, and that epistemology simply shows that these deductions are not valid. But admitting that people's actual deductions are invalid amounts to giving up deduction as a competence theory of human reasoning. This is because, by assumption, people's actual deductions are not valid, and hence their reasoning behaviour cannot be characterized by deductive logic. Moreover, the fact that human reasoning about the world is often successful is left entirely mysterious on the view that human reasoning is merely bungled deductive logic.

We have seen that the view that deduction characterizes people's reasoning about the world at the computational level is epistemologically unviable. Reasoning about the everyday world *should not be*, and *is not*, deductively valid. This conclusion is reinforced by considerations from artificial intelligence.

Artificial intelligence

The philosophical considerations we have discussed strongly suggest that logic is not the appropriate tool with which to capture either scientific or everyday inference. If this is right, we would expect that probability, rather than logic, would be an appropriate tool with which to attempt to build computational models of everyday reasoning. Indeed, artificial intelligence provides an ideal testing ground for the hypothesis that reasoning is deductive, because it has adopted the practical project of attempting to formalize (fragments of) human knowledge and build computational systems that reason using this knowledge (e.g. Charniak and McDermott 1985). As we now see, research in artificial intelligence reinforces the conclusion from epistemology that deductive inference has little or no role in reasoning about the everyday world.

First, let us briefly consider inductive reasoning and inference to the best explanation, as they are studied in artificial intelligence. According to Hempel's (1965) deductive-nomological view of explanation and Popper's (1959) hypothetico-deductive approach to prediction and theory testing, deduction might be expected to play an important role in computational systems performing such reasoning. Similarly, according to Rips (1994) and Johnson-Laird and Byrne (1991), who argue that deduction plays an important role in almost all cognitive processes, it might be expected that deduction would have an important role to play. But, in fact, as might be expected in the light of the epistemological arguments outlined above, artificial intelligence has found no useful role for deduction in inductive and abductive reasoning. Induction, which is studied in the artificial intelligence and engineering literatures on 'machine learning' (e.g. Michalski *et al.* 1983) 'support vector machines' (Cristianini and Shawe-Taylor 2000), 'pattern recognition' (e.g. Duda *et al.* 2000), and 'neural networks' (e.g. Hertz *et al.* 1991), has no place for deduction. Inference to the best explanation, which we mentioned in the previous section, is known as 'abduction' in artificial intelligence. Artificial intelligence systems for abductive inference are generally non-deductive in character (Josephson and Josephson 1994). Furthermore, making predictions, where deduction at least seems *prima facie* to be appropriate, is no more deductive in the domain of common-sense reasoning than we found it to be in science.

Consider, for example, the prediction that if you drop an egg it will break, based on knowledge about eggs, the floor surface, the height from which you drop the egg, and so on. This inference is uncertain: you may catch the egg before it lands, you may have hardened the shell by artificial means, and so on. Alternatively, consider the inference that Tweety flies, from the general proposition that birds fly, and the knowledge that Tweety is a bird. This inference too is uncertain, since Tweety may be a penguin, may have an injury, be new-born, have clipped wings, and so on. Different areas of cognitive science, from cognitive psychology and philosophy to artificial intelligence, give many different labels to this phenomenon. Common-sense inference is 'context-sensitive' (Barsalou 1987), 'holds only relative to background conditions' (Barwise and Perry 1983), is 'defeasible' (Minsky 1977), 'admits exceptions' (Holland *et al.* 1986), 'lacks generality' (Goodman 1954), and has categories that are 'intention-relative' (Winograd and Flores 1986). Borrowing the standard term from artificial intelligence, we shall call inferences using rules that allow exceptions *default* inferences.

How can deductive logic, the calculus of certainty, be used to model the uncertainty of default inference? An initial suggestion is to deny that prediction really is uncertain; i.e. to claim that the conclusion follows deductively from the premises, and that the conclusion fails only when one or more of the premises do not apply. According to this view, prediction only appears to be uncertain because some of the premises are left unstated. In the case above, for example, additional premises such that the egg falls unimpeded, no one has artificially tampered with shell, and so on, are required to deduce the conclusion that the egg will break. If those premises are true, so the story goes, the conclusion follows with certainty.

We saw that this approach does not appear to be successful in the context of scientific reasoning, where we noted that because systems under study are open, there will always be indefinitely many unexpected factors that can defeat our predictions. Open systems are also the concern of common-sense reasoning about the everyday world, and so here too similar problems arise. In formalizing common-sense reasoning, as in formalizing science, it is not possible to restore certainty by including all these possible additional factors as extra premises in the argument. Even if we rule out the possibility that the dropped egg has an artificially hardened shell, or that you catch the egg before it lands, there remain possibilities such as that room is in free-fall, or is flooded, that the egg is caught by a net, and so on, that defeat the conclusion that the egg will break. Whatever additional premises we add, there are always further additional factors, not ruled out by those premises, that will overturn the conclusion.

It seems that the majority of inferences about the real world, whether common sense or scientific, are uncertain rather than deductive. In particular, we have seen that prediction in both science and common sense is non-deductive. Recent research in artificial intelligence, in contrast to the psychology of reasoning, has largely abandoned the attempt to model common-sense reasoning purely deductively and has recognized the need for a calculus of default reasoning that goes beyond deduction (Ginsberg 1987).

There are three broad approaches to dealing with uncertainty in artificial intelligence, none of which maintains that common-sense inference is deductively valid: the *logicist* approach, the *proceduralist* approach, and the *probabilistic* approach. We shall look at each in turn.

The logicist approach

This approach, which we introduced in a more general context in Chapter 1, attempts to develop non-monotonic logics (or related methods) where future premises can overturn conclusions, i.e. they sacrifice deductive validity (McCarthy 1980; McDermott 1982; McDermott and Doyle 1980; Reiter 1980, 1985). Within logic, there have been other attempts to extend logical methods so that they handle the uncertain, non-deductive character of inference concerning the real world—situation theory (Barwise and Perry 1983) being a notable example. We may view these approaches as broadening the notion of deduction, rather than abandoning it. We should not underestimate the magnitude of the change, however. From an epistemological point of view, giving up certainty is, of course, of fundamental significance; from a formal and computational point of view, non-monotonic reasoning has different properties from standard monotonic reasoning, partly because these systems must continually re-evaluate past conclusions in the light of new information, to see if they still follow (Brachman and Levesque 1985; Ginsberg 1987; Harman 1986; Oaksford and Chater 1991). As noted above, we restrict 'deduction' to monotonic reasoning, as this is the sense used in the psychology of reasoning; according to this usage, these non-monotonic reasoning schemes are not deductive. Indeed, psychologists of reasoning have generally rejected the use of non-monotonic logics (Johnson-Laird 1986; Johnson-Laird and Byrne 1991; Rips 1994). Indeed, Johnson-Laird and Byrne (1991) and Garnham (1993) suggest that the psychology of reasoning does not need to appeal to non-monotonic logics to understand how people carry out non-monotonic reasoning.

We have been particularly critical of this approach, especially with respect to the way that the problems revealed in artificial intelligence for non-monotonic reasoning also affect many current psychological theories of human reasoning (e.g. Chater 1993; Chater and Oaksford 1993; Oaksford 1993; Oaksford and Chater 1991, 1995b, 1998a). The first problem is what we term the problem of *completeness** (Oaksford and Chater 1991). A non-monotonic, logicist account must be capable of characterizing the defeasible inferences implicated in human cognition. That is, the logical rules it proposes must capture what we take pre-theoretically to be the semantically appropriate defeasible inferences. In Susan Haack's (1978) terminology, the logic(s) should be capable of respecting the appropriate *depraved semantics* (Haack 1978, p. 188). So in the case of a non-monotonic logic for defeasible reasoning, the interpretation of the formalism must map appropriately onto our common sense or *depraved* understanding of defeasible inference. Some suitable non-monotonic logic must therefore capture the range of inferences that common sense licenses or, in other words, it should be *complete* with respect to the depraved semantics. By loose analogy with the notion of completeness in classical logic with respect to a standard formal semantic interpretation, we called this the *completeness* criterion* (Oaksford and Chater 1991). So a complete* logicist explanation in some domain must provide a logical language and set of inferential rules which at least roughly captures our intuitions about the defeasible inferences in that domain. However, there are strong reasons to doubt that this is possible

Let us reconsider perhaps the most well-known approach to this problem within artificial intelligence, Reiter's (1985) default logic. Problems arise when the inferences that can be made from one rule intuitively conflict with the inferences that can be made from another. For example, knowing that Tweety is a sparrow leads to the conclusion that Tweety flies, whereas knowing that Tweety is one second old leads to the conclusion that Tweety cannot fly. This leads to the problem of what we infer when we learn that Tweety is a one-second-old sparrow. It is intuitively obvious that a one-second-old sparrow cannot fly. Although this is intuitively obvious, formally, it not obvious how to capture this conclusion. Formally we can regard these two pieces of information as two conditional rules: *if something is a bird it can fly*; and, *if something is one-second-old it cannot fly*. Formal proposals in artificial intelligence (Reiter 1985) appear unable to break the symmetry between these rules and specify which of these conflicting conclusions we should accept. That is, these proposals do not respect our intuitive understanding of these default inferences. The point here is that in the example it is our knowledge of what the rules mean and how the world works that indicate that a one-second-old sparrow is not going to fly.

It is not the formal properties of conditionals that determine which conclusion to draw. What matters is the *content* of the rules, to which the formal procedures for inference in Logicist artificial intelligence do not have access.

The second problem encountered by the logicist approach is *computational intractability* (McDermott 1986; Oaksford and Chater 1991). Most artificial intelligence programs require knowledge to be represented and accessed. We return to our standard example: *all birds can fly*. From this rule and the knowledge that *Tweety is a bird* you may infer that *Tweety can fly*. However, as this rule is defeasible, if you subsequently learn that *Tweety is an ostrich*, then the conclusion that *Tweety can fly* is defeated. Note that, strictly speaking, that ostriches cannot fly is a *counter-example* to the original generalization. That is, the generalization is false, and hence no valid conclusions can be drawn from it. This may suggest that only exceptionless generalizations should form the contents of world knowledge. However, at least at the level of people's commonsense classification of the world, such exceptionless generalizations would not appear to be available to characterize their everyday world knowledge. Moreover, if such generalizations were treated as false, then they would have to be expunged from the knowledge-base and would no longer be available to draw reasonable inferences about the world.

The standard approach in artificial intelligence (e.g. Reiter 1980, 1985) has been to argue that a closed-world assumption should be made. That is, inferences are drawn, based on what is in the knowledge-base *now*. Informally, when it is learnt that *Tweety is a bird*, as long as a counter-example cannot be generated from the current contents of the database, i.e. *Tweety cannot fly* cannot be established, then it is reasonable to infer that *Tweety can fly*. Observe that this means that every time a conclusion is drawn from a default rule, the whole of the database must be exhaustively searched to ensure no counter-example is available. This is equivalent to checking the consistency of the database. Consistency checking reduces to the satisfiability problem and is therefore computationally intractable (Garey and Johnson 1979), i.e. all known algorithms require exponentially increasing resources as the length of the input increases. In consequence *a computationally intractable problem has to be solved every time a default rule is invoked*. Since in the human case, the database may consist of the whole of world knowledge, a logicist account looks unpromising.

The proceduralist approach

This approach involves devising procedures that solve particular inference problems, but without attempting to ground such procedures in any formal theory of inference (McDermott 1987). *A fortiori*, this approach rejects the reconstruction of common-sense inference as *deductive* inference.

Interestingly, this approach, which is perhaps the most explicit in its rejection of a deduction, has been most in evidence in cognitive psychology, which has used artificial-intelligence models to provide theoretical proposals about how to organize world knowledge to support common-sense reasoning. We now discuss three by now quite old approaches that have been influential in psychology: semantic networks, schemas, and production systems. All of these approaches contain mechanisms for dealing with default inference. We argue that all are examples of the proceduralist approach and consequently one might have expected that cognitive psychologist would have come to an early realization that much of human inference is not deductive in character.

Semantic networks (e.g. Collins and Loftus 1975; Collins and Quillian 1969) use a hierarchical organization of knowledge and associate properties of objects with nodes in the hierarchy. Suppose that the BIRD node is associated with the property of FLYING; but that the PENGUIN node is associated with the property of NOT_FLYING. On encountering Tweety, a specific penguin, the system can infer both that Tweety cannot fly (because Tweety is a penguin) and that Tweety can fly (because Tweety is a bird). To resolve the conflict, the system assumes that information lower in the hierarchy (i.e. more specific information) takes precedence. Thus the system infers that Tweety does not fly. This method involves a particular approach to a certain kind of default rule—rules that apply to most of the objects in a class, but not to some subclasses of that class (rather than default rules that intervening external factors may over-ride, such as those we discussed in the section on epistemology). However, as it stands, the approach is very unconstrained. For example, the label NOT_FLYING may apply to all varieties of bird, although FLYING may still attach to the class BIRD, and other bizarre possibilities (for related discussion see: Woods 1975).

Schema theories and production systems use essentially similar mechanisms for dealing with default inference. In schema or frame theories (e.g. Minsky 1977; Schank and Abelson 1977), incoming information fills 'slots' in rules that are organized into domain-specific compartments or 'schemas'. Slots have associated default values, which further information can over-ride. For example, Tweety may fill the BIRD slot in a rule such as IF **hears** (*BIRD, bang*), THEN **flees** (*BIRD*) (i.e. if a bird hears a bang it flees). The slot for BIRD will carry the default assumption that birds fly, and hence that Tweety can fly. This may lead, for example, to the inference that Tweety will flee by flying away on hearing the bang. But if you know Tweety is a penguin, then this will over-ride the default using much the same mechanism as in the semantic network, and you may infer that Tweety will waddle rather than fly away.

Production systems (e.g. Anderson 1983; Newell 1990) encode knowledge in conditional rules much as in the example above. Default inferences arise out of conflicts between different conditional rules; for example, between the rule that IF **bird** (x), THEN **flies** (x) and IF **penguin** (x), THEN NOT (**flies** (x)). On encountering Tweety, to which both rules apply, the system resolves the conflict by choosing the most specific rule, as with semantic networks. Production systems also embody a variety of other procedures, in addition to specificity, for resolving conflicting defaults, including use of production *strength*, goodness of match with the antecedent of the conditional, and so on (Anderson 1983).

Semantic networks, schemas, and productions are all procedural approaches in the sense discussed above, specifically in regard to their approach to default reasoning. They handle defaults by simple procedural strategies, such as pre-ferring rules whose antecedents are at a lower level in a default hierarchy. Although the non-default aspects of some of these systems can be formalized using standard monotonic logic (for example, regarding semantic networks, see: Woods 1975; for schemas, see: Hayes 1979), the default inferences are sim-ply treated as procedures without any logical justification. For this reason, none of these systems simply implement logical inference. Hence, since almost all knowledge is defeasible, as we have already discussed, the majority of inferences drawn will be non-deductive in character.

The emergence of rational analysis (e.g. Anderson 1990) was partly a reac-tion against the proceduralism of these approaches. These models gave no account of why they were as they were. As Anderson (1990) pointed out, such models were like Heath Robinson (UK) or Rube Goldberg (US) machines: you could see how they worked but not why, i.e. what was their function? Our view is that the last approach adopted in artificial intelligence represents the way forward in establishing rational analyses of human reasoning performance.

The probabilistic approach

This approach to uncertainty in human reasoning uses the mathematical the-ory of uncertainty: probability theory, or related formalisms (Dempster 1967; Pearl 1988; Shafer 1976). This approach reconstructs common-sense infer-ences as establishing that a conclusion is probable, rather than deductively cer-tain, given a set of premises. In cases in which conditional probabilities are close to one, then the probabilistic style of reasoning becomes increasingly close to logical inference. Pearl (1988) exploits this fact in developing a non-monotonic logic- which he justifies as a limiting case of probabilistic infer-ence. This approach has the advantage of dealing with defeasibility naturally without many of the problems inherent in the non-monotonic logic approach (Oaksford and Chater 1998a). Moreover, it provides a set of normative princi-ples against which to assess human rationality. In subsequent chapters, we will show that this approach permits us to re-interpret some important results in the psychology of reasoning that had previously been thought to impugn human rationality. We show that these results conform to the normative principles of probability theory (Oaksford and Chater 1994b).

Summary

We began by considering the view that deductive reasoning is central to human cognition. However, we have found that the scope of deductive reasoning is remarkably limited. When we considered the acquisition and organization of knowledge in epistemology and artificial intelligence, it became clear that it is non-deductive, uncertain reasoning that appears to be cognitively ubiquitous. We concluded that the currently emerging probabilistic approach in artificial intelligence is a much more promising line to pursue than logicist attempts to construct non-monotonic logics or to pursue proceduralist approaches. In the next chapter, we argue that the move to a probabilistic approach is an emerging theme across a range of areas in the cognitive sciences.

Chapter 4

The probabilistic turn

Perhaps the single most striking conclusion in the psychology of deductive reasoning over the last forty years, in relation to the centrality of the concept of rationality in understanding human behaviour, is that people seem, by logical standards at least, to be remarkably *ir*rational. These empirical results have served as a substantial intellectual shock in discussions of rationality, both in psychology and philosophy (e.g. Cohen 1981; Stich 1985). Moreover, these results have led psychologists of reasoning to come away with the conclusion that human thinking is remarkably confused and riddled with error. Because of this, psychologists of reasoning have placed little emphasis on the remarkable achievements of human intelligence—and the fact that even the most modest aspects of human common-sense reasoning appears to be far beyond the reach of current computational-reasoning systems (as we saw in Chapter 3).

We advocate, in this book, the opposite viewpoint. We suggest that human reasoning is well-adapted to the uncertain character of everyday reasoning—to integrating and applying vast amounts of world knowledge concerning a partially known and fast-changing environment. If the real purpose of human reasoning processes is dealing with high levels of uncertainty, then it is perhaps not surprising that these processes are less effective in the context of certain deductive thought. It is rather as if we are surprised to find that a flipper turns out to be rather poor when used as a wing! The cognitive system is simply being tested by standards, and in a context, that is totally inappropriate. But taken at face value, this line of argument would appear to lead to the rejection of the psychology of deductive reasoning as an interesting domain of inquiry. This would appear to follow, because studying a system's operation in a totally inappropriate context is, in general, not likely to yield useful insights into its normal operation. To continue our analogy, it would seem likely that the study of how people carry out deductive-reasoning tasks might be no more interesting than the study of how well seals can learn to fly by flapping their flippers as fast as possible!

But, in the case of the psychology of deductive reasoning, the situation is not so simple. The reasoning tasks that people are asked to carry out are artificial, to be sure; but they concern the processing and manipulation of knowledge represented in a linguistic form (e.g. dealing with premises such as conditionals, quantified statements, and so on), which is a normal part of everyday cognition. Hence reasoning with statements of this kind is, presumably, a central aspect of everyday cognition—and something that the cognitive system is well-adapted to do. So the cognitive system may not be well-adapted to carrying out deductive reasoning; but it may, nonetheless, be well-adapted to reasoning with the linguistic materials used in deductive reasoning problems.

This suggests the following radical possibility, which we hinted at in Chapter 3. Perhaps the 'logical' renditions of everyday statements, which are typically assumed without question by psychologists of reasoning, are mistaken. Moreover, if uncertainty is at the core of understanding human reasoning, a better rendition of the meaning of such statements might be framed in terms of probability theory. If this is the case, then it may be that what have typically been viewed as deductive-reasoning tasks by experimenters are not actually deductive tasks at all, from the perspective of the experimental participant. The contrast between the experimenter's and the participant's perspective may, on this view, be quite stark. The experimenter devises the task with a great deal of theoretical background in mind—including, most particularly, a particular logical analysis of language. But the participant may be expected to attempt to assimilate the materials in terms that are appropriate in everyday discourse, and attack the problem using strategies that are appropriate in everyday reasoning. This suggests that people may be doing some form of uncertain, and perhaps probabilistic, reasoning, even when they are tackling putatively *deductive* reasoning tasks.

This interpretation presents a considerable challenge to advocates of the probabilistic approach to reasoning: to provide a probabilistic theoretical framework to account for the large body of empirical data that has been accumulated. And if the probabilistic approach is right, then it should be possible to show that, despite appearances, when viewed from a probabilistic standpoint, human reasoning is predominantly rational, after all.

This chapter aims to outline what we view as the 'probabilistic turn'—a move from using logic to using probability theory as a framework for understanding human thought (later, we shall also use some concepts from the closely related mathematical field of information theory). This probabilistic turn has occurred primarily over the last ten to fifteen years across a range of disciplines. We shall begin by considering the probabilistic turn in the semantics of natural language—i.e. the project of specifying a formal theory of meaning for natural language statements, and thus specifying which inferences follow from such statements. Natural language semantics has typically been analysed in logical terms, and the programme of developing a probabilistic semantics for aspects of natural language is very underdeveloped. Nonetheless, making a shift to a probabilistic analysis of the meaning of natural language statements is of critical importance in the programme of theoretical work outlined later in the book. We then consider how probabilistic approaches have become prevalent in the three areas that we have considered in relation to logic-based methods. In each of these areas, theories of scientific inference, artificial intelligence, and psychology, the discussion will be broadened to consider relevant research across related disciplines. This chapter thus provides historical and technical background for the development of the specific probabilistic theories of performance on the three key areas of human reasoning: conditional reasoning, the selection task, and syllogistic reasoning, that we discuss in detail in Chapters 5, 6, and 7.

A probabilistic semantics for natural language?

We noted earlier in this book that there is a strong inter-relationship between the project of interpreting representations and the project of discovering what inferences people draw over those representations. This is because the meaning of a representation determines what inferences follow from it; and the inferences that can be drawn on the basis of a representation reveal its meaning. In the case of natural language, the point is simply that the meaning of word, phrase, or sentence crucially affects what can be inferred from it; and by watching how people draw inferences can help us discern the meaning that they must have in mind. Thus, if we hear an unfamiliar word, we attempt to reconstruct its meaning from the things that people take it to imply. For example, I might decide that a 'burble' is a kind of bird because I hear a person mentioning that one can be sure that burble's always build their nests on the sides of streams. But, of course, to understand the kinds of inferences that are being drawn also depends on understanding the meanings of the words being used. The influence, then, between the problem of assigning meanings to sentences and deciding what inferences people endorse is two-way.

The psychology of reasoning typically borrows the interpretations of the sentences used in laboratory reasoning tasks directly from logical interpretations of language. That is, the natural language statements are viewed as equivalent to logical formulae, so that, for example, 'fish swim' is interpreted as:

$$\forall x(Fish(x) \Rightarrow Swims(x)).$$

Once the premises and conclusions of an argument have been translated in to logical terms, the validity or otherwise of the argument can be assessed, by the pure application of the mathematical methods of formal logic. Then the psychological question is: can people spontaneously draw conclusions that deductively follow from the premises? And, equally, can people distinguish between valid and invalid natural language arguments? But in making these assumptions, it is easy to lose sight of the fact that it is an *assumption* that natural language sentences can be interpreted in logical terms at all.

This assumption is, it is true, the dominant formal approach to analysing the meaning of natural language statements. The logical analysis of natural language is now known as formal semantics (e.g. Kamp and Reyle 1993). Moreover, this project arises from a much longer tradition in philosophy of attempting to capture the underlying 'logical form' of sentences, with the hope of distinguishing between good and bad natural language arguments—a tradition that reached maturity with Frege's development of so-called 'first-order' logic. The assumption that natural language should be modelled in logical terms is so deep rooted that it is often forgotten, particularly in the psychology of reasoning, that it is an assumption at all. The resulting consensus on a logical analysis of language builds in a powerful and unseen bias in favour of the logical view of inference.

Problems for logic

Despite being strongly entrenched, the logical analysis of natural language produces well-known and powerful clashes with pre-theoretic intuitions. Thus, for example, the simplest way to render the conditional, *if ... then*, is in terms that are known in logic as the *material conditional*, which can be explicated using what is known as a 'truth table'. A truth table specifies the truth value (i.e. 'true' or 'false') of a compound statement in terms of the truth values of its components. The truth table for the material conditional is shown in Table 4.1. This truth table indicates that, according to the material conditional interpretation, *if ... then* is false only when the antecedent is true and the conclusion is false; but it is true otherwise.

It is apparent from everyday usage, however, that the natural language conditional is much more restrictive than this. For example, according to the material conditional interpretation, of ... *then* statements, such as *if the moon is blue, then cows eat fish*, or even sentences such as *if the moon is blue, then the moon is green* are true, simply in virtue of the fact that the antecedent statement is false. Equally, statements such as *if seven is a prime number, then Leonardo was borne in Italy* are true purely in virtue of the fact that both antecedent and consequent are true. But no-one would endorse the natural languages sentences corresponding to conditionals like this—indeed they would be rejected as patently absurd. Typically, in natural language conditional

Table 4.1 Truth table for the material conditional.

A	B	if A then B
T	T	T
T	F	F
F	T	T
F	F	T

T stands for 'true' and F stands for 'false.'

sentences, there is some informational *dependency* between the antecedent and consequent, such that the truth of the antecedent determines, or is at least informative about, the likely truth of the consequent. Thus, consider the following: *if the burglar entered through the window, there are footprints in the flowerbed.* Here there is a causal connection between the antecedent and the consequent—the process of entering through the window *causes* the footprints. Or consider this: *if there are footprints in the flowerbed, the burglar entered through the window.* Here the connection is reversal—learning about the presence of footprints carries information about how the burglar entered. Specifically, if the footprints were not there, then we should presume that the burglar had not entered through the window. Any such connection is clearly entirely lacking in the examples of true instances of material implication above.

The concern about the logical interpretation of the natural language conditional has been widely recognized by philosophers and formal semanticists. For example, a vast range of alternative logical analyses of the natural language conditional *if ... then ...* have been proposed, which attempt to take account of some of the intuitions described above (for the most recent summary of these attempts, see: Bennett 2003; but also: Edgington 1995; Nute 1984; Veltman 1985). Three points are worth stressing, in the present context. First, by common consent, no current analysis of the conditional provides a satisfactory account of the wealth of natural language conditional sentences (Bennett 2003). Thus, the logical analysis of this most central of terms remains at best partial. Second, in the psychology of reasoning, recent logical developments have, in any case, frequently been ignored. We shall see later that researchers have often assumed a 'rational' or 'logical' solution to conditional reasoning problems that only makes sense if we presuppose that the natural language conditional is interpreted as material implication (although, see Evans and Over 2004, which we consider in Chapter 5). Third, notice that the interpretation of the conditional as material implication, combined with other logical machinery, does not allow conditional statements to admit exceptions.

The standard logical interpretation of a statement such as *birds fly*, involves the conditional in an essential way. The logical structure is presumed to be paraphrased as: *for all objects, x, if that object is a bird, then it flies.* Translating this into standard logical notation, we obtain:

$$\forall x(Bird(x) \Rightarrow Flies(x)).$$

This statement is false if there is a single exception to it. But since almost all natural language rules are defeasible, as we have discussed extensively above, this immediately means that, according to this logical interpretation, the corresponding natural language statement is false. But then we face the deep puzzle concerning how it is possible for the cognitive system systematically and successfully to rely upon a store of knowledge, almost all of which consists of false statements! And logic is no help here, of course, because nothing useful can be inferred from a *false* statement, including, of course, a false conditional statement.

Just as we mentioned above, attempts to overcome this difficulty have involved trying to develop richer logical notions of the conditional than is embodied in the material conditional. But as before, it is widely agreed that none of these attempts is fully successful. Indeed, the attempt to provide a logically appropriate analysis of quantified conditional sentences (e.g. Barwise and Perry 1983) is closely related to the project of defining an appropriate logic for default inference (Fuhrmann 1998; Wobcke 1995) and we will explore this intimate connection more closely in Chapter 5. However, as we saw in Chapter 3, in artificial intelligence, at the end of the 1980s the project of devising a non-monotonic logic had been shown to raise profound problems about capturing intuitive patterns of defeasible inference, the *completeness** problem (Oaksford and Chater 1991) or McDermott's (1987) *you don't want to know* problem, and about computational intractability, McDermott's (1987) *you can't know* problem. Thus the project of providing a logical account of the conditional raises profound problems for computational and hence psychological accounts of conditional reasoning.

Non-monontonic logic vs. probabilities

Since Oaksford and Chater's (1991) original critique of logicism (the title of the paper was 'Against logicist cognitive science'), things have moved on both in the investigation of probabilistic accounts of knowledge and reasoning and in non-monotonic logic. Indeed work in these areas has flourished so much during the 1990s that summarizing it and indexing its relevance to the psychology of conditional reasoning would be a book length project in itself, which would go beyond our competence. But using broad strokes a picture can be painted that locates our position within this burgeoning literature.

The first point to make is that some of the earliest work on non-monotonic reasoning explicitly focused on probabilities (Adams 1975; Kyburg 1961) and on the conditional in particular (Adams 1975; again, we return to this point in Chapter 5). More recently, 'most advocates of non-monotonic formalisms insist that they model a wider class of phenomena than can be captured by ordinary probability functions' (Fuhrmann 1998, p. 31). Some of these formal systems explicitly include some measure analogous to probability (Fox and Parsons 1998; Gabbay 1996; Pollock 2001; Prakken and Vreeswijk 2002) from which they draw their nice default properties. Here the root of the rejection of probability is what is known as Theophrastus' rule: the strength that a chain of deductively linked arguments confers on the conclusion cannot be weaker than the weakest link in the chain (Walton 2004). This is a condition that cannot be guaranteed by the probability calculus. Examples that seem to conform to Theophrastus' rule but not to the probability calculus, have persuaded, for example, Walton (2004) and Pollock (2001), that a third form of reasoning should be countenanced in addition to deductive and inductive/probabilistic reasoning, i.e. *plausibilist* reasoning (and in endorsing a non-monotonic logic approach to human reasoning, some psychologists seem to endorse this position; Stenning and van Lambeglen 2003).

Problems for attempts to create a plausibilist theory of reasoning arise from two directions. First, unlike deduction and probabilistic reasoning there are a wide variety of calculi proposed to deal with plausibilities. In some accounts (e.g. Pollock 2001) plausibilities are assumed to range from 0 to ∞, whereas in others they are treated as qualitative categories with varying numbers of bins, e.g. ++, +, −, − − (Fox and Parsons 1998; see also some the work reviewed in Prakken and Vreeswijk 2002). In the latter case, plausibilities can combine like multi-valued truth tables. Some of these rules for combining qualitative plausibilities are consistent with the probability calculus (Fox and Parsons 1998) but some are not. Thus there would not appear to be a single consistent formal plausibility calculus in existence.

Second, it has been argued that wherever one starts in developing an account of uncertain reasoning, the resulting theory will be equivalent to the probability calculus (for fuller discussion and references, see: Howson and Urbach 1989). Consequently, one may as well stick with this well-understood formalism rather develop something new. If there are compelling examples that argue against a probabilistic framework then one must consider the consequences. Are these examples so ubiquitous and compelling that they require abandoning a well-established formal theory that works well for the majority of cases? That is, are such cases counter-examples or exceptions? Many of the alternative accounts have arisen in the context of the attempt to better understand non-monotonic reasoning. However, in response to these possible counter-examples, we follow Pearl's (1988, p. 20) view on whether it is necessary to supplant probability theory:

> ... we find it more comfortable to compromise an ideal theory [i.e. probability theory] that is well understood than to search for a new surrogate theory, with only gut feeling for guidance.

In short, deep problems are created by the interpretation of conditionals and its relationship to non-monotonic reasoning. Following Pearl (1988, 2000) and Adams (1998a), we advocate sticking with probabilities.

Alternative probabilistic semantics

Psychologists of reasoning have widely assumed the crudest, and most clearly inadequate, logical model of the conditional, material implication, to be correct (but see: Oaksford 1989; Evans and Over 2004). The difficulties we have sketched with the conditional could be amplified considerably—the paradoxes and difficulties associated with such an analysis are numerous and well-known (and we discuss them in depth in Chapter 5). Moreover, the same types of difficulties can be raised with the interpretation of other natural language terms with an apparent direct connection to terms of elementary logic—*all, some, not, and, or*, appear to be only distantly related to the logical meanings of $\forall, \exists, \neg, \wedge, \vee$, respectively.

These considerations should, at the very least, put the interpretation of statements used in experimental reasoning tasks up for debate. In a conditional reasoning task, or in Wason's selection task, what exactly does the participant understand by the natural language conditional? In a syllogistic reasoning task, how does the participant interpret syllogistic premises or conclusions involving *all* or *some ... not ...*?

More interestingly, this raises the possibility that a non-logical analysis of some of these statements may be appropriate. We shall see in the following chapters that such a simple probabilistic analysis can indeed be developed and that this appears to do a good job of capturing reasoning performance. The essential ideas are extremely simple. A conditional statement can be interpreted as expressing a *conditional probability*. A strict interpretation would be that if p then q means that the probability that q is true, given that p is known to be true, $P(q|p)$, is 1. But a rather looser interpretation may be appropriate in contexts where defaults are allowed—in these cases, the constraint might be simply that $P(q|p)$ is high. Similar probabilistic interpretations may be given to the quantifiers. For example, 'some X and Y' can be viewed as stating that the probability that an arbitrarily chosen object has both properties X and Y is greater than 0. We shall consider the probabilistic semantics for quantified statements in more detail in Chapter 7 in developing a theory of how people reason with syllogisms.

As we have seen, this kind of probabilistic semantics for natural language is by no means new. In philosophy, Adams (1966, 1975, 1998; see also, Edgington 1995) has developed a detailed formal analysis of the natural language conditional in terms of conditional probability. Moreover, in psychology, Anderson (1995) conducted a preliminary exploration of the implications of modelling the conditional in terms of conditional probability for the empirical data on conditional reasoning (for such earlier work, see also: George 1997; Liu *et al.* 1996; Stevenson and Over 1995). This work is a precursor to the analysis of conditional reasoning data presented in the next chapter.

How much do we gain by the shift to conditional probability? Conditional statements with false antecedents and consequents are no longer automatically true under this interpretation—the probability that, for example, the moon is green given that the moon is blue is not 1 or close to 1, but it is 0, and hence this corresponding conditional can now be rejected as false. Moreover, the shift to probability immediately allows the possibility that conditionals can, at least under many circumstances, allow exceptions. Problems remain, of course. For example, a statement such as *if seven is a prime number, then Leonardo was born in Italy* remains potentially problematic, because the probability P (*Leonardo is Italian*|*7 is prime*) is nearly one. What seems to be wrong about this kind of statement is that the conditional probability is high *for the wrong reasons*. That is, it is high because of our background knowledge, rather than in virtue of our having learned that the antecedent is true. In the context of causal reasoning (Cheng 1997, Lober and Shanks 2000; Shanks 1995) this has led psychologists to consider the difference between the conditional probability of the consequent, given that the antecedent is true, compared with the conditional probability of the consequent, given that the antecedent is false. The idea is, in the context of causal relations at least, that what is crucial is the difference between these two probabilities (or some more complex, but related function—see, for example, Cheng 1997).

In the rational analyses below, we do not attempt the very difficult problem of formulating a fully adequate probabilistic semantics for the conditional (however, see Adams 1998). Instead, we have adopted the pragmatic strategy of using the simplest probabilistic semantics that is needed to model the empirical data. But the close inter-relationship between the project of interpreting language and the project of characterizing human inference ensures that, to the extent that the probabilistic analysis of reasoning developed below is successful, the corresponding probabilistic semantics for natural language should be taken seriously. Thus, the results developed in this book, while directly aimed at providing a new perspective on the psychology of reasoning, may also indicate that the emphasis on logic as the foundation for natural language semantics may also have to be re-thought.

In the next three sections of this chapter, we outline the growing focus on probabilistic models of uncertain reasoning, dividing the discussion into three parts. The first considers probabilistic models of scientific inference—traditionally the domain of philosophy of science and statistics. The second considers probabilistic models in artificial intelligence, and the third describes the rise of probabilistic accounts of mental processes. The divisions between these sections are, however, somewhat arbitrary. One of the most exciting aspects of the resurgence of probabilistic ideas is that it has spilled across traditional research domains—abstract models of brain function have been used as computational tools; theories of machine learning have been related to problems in the philosophy of science; and so on. The following sections aim to introduce some of the most important developments across these areas.

The probabilistic turn in models of scientific inference

In Chapter 3, we noted that close parallels are frequently drawn between scientific inference and human reasoning (e.g. in viewing the child as 'scientist', e.g. Carey 1988; Karmiloff-Smith 1988). We noted, too, that there was a long tradition of attempting to model scientific inference in logicist terms. We saw, however, that it has not proved possible to force the uncertain character of such inference into the mould of certain logical inference, despite the exercise of considerable ingenuity. The essential difficulty is that scientific inference, like everyday inference, is irremediably uncertain, and logical methods are suited to dealing with certain reasoning rather than uncertain reasoning. A natural way to face the uncertainty of scientific reasoning head-on is to view scientific reasoning as a type of probabilistic reasoning. But how might a probabilistic analysis of scientific reasoning look?

At first sight, the analysis of scientific reasoning can be captured immediately, by the application of probability theory. As we saw in Chapter 1, the subjectivist interpretation of probability holds that probabilities are degrees of belief. Degrees of belief can be attached to propositions of any kind—whether those propositions are about data, or about hypotheses that may be used to explain the data. The ability to treat data and hypotheses in a uniform way allows a direct application of the theory of probability, as we shall now see.

To begin, let us consider arbitrary propositions A and B. The conditional probability $P\,(A|B)$ means the probability of A being true, given that B is true. Clearly, both A and B are true if B is true and if A is true given that B is true. Therefore, the probability that A and B are true, $P\,(A, B)$, is the product of the probability of A given B, $P\,(A|B)$, multiplied by the probability of B, $P\,(B)$. An exactly similar argument says that $P\,(A, B)$ also equals the probability of A, $P\,(A)$, multiplied by the probability of B, given A, $P\,(B|A)$. Summing up, an immediate consequence of the definition of conditional probability is that, for any A and B:

$$P(A, B) = P(A\,|\,B)\,P(B) = P(B\,|\,A)\,P(A)$$

and, rearranging, we obtain the standard formulation of the Bayes' celebrated theorem:

$$P\left(A\,|\,B\right) = \frac{P\left(B\,|\,A\right)P\left(A\right)}{P\left(B\right)}$$

Now suppose that we apply Bayes' theorem to the relationship between a scientific hypothesis or theory, H_i, and a piece of data D, to obtain:

$$P\left(H_i\,|\,D\right) = \frac{P\left(D\,|\,H_i\right)P\left(H_i\right)}{P\left(D\right)}.$$

This is the key formula underpinning the probabilistic approach to the philosophy of science. The impact of a piece of data is determined by the degree to which the hypothesis predicts that data, $P\,(D|\,H_i)$, and the probability of that hypothesis, before the data was collected, $P\,(H_i)$. This means that hypotheses that predict data well, but are also plausible given prior knowledge (e.g. do not involve wilful appeal to the intervention of aliens; or to hitherto unknown laws of physics, and so on), will be favoured.

The final influence on the probability of a hypothesis, given data, is the $P\,(D)$, the probability of the data itself. Again, by elementary probability theory, this can be expressed as:

$$\sum_j P\left(D\,|\,H_j\right)P\left(H_j\right).$$

This makes intuitive sense—data is probable to the extent that it is well predicted ($P(D| H_j)$ is high) by a theory or theories that have high prior probability ($P(H_j)$ is high). Indeed, this term embodies the fact that, according to a probabilistic conception of scientific inference, science is a matter of competition between theories. What matters is how much better one theory predicts the data, in relation to the other theories. Roughly, if it does better than all or most of the competing theories, then its probability will be revised upwards; if it does worse, then its probability will be revised downwards.

In some contexts, it is useful to have a *measure* of the degree to which a theory is confirmed (or disconfirmed) by a particular piece of data—developing and studying such measures is the subfield of philosophy of science known as confirmation theory. A large range of measures of confirmation have been proposed, most of which are formulated in probabilistic terms (Good 1984; Jeffrey 1992; Kyburg 1983; Mackie 1969; Milne 1996). For example, a popular choice of confirmation measures is the log ratio of the probability of the hypothesis before and after the data is encountered (see, e.g. Milne 1996, for an axiomatic argument for this viewpoint; and Fitelson 1999, for an alternative viewpoint):

$$\log \frac{P(H_i \mid D)}{P(H_i)}$$

So far, the probabilistic approach to the scientific inference may seem suspiciously straightforward and uncontroversial. After all, it seems to be based entirely on the laws of probability theory, and especially an elementary consequence of those laws, Bayes theorem; and few people would wish to challenge the laws of probability. Why is the probabistic approach controversial?

The probabilistic approach runs into three, somewhat inter-related, sources of controversy: concerning the meaning of probability; whether relevant probabilities are actually available or well-defined; and whether the approach actually captures patterns of good scientific inference successfully. Let us consider each of these in turn.

Subjective probabilities

Though few people disagree about the probability calculus, there is substantial disagreement about what probabilities *mean*. For example, consider the frequentist (von Mises 1939) interpretation of probability, according to which a probability corresponds to the limiting proportions of the outcomes of a long sequence of identical trials in an 'experiment'. According to this viewpoint, to say that a biased coin has a probability 0.6 of coming up heads is to say that, if the coin were to be flipped indefinitely often, in the long run, the proportion of times that it comes up heads will be roughly 60%.[1]

According to the frequentist viewpoint, the Bayesian approach to the philosophy of science makes no sense. In the actual world, a hypothesis, H_i, is either true or not—there is no question of an infinite sequence of experiments in which it may be true or not, in some proportion. So it makes no sense to speak of quantities such as P (H_i) or P $(H_j|D)$—and hence the entire probabilistic approach founders.

Similarly, 'objective' or 'propensity' interpretations of probability (Mellor 1971; Popper 1959), according to which probabilities capture properties of physical objects (such as dice and coins), cannot be applied to define probabilities for abstract 'hypotheses'—and again, according to this interpretation of probability, a probabilistic philosophy of science makes no sense.

To make sense of the probabilistic approach to scientific inference requires that we interpret probabilities as *degrees of belief*, where 0 corresponds to complete certainty that a state of affairs does not hold; and 1 corresponds to complete certainly that it does. A wide range of arguments, starting from different sets of fairly minimal assumptions, have been used to show that degrees of belief should precisely obey the standard laws of probability (De Finetti 1972; Earman 1992; Fitelson 1999). According to this viewpoint, it makes perfect sense to talk about degrees of belief in hypotheses; and how those degrees of belief may be revised in the light of new data. This 'subjectivist' view of probability has a number of flavours, depending on the precise way in which degrees of belief are conceived (e.g. Keynes 1921). But once the subjective view of degrees of belief is adopted; and if it is assumed that a primary goal in science is to revise degrees of belief in response to the data collected, then a probabilistic view of scientific enquiry follows.

Before turning to the further controversial aspects of the probabilistic approach to scientific inference, two points are worth stressing in the light of this discussion. The first is that, while the probabilistic approach to scientific

---

[1] More strictly, and perhaps somewhat circularly, the relevant mathematical result, the weak law of large numbers, says that this will occur with high probability—indeed this probability can be arbitrarily high, as the sequence becomes arbitrarily long. We do not pursue further the fact that the frequentist view itself appears to invoke probability in its own explication of probability, in a way that may be difficult to eliminate, in purely frequentist terms.

inference is often called the Bayesian approach, because of the extensive use of Bayes' theorem that it entails, the distinctive feature of the approach is the subjective interpretation of probability. Bayes' theorem, of course, is an elementary theorem of the probability calculus and universally acknowledged.[2]

The second point is that the subjective interpretation of probability is essential, not just for the application of probability to scientific inference, but to the application of probability to *cognition*. In typical applications, as we shall see below, the cognitive system is viewed as weighing up evidence, e.g. from perception or memory, concerning whether or not some hypothesis, categorization, or causal relation holds. This can be understood in terms of degree of belief—but not, of course, in terms of limiting frequencies, or objective properties of the external world.

Identifying probabilities

One source of controversy concerning the probabilistic approach, then, concerns the legitimacy of the subjectivist interpretation of probability. A second source of controversy concerns whether the probabilities required for the Bayesian calculation are actually well-defined and measurable. One approach to getting at subjective degrees of belief would be to ask individual scientists, or perhaps groups of scientists, to simply put numbers on their degrees of belief directly. Or more indirect means might be used to elicit probability judgements—e.g. asking scientists to choose between gambles concerning hypotheses, or the data that they predict. But the psychological literature on probabilistic reasoning and decision-making indicates that this is likely to be a hopeless endeavour—experts, like people at large, do not appear able to assign probabilities to events that are even remotely consistent with the probability calculus. And the inconsistencies in their judgements appear to reflect not merely uncertainty or 'noise', but systematic non-rationalities in the explicit analysis of probabilistic tasks (Baron 2000). Such phenomena are, at a practical level, well-known by, and problematic for, researchers building probabilistic expert systems—experts, presumably including research scientists—do not seem to be able to coherently express their knowledge in terms of numerical probabilities. These issues are presumably particularly difficult in the

---

[2] While this point causes no confusion in the philosophy of science and the foundations of statistics, it does cause confusion in adjacent disciplines—for example, in psychology, the misapprehension that the Bayesian approach is centred on Bayes' theorem is not uncommon (e.g. Laming 1996).

context of assigning prior probabilities to scientific hypotheses—to some degree, of course, todays 'prior' is the outcome of processing yesterday's data. But the process has to start somewhere—and its unclear how to 'ground' prior probabilities in a non-arbitrary way.[3]

Practical success

The final source of controversy concerning the probabilistic approach to the philosophy of science concerns the question of its practical success as a theory of good scientific inference. Advocates of the probabilistic approach argue that it provides an elegant synthesis of a range of well-known features of scientific inference (for example, Bovens and Hartmann 2003). Detractors claim that the approach faces a series of difficulties—such as the problem of explaining how 'old' or known data can have any evidential impact on hypotheses that are currently being entertained (Earman 1992; Glymour 1980); on explaining why diverse evidence for a theory is more convincing than endless repetitions of the same experiment (Franklin and Howson 1984; Horwich 1982; though see Wayne 1995).

Rather than attempt to adjudicate these debates here, we simply note that the probabilistic approach to the philosophy of science has now grown to be the dominant approach in the field.

Much literature in the field, and in related areas such as the foundations of statistical inferences, are not so much concerned with the validity of the probabilistic standpoint, but with developing and broadening the approach (e.g. Eells and Fetzer, 2005). For now, the important point is that there has been a probabilistic revolution in the philosophy of science, which, as we shall see, is paralleled in similar upsurges of probabilistic analysis, in distinction from logical approach, in artificial intelligence and psychology. While sufficient to establish the probabilistic turn in the philosophy of science, we now illustrate the practical success of a probabilistic approach in accounting for how auxiliary hypotheses (see, Chapter 3) impact scientific inference.

One of the core arguments of this book is that human everyday inference is irremediably uncertain—and hence that probability theory, the calculus of

---

[3] A great deal of attention is given to the question of assigning priors in a 'fair' or 'reasonable' way in the statistical literature; the emphasis in this literature is not to capture people's actual prior assumptions, but instead to articulate what would be 'defensible' and 'neutral' prior assumptions. Methods such as maximum entropy, the use of the Jeffreys priors (Jeffreys 1939), and minimum description length (Grünwald et al. 2005; Rissanen 1987) attempt to address this problem.

uncertainty, is a better candidate for modelling thought than logic, which focuses on inferences that are certain. In the philosophy of science, the attempt to hold onto a logical viewpoint forced Popper's emphasis on falsification—because it was assumed that data could falsify theories for certain (where the theory and data are logically inconsistent). On the other hand, it is clear that confirmation of a theory, however extensive, never gives rise to certainty, because the critical disconfirmation could arise at any time, and hence that confirmation can never be a matter of logical inference. But, as we saw in Chapter 3, the attempt to force a logical relation of disconfirmation between theory and data cannot succeed, because there are always indefinitely many auxiliary hypotheses, however wild and implausible these might be, that can be drawn upon, according to which the hypothesis and data are consistent. Hence, even the relation of disconfirmation, as well as that of confirmation, is uncertain. From a probabilistic perspective, as might be expected, the presumed asymmetry between disconfirmation and confirmation disappears—both notions are modelled in probabilistic terms; and indeed in a completely uniform way. The only difference between them is the sign of the change in the probability of a hypothesis, after the data is encountered—if the probability of the hypothesis increases, we have a case of confirmation; if it reduces, we have a case of disconfirmation.

But can the probabilistic approach to scientific inference itself deal with the problem of auxiliary hypotheses that created such difficulties for the logical viewpoint? In reality, the probabilistic approach does not really solve this problem—rather it side-steps it. In order to derive predictions from any scientific hypothesis or theory, we need to add assumptions about the present or past state of the system under study (depending on the context, these are known as boundary conditions, or initial conditions). But, crucially, we also need to make implicit assumptions concerning what is *not* relevant to the behaviour of the system under study—that is, we need to assume that the system that we are interested in is, for the purposes of our analysis, closed to other influences. In reality, of course, any real, physical system will necessarily be, to some degree, open: open to the influence of forces and objects that scientists ignore, or of which they may be unaware. Thus, there is a critical step of idealization—of constructing an idealized model of the system; and only on this assumption, which is know to be strictly false, can predictions concerning the behaviour of the system be derived. This applies irrespective of whether those predictions are derived using logic or probability. To give a probabilistic example, to predict the behaviour of a coin, we must adopt a particular idealization of its behaviour—e.g. that it is a fair coin, and that the outcome of each throw is independent of the previous outcomes. This, like any other idealization, will inevitably not be precisely correct—the hope with such idealizations is that they need to be good enough, most of the time, to produce useful results.

So, as for logical theories, it will always be possible to 'save' a theory by introducing an auxiliary hypothesis, to modify the current idealization of the system under study. But at least the probabilistic approach has a mechanism that may potentially penalize the wanton introduction of such hypotheses. Any such hypothesis will have its own probability value—and the smaller that probability, the smaller the probability of the explanation of the data provided by the conjunction of that auxiliary hypothesis with the theory under test. It turns out that, to the extent that a theory can only be saved by introducing an auxiliary hypothesis with independently low probability, that theory will be disfavoured. Hence the probabilistic approach at least has some machinery with which to attempt to address the problem of auxiliary hypotheses. We shall touch on these issues again, below, in discussing the frame problem in artificial intelligence.

In sum, then, philosophy of science has undergone a probabilistic revolution. Logic-based conceptions of scientific inference, in which falsification has priority over confirmation, have become unfashionable. In their place, the probabilistic, Bayesian, viewpoint treats confirmation and disconfirmation alike as emerging immediately from the application of the laws of probability, where probabilities are interpreted as degrees of belief. The next two sections show how this probabilistic 'turn' has been paralleled in artificial intelligence and psychology.

The probabilistic turn in artificial intelligence

In Chapter 3, we noted that the uncertain character of everyday inference seemed to be a poor match with the logic-based knowledge representation schemes used in many areas of artificial intelligence. For example, a conditional rule, such as 'if you put 50p in the coke machine, you will get a coke' seem to succumb to all kinds of counter-examples—there are innumerable possible factors that may block this inference (power failure, the machine is empty, the coin or the can get stuck, and so on). These factors are analogous to the auxiliary hypotheses in the discussion of philosophy of science above. Thus, you can put the money in, and no can of coke may emerge. This possibility could be interpreted as indicating that, from a logical point of view, the conditional rule is simply false—because it succumbs to counter-examples. But as we discussed in Chapter 3, this seems to be an excessively rigorous standpoint, in terms of which almost all conditionals that appear to govern people's everyday thought and action will be discarded as false. And, given this, it becomes unclear why relying on a plethora of false conditional statements could ever be a useful basis for action.

The probabilistic standpoint on knowledge representation takes the view that relations between pieces of knowledge will, in general, be probabilistic. As we noted in our discussion earlier in the chapter, one aspect of this is to view conditional statements as expressing conditional probabilities. But the goal of knowledge representation in artificial intelligence is, of course, far more general than merely rendering particular natural language statements. What is required is a formalism for capturing common-sense knowledge over which patterns of everyday inferences can be correctly defined, and efficiently computed.

Graphical models

A crucial step in this direction has been the development of so-called 'graphical' models of probabilistic relationships (e.g. Lauritzen and Spiegelhalter 1988; Pearl 1988) (in Chapters 5 and 7, we shall use some extremely simple graphical models in providing a probabilistic explanation of data apparently concerned with 'logical' reasoning.). Each node in a graphical model corresponds to a set of possible states of some variable; direct influences between variables are expressed by links (in some contexts, directed arrows) between variables (see Fig. 4.1). Graphical models are, in general, interesting to the extent that they are sparsely interconnected—that is, to the extent that the relationships between the variables can be broken down into a reasonably small number of pairwise connections. Where this is the case, the specification of a relatively simple graphical structure provides a very efficient framework for capturing the huge number of probabilistic relationships between the variables represented.

Probabilistic relationships can usefully be captured in a number of related graphical formalisms. Here, nodes represent *variables*: aspects of the world that can take on a number of states. Here all variables are binary: a car brakes or does not; the road is wet or dry; etc. The structure of the diagram indicates which variables depend on which. For example, variable **A**, whether the car avoids the car in front depends on **S**, whether the car slows; and indirectly on whether the brakes are applied, **B**. But the influence of the, **B**, brakes is mediated via the slowing, **S**. If **S** is held fixed, **A** is independent of **B**. These independence relations allow us to 'factorize' the joint probability distribution across the variables accordingly:

$$\Pr(\mathbf{B}, \mathbf{R}, \mathbf{H}, \mathbf{S}, \mathbf{T}, \mathbf{A}) = \Pr(\mathbf{B})\Pr(\mathbf{R})\Pr(\mathbf{H}|\mathbf{B})\Pr(\mathbf{S}|\mathbf{B}, \mathbf{R})\Pr(\mathbf{T}|\mathbf{S})\Pr(\mathbf{A}|\mathbf{S}),$$

where each item depends directly only on its causes (indicated by the direction of the arrows). Moreover, interpreting the arrows as causal (Pearl 2000),

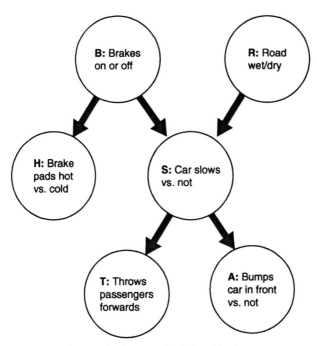

Fig. 4.1 A simple belief network. The causal relationships between events are indicated by arrows. The network provides a compact description of the probability distribution over these events; and also the starting point for a distributed computational architecture for updating probabilities over this distribution.

we note, e.g. that *observing* whether the brake pads are hot, **H**, is *informative* about whether the passengers are throw forward, **T**. But *making* the brake pads hotter (intervening to change **H**) will not impact **T**. Causal influence only flows in the direction of the arrows. Pearl (2000) provides a probabilistic calculus to capture the impact of causal interventions, and explaining the contrast with observation (for a discussion in the context of cognitive science, see: Sloman 2005).

To see this, note that an arbitrary probability distribution over a set of n variables, each of which has s possible states, has $s^n - 1$ degrees of freedom— this value increases exponentially with the number of variables.[4]

---

[4] That is, a joint probability must be specified for each combination of states across the variables, i.e: $P(x_1 = x_1, x_2 = x_2, \ldots x_n = x_n)$. There are $s.s \ldots s = s^n$ of these values; which, as these outcomes are mutually exclusive and exhaustive, must sum to 1, giving $s^n - 1$ degrees of freedom. Given the joint probability distribution, of course, any other conditional or unconditional probabilities can readily be calculated.

By contrast, for a graphical model, the number of degrees of freedom is linear in the number of nodes and links.[5]

One implication of this result is that the class of probability distributions that can be factored into graphical models is extremely restricted, in relation to the class of all possible probability distributions over a set of variables. If the dependencies that the cognitive system can represent are typically highly local, then this restriction would seem to be entirely the right kind. But is it? An interesting line of argument suggesting that the locality assumption may be correct is based on the idea that *causal* dependencies determine the structure of graphical models (Pearl 2000). If the causal structure of the world is local, then so might the representation of probabilistic information—because links are only required, to a first approximation, where there are causal linkages between the relevant variables. This viewpoint does not, notice, require a strong view of locality, according to which knowledge can be partitioned into separate bundles, which are not interested in each other. After all, graphical models can involve full connections between all the variables under consideration. The constraint is, instead, that the number of such connections is relatively sparse.

Graphical models are, in a sense, just a notation for expressing a particular (and perhaps particularly interesting) class of probability distributions. But graphical models also appear especially interesting, from the point of view of artificial intelligence, in at least three respects.

First, an immediate attraction of the approach is the possibility that graphical models may map, in a transparent way, to chunks of knowledge that might be used by, and perhaps elicited from, people. Variables may correspond to different possible events; and as we have noted, links between nodes, at least in some circumstances, may be interpreted in terms of causal relationships

---

[5] Specifically, for a model with n variables, and l links between them, the number of degrees of freedom is roughly the sum of the unconditional probabilities: $P(x_1 = x_1, x_2 = x_2, \ldots x_n = x_n)$, of each of the s states of the n probabilities, of which there are n $(s-1)$; and the joint probabilities between each of the states of the l pairs of variables that are linked, of which there are $l.s.$ $(s-1)$. If we assume that links in a putative representation of a graphical network are reasonably 'local', then as we consider networks of increasing size, then the number of links will increase roughly linearly with the number of variables, n. This implies that the number of degrees of freedom that must be stored for a graphical network, roughly n $(s-1) + l.s.$ $(s-1)$, will be linear in the number of variables. This contrasts with the case of an unrestricted probability distribution, where, as we have seen, the number of degrees of freedom increases exponentially with the number of variables. Note that the precise details of this calculation depend on the specific type of graphical model that is being considered—but the general conclusion remains the same.

between the corresponding events (see Fig. 4.1). Thus, the graphical model approach promises to carry over some of the appeal of logic-based approaches in artificial intelligence—that the knowledge-base has a clear interpretation. A related point is that, because knowledge is localized in particular nodes and connections in a graphical model, it seems possible, at least in principle, to see how knowledge might be added or modified in a piecemeal way by the learning system itself in *response to linguistic input*. In contrast, the highly distributed and opaque codes typically created in neural network learning do not have this property—there is no way of locally modifying the network so that it behaves as before, except that it takes account of some specific new piece of knowledge. Thus, although distributed representations are sometimes viewed as a virtue of neural network models, from the point of view of understanding how people represent knowledge, and can locally revise that knowledge through relevant linguistic input, such representations are a major disadvantage. The transparency and locality of information in graphical models can, therefore, be viewed a key attraction of the approach.[6]

Second, while one attraction of graphical models is their transparency, which implies that artificial intelligence systems may, to some degree, be hand-crafted using expert knowledge, just as in traditional logic-based artificial intelligence, another appeal of graphical models is that they have straightforward learning algorithms that allow them to learn from exposure to empirical data. Learning a graphical model has two aspects—learning the approach network structure (that is, according to the causal interpretation of that structure, learning the causal dependencies between variables); and, second, learning the appropriate probabilities that should be associated with that structure (specifically, the 'base-rate' probabilities associated the states of each variable; and the joint probabilities of states in variables that are directly connected by a link).

----

6 On the other hand, it worth noting that while the probabilistic approach is more expressive than the logic-based approach to knowledge representation in one sense (because probabilities can express relationships between events of different *strengths*), it is also less expressive in a different way. For example, probability theory does not have the machinery of quantifiers and bound variables with which to represent arbitrary general statements; similarly, there is no probabilistic version of modal operators for reasoning about possibility and time. For a knowledge-base to be updated in line with linguistic input, it seems a minimal condition that the form of representation is expressive enough to capture the meanings of linguistic statements—for which the rich logical notions beyond the expressive power of graphical models appear to be necessary. The technical project of fusing developments in logic into probability theory in a cohesive way appears to be a very challenging one (for some early attempts, see: Carnap 1950).

These problems can, to some extent, be addressed separately. Learning graphical structures from correlation data is now associated with a well-developed literature (e.g. Glymour and Cooper 1999; Pearl 1988, 2000; Spirtes *et al.* 1993), which has found applications across a broad range of practical statistical problems (e.g. Glymour and Cooper 1999). The problem of learning parameters for such models has also been extensively studied (e.g. Jordan 1998; Pearl 1988) and many approaches to the problem are closely related to neural network learning algorithms (e.g. Neal 1996).

Third, another appeal of graphical models is that they can be implemented in parallel, somewhat 'neuron-like' hardware (e.g. Neal 1996). Specifically, variables can be viewed as nodes; links between variables can be associated with sets of weighted links between nodes. And the probabilistic computations of graphical models can be viewed as the propagation of activation from node to node, across these links, which can operate in parallel, and with no need of the supervision of a central 'controller.' Thus, graphical models have many of the attractions, from a computational and psychological point of view, of standard neural networks models (e.g. Rumelhart and McClelland 1986).

Other probabilistic trends

Graphical models are part, though an important one, of a wider trend towards the use of probabilistic methods in artificial intelligence. For example, in machine learning, there has been an increasing focus on Bayesian, and related, analysis of the learning problem—for example, many neural-network learning models and their learning algorithms, including back-propagation, can be understood in probabilistic terms. Roughly, the network is interpreted as a model of a probability distribution (which might be a *conditional* probability distribution of output patterns, given a specific input pattern)—the weights in the network are model parameters that must be fitted to the data; and a neural-network learning algorithm is interpreted as a process of Bayesian statistical inference from input/output data to appropriate weight values (e.g. MacKay 1992; Neal 1992; for general discussion, see: Chater 1995; McClelland 1998). More broadly, new developments in these fields have typically derived from developments in statistics. For example, one of the most important new learning methods, support vector machines (Cristianini and Shawe-Taylor 2000), is derived directly from fundamental statistical work on so-called VC-dimensions and related concepts by Vapnik and Chervonenkis (Vapnik 1998). Similarly, in computational linguistics, the emphasis has shifted from a primary focus on symbolic parsing methods, rooted in generative linguistics, to much simpler statistical models of language processing and learning; and in parallel there has been an increasing focus on the statistical analysis of corpora of natural language (e.g. Manning and Schütze 1999). To take a final example, the field of computer vision has, similarly, shifted towards probabilistic models of image structure (e.g. Geman and Geman 1984; Yuille and Kersten, 2006) and intense interest in the statistical structure of natural images (e.g. Simoncelli and Olshausen 2001).

The probabilistic turn has transformed many areas of artificial intelligence. From a logicist point of view, the statistical structure of the environment is typically viewed as peripheral to the operation of intelligent systems. The problem of vision, language processing, or reasoning can be addressed, in the first instance, by abstracting away from such statistical structure (by defining noiseless language fragments, working with the interpretation of geometric forms, reasoning about abstract scenarios). According to this approach, if the problems of cognition could be solved under such ideal conditions, the statistical 'noise' of the real world could then be addressed, as a secondary matter. From the probabilistic view of artificial intelligence, the statistical structure of the environment cannot be idealized away—it is critical to defining the problem that intelligent systems face; and probability theory is critical to providing a solution to those problems. Thus, visual scenes are viewed as generated by mixtures of probabilistic processes (Yuille and Kersten, 2006); language is considered to be the output of stochastic grammars (Chater and Manning, 2006); and reasoning is viewed as centrally concerned with probabilistic evidential relationships between propositions, rather than with logical connections (Pearl 1988, 2000).

We have presented a simple picture of an historical trend of the replacement of logical notions with probabilistic notions across artificial intelligence. But of course this is too simple. Probabilistic ideas have always, in some measure, played a role in artificial intelligence—even if used in heuristically rather than following precise Bayesian calculations, as in early expert systems (e.g. Wallis and Shortliff 1985). Moreover, logical work is still vigorous and important in many areas of artificial intelligence. To a rough approximation, we suggest, logical work is most vigorous in those research areas where intelligent behaviour is most closely allied to mathematical, rather to everyday or scientific, reasoning.

Completeness* and intractability again

In the last Chapter we raised central difficulties for logicist approaches that are presently unsolved by the probabilistic methods described in the present chapter. We identified two types of problem for the logicist approach: completeness* and intractability. Completeness* concerned the problem of providing a formal characterization of everyday knowledge that picks out all, and only, the common-sense inferences that people endorse. From the point of view of probability theory, providing such a characterization, in a particular domain, involves specifying a probabilistic model. For example, suppose that we consider reasoning about a game of dice; then, if the dice are unbiased, then a probabilistic model specifying that each throw as independent, and having identical probability distribution over the faces (in this case, a probability of one in six, for each face being uppermost), will serve for some aspects of reasoning about the game. But this model is both too strong and too weak. It is too strong, because it generates all manner of subtle mathematical predictions, concerning, say, the relative probabilities of rolling at least one six out of six dice rolls versus rolling at least two sixes out of twelve dice rolls, that are not available to everyday intuition.[7]

And it is too weak, in the sense that it embodies a very simple idealized model, which ignores many factors of crucial importance in everyday reasoning. For example, in observing a dice being thrown, we have not only a model of the probability that each face will be uppermost, but a rough model of where it will land, how likely it is to fall off the table, how loud that impact is likely to be, how another player is likely to react to a particular outcome, given their temperament, and the gamble they have placed, and so on.

This observation implies that, if the cognitive system is indeed building probabilistic models of the world, then it is building models of considerable complexity—models that can take into account any aspect of knowledge, from naïve physics to folk psychology. This implies that the probabilistic turn does not resolve the difficulty of representing knowledge—rather it provides a framework into which this knowledge must be integrated. The advantage of the probabilistic viewpoint, though, is that it appears to provide an appropriate framework for dealing with a world that is uncertain; and, indeed, for assessing competing explanations of observed phenomena (competing interpretations of the visual world; competing grammars; alternative readings of a sentence, story, or court-case). Moreover, note that probabilistic models of complex domains do not need to be fully specified, at a numerical level—most critical is that the *functional* relationships between pieces of information are represented. What tends to cause what? What is evidence for what? The precise numerical values may, in many contexts, be unknown, but the direction and existence of functional dependencies between pieces of information may nonetheless be known. Thus, probability theory can provide a framework for

---

[7] The former is more probable, as Newton wrote to Pepys (Schell 1960).

qualitative reasoning, without using numerical values. In terms of graphical models, described above, the qualitative aspects of reasoning may be determined by the structure of the graphical model, independent of the precise numerical values of the prior and conditional probabilities that may be defined over it.

We tentatively suggest that much of the power, and the limitations, of human reasoning about the everyday world may flow from this qualitative style of reasoning. In particular, such qualitative probabilistic reasoning may allow the cognitive system to reason over domains where precise numerical information is not available. This may be the typical case, when reasoning about complex everyday situations that are unique or rarely recur. For example, in reasoning about what would happen if a large ash tree in the garden might fall on one's house, one can qualitatively evaluate the likelihood of various outcomes (comparative chances of minor damage vs. complete demolition; relative chance of injury depending on which room one was in at the time; and so on), without any grasp of relevant numerical probabilities. But this particular tree has never actually fallen; and indeed, most of us have little experience of trees falling on houses more generally; so precise numerical probabilities are clearly not available to the reasoning system. What makes the human reasoning system so effective, we suggest, is that it is able to give qualitative insights that can guide behaviour, without having to rely on precise numerical values. Thus, if we know that the falling tree is more likely to damage one side of the house, we can run to the other side, with no need to know the absolute probabilities of either outcome. We stress, though, that the problem of representing, learning, and using the knowledge that underlies such qualitative patterns of inference is not solved—probabilistic methods, such as graphical models, make a start in helping to analyse simple cases of qualitative probabilistic reasoning (e.g. Pearl 1988); and probabilistic methods seem to extend to increasingly complex cases in a natural way (whereas logical methods, with their emphasis on certainty, and difficulties with non-monotonicity, do not); but the creation of a probabilistic theory of knowledge representation has only begun (e.g. Pearl 1988, 2000).

From this point of view, it is perhaps not surprising that people are not good at explicit reasoning with probabilities—indeed, they fall into probabilistic fallacies just as readily as they fall into logical contradictions (e.g. Kahneman *et al.* 1982), as we noted in Chapter 1. The probabilistic mind is not, of course, a machine for solving verbally or mathematically specified problems of probability theory. Instead, we suggest, the mind is probabilistic, in the sense that the rational analysis of human reasoning requires understanding how the mind deals qualitatively with uncertainty—and probability theory is the calculus of uncertainty. As we stressed in Chapter 2, this does not imply that the mind is a probabilistic calculating machine (although it may be); still less does it imply that the mind can process probabilistic problems posed in a verbal or mathematical format. Nonetheless, the concepts of probability are, we suggest, as crucial to understanding the human mind as the concepts of fluid dynamics are in understanding the operation of a bird's wing.

We have argued that, according to the criterion of capturing correct everyday inferences (completeness*), probability is a better framework than logic. What, though, of the problem of computational intractability, addressed in Chapter 3? Exact probabilistic calculations are, as might be expected, computationally intractable in general, as the complexity of the probabilistic model being considered increases (e.g. Paris 1992). But the crucial question, in the light of our previous discussion, is how rapidly qualitative probabilistic calculations can be carried out, over the knowledge-base relevant to human reasoning? There are indications that probabilistic methods may be able to give rapid, approximate answers at least under some conditions. As we have noted, graphical models permit a parallel, distributed style of processing; and a small number of iterations of such processing may give useful approximate probabilistic answers (Frey 1998; Neal 1996; Pearl 1988). Given the slowness of neural components in the brain, Feldman and Ballard (1982) famously postulated the 'hundred-step constraint'—that any cognitively primitive operation (e.g. of a duration in the order of hundreds of milliseconds) must involve at most 100 computational steps. The fact that the parallel, distributed quality of graphical networks seems to map naturally on the parallel, distributed structures of the brain, suggests that probabilistic methods at least have the hope of being compatible with this constraint. By contrast, logic-based methods typically do not parallelize as straightforwardly and typically require too many computational steps to be implemented in the brain (for example, see Chater and Oaksford (1990) on Fodor and Pylyshyn's (1988) defense of the logicist viewpoint).

Artificial intelligence, like the philosophy of science, has been transformed by probabilistic ideas. In particular, logic-based approaches to reasoning about uncertainty have been replaced by the application of probability theory. Just as in the philosophy of science, a subjectivist view of probability is to the fore—probabilities are viewed as expressing degrees of belief, rather than as, for example, limiting frequencies. Typically, uncertain reasoning concerns situations that have never or rarely occurred; the relevant limiting frequencies are therefore not available. We now consider how far work in cognitive psychology has followed these developments. To the extent that the cognitive processes are really viewed as analogous to naïve science, and to the extent that attempts to construct intelligent computational systems inspire theorizing about how cognitive processes operate, we should expect that cognitive psychology too, might take a probabilistic turn. In the next section, we consider how far this has been the case.

The probabilistic turn in cognitive psychology

Most interesting problems faced by the cognitive system involve dealing with uncertainty. In this section we review a few areas of cognitive psychology, where a probabilistic turn has been adopted.

Perception

Consider, for example, the problem of inferring the structure of the world, from perceptual input. There are, notoriously, infinitely many states of the environment that can give rise to any perceptual input (e.g. Freeman 1994)–this is just a special case of the well-known observation in statistics that an infinite number of curves can fit any particular set of data points; or in the philosophy of science, that infinitely many theories can predict any body of scientific data. Deciding which of this infinite set of interpretations is most likely, is a problem of probabilistic inference *par excellence*. The idea that the perceptual system seeks the most likely interpretation can be traced to von Helmholtz (1910); more recently, it has been embodied in the Bayesian approach to (particularly visual) perception that has become prominent in psychology and neuroscience. This viewpoint has been backed by direct experimental evidence (e.g. Rock 1983); and also by the construction of detailed theories of particular aspects of perceptual processing, from a Bayesian perspective, including low-level image intepretation (Weiss 1997), shape from shading (Adelson and Pentland 1996; Freeman 1994), shape from texture (Blake *et al.* 1996), image segmention and object recognition (Tu *et al.* 2005), to interpolation of boundaries (Feldman 2001; Feldman and Singh 2005). Moreover, the functions of neural mechanisms involved in visual perception have also been given a probabilistic interpretation—from lateral inhibition in the retina (e.g. Barlow 1959b), to the activity of single cells in the blow-fly (Snippe *et al.* 2000).

Furthermore, the scope of the probabilistic view of perception may be somewhat broader than at might first be thought. Although apparently very different from the probabilistic view, the simplicity principle in perception, which proposes that the perceptual system chooses the interpretation of the input that provides the simplest encoding of that input (e.g. Attneave 1954; Hochberg and McAlister 1953; Leeuwenberg 1969, 1971; Leeuwenberg and Boselie 1988; Mach 1959; Restle 1970; Van der Helm and Leewenberg 1996) turns out to be mathematically equivalent to the probabilistic approach (Chater 1996).

Specifically, under mild mathematical restrictions, for any probabilistic analysis of a perceptual inference (using a particular prior probabilistic assumptions) there is a corresponding simplicity-based analysis (using a particular coding language, in which the code-length of an encoding of perceptual data in terms of an interpretation provides the measure of complexity), such that the most likely and the simplest interpretations co-incide (Chater 1996; although see Van der Helm 2000). Thus, theories of perception based on simplicity and coding, and theories of neural function based on decorrelation and information compression (e.g. Barlow 1959a) can be viewed as part of the Bayesian probabilistic approach to perception.[8]

Categorization

Probabilistic analyses have also been extensively developed in categorization. This seems natural, both to the extent that categorization is simply a high-level aspect of perception; and because categorization is a well-studied problem in statistics and machine learning, typically modelled in probabilistic terms (Cristianini and Shawe-Taylor 2000; Duda *et al.* 2000). For example, leading theories of supervised categorization (i.e. concerning the question of how people learn to associate items with category labels), are all formulated probabilistically. The exemplar view (Lamberts 2000; Medin and Shaffer 1978; Nosofsky 1984, 1986), which assumes that the categorization of new items is based on the category of similar items, and variants on the prototype view

---

[8] Advocates of 'direct' perception (Gibson 1966, 1979; Kugler and Turvey 1987) have argued that the idea that perception involves uncertain inference is incorrect—rather, they argue that the richness and regularity of the natural environment are sufficient to remove such ambiguity; and moreover they argue that the perceptuo-motor system can be 'attuned' to these regularities to drive action, without requiring that any representation of the external world be constructed. We agree that ambiguity can, typically be resolved by the perceptual system—after all, most perceptual inputs, aside from those constructed in perceptual experiments, do give rise to a single interpretation. Yet being 'attuned' to this single interpretation requires some mechanism for systematically alighting upon the appropriate interpretation—and this seems to be a matter of inference. Moreover, such inference is, even for rich perceptual stimuli, uncertain—alternative organizations are not impossible, merely very unlikely (sometimes astronomically so). Finally, the attempt to build a direct link between perception and action, without any mediating representation of the environmental structure (and hence, apparently, avoiding the inferences that appear to be required in constructing such a mediating structure) appears in general inadequate to explicate the flexible control of action in response to the goals of the agent. To figure out how to act, an agent needs to know not just what it wants; but how the world is; but delivering this last representation is precisely what is not countenanced by direct theories of perception (see Fodor and Pylyshyn 1981; Ullman 1980).

(e.g. Ashby and Gott 1988; Ashby and Townsend 1986; Fried and Holyoak 1984), which assumes that new items are categorized according to a parametric probability distribution for each category that is fitted on the basis of past items, can be viewed as lying on a continuum of probabilistic models. Moreover, there are close connections between Nosofsky's model and Anderson's (1991b; Nosofsky 1991) rational analysis of categorization, which has an explicitly probabilistic interpretation. Similarly, work on unsupervised categorization, in which people spontaneously group items, rather than learning pre-defined labels, also treats the problem in probabilistic terms. One idea is to try to model the items as a produced by a mixture of different probability distributions, each associated with a category (for related approaches see, for example: Corter and Gluck 1992; Gosselin and Schyns 2001; Pothos and Chater 2002; Rosch 1977).

Animal learning and human causal judgement

There has, too, been increasing interest in probabilistic models in animal learning and human causal judgement. Processes of learning about environmental structure from data are paradigm problems in mathematical statistics—and hence are naturally considered in the light of probabilistic techniques. Moreover, the problem of discerning structure in the world on the basis of observation and intervention is also immediately analogous to the problem faced by the scientist. It is perhaps not surprising, therefore, that psychologists have increasingly drawn on probabilistic ideas in building theories in these areas. For example, Cheng has proposed a 'probabilistic contrast' model of human causal judgement (Cheng 1997). Roughly, the contrast between the probability of an effect given that a specific cause is present, and the probability of an effect given that the cause is absent. Similarly, Fiedler (2000) has argued that social judgements concerning attributions of traits to people based on their observed behaviours, can be well accounted for by assuming that people apply a simple probabilistic analysis. Fiedler argues that many biases in social judgement are results, not of probabilistic miscalculations given the information that people receive—but rather, result from biases in the sample of information that people do receive. Biases in social judgement are then viewed as arising from people's lack of awareness of, or inability to counteract, such sampling biases (Fiedler and Juslin, 2006). Moreover, both Fiedler and Cheng represent the latest in a long history of researchers arguing that understanding the physical and social world is essentially a statistical problem (e.g. Alloy and Abramson 1979; Kelley 1967), and hence to be addressed by probabilistic, rather than logical, methods. The same style of explanation has also been widely applied to animal learning (e.g. Gallistel and Gibbon 2000; Kakade and Dayan 2002; Rescorla and Wagner 1972; Sutton and Barto 1981).

Moreover, there have recently been direct attempts to investigate how far graphical models, as described in the previous section, are a useful general model of causal reasoning (e.g. Griffiths and Tenenbaum, 2005; Sloman 2005; Sobel *et al.* 2004; Waldmann and Martignon 1998).

Memory

The psychology of memory might seem a less promising area for probabilistic analysis—naïvely one might suppose that memories are either present or absent, leaving no room for probabilistic analysis. But probability enters into memory in a number of ways—in theories that assume that memory is organized to make ease of memory retrieval correlate with the probability that an item will be needed (Anderson and Schooler 1991); theories that consider the integration of different memory cues (Shiffrin and Steyvers 1998); and how memories can be reconstructed from partial information, based on an underlying probabilistic model of how different pieces of information in memory are inter-related (e.g. Rumelhart *et al.* 1986).

Language processing

As a final example, consider language processing. Traditional approaches to understanding language and language structure have attempted to abstract away from probabilistic aspects of language. A language is viewed as a set of well-formed strings, generated according to formal rules; and these strings are associated with phonological and semantic representations. From this perspective, language understanding requires, among other things, mapping from phonology to semantics; language production requires, among other things, mapping from semantics to phonology. These computational problems seem fully specified without reference to any probabilistic factors. However, as with memory, probability seems to be crucially involved in language and language processing in a number of ways.

First, speech processing, in which the goal is to convert a hugely complex acoustic waveform into a discrete symbolic representation of what has been heard, must necessarily deal with uncertainty—as with any signal processing problem. Not surprisingly, leading methods in this area involve a variety of probabilistic learning methods, including hidden Markov models, and neural networks (Rabiner and Huang 1993). Probability enters, for similar reasons, where the language processor has to deal with errorful linguistic output—error correction requires a probabilistic model of the language output and the processes by which errors can occur.

Second, because of the ubiquitous ambiguity throughout language, merely enumerating possible interpretations of a sentence is not sufficient—the hearer needs also to figure out which is most likely to be that intended by the speaker. This, too, appears to be a probabilistic inference problem, which is analogous, at an abstract level, to the problem of associating an interpretation with highly ambiguous perception inputs, described above. Some theories of parsing assume that the parser does not, nonetheless, use a probabilistic solution—at least in the case of syntactic ambiguity, such theories assume that the ambiguity is resolved purely in accordance with the structure of competing syntactic parses (e.g. Frazier 1979). Nonetheless, recent research has increasingly viewed the parser as engaged in probabilistic calculations over a range of sources of evidence about which parse is the most probable (MacDonald *et al.* 1994; McRae *et al.* Tanenhaus 1998).[9]

Third, there has been increasing interest in the statistical cues that may underpin aspects of the processing and acquisition of aspects of phonology, syntax, and semantics. For example, statistical analysis of the contexts in which words occur can be used to classify them into syntactic classes (e.g. Redington *et al.* 1998) or semantic classes (e.g. Landauer and Dumais 1997; Lund and Burgess 1996). The richness of these statistical cues may indicate that they may be able to substantially facilitate language processing and acquisition (e.g. Dennis 2005; Redington and Chater 1998).

Summary

We have argued that cognitive psychology has increasingly adopted a probabilistic view of mental life. This is, in a sense, a return to the roots of probability theory. As we saw in Chapter 1, probability theory was viewed, from the start, both as a normative theory of how people should reason about uncertainty; and as a descriptive theory of how good reasoners actually do reason (Gigerenzer *et al.* 1989).[10]

Moreover, recall too from Chapter 1, that according to one leading interpretation of probability, probability expresses *subjective degree of belief*—thus, the very subject matter of probability, from this point of view, seems to be necessarily psychological. But there is a sense, too, in which emphasizing this pedigree is misleading—because it suggests that the cognitive psychologists view the mind as a machine that directly and consciously tackles probabilistic reasoning problems. But people are, of course, hopelessly poor at explicit verbal or numerical mathematical reasoning about probability—as is evident from the enormous

---

[9] However, see Chater *et al.* 1998 for a refinement of the preference for the most probable interpretation in local ambiguity resolution.

[10] Indeed, as we noted, the normative/descriptive dichotomy is relatively recent.

intellectual effort required to construct modern probability theory, and the struggle that each new generation of student must go through to assimilate it.

The role of probability in cognitive psychology is, rather, to explicate the nature of the problems that the cognitive system faces, whether these be constructing an interpretation for a scene or a sentence; learning causal structure from experience; or categorizing visual objects. That is, probability plays a key role in the rational analysis of human cognition, as described in Chapter 2. By understanding the nature of the problems that cognitive processes must solve, we can thereby say quite a lot about the outputs of cognitive processes—just as, with a theory of how to play good chess, one will automatically make good predictions about the moves that good chess players typically make.

Now, of course, it may be that cognitive processes solve the probabilistic problems that they face by engaging in explicit probabilistic calculation—although this is certainly not necessarily the case. But whatever their nature, the relevant calculations (in the domains we have described) are clearly not consciously accessible. If we have machinery for probabilistic inference in common-sense reasoning, perception, categorization or language processing, it is not, therefore, surprising that we cannot recruit it to help us solve mathematical probability problems. In this book, we shall focus on the core issue of the rational analysis of human reasoning.[11]

We focus on rational analysis, because we have to understand *what* the cognitive system is doing, before having much chance of discovering how it might be doing it; and we focus on reasoning, rather than, say, perception, language processing, or categorization, because here the question of the correct normative pattern of thought is most clearly in focus; and, moreover, reasoning problems are intended to engage central cognitive processes involved in common-sense reasoning about the world, rather than engaging what might potentially be quite specialized 'modular' cognitive processes (e.g. Fodor 1983). In the second half of this book, we develop probabilistic accounts of three key reasoning problems—conditional inference, Wason's selection task, and syllogistic reasoning. All of these have traditionally been assimilated within a logicist framework; all of these can be illuminated, we argue, from the point of view of the probabilistic mind; and all are, we suggest, illustrative of the probabilistic character of the mind.

---

[11] Although we will also describe some proposals concerning the algorithms that may be used to carry out certain reasoning problems—in particular, in Chapter 7, we shall suggest that syllogistic reasoning may be carried out using a simple 'fast and frugal' set of heuristics, which give a good approximation to a normative probabilistic standard.

Chapter 5

Does the exception prove the rule? How people reason with conditionals

In this chapter we turn to the task of showing how a probabilistic perspective can resolve many of the outstanding issues in reasoning research. Our goal is to show that many of the errors and biases seen in experiments on human reasoning are the result of people applying probabilistic strategies used for coping with their uncertain world. In the psychology of reasoning it has been standard to take logic as the normative theory against which performance is assessed. However, as we first discuss, standard logic has long been known not to provide an adequate account of reasoning. The key logical term where this issue arises is the conditional, *if...then*. This simple expression is probably the most important to all systems of reasoning. It has long been observed in the philosophy of language and logic that there is a mismatch between how logic treats the conditional and how it is used in natural language and in everyday argument. We first argue that this mismatch suggests a probabilistic approach to the conditional. We then show that adopting this approach allows us to explain much of the data on conditional inference.

Logicism and uncertainty

Within philosophy, linguistics, logic, and computational theory there is general convergence on the view that standard first-order logic is inadequate to capture everyday reasoning about the real world. Although many psychologists are well aware of these literatures, the implications of this work for the scope of first-order reasoning have not been fully recognized. Indeed, the very fact that the two leading formal psychological theories of reasoning, mental logic (e.g. Rips 1994) and mental models (e.g. Johnson-Laird and Byrne 1991) both retain the standard logical apparatus suggests that the inadequacies of first-order logic as a model for human reasoning are not universally accepted. We focus our discussion in this chapter on the conditional, *if...then*. We first sketch the standard logical treatment of the conditional, and then consider its problems and attempted solutions to these problems within a logical framework.

The standard logic of the conditional

The standard approach within formal semantics of natural or logical languages is to provide a recursive definition of the truth of complex expressions in terms of their parts. The natural language phrase *if p then q* is standardly rendered as the material conditional of logic. The material conditional $p \Rightarrow q$ is true if and only if p (the antecedent) is false or q (the consequent) is true (or both) (see Table 4.1). This semantics licenses the valid rules of inference, *modus ponens* (MP) and *modus tollens* (MT):

$$(\text{MP}) \quad \frac{p \Rightarrow q, \ p}{\therefore q} \qquad (\text{MT}) \quad \frac{p \Rightarrow q, \ \neg q}{\therefore \neg p} \qquad (5.1)$$

These inference schemas read, given the propositions above the line ($p \Rightarrow q$ and p, for MP) are true then the truth of the propositions below the line can be deduced, (q for MP). This is because, according to the truth table in Chapter 4 (Problems for logic), if the propositions above the line are true, i.e. $p \Rightarrow q$ and p are true, then so must be the propositions below the line, i.e. q must be true.

There are certain well-known counter-intuitive properties of this semantics for the conditional that have become known as the 'paradoxes of material implication', which we have noted before (Oaksford 1989; Oaksford and Chater 1998a, 2001, 2003d) but which have largely been ignored in the psychological literature (see, Johnson-Laird and Byrne 2002; but more recently, see: Evans and Over 2004). For example, material implication implies that any conditional with a false antecedent is true—thus, the sentence, *if the moon is striped, then Mars is spotted*, is true according to the material conditional simply because its antecedent is false. But intuitively it is either false or nonsensical.

Further problems arise because the material conditional allows *strengthening of the antecedent*. That is, given the premise *if p then q*, we can conclude that *if (p and r) then q*, for any *r*. Strengthening of the antecedent seems appropriate in mathematical contexts. *If it is a triangle, it has three sides*, does imply that, *if it is a triangle and it is blue, it has three sides*. Indeed, this is a crucial feature of axiomatic systems in mathematics—axiomatization would be impossible if adding new axioms removed conclusions that followed from the old axioms. However, strengthening of the antecedent does not apply to most natural language conditionals, which as we have argued are uncertain. Indeed, conditionals for which strengthening of the antecedent holds are monotonic.

But as we have seen in previous chapters, everyday conditionals are *defeasible* and so *non-monotonic*. For example, *if it is a bird, then it flies*, does not allow you to infer that, *if it is a bird and it is an ostrich, then it flies*. That is, for natural language conditionals conclusions can be lost by adding premises, i.e. strengthening of the antecedent does not hold.

Further, note that whether some additional information *r* has this effect or not is content dependent. For example, if you learn that this bird is a parrot, the conclusion that it can fly is not lost. As we have argued in previous chapters, the distinction between inference systems in which strengthening of the antecedent does or does not hold, is of central importance to knowledge representation in artificial intelligence. Roughly, inference systems where strengthening of the antecedent holds are known as monotonic systems (continuously adding premises leads to continuously adding conclusions, without removing any); inference systems where strengthening of the antecedent does not hold are non-monotonic. As we have argued in Chapters 3 and 4, it is almost universally accepted in artificial intelligence that human everyday reasoning is uncertain and thus non-monotonic, and that developing systems for non-monotonic reasoning is a major challenge (e.g. Fuhrman 1998; Ginsberg 1987; McCarthy and Hayes 1969).

We have previously addressed alternative logical approaches to the conditional with respect to the philosophy of mind (Oaksford and Chater 1991) and the cognitive science of conditional reasoning (Chater and Oaksford 1993; Oaksford 1989; Oaksford and Chater 1991, 1995b, 1998a) As we pointed out in Chapters 3 and 4, the problems that these accounts of the conditional inevitably lead to when construed as computational psychological theories are those confronted by artificial intelligence in dealing with defeasibility. However, given the recent literature on the psychology of conditional reasoning, where these connections are not discussed (Evans and Over 2004), it is worth surveying these issues in some detail. In the following sections we explore different logical and formal semantic approaches to dealing with the problems we have noted for the material conditional. We begin with approaches that focus on relevance.

Relevance

Regarding our first problem with material implication, that a false antecedent guarantees the truth of a conditional, an intuitive diagnosis is that material implication fails to specify that there be any connection between the antecedent and consequent—they can simply be any two arbitrary propositions. Within the logical literature, relevance logic has tried to capture this intuition.

Relevance logic, as its name implies, demands that there is a relationship of 'relevance' between antecedent and consequent, where this is defined in terms of the proof of the consequent involving the antecedent (Anderson and Belnap 1975). So *if the moon is striped, then Mars is spotted* is non starter because the assumption that the moon is striped could never figure in a proof that Mars is spotted. From a logical point of view, systems of relevance logic are not well-developed. For example, it has been very difficult to provide a semantics for relevance logics (Veltman 1985), which means that it is not clear quite what notion of relevance is being coded by the syntactic rules used in particular relevance logics. But in any case, the relation of relevance would not appear to be reducible to notions of proof, particularly not in everyday contexts, because the uncertain character of reasoning means that proofs are never possible. So relevance logics do not appear to be a useful direction for developing a notion of the conditional that applies to everyday reasoning. However, in the psychology of reasoning, Braine (1978) has advanced a relevance-based account, arguing that people naturally only assert conditionals when the consequent is deducible from the antecedent.

Causality and situation semantics

The idea that conditionals are usually only asserted when there is some kind of relationship between antecedent and consequent has been pursued in *situation semantics*. Barwise and Perry (1983) attempted to develop a formal semantics for natural language based on the idea that conditionals are not truth functions, but terms that refer to a causal or other law-like relationship between antecedent and consequent. Philosophers tend to gloss 'causal or other law-like relation' in terms of a relationship being *counter-factual supporting*. Explicating this notion will also introduce the two fundamental types of conditional.

Causal relations are clearly counter-factual supporting. So take the standard *indicative* conditional:

If you turn the key, the car will start. (5.2)

The truth of 5.2 supports the truth of the corresponding *counter-factual* conditional:

If you had turned the key, the car would have started. (5.3)

The only reason for believing that 5.3 is true is because of the existence of the causal or law-like regularity that underlies 5.2 that would have guaranteed that the car started had you turned the key. The fact that the truth of a counter-factual conditional may depend on the truth of the corresponding indicative suggests a close relationship between them. And indeed some logicians propose a unified analysis of both types of conditional (Edgington 1995), while others believe that they require distinct analyses (Bennett 2003). As some authors have pointed out (e.g. Bennett 2003), the falsity of the antecedent is not necessary in the case of 5.3, all that is required is that the person who utters 5.3 *believes* it to be false, so 'counter-factual' is really a misnomer. A more often used term for conditionals like 5.3 is *subjunctive* because of the mood of the consequent indicated by 'would.' We will largely side-step the issue of the relationship between the indicative and the subjunctive by concentrating on the indicative.

While 5.2 is clearly causal, non-causal relationships can be counter-factual supporting. For example, take the conditional promise:

<blockquote>If you mow the lawn, I'll pay you £10.   (5.4)</blockquote>

The truth of 5.4 seems to support the truth of the corresponding counter-factual (5.5) in just the same way as 5.2 supports 5.3:

<blockquote>If you had mown the lawn, I would have paid you £10.   (5.5)</blockquote>

As long as the promise in 5.4 was entered into in good faith, it supports the truth of counter-factual in 5.5. However, there are clear problems with the idea that indicative conditionals *refer* to law-like relations like this, as promises do not seem to be things in the world that can be referred to. But then again, as Hume (1748) famously observed, the same could be said for causes (for further discussion, see: Oaksford 1989). Situation semantics is irredeemably realist about causes and the problems lie in whether it makes sense to be similarly realist about other dependencies in the world, such as promises, legal obligations, or habits.

Some of these problems for situations semantics were discussed in Oaksford (1989) who also applied this semantic theory to the psychology of reasoning. The idea behind situation semantics was that causal and other constraints allow conditionals to express *information-gaining* relationships. So, for example, if you know that, *if there is smoke there is fire*, then on discovering that there is smoke, you gain the information that there is fire. Again conditionals like, *if the moon is striped, then Mars is spotted*, is a non-starter because there is no constraint between the antecedent and consequent, such that learning that the antecedent was true could provide information about the consequent.

Moreover, problems like strengthening the antecedent could potentially be dealt with because information gain was relative to a *situation*. The ontological status of *situations* is problematic, but for our purposes we can just think of them in the everyday sense. Situations can be big or small, the situation *at my desk, in my house, at work,* and so on. Situations *support* causal or law-like *constraints.* But people might not be perfectly attuned to the constraints a situation supports. So, at the theatre, a young child may believe there is a fire because there is smoke on the stage not realizing that this situation does not support the, *if there is smoke, there is fire* constraint (as dry ice is causing the smoke). Situations introduce the concept of *partial interpretation.* That is, being relatively small bits of the world, they are silent on issues outside their domain. So there is nothing in my situation, sitting at my desk at home, which could resolve the truth or falsity of the proposition that *Tony Blair is eating a burger.* In my situation this proposition cannot be assigned a truth value, my situation does not support either a true or a false valuation, which suggests that in many cases people may not be in a position to assign *true* or *false* to all the propositions that might be relevant to a particular passage of reasoning. With respect to a conditional, the constraint it describes can only be informational in a situation if it supports the truth of the antecedent.

As an account of conditionals, problems for situation theory concerned the lack of a corresponding logic to determine those inferences that were and were not permitted (Oaksford 1989) and the problem of below causal constraints. However, some of the ideas that were part of situation semantics will crop up later on. Oaksford and Chater (1994b) went on to develop a probabilistic account of *information gain* that they applied to the Wason selection task (see Chapter 6). Moreover, more recently, as we discussed in Chapter 4, probabilistic graphical models have been used by Pearl (2000) to formally capture the concept of causation, i.e. to provide a semantics for causal statements and an account of the inferences such statements allow. In Chapter 7, we will use similar, albeit very simple, probabilistic graphical models to capture syllogistic reasoning.

Modality and the Lewis–Stalnaker conditional

One of the most important approaches to the conditional employs modal notions, such as necessity and possibility. Syntactic systems of modal logic and so-called strict implication based on them were first suggested by C. I. Lewis (1918). Semantic theories for modal logics were developed much later by Kripke (1963), which permitted an understanding of the notions of necessity and possibility that were encoded in the syntactic rules. Specifically, Kripke provides a semantics in terms of 'possible worlds.' The idea is that different modal logics can be understood in terms of different relations of *accessibility* between possible worlds. In these terms, a proposition is necessary, if it is true in all accessible possible worlds, and it is possible if it is true in some accessible possible world.

The most philosophically important account of conditionals was given by the Lewis–Stalnaker possible world semantics for the counter-factual conditional (Lewis 1973; Stalnaker 1968). As we saw above, a counter-factual conditional is one in which the antecedent is known (or believed) to be false: e.g. *if the gun had gone off, he would have been killed*. According to material implication, such claims are always true, simply because their antecedents are false. But clearly this cannot be correct—under most circumstances, the counter-factual, 'if he had stubbed his toe, he would have been killed', will be judged unequivocally false. Looking at the Lewis–Stalnaker semantics for such claims reveals all the problems that logical approaches to everyday reasoning must confront in philosophy and in artificial intelligence.

The intuitive idea behind the Lewis–Stalnaker semantics for a conditional such as *if the gun had gone off, he would have been killed*, is based on the idea that in the possible world minimally different from the actual world but in which the gun went off, he died. Clearly, the major issue here is what counts as the world minimally different from the actual one. One important criterion is that the physical laws are the same, so that speeding bullets still tend to kill people, the gun is pointing in the same direction, and so on—the only difference is that the gun went off in this world, whereas it did not in the actual world. But there is a vast range of specific problems with this account. For example, it is not at all clear how to construct a world where only a single fact differs from the actual world. This is problematic because for this to be true (assuming determinism) the difference in this crucial fact either implies a different causal history (the bullet was a dud, the gun was faulty, etc.), or different causal laws (pulling triggers does not make guns go off in this possible world). Moreover, a different causal history or different causal laws will have different causal consequences, aside from the single fact under consideration. Thus, it appears inevitable that the so-called minimally different world differs in many ways, rather than just about a single fact, from the actual world. So by changing one thing, we automatically change many things, and it is not at all clear what the inferential consequences of these changes should be. These kinds of difficulties are partially addressed by D. Lewis's (1973) gloss that, in assessing a counter-factual, we should assume that a 'small miracle' occurs, in local contravention to normal causal laws, that brings about the truth of the antecedent, without modifying past causal history, or the future operation of causal laws. Even so, how far it is possible to change one thing, without simultaneously bringing about changes in many others, is not at all clear.

These problems aside, this semantics for the counter-factual (i.e. where the antecedent—the gun going off—does not apply in the actual world) has also been applied to the indicative case (where the gun may or may not have gone off).

Simplistically, the hypothetical element of an indicative statement such as 'if the gun goes off, he is dead' seems to be captured by the same semantics—the only difference is that we do not know whether the actual world is one in which the gun goes off or not. Nonetheless, this kind of semantic account does avoid some of the absurdities of material implication. Thus, for example, sentences like 'if the moon is striped, then Mars is spotted' are now clearly false—in worlds minimally different from the actual world in which the moon is striped, Mars will still look red. Crucially, it is intuitively clear that strengthening of the antecedent can no longer hold. For example, *if it's a bird, then it flies* does not allow you to infer that, *if it is a bird and it is an ostrich, then it flies*. The worlds at which the antecedents are evaluated will clearly differ—the world most similar to the actual world in which something is a bird is not the same as the world most similar to the actual world in which something is an ostrich. In particular, in the first world, the thing will most likely fly (because most birds fly); but in the second world, the thing will not fly (because ostriches cannot fly). These examples suggest that the Lewis–Stalnaker semantics may provide a more descriptively adequate theory of conditionals than the material conditional.

An important distinction between the Lewis–Stalnaker conditional and the material conditional is that while both are *truth conditional*, only the latter is *truth functional*. That is, the material conditional specifies the truth of the conditional to be a Boolean function of the truth or falsity of the antecedent and consequent. However, the Lewis–Stalnaker conditional does not describe the truth of the conditional in these truth-functional terms. Whether the conditional is true or false depends on the *selection function* that selects possible worlds minimally different to the actual world in which the antecedent is true. This has the consequence that when the antecedent is false, the conditional could be true or false. It depends on how close the truth table cases are to the worlds in which the conditional is determinately true and determinately false. Take the rule *if you turn the key, the car starts* and let world w_{TT} be the minimally different world from the actual world in which the car starts. There will also be a more distant world w_{TF} in which the car does not start. Whether the false antecedent cases, where the key is not turned, make the rule true or false then depends on how close w_{FT} and w_{FF} are to w_{TT} and w_{TF}. If they are closer to w_{TT} than w_{TF} then these truth table cases make the rule true. If they are closer to w_{TF} than w_{TT} then the cases make the rule false. Either way the truth of the Lewis–Stalnaker conditional does not depend on the way the world is, i.e. it is not *extensional*, but on possible ways the world might be, i.e. in philosophical terms it is *intensional* (with an *s*).

For psychological purposes, talk of possible worlds may seem obscure. But this formal mathematical concept is motivated from an earlier informal treatment that is more obviously psychological; this is the Ramsey test (Ramsey 1931) in which talk of possible worlds is replaced by talk of knowledge or belief states. It is worth citing the Ramsey test in full as it will figure in our subsequent discussions (Ramsey 1931, p. 143):

> If two people are arguing 'if A will C' and are both in doubt as to A, they are adding A hypothetically to their stock of knowledge and arguing on that basis about C ....
> We can say that they are fixing their degrees of belief in C given A.

There has been debate over precisely what Ramsey had in mind in this passage (e.g. Levi 1996; Slater 2004) but we follow Bennett's (2003) exposition. Some logicians by and large ignore the last sentence (to which we shall return below) and suggest that people assess the conditional by supposing A to be true, making minimal changes to their current beliefs to accommodate A, and then checking whether C is assessed as *true* in the resulting belief state (e.g. Gärdenfors 1986). We must be careful about talk of 'belief states' because supposing A to be true is not the same as actually believing it to be true. Using Bennett's (2003) example, an atheist presumably thinks that the proposition that God exists is false, and may not revise that opinion on supposing that she has a terminal illness. However, on actually being told that she has a terminal illness, she may nonetheless come to believe that God exists, perhaps out of fear and weakness. One way round this potential confusion is to use the neutral AI term *database* to refer to our stock of beliefs about the world. We can then use 'suppose' and 'believe' as attitudes to the results of performing operations over that database. An attitude of belief automatically connects the result of those operations to affective and action systems in a way that supposing does not. For example, our atheist supposing she has a terminal illness will not have the emotional responses or act so as to try and ensure an afterlife or to make arrangements for one's nearest and dearest in the same way as if she came to believe she was terminally ill.

Some form of the Ramsey test has been influential in all the most important alternatives to the material conditional. Moreover, as we shall discuss further below, recently Evans and Over (2004) have appealed to this test as part of a psychological account of conditionals. However, as we shall also argue later, the psychological/computational problems raised by the Ramsey test are exactly those that confront theories of defeasible reasoning in AI, i.e. intractability and completeness*, which we have already discussed. Later we also discuss a recent computational theory of our own that attempts to use *constraint satisfaction* neural networks to model the Ramsey test. However, first we explore another older approach to conditionals that can be given a far richer justification using probability theory. This will lead in to a discussion of perhaps the currently most important account of the indicative conditional due to Adams (1966, 1975, 1998).

Conditional assertion

The idea that conditionals do not assert a conditional but rather make a conditional assertion, goes back at least to Quine (1950, *Methods of logic*). So rather than asserting *if p then q*, a conditional asserts *q* on the assumption that *p* is true. Conceiving of conditionals in this way immediately seems to get round the problem that when construed as material conditionals, everyday conditionals come out true if their antecedents are false, which as we have seen violates intuition. However, the question is then how to formalize this idea. There have been a variety of accounts (see, in particular, Belnap 1970) but the most obvious way is to introduce an extra truth value. Some logics do this by introducing an *indeterminate* truth value, which may be assigned when the antecedent of a conditional is false. However, in such *multi-valued* logics, decisions have to be made about how this new truth value ramifies through the logical system to determine new multi-valued truth functions for all connectives, and this in turn also affects which logical laws hold and which do not. Haack (1974) provides an overview of some of these systems. Problems arise because the decisions made tend to depend on why an extra truth value has been introduced in the first place and these reasons have been varied. For example, in *quantum* logic (see, Reichenbach's (1944) *quasi implication*), indeterminate values arise because of causal anomalies, where wave-particle duality seems to lead to contradictory descriptions of events (see, Haack 1974, chapter 8). As we will see in the next section, the idea that conditionals cannot be assigned true or false when the antecedent is false, receives full justification in Adams' (1966, 1975, 1998) *probability logic* without the need to propose multi-valued logics with *indeterminate* truth values. First, however, we briefly argue that some results in the psychology of reasoning are consistent with conditional assertion.

In discussing conditional assertion, Oaksford (1989) pointed out that work in the psychology of reasoning on truth-table tasks (Evans 1972; Evans *et al.* 1993; Oaksford and Stenning 1992), seemed consistent with multi-valued systems. In these experiments, participants either evaluate or construct the truth table cases that make a conditional true or false. So for example, given a rule, *if there is a green square on the left, there is a blue circle on the right*, and an array of coloured shapes, participants would be asked to select pairs of shapes that made the rule true or false (Evans 1972; Oaksford and Stenning 1992). Participants were pretty uniform in identifying that the true antecedent and true consequent case make the conditional true and that the true antecedent and false consequent case make it false. However, they rarely constructed false antecedent cases as making the rule true or false, and when asked to evaluate these cases they would usually treat them as irrelevant.

This led researchers to the conclusion that people have a *defective* truth table for the conditional. Oaksford (1989) pointed out that this was compatible with the idea that people treat the conditional as a conditional assertion in a multi-valued logic. The same point about the defective truth table has been picked up again more recently by Evans and Over (2004), who also point out that this empirical observation is compatible with Adams *probability logic*.

Probability logic

Adams (1966, 1975, 1998) probability logic provides a sound justification for why conditionals should be treated as conditional assertions. The core of probability logic for the conditional is what Edgington (1995) refers to as 'the Equation', which equates the probability of an everyday indicative conditional with the conditional probability:

$$P(p \rightarrow q) = P(q \mid p), \text{ where } P(p) < 0. \tag{5.6}$$

Where $P(q|p)$ is given by the *Ratio formula*:

$$P(q \mid p) = \frac{P(p \wedge q)}{P(q)}. \tag{5.7}$$

Importantly, the Ratio formula is not to be interpreted as a definition of conditional probability, which is regarded as more primitive. Our understanding of $P(q|p)$ is given by the subjective interpretation provided by the Ramsey Test. As Bennett (2003, p. 53) says:

> The best definition we have [of conditional probability] is the one provided by the Ramsey test: your conditional probability for q given p is the probability for q that results from adding $P(p) = 1$ to your belief system and conservatively adjusting to make room for it.

The immediate consequence of the Equation is that false antecedent instances are irrelevant. This is because, according to the Ramsey test, assessing the conditional probability assumes that $P(p) = 1$. Another route to the same conclusion is that the Ratio formula indicates that in calculating the probability of the everyday conditional, all that matters are the probabilities of the true antecedent cases, i.e. $P(p \wedge q)$ and $P(p \wedge \neg q)$ $[P(q) = P(p \wedge q) + P(p \wedge \neg q)]$. Note that the Ramsey test is the best available definition of conditional probability and that the Ratio formula, as Bennett demonstrates, can be shown to conform to the Ramsey test. Combining the Ramsey test and the Ratio formula shows that everyday indicative conditionals are *zero-intolerant* (Bennett 2003). That is, they are not acceptable when $P(p) = 0$, because the consequence is that you should 'believe $p \rightarrow q$ to the extent that you think that $p \wedge q$ is nearly as likely as p' (Edgington 1991, p. 189). So when $P(p) = 0$, you should not accept $p \rightarrow q$.

There are many examples demonstrating why it makes sense to treat the probability of a conditional as the conditional probability (again, see Bennett 2003). However, there have also been detractors (e.g. Lewis 1976) who point to some of the counter-intuitive consequences of adopting the Equation. The first consequence is that not only is the *probability conditional*, as Adams (1998) refers to it, not truth functional, it is not truth conditional either, i.e. conditionals are not propositions that can have a truth value. If they were propositions, then when we ask about their probability, $P(p \rightarrow q)$, we are asking about the probability that '$p \rightarrow q$' is true. But from the Equation, $P(p \rightarrow q) = P(q|p)$, and so we are asking a question about the probability that $q|p$ is true. However, '$q|p$' is not a stand-alone claim about the world, i.e. it does not make sense to ask whether this is true or false. According to the Ramsey test, this expression relates to a mental process, not a fact about the world that could be true or false.

If conditionals do not have truth conditions, then other apparently counter-intuitive consequences follow. For example, it means that conditionals cannot be embedded in truth functional compounds. For example, one might deny that turning the key will start this car by asserting, *it is not the case that if you turn the key, the car will start*, i.e. $\neg(p \rightarrow q)$. But as we have seen, $p \rightarrow q$ is equal to $q|p$ and so $P\neg(p \rightarrow q)$ should equal $P(\neg(q|p))$ but '$P(\neg(q|p))$' is not formally defined and is meaningless. One might imagine that this apparent limitation would set bounds on the expressiveness of a system embodying the probability conditional, such that it could not capture important aspects of natural language. However, denying that turning the key will start the car, is expressed most naturally by saying, 'no it won't'. That is, *if you turn the key, the car will not start*. But in the standard logic of the material conditional $p \Rightarrow q$ and $p \Rightarrow \neg q$ are consistent, one is not the denial of the other. For the probability conditional, in contrast, they are *probabilistically inconsistent*. This is because $P(q \mid p) + P(\neg q \mid p) = 1$, so asserting that $p \rightarrow \neg q$ has a high probability simultaneously means that $p \rightarrow q$ has a low probability. Thus, there may be no lack of expressiveness by moving to the probability conditional. Adams (1975) argues that the move to the probability conditional suggests that there may be constraints on the way conditionals can be embedded in truth functional compound sentences. Moreover, Bennett (2003) argues that this move seems to disarm some of the strongest criticisms of the Equation due to Lewis (1976). And there seems to be linguistic evidence that the constraints on embeddings recommended by the probability conditional may be reflected in natural languages (Bennett 2003).

If indicative conditionals do not have truth values, then it would seem that it is impossible to define any valid inferences that follow from them. This is because if they have no truth value then there can be no transfer of truth from premises to the conclusion of an argument that has an indicative conditional as a premise. However, while classical validity is therefore impossible for arguments involving conditionals, they may possess another virtue, *probabilistic validity* or *p-validity*. Adams (1975) discovered that all classically valid arguments also possess a property that can best be formulated using the concept of *uncertainty*. The uncertainty of a proposition p, $U(p)$, is simply $1 - P(p)$. The property he discovered was that, 'in a classically valid argument the uncertainty of the conclusion cannot exceed the sum of the uncertainties of the premises' (Bennett 2003, p. 131). That is,

$$\text{If } p_1 \ldots p_n \text{ entail } q, \text{ then } U(q) \le \sum_{i=1}^{n} U(p_i) \tag{5.8}$$

An argument fulfilling this condition, Adams (1975) calls *p-valid*. Arguments containing indicative conditionals, while not candidates for classical validity, may be *p*-valid and so can be evaluated on that basis.

Evaluating some of the paradoxes of material implication, immediately indicate that they are not *p*-valid. For example, according to the material conditional, a conditional is true if the antecedent is false, or the consequent is true. That is, the following inference schemas are valid:

$$\frac{\neg p}{\therefore p \Rightarrow q} \qquad \frac{q}{\therefore p \Rightarrow q}. \tag{5.9}$$

In case of the left-hand schema $P(p) = 0$, and so, as we have seen, no value can be assigned to the probability of the conditional in the conclusion because of *zero-intolerance*. However, when $P(q) = 1$, then $P(p \rightarrow q)$ should also be 1, which means their uncertainties are equal. However, *p*-validity requires the inequality in 5.8 to hold whatever the value of $P(q)$. But suppose q is *my car starts*, which has a probability of 0.98, and p is *I turn the key*. Suppose also that I know that I have no gas. Although q is high, supposing $P(p) = 1$, means I must assign 0 probability to $p \rightarrow q$ because I know I am out of gas, which violates *p*-validity. Thus the paradoxes of material implication are not *p*-valid.

Four further inferences that are classically valid for the material conditional turn out not to be *p-valid* for the probability conditional. These are *strengthening the antecedent, transitivity, contraposition,* and *or-to-if:*

$$\text{Strengthening} \quad \frac{p \rightarrow q}{\therefore (p \wedge r) \rightarrow q}. \qquad \text{Transitivity} \frac{(p \rightarrow q),(q \rightarrow r)}{\therefore p \rightarrow r}. \qquad (5.10)$$

$$\text{Contraposition} \quad \frac{p \rightarrow q}{\therefore \neg q \rightarrow \neg p}. \qquad \text{Or-to-if} \qquad \frac{p \vee q}{\therefore \neg p \rightarrow q}$$

Counter-examples to the *p*-validity of all these inferences involve, of course, showing that the uncertainty of the conclusion can be greater than the uncertainty of the premises (or their sum in the case of transitivity). Examples abound for strengthening the antecedent. Although it makes sense to assign a high probability to *if Tweety is a bird, then Tweety can fly*, because most birds fly, any one would assign a very low probability, i.e. 0, to *if Tweety is a bird and Tweety is one second old, then Tweety can fly* (how old Tweety is can be adjusted to produce probabilities for the conclusion that are greater than 0). Thus the uncertainty of the conclusion (1) is greater than the uncertainty of the premise. Transitivity entails and is entailed by strengthening the antecedent (Bennett 2003), so they stand *and* fall together. Contraposition also seems to succumb readily to counter-examples. Although it makes sense to assign a high probability to *if you turn the key, your car starts*, because it most often starts when you turn the key, in any pragmatically natural context, any one would assign a low probability to *if the car does not start, then you did not turn the key*, because the only reason to expect the car to start in the first place is that you turned the key. Or-to-if also fails. For example, someone may assign a high probability to *Oswald shot Kennedy or Mars is striped* because they believe that Oswald was the gunman, however they would still assign a low probability to *if Oswald did not shoot Kennedy, then Mars is striped.*

Although these inferences are not *p*-valid, they may be *probabilistically secure*. That is, in the conditions under which it would make sense to assert these conclusions they may not be as uncertain as the above counter-examples seem to show. Notice that the conclusions of all these inferences are themselves conditionals. Adams (1975) *security thesis* is as follows (quoted from Bennett 2003, p. 141):

> *Security Thesis*: If X is an argument whose conclusion is an indicative conditional $p \rightarrow q$, and if what results from replacing $\rightarrow$ [the indicative] by $\Rightarrow$ [the material conditional] throughout X is a classically valid inference, then X is probabilistically secure to the extent that $P(p)$ is high.

So, in our contraposition example, one could argue that the conclusion would only be asserted when the intention is to (implicitly) quantify over all times, rather than car starting attempts. If so, the probability of the car not starting will be high, simply because most of the time no one is trying to start it by turning the key. Probabilistic security is of course a matter of degree. An argument is probabilistically secure as long as the uncertainty of the conclusion does not exceed the sum of the uncertainties of the premises *by too much*.

In psychological experiments, the most common inferences investigated are *modus ponens* (MP) and *modus tollens* (MT; see, 5.1) together with the fallacies of *denying the antecedent* (DA; $p \rightarrow q$, $\neg p$, $\therefore \neg q$) and *affirming the consequent* (AC; $p \rightarrow q$, q, $\therefore p$) which we discuss in 'A computational level model'. In probability logic, both MP and MT are *p*-valid. However, this simple statement covers over a range of important issues. For Adams (1975, 1998), the whole point of the indicative conditional is to perform MP inferences, i.e. conditionals are *inference tickets*—an idea that goes back to Ryle (1949)—that allow us to update our beliefs given new information. So if I assign a high probability to *if x is a bird, x flys*, then on acquiring the new information that *Tweety is a bird*, I should revise my degree of belief in *Tweety flies* to my degree of belief in *Tweety flies given Tweety is a bird*, i.e. my degree of belief in the conditional. So using P_0 to indicate *prior* degree of belief and P_1 to indicate *posterior* degree of belief, then:

$$P_1(q) = P_0(q \mid p), \text{when } P_1(p) = 1. \tag{5.11}$$

This result can be generalized (Hailperin 1996; Sober 2002) to the case when the new information is not that $P_1(p) = 1$, but that $P_1(p)$ equals some probability b, then assuming $P_0(q \mid p) = a$, the best possible bounds on $P_1(q)$ are:

$$ab \leq P_1(q) \leq ab + 1 - b \tag{5.12}$$

There are important conditions on when updating beliefs using *probabilistic modus ponens* is appropriate. The main condition is the *rigidity* condition: $P_1(q \mid p) = P_0(q \mid p)$ (Jeffrey 1983). In terms of our example, this means that learning that *Tweety is a bird* does not alter your degree of belief in the conditional *if x is a bird, x flys*. The issues here are related to the problem that, although MP is *p*-valid, it is only valid in a restricted sense because *strengthening of the antecedent* is not valid. Consequently, if you then discover that *Tweety is a penguin*, you would have to assign an uncertainty of 1 to the conclusion of the original MP inference, i.e. *p*-validity would be violated. So in the context that I learn that *Tweety is a bird* ($P_1(p) = 1$), this must not be a context in which this fact gives me grounds to alter my degree of acceptance of the conditional, e.g. it must not give me grounds to accept *Tweety is a penguin*.

Contexts like this are not unimaginable. For example, on being told that an islander's pet, Tweety, is a bird, an ornithologist on Penguin Island might refrain from using his normal inference ticket to infer Tweety can fly because Tweety is most likely a penguin. This is presumably because in a context where most birds are penguins, the conditional probability of a pet flying, given it is a bird, is much lower than normal. Moreover, in drawing the distinction between *supposing* and *believing*, we explicitly introduced conditions where this might happen. If I suppose I have an incurable disease, this may not increase my degree of belief in the existence of God. However, being given this information as a fact may alter the probability I assign to the existence of God. So it seems at least possible that a conditional probability arrived at by the Ramsey test when *supposing* the probability of the antecedent is 1 ($P_0(p) = 1$) might differ when the same probability is assessed when you come to *believe* the probability of the antecedent is 1 ($P_1(p) = 1$). The issues surrounding the rigidity condition are complex and still a matter of active debate in the logical and philosophical literature (for example, see Adams 1998, chapter 5, on *scope*).

Sober (2002) argues that a *probabilistic modus tollens* would have to be invalid. Sober's arguments are primarily about how evidence e impacts on hypotheses, H. He assumes that the given conditional probability is the likelihood of the evidence given the hypothesis, $P_0(e|H)$, and that you now receive evidence that $\neg e$, i.e. $P_1(\neg e) = 1$. The MT inference involves updating your probability for $\neg H$ by conditionalizing on $\neg e$ to reach the conclusion that $P_1(\neg H)$ is high. However, as Sober (2002) observes, such *probabilistic modus tollens* requires $P_0(\neg H|\neg e)$ for $\neg e$ to conditionalize on, but the premises— $P_0(e|H)$ is high and $P_1(\neg e) = 1$—do not entail a value for $P(\neg H|\neg e)$.

However, more recently, Wagner (2004; see also, Sobel 2004), has derived bounds similar to 5.12 for *modus tollens* (MT). As we shall see in 'Oaksford and Chater's (2000) probabilistic approach', the conditions under which Wagner (2004) achieves this result are very similar to the probability models used by Oaksford *et al.* (2000) to capture empirical data on conditional reasoning.

We have spent some considerable time rehearsing the basics of probability logic. This is because this account of indicative conditionals is now the dominant view in the logical and philosophical literature and hence it was important to show how different probability logic is from the standard truth functional logical account encountered in textbooks on the psychology of reasoning. Many aspects of probability logic are related directly to our psychological proposals about a probabilistic account of human reasoning and we shall continue to draw out these relationships. Moreover, recently Evans and Over (2004) have also appealed to the probability conditional as more psychologically realistic than the material conditional. They have also shown empirically that people treat the probability of an indicative conditional as the conditional probability and *not* as the probability of a material conditional, i.e. $P(p \wedge q)$ + $P(\neg q)$ (Evans *et al.* 2003; see also, Oberauer and Wilhelm 2003). We consider Evans and Over's approach further below.

Non-monotonic reasoning, databases, and Ramsey tests

In Chapters 2 to 4, we have been critical of logicist attempts to deal with non-monotonic reasoning: non-monotonic logics fail to derive the right inferences, they are not complete*, and they are computationally intractable. However, there have been attempts to implement these theories as practical computational systems and recently more tractable systems have been developed (e.g. Horty *et al.* 1990; Niemelä and Rintanen 1994). But complexity results for these logics are only relevant to small classes of non-monotonic reasoning problems. The general problem of default reasoning is often called the *frame problem* in artificial intelligence (Pylyshyn 1987), which we have discussed in Chapters 2 and 4. Until there is some resolution of this problem, it is reasonable to remain fairly sceptical of claims to have a tractable computational solution to the general problem of defeasible inference. Moreover, some claims that non-monotonic logics actually get the right conclusions for problems where there are conflicting default rules (see Chapter 3, on 'The logicist approach'), seem to be simply wrong (Niemelä and Rintanen 1994; Schöter 1996). The suggestion is that given you know that *Tweety is a bird and one second old*, you should conclude that either *Tweety can fly* or *Tweety cannot fly*. We suspect that most people would wager a very large sum that *Tweety cannot fly* and consequently the tautological conclusion is too cautious, aside from being vacuous.

Nonetheless, there have been recent attempts to apply non-monotonic logics to the psychology of reasoning (Stenning and Lambalgen 2004). The current trend, both in the philosophy of logic and language, and in artificial intelligence, is towards the probabilistic treatment of the conditional embodied in the Equation. We also touched on this issue briefly in Chapter 4 ('Non-monontonic logic vs. probabilities'), where we argued that sticking with probabilities is the conservative option proposed by Pearl (1988, 2000). Moreover, we interpret all the arguments mustered by Bennett (2003) and Edgington (1995) as strong arguments that a probabilistic construal of the conditional is likely to provide the most psychologically realistic, computational-level account of the conditional. For the moment, we adopt this as an article of faith; we hope to demonstrate that it is well-founded in the remainder of this chapter.

So much for the differences between a probabilistic approach and non-monotonic logics. In the rest of this section, we concentrate on their common problems. In particular, we point out that the problems we have highlighted in the psychological literature for non-monotonic logic (Chater and Oaksford 1993, 2001; Chater *et al.* 2005; Oaksford and Chater 1991, 1993, 1998b) must recur for an account of the conditional based on the Ramsey test.

The programme of attempting to mechanize reasoning about the way the world might be has been taken up by the study of knowledge representation in artificial intelligence. The starting point, as we have seen, is the notion of a *database*, which contains representations of a cognitive agent's beliefs about the world. This approach involves formal, logical representations and formal proof procedures that operate over these representations, which can be implemented computationally. In the case of human long-term memory, the contents of the database would be the collection of logical *theories* that constitute our knowledge of the world. Logical theories include logical statements like $\forall x(Bird(x) \Rightarrow Flys(x))$, which make up a set of *non-logical axioms*, i.e. statements whose truth is not a matter of logic. These statements can be combined with new information and *logical axioms* about the behaviour of the logical terms *all*, *some*, *if...then*, etc., to draw inferences. For this to be possible it is important that the database contains no contradictions.

We now argue that standard default inference in Reiter's (1985) *default logic* involves very similar computational operations to those required by the Ramsey test. Reiter's default logic contains an *M*-operator (which can be given a possible worlds interpretation; see, Fuhrman 1998). People's knowledge that *birds fly* would then be represented in a default rule:

$$\forall(x)[Bird(x) \wedge M(Flys(x)) \Rightarrow Flys(x)] \tag{5.13}$$

The interpretation of the *M*-operator is that the denial of *Flys*(*Tweety*) cannot be deduced from the conjunction of the database (Γ) and *Bird*(*Tweety*) ($\neg[Bird(Tweety) \wedge \Gamma \rightarrow \neg Flys(Tweety)]$). So another way of describing a default rule is that the antecedent (*Bird* (*Tweety*)) is added to the database and it is then checked to see if *Flys*(*Tweety*) is consistent with the revised database. If it is, then you can provisionally conclude *Flys*(*Tweety*). According to this viewpoint, the conclusion of a default rule can be derived, unless the negation of this conclusion can be derived from existing knowledge—i.e. we accept the consequence from applying a default rule unless there is some specific reason to the contrary.

Consistency checking can be achieved in a variety of ways. The truth-table method provides one formal procedure but it is clearly computationally prohibitive because, as the number (n) of propositions increases, the number of lines in the truth table increases as 2^n, and so it is feasible only for very small databases. This is simply to say, as we have argued in Chapters 2–4, that everyday reasoning is computationally problematic because of its apparent reliance on checking the consistency of default conclusions with the current contents of the database.

The default conclusion reached is only a *subjective* judgement because people's databases rarely achieve *epistemic closure* with respect to a particular topic. That is, it is rarely the case that anyone possesses all the relevant knowledge to draw inferences involving non-logical axioms with certainty. Consequently, default inference relies on a *closed world assumption*, i.e. it is *assumed* that the database is epistemically closed. This means that negation is not *classical*, rather it is *constructive*: one concludes ¬p because p cannot be proved from what you know (i.e. $M(\neg p)$). One might argue that a more cautious conclusion is that you do not know whether p is true or false, or that you can only assign a certain probability to the truth of p.

This account is a case of default *inference*. In contrast, the Ramsey test is a way of determining the subjective probability of a conditional. As we have just seen at the end of the last section, the principle difference concerns *supposing* versus *believing* the antecedent to have a probability of 1 (or to be true). However, other than the attitude adopted to the operations performed over the database and the need to undo any intermediate conclusions added— consequent on *supposing* (rather than believing) the antecedent to be true— similar consistency checking operations must be performed. The primary difference is that in a default logic database no uncertainty is allowed, either the consequent is consistent with the revised database $(P(Flys(x)|Bird\,(x)) = 1)$ or it is not $(P(Flys(x)|Bird(x)) = 0)$. Consequently, it would not be unreasonable to describe the processes required to implement the *M*-operator as performing a *deterministic* Ramsey test. Indeed this interpretation is consistent with Gärdenfors' (1986, p. 81) interpretation of the Ramsey test (Slater 2004):

> Accept a proposition of the form 'if A then C' in a state of belief K if and only if the minimal change of K to accept A also requires accepting C.

Later on in this chapter we will explore a neural-network model (Oaksford 2004) that may provide a more graded implementation of the Ramsey test and of conditional inference.

The reason why one would expect there to be close relationships between *probability logic*, *belief revision*, and *non-monotonic logic* is that they all share a common root in the Ramsey test (Fuhrmann 1998; Slater 2004) as we discussed in Chapter 4 ('Non-monontonic logic vs. probabilities'). Given their common roots one might expect non-monotonic logic and a probabilistic approach to conditionals to share the common problems we have just raised. Oaksford and Chater (1991, 1993, 1995b, 1998a) described the problems raised by non-monotonic or default reasoning for the philosophy of mind (Oaksford and Chater 1991) and for the psychology of reasoning (Chater and Oaksford 1993; Oaksford and Chater 1995b, 1998a) in their critique of *logicist cognitive* science. As we have repeatedly argued, the main problems are those surrounding the *world knowledge problem* that we were warned against as postgraduate students (see *Preface*) and which we have returned to many times in discussions of the psychology of reasoning (Chater and Oaksford 2001; Chater *et al.* 2005; Oaksford and Chater 1991, 1993, 1995b, 1998a). Default inference and the Ramsey test require access, not only to immediately given premises but to relevant world knowledge. Unless we have a theory of how information can be added to a database (either as a supposition or a new belief) and of how that database can be revised to provide new information, we will not be in possession of a satisfactory theory of human reasoning. We have discussed the deep problems that arise here in artificial-intelligence knowledge representation in Chapters 2–4 and in a previous book (Oaksford and Chater 1998a, chapter 16, 'Rationality reconsidered') where we also pointed out that the problems recur for probabilistic approaches. It is worth re-iterating these points, given the resurgence in interest in the application of the Ramsey test in the psychology of reasoning (Evans and Over 2004), from a standpoint that has not focused on the computational/psychological problems that arise for this approach.

In the next section, we outline our probabilistic account of conditional inference, how it relates to probability logic, and how it accounts for a variety of effects in the psychological literature.

Oaksford and Chater's (2000) probabilistic approach

Several authors have suggested that human conditional inference has a significant probabilistic component (Anderson 1995; Evans *et al.* 2003; George 1997; Liu 2003; Liu *et al.* 1996; Oaksford and Chater 1994b, 1998, 2003a, b, c; Oaksford *et al.* 2000; Oberauer and Wilhlem 2003; Stevenson and Over 1995). Inevitably, all these approaches, at least implicitly, assume the Equation, whether they explicitly relate this assumption to normative work on probability logic or not. In this section, we present Oaksford *et al.*'s (2000) probabilistic computational-level model (Marr 1982) of conditional inference—but our own interest in probabilistic approaches to the conditional goes back substantially further.

The probabilistic treatment of the conditional presented in Oaksford *et al.* (2000) is a development of the account of conditionals first presented in an early version of Oaksford and Chater (1994; the published version focused only on the selection task, and did not provide a model of conditional inference, for reasons of space).

A computational-level model

In introducing Oaksford *et al.*'s account, it is useful at the outset to make the connection with the probability conditional discussed in 'Probability logic'. The core of Oaksford *et al.*'s (2000) probabilistic model was that the probability of the conclusion of a conditional inference is equal to the conditional probability of the conclusion given the categorical premise. For *modus ponens*, this prescription is identical to the account of probabilistic MP we discussed in 'Probability logic'. People derive an estimate for $P_0(q|p)$, i.e. the probability of the conditional premise $(p \rightarrow q)$, via the Ramsey test. The categorical premise, p provides the information that $P_1(p) = 1$, so $P_0(q|p)$ can now be conditionalized on, to provide the best estimate of $P_1(q)$, which—assuming *rigidity*—is $P_0(q|p)$. However, the problem for the remaining inference, i.e. *modus tollens* (MT), and the fallacies, *denying the antecedent* (DA) and *asserting the consequent* (AC) (see, 5.14), is that unlike MP, the premises alone do not entail a specific value for the relevant conditional probability, i.e. the premises entail no values for, $P_0(\neg q|\neg p)$, $P_0(p|q)$, or $P_0(\neg p|\neg q)$:

$$\text{DA} \quad \frac{p \rightarrow q, \neg p}{\therefore \neg q}, \qquad \text{AC} \quad \frac{p \rightarrow q, q}{\therefore p}. \qquad (5.14)$$

Consequently, there is nothing for the categorical premise, i.e. $P_1(\neg p) = 1$ (DA), $P_1(q) = 1$ (AC), or $P_1(\neg q) = 1$, to conditionalize on, as Sober (2002) pointed out for MT.

Recently, Wagner (2004) has proposed a probabilized version of MT which indicates the following bounds on the probability of the conclusion of this inference, i.e. $P(\neg p)$. Letting $P(q|p) = a$ and $P(\neg q) = b$:

$$\max\left[\frac{1-a-b}{1-a}, \frac{a+b-1}{a} \right] \leq P(\neg p) < 1, \text{when } 0 < a, \, b < 1; \qquad (5.15)$$

$$1 - b \leq P(\neg p) < 1, \qquad \qquad \text{when } a = 0 \text{ and } 0 < b \leq 1; \qquad (5.16)$$

$$b \le P(\neg p) < 1, \qquad\qquad \text{when } a = 1 \text{ and } 0 \le b < 1. \qquad (5.17)$$

This version of MT for conditional probabilities has some interesting properties. For example, 5.17 shows that $P(\neg p)$ tends towards 1, as $P(\neg q)$ and $P(q|p)$ tend towards 1; but 5.16 shows that $P(\neg p)$ also tends towards 1 as $P(\neg q)$ and $P(q|p)$ tend towards 0. Wagner (2004) shows that under the conditions in 5.15–5.17 (i.e. the *when* clause), these bounds arise if $P(\neg q)$, $P(q|p)$ and $P(p)$ are used to derive expressions for the joint probabilities, $P(p \wedge q)$, $P(p \wedge \neg q)$, $P(\neg p \wedge q)$, $P(\neg p \wedge \neg q)$. Letting $P(p) = c$, we show these probabilities in a standard contingency table:

$$
\begin{array}{c c c}
 & q & \neg q \\
p & ac & (1-a)c \\
\neg p & 1-b-ac & b-(1-a)c
\end{array} \qquad (5.18)
$$

The bounds in 5.15–5.17 arise because c must be subject to the restrictions of a probability model that all these joint probabilities are greater than or equal to zero and they must sum to 1.

In the terminology of belief updating, Wagner (2004) assumes that people have a prior estimate of $P_0(q|p) = a$ and they then ask given $P_1(\neg q) = b$, what constraints does the probability model in 5.18 place on $P_1(\neg p) = 1 - c$? Oaksford *et al.*'s (2000) approach was similar and can be characterized as follows. Assuming that people have prior estimates of $P_0(p) = c$, $P_0(q) = 1 - b$, and $P_0(q|p) = a$, what constraints does the probability model in 5.18 place on the relevant conditional probabilities?, i.e. the conditional probabilities required by AC, DA, and MT to conditionalize on. Bar a few notational differences, Wagner's (2004) contingency table in 5.18 is the same as that presented in Oaksford *et al.* (2000, table 1). The relevant conditional probabilities can be calculated as follows:[1]

$$\text{MP} \qquad P_1(q) = P_0(q|p) = a \qquad\qquad (5.21)$$

$$\text{DA} \qquad P_1(\neg q) = P_0(\neg q | \neg p) = \frac{b-(1-a)c}{1-c} \qquad\qquad (5.22)$$

---

[1] In Oaksford *et al.* (2000) the contingency table in 5.18 was parameterized in terms of $P_0(p)$, $P_0(q)$, and the conditional uncertainty $1 - P_0(q|p)$, which was referred to as the 'exceptions parameter'.

AC $\qquad P_1(p) = P_0(p|q) = \dfrac{ac}{1-b}$ $\hfill$ (5.23)

MT $\qquad P_1(\neg p) = P_0(\neg p|\neg q) = \dfrac{b-(1-a)c}{b}$ $\hfill$ (5.24)

Except for notational differences, 5.21–5.24 are the same as equations 1–4 in Oaksford *et al.* (2000, p. 884). So, by assuming that people also have prior beliefs about the marginal probabilities of the antecedent, $P_0(p)$, and the consequent, $P_0(q)$, appropriate conditional probabilities can be derived for the categorical premises of DA, AC, and MT to conditionalize on. This approach has the advantage that people are attempting to do exactly the same thing for each inference, i.e. update their beliefs about the conclusion by using the categorical premise to conditionalize on the relevant conditional probability. From now on, we will refer to the model in 5.21–5.24 as the *conditional probability model*.

In 5.21–5.24, it is assumed that the probability of the categorical premise is 1. However, as we discussed when looking at 5.11 and 5.12, this assumption can be relaxed. By Jeffrey, conditionalization (Jeffrey 1983), which assumes rigidity, MP, for example, becomes:

MP $\qquad P_1(q) = P_0(q|p)P_1(p) + P_0(q|\neg p)P_1(\neg p)$ $\hfill$ (5.25)

5.25 can be expressed in terms of the parameters, a, b, and c, and an additional parameter for $P_1(p)$. 5.25 also shows clearly why the bounds in 5.12 rely on varying $P_0(q|\neg p)$ between 0 and 1. For almost all the data we look at later on, the generalization in 5.25 is not needed because for these data, experimental participants are invariably told that the categorical premise holds with certainty, e.g. for MP, $P_1(p) = 1$.

Probabilistic models of conditional reasoning do not, of course, require that people actually carry out the mathematical computations in 5.22–5.24, as if they were doing mental arithmetic. Rather we assume that if the processes that implement a Ramsey test respect the laws of probability, at least to some degree of approximation, then, assuming rigidity, people's estimates for the corresponding conditional probabilities should be close to those indicated in these equations. However, given the asymmetry between MP and MT, noted by Sobel (2004), it might be naïve to expect peoples' inferences to be totally consistent with 5.22–5.24. But the alternative, which is just to treat each inference as an independent judgement, seems unpalatable as a empirical theory of conditional inference, as it implies no constraints between the values of $P_0(q|p)$, $P_0(\neg q|\neg p)$, $P_0(p|q)$, and $P_0(\neg p|\neg q)$, that might explain the observed patterns of inference. Below we will look at a possible implementation of the Ramsey test using a constraint satisfaction neural network (Oaksford 2004).

Model behaviour

We show how the model in 5.21–5.24 behaves in Fig. 5.1. Each panel shows how the relevant posterior probability of the conclusion—$P_1(q)$, $P_1(\neg q)$, $P_1(p)$, or $P_1(\neg p)$—varies with the prior probabilities of the categorical premise—$P_0(p)$, $P_0(\neg p)$, $P_0(q)$, or $P_0(\neg q)$—and the conclusion—$P_0(q)$, $P_0(\neg q)$, $P_0(p)$, or $P_0(\neg p)$—with $P_0(q|p) = 0.75$. For example, the panel on the left shows this information for the DA inference. The x-axis represents the prior probability of the conclusion $(P_0(\neg q))$. The posterior probability of the categorical premise was assumed to always be 1, i.e. for DA, $P_1(\neg p) = 1$. Each curve represents how the posterior probability of the conclusion, i.e. the probability of the obverse $(P_0(\neg q|\neg p) = P_1(\neg q))$, varies as a function of the prior probability of the conclusion $(P_0(\neg q))$ for different values of the probability of the categorical premise $(P_0(\neg p) = 1 - P_0(p))$. The prior probabilities of both the premise and the conclusion were varied from 0.1 to 0.9 in steps of 0.2. Where no value appears at a co-ordinate, this is because this combination of probabilities violates the assumptions of a probability model. As the prior probability of the conclusion of DA, AC, or MT increases so the probability that any of these inferences will be drawn also increases. That is, the higher the

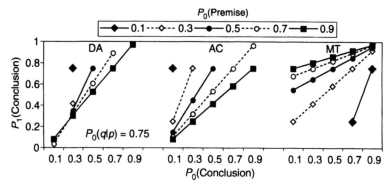

Fig. 5.1 How the posterior probability of the conclusion (P_1(Conclusion)) varies as a function of the prior probability of the conclusion (P_0(Conclusion)) and the prior probability at the categorical premise (P_0 (Premise)) for denying the antecedent (DA), asserting the consequent (AC), and for modus tollens (MT) with the posterior probability of categorical premise (P_1(Premise)) set to 1, i.e. P_1(Premise) = 1.

prior probability of the conclusion, the higher the prior conditional probability of the conclusion given the categorical premise. This relationship holds for all three inferences as long as $P_0(q|p) < 1$. If $P_0(q|p) = 1$, as we saw when discussing Wagner's (2004) probabilized MT, the probability of endorsing an MT inference ($P_0(\neg p|\neg q)$) is 1 and so MT should be drawn regardless of the prior probability of the categorical premise or conclusion.

There is also a relationship between the prior probability of the categorical premise and the posterior probability of the conclusion. However, the relationship varies between the inferences. For AC, the posterior probability of the conclusion is high when the prior probability of the premise is low (see Fig.5.1, AC). This relationship also holds for DA when $P_0(q)$ is less than $P_0(q|p)$ (see Fig. 5.1, DA). However, for MT the opposite relationship is found, i.e. the posterior probability of the conclusion is high when the prior probability of the premise is *high* (see Fig. 5.1, MT). This relationship also holds for DA when $P_0(q)$ is greater than $P_0(q|p)$ (see Fig. 5.1, DA).

In the following sections of this chapter, we review the data on conditional inference showing how the probabilistic model developed in the last section can explain that data. We do not present an exhaustive review of the data on conditional reasoning (for a comprehensive review, see: Evans and Over 2004).

The relationship between the present approach and that of Evans and Over is not entirely straightforward. They place some distance between their proposals and the present analysis. Nonetheless, the analysis above indicates that the proposal that they broadly favour, Adams' probability conditional, is consistent with the present probabilistic approach. We shall return to the question of how much agreement there is between Evans and Over's account and our own later on.

The standard abstract results

We begin with past research using abstract versions of the conditional-inference task, i.e. versions where simple alphanumeric stimuli are used (Schroyens *et al.* 2001a, b). The original experiments on conditional reasoning used these stimuli to try to minimize the effects of prior knowledge, which it was considered might be a confounding factor that would obscure the real nature of the underlying reasoning mechanism. In part, this was because of the expectation that the mind operates according to formal logical rules, to which content should be irrelevant. Using abstract material should allow researchers to uncover the logic of the mind. Of course, according to the Ramsey test, this procedure looks misguided as it is only by reference to prior knowledge that conditionals can be evaluated. It also raises the question of what people are doing when confronted with such abstract material.

Ramsey tests and abstract material

We have assumed that for abstract material, people adopt values for the relevant probabilities that reflect their normal experience and the discourse context of the experiment (e.g. Oaksford and Chater 1994b, 2003a). Considering the values that people might employ in conditional inference does not resolve the issues of what psychological mechanisms might be responsible for deriving these estimates when abstract materials are used and so prior knowledge, i.e. conducting a Ramsey test, would seem to be irrelevant. As we discuss further below, it seems that this situation is not that different to acquiring new conditional beliefs *with* content that relates to prior knowledge but of which we have had no experience. Mental representations of the conditional have to be recruited and estimates for the relevant probabilities need to be made by reference to prior knowledge—or some relevant subset of prior knowledge—and to the discourse context in which the belief was acquired. For example, on your first flying lesson, you might be told *if you give it too much choke, the engine will stall.* Generalizing from past experience with your old cars (that still had choke controls) might lead you to underestimate how little choke you need to stall an aero-engine, but it would still be a reasonable initial extrapolation. Without content, determining *relevant* prior knowledge is not feasible. Nonetheless, estimates can still be obtained by sampling previous memories of conditional beliefs at random or sampling those most recently experienced (see Stewart *et al.* 2003). However, for the moment we leave these issues until we are ready to discuss possible algorithmic theories that might implement the Ramsey test in the mind. Before doing this we can still answer the question, is the existing data on conditional inference consistent with the approach we outlined in 'Oaksford and Chater's (2000) probabilistic approach'?

Frequencies and ratings

As we suggested in 'A computational level model', the conditional probability model really amounts to the claim that people's conditional inferences are probabilistically consistent. Consequently, fitting the equations in 5.21–5.24 to the data should provide good fits, if people are consistent and the rigidity condition holds, i.e. $P_0(q|p)$, $P_0(p)$, or $P_0(q)$ do not change between inferences (at least in the absence of an explicit manipulation that should change these values). To fit this model requires data on the probability that each inference is drawn. This potentially introduces a problem.

In most experiments on conditional inference, people are asked whether they endorse a particular inference or not. They are not explicitly asked to rate the probability with which they think the inference goes through (although more recently this procedure has been adopted more widely). Consequently most of these experiments only result in a single probability for each inference, i.e. the relative frequency of participants endorsing it. Modelling this kind of aggregated data could result in finding good fits, while the model fails to fit any particular individual participant's pattern of responding. Fortunately, as Evans and Over (2004, p. 112) observed, experiments where people are asked for probability ratings produce very similar results to experiments that collect relative frequencies of endorsement.

Model fitting: the standard results

Schroyens et al. (2001b) reported a meta-analysis of 65 experiments using abstract material with the conditional-inference task. In these tasks, participants are simply provided with inferences like:

If A then 2

A

$\qquad$ 2?

They are then asked to decide whether given the rule and the statement, A, they would endorse the conclusion, 2. Results of fitting the model (5.21–5.24) to these data are discussed in Schroyens and Schaeken (2003) and in Oaksford and Chater (2003b). For each experiment, Schroyens and Schaeken (2003) fitted the model to the data by minimizing the coefficient of variation (R^2) between the predicted probabilities of endorsing each inference, i.e. $P_0(q|p)$, $P_0(\neg q|\neg p)$, $P_0(p|q)$, and $P_0(\neg p|\neg q)$, and the data on the frequency of MP, DA, AC, and MT endorsement, respectively, as in Oaksford et al. (2000). The coefficient of variation expresses the deviation of the model from the exact data values as a proportion of the variance in the data. The average R^2 over the 65 studies was .85 (SD = 0.14) indicating that on average the model accounted for 85% of the variance in the data. Figure 5.2 (panel A) shows the mean values and the 95% confidence intervals for the data and the model. The average best fit parameter values were $P_0(q|p) = 0.89$ (SD = 0.05), $P_0(p) = 0.54$ (SD = 0.15), and $P_0(q) = 0.73$ (SD = 0.08). As an index of how far the predicted values differed from the exact location of the data points, Schroyens and Schaeken (2003) reported the average root mean squared deviation (RMSD) which was 0.06 (SD = 0.03). In sum, the probability model provides a good account of the data.

Remember that no assumptions have been made about the cognitive processes that implement the Ramsey test. Schroyens and Schaeken's (2003)

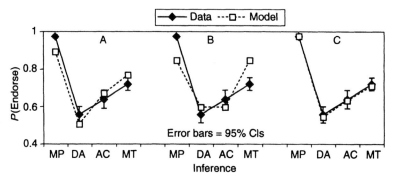

Fig. 5.2 The fit of the conditional probability model to the data (panel A); the fit of the logical model to the data (panel B); the fit of the revised conditional probability model to the data (panel C), see next section). CI = confidence interval.

model fits show that an account of conditional inference based solely on probability theory and the assumption that people are consistent across the four inferences in the values of $P(q|p)$, $P_0(p)$, and $P_0(q)$ that they assign, can account for a large proportion of the variance in the data. Few normative theories in psychology have faired this well in the psychology of reasoning and decision-making. For example, Oaksford and Chater (2003b) showed that standard logic provides a far worse account of these data (see Fig. 5.2, panel B). Even allowing for errors, they showed that standard logic only accounts for 56% of the variance in the data on average with RMSD = 0.10 (SD = 0.05). That is, the probability model accounts for an additional 29% of the variance and so explains far more of the data within a rational normative framework. However, there have been objections to this account of the conditional reasoning data to which we now turn.

The asymmetry between MP and MT

Schroyens and Schaeken's (2003) model-fitting exercise was actually conducted in the framework of a critique of the probabilistic model. They note that when looking at Fig. 5.2 (panel A) it seems that the model underestimates the probability of endorsing MP and over-estimates the probability of endorsing MT. Indeed Schroyens and Schaeken (2003) go as far as to claim that the relatively high observed endorsement rate for MP falsifies a probabilistic account. However, there may be good normative reasons why fitting the original conditional probability model leads to this result.

Sober (2002) pointed out that a probabilized version of MT seems to have some odd consequences:

> It is easy to find counterexamples to this principle. You draw from a deck of cards. You know that if the deck is normal and the draw occurs at random, then the probability is only 1/52 that you'll obtain the seven of hearts. Suppose you *do* draw this card. You can't then conclude just from this that it is improbable that the deck is normal and the draw was at random.

However, Sobel (2004) observes that this probabilized version of MT is subject to *rigidity* restrictions just as for MP. The probability that you would *not* draw the seven of hearts before drawing a card, given the deck is normal and the draw random is 51/52, i.e. $P(\neg 7$ of hearts|RandomNormal$) = 51/52$. But if you are sure you drew the seven of hearts, then the probability you did not, $P(\neg 7$ of hearts$)$, is 0; consequently the probability that you do not draw the seven of hearts, given the deck is normal and the draw random, is now 0, i.e. $P(\neg 7$ of hearts|RandomNormal$) = 0$. This is a very large change in the relevant likelihood and a clear violation of the rigidity condition. Sobel (2004) observes that most counter-examples to probabilized MT violate rigidity in this way. However, he also points out that,

> In striking contrast [to probabilized MP] it is very difficult to assemble cases in which there are reasons to think that the likelihood for a person 'beforehand' of some likely evidence on a theory is not perturbed when this person learns that this evidence has failed to materialise.

That is, it is difficult to arrive at conditions whereby probabilized MT would be appropriate because of the high likelihood that the rigidity condition is not met. What this shows is that although MP and MT are *p*-valid, they are valid only in the restricted sense given by the rigidity condition. Moreover, because satisfying this condition is likely to be rarer for MT, there is an asymmetry between MP and MT. It should be clear that the problem of *which* conditional probabilities are rigid, in relation to the addition of a new piece of information, and which should change, is another version of the notorious frame problem, that we discussed in Chapters 2 and 4. Thus, in real-world contexts, the issue of rigidity is likely to be extremely tangled. Nonetheless, a probabilistic approach can make some headway with explaining the relevant empirical data.

Consider, for example, the possible effects of the failure of rigidity, which can be illustrated using a simple everyday conditional, i.e. what happens if you believe that *if you turn the key (p) the car starts (q)* and that on this occasion *the car did not start*. There would seem to be little reason to expect the car to start unless one was reasonably confident that the key had been turned. Put another way, the assertion of the categorical premise of MT only seems to be informative against a background where the car was expected to start—otherwise, the assertion that the car did not start would seem pragmatically bizarre.[2] So this seems like a case where rigidity might be violated, i.e. it is a counter-example, and so $P_0(q|p)$ needs to be adjusted.

The revision can be carried out by Bayesian updating, assuming as a foil a hypothesis where turning keys and cars starting are independent (Oaksford and Chater 1994b, 1996, 2003e). In previous discussions of the hypothesis-testing model (Evans and Over 1996; Klauer 1999), which we introduce in the next chapter, it has been proposed that $P_0(q|p)$ should be related to the degree of belief in the hypothesis under test.[3]

Assuming that $P_0(q|p) = 0.97$ (as in the meta-analysis of Schroyens and Schaeken's 2003), this is also the prior degree of belief assigned to the hypothesis that, *if you turn the key the car starts* (by the Equation), and so a prior degree of belief of 0.03 is assigned to the independence hypothesis. Let us assume that $P_0(p) = P_0(q) = 0.5$ and so in the independence hypothesis, $P_0(q|p) = 0.5$, then on updating, $P_1(q|p) = 0.67$. Moreover, using this value in 5.24, the relevant conditional probability for MT and so $P_1(\neg p)$ will also be 0.67 (this is simply because in this example $b = 1 - c$). This example suggests that the effect of the greater possibility of violations of rigidity for MT is to reduce the value of $P_0(q|p)$ used to calculate the relevant conditional probability. The notation $P_0^R(q|p)$ will be used to denote this revised probability.

To adequately account for the data, we need to adjust the model to take account of the fact that people are more likely to endorse MP. One way to achieve this is to allow the model to always capture the MP inference and then fit the model for just for DA, AC, and MT. To model the data it was also assumed that people are always maximally uncertain about $P_0(p)$ and so assign a value of 0.5. Given the abstract material used in the experiments in Schroyens and Schaeken's (2003) meta-analysis, this seems appropriate. Participant's know they are to assume the rule is asserted in this context and so $P_0(p) > 0$ (by the Ratio formula). But as the context is not specified, they

---

[2] This is an instance of a pre-suppositional use of negation, i.e. the assertion of the categorical premise denies the presupposition that the car should have started (Wason 1972), presumably because it is highly likely that the key was turned.

[3] The hypothesis is expressed as a contingency table, which is completely specified by $P_0(q|p)$, $P_0(p)$, and $P_0(q)$. Evans and Over (1996a) and Klauer (1999) argued that the degree of belief in this hypothesis, $P(H_D)$, should be directly related to the possibility of exceptions, i.e. $P_0(p, \neg q)$. This means that $P_0(q|p)$ and $P(H_D)$ should rise and fall together. Here we make the assumption that $(H_D) = P_0(q|p)$.

remain uncertain about its precise value. Setting $P_0(p) = 0.5$, also meant that only two parameters were free to vary. So, as in the original model fits in Schroyens and Schaeken (2003) and in Oaksford and Chater (2003a), there was one degree of freedom, i.e. one less parameter than data points. The model was fitted to the data in the same way as for standard logic and the original model (see Fig. 5.1, panels A and B).

Before reporting the fit there is one important observation to make. Eight conditions were included in Schroyens and Schaeken's (2003) meta-analysis from a single study that investigated the effects of changing the order in which the premises and conclusions were presented to participants (Evans *et al.* 1998). Oaksford and Chater (2003d) have observed that there are good pragmatic reasons why the non-standard orders in these experiments lead to higher probabilities than normal, certainly higher than the 0.5 at which the value for $P_0(p)$ was fixed for this revised model. Five of the conditions in Evans *et al.* (1998) were therefore excluded; these conditions involved either a reversal of the order of premises and conclusion, or the order of the premises so that the categorical premise was presented before the conditional premise; or both.

The average R^2 was 0.91 (SD = 0.11) and RMSD was 0.05 (SD = 0.04). The average best fit parameter values were so that $P_0^R(q|p) = 0.77$ (SD = 0.16) and $P_0(q) = 0.62$ (SD = 0.12) (see Fig. 5.2, panel C). The probability model, when revised to take account of perceived rigidity violations, provides a good account of the data and on average explains a further 7.5% of the variance, a significant improvement, t (59) = 3.30, $p < 0.0025$ (the original model's fit was largely unaltered by removing the non-standard orders for Evans *et al.'s* (1998) study, i.e. R^2 was .84). Moreover, Fig. 5.2, panel C, shows that this revised model provides a much improved account of the MP–MT asymmetry and simultaneously ceases to over-estimate the AC–DA asymmetry. The model's predictions also all now fall well within the 95% confidence intervals for the data. Consequently, it would appear that there are good normative reasons to expect an MP–MT asymmetry like that observed in the data, i.e. this behaviour is *normatively defensible* (McKenzie 2004).[4]

We have argued that the change in $P_0(q|p)$ to $P_0^R(q|p)$ may come about by Bayesian updating because rigidity violations for MT suggest a possible counter-example, on pragmatic grounds. The relationship between $P_0(q|p)$

---

[4] Better fits would be obtained if instead of assuming point values for the probabilities, they were treated distributionally using diffuse Bayesian priors (as in Anderson 1990).

and $P_0{}^R(q|p)$ was therefore investigated on the assumption that participants update on the evidence of a single p, $\neg q$ counter-example. The priors, $P_0(q|p)$, are given by the endorsement rate for MP and the posteriors, $P_0{}^R(q|p)$, by the best fit values. The *likelihood ratio* maps the prior odds onto the posterior odds. Given the same assumptions made above, the likelihood ratio for this counter-example is:

$$LR = \frac{P(p,\neg q|M_D)}{P(p,\neg q|M_I)} = \frac{.5 - .5P_0(q|p)}{.5(1 - P_0(q))},$$
(5.26)

where M_D stands for the dependence model, M_I stand for the independence model, and $P_0(q)$ is again the best fitting parameter value. This means that:

$$\frac{P_0^R(q|p)}{1 - P_0^R(q|p)} = \frac{1}{k} \cdot \frac{.5 - .5P_0(q|p)}{.5(1 - P_0(q))} \cdot \frac{P_0(q|p)}{1 - P_0(q|p)} = \frac{1}{k} \cdot \frac{P_0(q|p)}{1 - P_0(q)}.$$
(5.27)

Because of the Equation, the conditional probabilities of interest also correspond to the degrees of belief in the different hypotheses. This has the consequence that the prior is also part of the likelihood ratio. A learning rate parameter, k, is included as people do not necessarily learn as rapidly as Bayes' theorem dictates.[5]

The parameter, k, is the focus of the analysis. If people were perfectly Bayesian, then this parameter should be 1. For each of the sixty studies in the meta-analysis, the equation (5.27) was solved for k. For those studies where the probability of endorsing MP was 1, $P_0(q|p)$ was set to 0.9999 because otherwise the likelihood ratio is zero. If k is less than one, this means that to obtain $P_0{}^R(q|p)$, $P_0(q|p)$ is adjusted by less than it should be according to Bayes' theorem. Overall, $k = 0.86$ (SE = 0.10), which was not significantly different from 1, $t (59) = 1.39$, $p = 0.17$. The studies were also split into those where the probability of endorsing MP was 1 (mean $k = 0.72$, SE = 0.11, $N = 22$) and the rest (mean $k = 0.95$, SE = 0.14, $N = 38$). There was no significant difference between these groups, $t (58) = 1.14$, $p = 0.26$. However, for the

[5] k is in the denominator because, given negative evidence, the posterior odds should go down, so $k < 1$, means that learning is not as fast as it should be.

group where the probability of endorsing MP was 1, k was significantly less than 1, $t\,(21) = 2.63, p < .025$.[6] This means that when $P_0(q|p)$ is very close to 1, the priors are revised by less than Bayes' theorem dictates.[7]

This result is consistent with the view that when someone is very highly convinced of a hypothesis, they are less willing than they should be to reduce their degree of belief in it when confronted with a counter-example, i.e. they are more conservative (Phillips and Edwards 1966). In contrast, at 0.95, k was very close to 1 for the rest of the studies, $t\,(37) = 0.37, p = 0.72$. That is, for those studies where the prior is less than one, $P_0(q|p) < 1$, the values of the posterior, $P_0^R(q|p)$, used to calculate the probability of drawing DA, AC, and MT can be seen as rationally derived from the prior by Bayesian updating.[8]

This analysis is consistent with the view that the effect of possible rigidity violations is to suggest that the instance under consideration may be a counter-example.

Rarity

Schroyens and Schaeken (2003) observed that relatively high values of $P_0(p)$ and $P_0(q)$ were found to provide the best fit to these experiments. They observe that this finding appears to be at odds with the fact that in modelling another task, the Wason (1968; see Chapter 6) selection task, Oaksford and Chater (1994, 1996, 1999, 2003a) assume that these values are low. This is called the *rarity assumption* (Oaksford and Chater 1994). Evan and Over (2004) also comment on this perceived discrepancy, arguing that it seems to count against our general probabilistic approach. This is despite the fact that they also endorse the probability conditional as the most psychologically viable normative approach to the conditional. In our view, Evans and Over (2004) argument is inconsistent in several respects.

....

[6] The values of k do not alter if the values of $P_0(q|p)$ are made to more closely approximate 1.

[7] It was assumed that no probabilities are actually 1, i.e. absolute certainty is not possible in the real world (for the application of a similar assumption to default reasoning, see: Pearl 1988).

[8] Another way of looking at this issue is to compare the values of $P_0^R(q|p)$ obtained by Bayesian updating and those obtained in the model fitting exercise. Collectively, and taken separately as groups, the normative value had a mean of 0.72 (SE = 0.01). However, for the studies where the probability of endorsing MP was 1, the mean best fit value was 0.80 (SE = 0.03), a highly significant difference from the normative value, $t\,(21) = 3.32$, $p < 0.005$. In contrast, for the rest of the studies (mean = 0.76, SE = 0.03) this difference was not significant, $t\,(37) = 1.60, p = 0.12$.

First, Oaksford *et al.* (2000) described their model using the conditional uncertainty $(1 - P_0(q|p))$, which we called the 'exceptions parameter' (ε), rather than $P_0(q|p)$. Evans and Over (2004, p. 144) say that, 'In illustrating the behaviour of their model (their figure 1) [Oaksford *et al.*] set the exceptions parameter, ε to .75.' This is not correct: Fig. 5.1 above was Oaksford *et al.*'s (2000) figure 1 and, as in that paper, ε was set to 0.25, i.e. $P_0(q|p)$ was set to 0.75.

Second, Evans and Over (2004, p. 144) argue that they are unconvinced by Oaksford and Chater's (2003b) argument that 'the pragmatic context of the task [i.e. conditional inference] over-rides the default rarity assumption'. Oaksford and Chater (2003b) suggested that in inductive inference, the goal is to establish generalizations that hold across contexts. In contrast, drawing conditional inferences is only something one would need to do in contexts where $P_0(p)$ and $P_0(q)$ are fairly high (Oaksford and Chater 2003b, p. 154):

> For example, suppose you know that swans are aggressive. It seems unlikely that this information will be available unless someone is in a context where s/he is more likely than normal to encounter swans, i.e. $P(x$ is a swan) is higher than its default rarity value. While this is true for inference, Wason's selection task engages *inductive* reasoning. The goal is to establish generalities, such as, for example, swans are aggressive, that are generally true across contexts. Across contexts, swans and aggressive things are rare.

Evans and Over (2004) agree that pragmatic factors imply fairly high values for $P_0(p)$ and $P_0(q)$. They argue that the reason 'lies in the assertion of the conditional itself' (Evans and Over 2004, p. 144) and that, '*If p then q* is not assertable—or at least has low relevance—in most contexts if $P_0(p)$ is too low or $P_0(q|p)$ is too low' (Evans and Over 2004, p. 145). They then argue that, 'Unfortunately for Oaksford and Chater, however, precisely the same argument would apply to the assertion of a conditional on the Wason selection task.'

This argument does not go through, however, because in the context of the inductive reasoning that is involved in the Wason selection task, the conditional sentence is not *asserted* it is introduced as a *conjecture*, i.e. whether $P_0(q|p)$ is high, and crucially greater than $P_0(q)$, is exactly what is at stake. *Asserting* and *conjecturing* are different speech acts (Bach and Harnish 1979). So, Evans and Over's observation that the conditional is asserted in the conditional-inference task is exactly right. However, they do not extend their useful pragmatic speech act analysis appropriately to the selection task. Doing so shows why the default rarity assumption holds for the inductive task but not the conditional-inference task.

Third, it could be argued that the reason for Evans and Over's proposal that the conditional is also asserted in the Wason selection task is that they do not regard this task to be an inductive task, rather they view it as a deductive task. This proposal seems to be belied by their apparent approval of probabilistic accounts of the selection task that immediately follows the above quotations (Evans and Over 2004, pp. 145–147). Indeed, at one point, Evans and Over (1996a) explicitly advocated an account of the Wason selection task which, while proposing a different measure of what data to select to test a hypothesis, relied on the rarity assumption in exactly the same way as Oaksford and Chater's (1994) analysis. In sum, Evans and Over's (2004) and Schroyens and Schaeken's (2003) arguments miss their mark. There is no inconsistency between our probabilistic analyses of the conditional-inference task and the rarity assumption in the selection task.

In the next section we turn to assessing whether other accounts of the standard results on the conditional-inference task can explain these data better than our normative probability model.

Mental models and validating search

One of the main psychological theories with which we will compare our probabilistic approach is the mental models theory of Johnson-Laird and colleagues (Johnson-Laird 1983; Johnson-Laird and Byrne 1991, 2002). Mental models theory argues that people reason over pictorial representations of what those sentences *mean*. These representations concern the different *possibilities* that a logical expression may allow. This is familiar from our discussion of truth tables (Chapter 4, 'Problems for logic'). Each row of a truth table corresponds to a different possibility depending on whether p and q are true or false, which leads to four possibilities. One way of thinking about the connectives is that they exclude different possibilities. So for example, if *if p then q* is true, then the possibility where p is true and q is false is excluded, leaving three other possibilities. These possibilities are held in working memory, which has limited capacity. This means that people may not represent all these possibilities at once when interpreting a conditional. Rather there may be a preferred initial representation. This is the core of the mental models theory. In this account each possibility is referred to as a 'mental model'. How people manipulate these mental models explains their reasoning performance. People initially represent the conditional, *if p then q*, in working memory as:

$$[p] \qquad q$$
$$\ldots \tag{5.28}$$

The ellipsis indicates that there might be other conditions that can 'flesh out' this representation and the square brackets indicate that p is exhausted and is not paired with anything else. Each line in a mental model is like the lines of a truth table. Note, however, that the uses of 'p' and 'q' in mental models theory are not to be confused with propositional variables. Most indicative conditionals used in psychological experiments are implicitly universally quantified, i.e. they relate to a domain of objects that might satisfy the antecedent or consequent. Consequently, the mental models notation treats these symbols in 5.28 as arbitrary exemplars of the predicates mentioned in the antecedent (p) or consequent (q). Somewhat confusingly, however, when a conditional is specific, e.g. *if Oswald did not shoot Kennedy someone else did*, exactly the same notation is used.

Given the premise p, the representation in 5.28 indicates that the conclusion q is licensed because it indicates that *all* the objects (indicated by [ ]) that are p are also q. Consequently, people are happy to draw the MP inference. However, nothing can be inferred given the premise $\neg q$ as it does not match anything in working memory. MT can only be drawn when this representation is 'fleshed out' with the remaining two combinations that make the rule true:

$$\begin{array}{cc} p & q \\ \neg p & q \\ \neg p & \neg q \end{array} \qquad (5.29)$$

From this representation it can be seen that $\neg q$ can only be paired with $\neg p$, so the MT inference can be made.

In mental models theory, the material bi-conditional interpretation is also allowed. The initial model for material equivalence is:

$$[p] \qquad [q] \\ \dots \qquad (5.30)$$

which licenses the MP and AC inference. When fleshed out as in 5.31:

$$\begin{array}{cc} p & q \\ \neg p & \neg q \end{array} \qquad (5.31)$$

all four inferences can be made. So according to this theory there are only four possible response patterns: endorse the MP inference only (conditional/initial model), endorse the MP and AC inferences (bi-conditional/initial model), endorse the MP and the MT inference (conditional/fleshed out), and endorse all four inferences (bi-conditional/fleshed out). There are two choice-points in processing this information. The first is whether a conditional or a bi-conditional interpretation is adopted, and the second is whether the representation is fleshed out.

This model can account for various aspects of the data like the MP–MT asymmetry. The MT inference will only be drawn if people flesh out their initial models. This account of conditional inference proposes that aspects of the data that deviate from standard logic should be explained by an algorithmic level theory of how the mind represents and processes information. The upshot of the section 'Logicism and uncertainty' was that recent normative approaches to the conditional seem to have converged on the view that the probability conditional provides the currently most viable account of the conditional. This mismatch suggests that the attempt to explain these patterns in the data by appeal to the algorithmic level may be premature. If an alternative normative account can provide at least as good an account of the data as a processing account like mental models then it should be preferred.

Oaksford and Chater (2003a, d, e) have shown that their model based on the probability conditional provides as good an account of the data as the algorithmic theory provided by mental models. They parameterized the mental models account in terms of two probabilities: the probability that people adopt a conditional interpretation (P_C) and the probability that they flesh out their initial representation (P_F). In a processing tree model, P_C and P_F are assumed to be independent (Batchelder and Riefer 1999). This is certainly the simplest instantiation of the model. Moreover, it is typically assumed that these processes are independent, although investigating models where the independence assumption is not made might be of interest. Oaksford and Chater (2003a) also allowed for the possibility of error for the MP inference because it would be unreasonable to expect any psychological theory to be committed to a 100% response rate. An error parameter, P_E, was therefore introduced for the MP inference. The equations for the probability of drawing each inference in the conditional-inference task were:

$$P(\text{MP}) = 1 - P_E \qquad P(\text{DA}) = P_F (1 - P_C)$$
$$P(\text{AC}) = 1 - P_C \qquad P(\text{MT}) = P_F. \tag{5.32}$$

Looking at the fit to Schroyens *et al.*'s (2001a) meta-analysis, this model provided no better account of the data than the probability model (mean $R^2 = 0.90$, SD $= 0.13$). As we computed R^2s for each of the sixty studies, we can statistically compare the result for the probability model (mean $R^2 = 0.91$, SD $= 0.11$) with this result. There was no significant difference, $t (59) = 0.46$, $p = 0.65$. Consequently, the move to the algorithmic level in mental models theory provides no better a fit to the data than sticking with normative probability theory.

However, recently Schroyens and Schaeken (2003; see also: Schroyens *et al.* 2000a,b; Schroyens *et al.* 2001a,b) have proposed an alternative mental models account, although they regard it more as a supplement to mental models rather than as a wholesale replacement. They propose that after people have constructed a mental model of the conditional rule, and perhaps fleshed it out, they then perform a *validating search* of long-term memory for potential counter-examples. So for example, their initial model will suggest that they can make the MP inference to the conclusion that *the car starts*, from the premises, *if you turn the key the car starts*, and *you turn the key*. But rather than just go with this conclusion they then search long-term memory for a possible counter-example where the car failed to start even though the key was turned $(p, \neg q)$. If they find one then they either do not make the inference or they make it with less confidence. Thus the validating search process supplements the construction and manipulation of mental models.

Schroyens and Schaeken (2003) parameterized this account and fitted it to the same conditional inference data we discussed above. They provided the following equations for each inference:

$$P(\text{MP}) = 1 - CE_{TF} \qquad P(\text{DA}) = W_{FF}(1 - CE_{FT})$$

$$ \tag{5.33}$$

$$P(\text{AC}) = 1 - CE_{FT} \qquad P(\text{MT}) = W_{FF}(1 - CE_{TF})$$

where CE_{TF} is the probability of finding a $p, \neg q$ is a counter-example, CE_{FT} is the probability of finding a $\neg p, q$ is a counter-example, and W_{FF} is the probability of finding a $\neg p, \neg q$ instance.

Apart from the MT inference, this model is formally equivalent to the mental models account, under the following translation rules: $CE_{TF} = P_E$, $CE_{FT} = P_C$, $W_{FF} = P_F$ (Oaksford and Chater 2003d). What this means is that, although under each model people are regarded as engaging in very different activities, their ability to fit the data is very similar. The additional wrinkle for the MT inference does improve the fit (mean $R^2 = 0.92$, SD $= 0.10$), but by only 2.0% of additional variance explained, which is not a significant improvement, $t(59) = 1.16$, $p = 0.25$. This seems to suggest that either constructing and manipulating mental models or the validating search process are explanatorily redundant; either process can adequately explain the data without needing to invoke the other. Moreover, as for standard mental models, the fit is not significantly better than that achieved by the normative probability model, $t(59) = 0.60$, $p = 0.55$. Oaksford and Chater (2003b, d) provided a variety of further criticisms of the validating search model. For example, under the interpretation given above for the parameters of this model, people must be attributed with inconsistent beliefs. This is because if the parameters do correspond to the probabilities that the counter-examples, $p, \neg q$ and $\neg p, q$ exist, and that the $\neg p, \neg q$ instance exists, then the best fit values must sum to less than one. However, they typically sum to greater than one, which means that the probability of the p, q instance must be negative!

While we might disagree with Schroyens and Schaeken (2003) on the appropriate normative theory of the conditional, we agree on the importance of prior knowledge in human reasoning. Indeed, as we saw in Chapters 1 to 4, this has been the basis of our critique of psychological theories in this area for fifteen years (Chater and Oaksford 1990, 1993, 2001; Oaksford and Chater 1991, 1995b, 1998a, 2001). The subjective probabilities that figure in our models are derived from prior knowledge stored in long-term memory, which is also the source of the parameters of Schroyens and Schaeken's validating search procedure. And, as we have seen, operations over prior knowledge also provide the basis for the Ramsey test. So, if psychological theories of abstract reasoning tasks have any aspirations to generalize to real, everyday conditional inferences, it is a good thing that some consensus is emerging on the importance of probabilistic prior knowledge.

To conclude this section, there is no need to invoke algorithmic-level theories like mental models (supplemented with a validating search process or not) to capture the standard abstract results on conditional inference, when a simple normative probability model captures the data equally well. That is, we do not have to argue that people are capable of logical performance but fall in to systematic error because of their cognitive processes, when their reasoning is perfectly rational according to an alternative probabilistic standard.

Suppression effects

As we have seen in Chapters 1 to 4, a general property of everyday inferences is that they can be defeated (Oaksford and Chater 1998). There have been many experiments investigating these aspects of everyday reasoning. They show that the inferences, MP and MT, and the fallacies, DA and AC, can be *suppressed* by providing information about possible defeaters. For example, if you are told that, *if the key is turned, the car starts* and that *the key is turned*, you are likely to endorse the MP inference to the conclusion that *the car starts*. However, if you are also told that *the petrol tank is empty*, you are less likely to endorse this conclusion, because the car will *not* start if the petrol tank is empty. An empty petrol tank provides an *exception* to the rule. This exception would also mean that you are less likely to endorse MT. If you knew that *the car did not start* you may not infer that *the key was not turned* because the empty petrol tank may be the cause of the car not starting. These exceptions have been called *additional antecedents* (Byrne 1989).

Other information can suppress DA and AC. For example, if you are told that, *if the key is turned, the car starts* and that *the key is not turned*, you might endorse the DA inference to the conclusion that *the car does not start*. However, if you are also told that *the car was hot-wired*, you may be less likely to endorse this conclusion because the car may start even though the key was not turned, because it has been hot-wired. This condition would also mean that you are less likely to endorse AC. If you knew that *the car started* you may not infer that *the key was turned* because the car starting may have been caused by being hot wired. These conditions have been called *alternative antecedents* (Byrne 1989).

Explicit suppression effects

Byrne (1989) demonstrated all these effects by providing participants with explicit rules containing this additional information Table 5.1). The results of Byrne's (1989) experiment 1 are shown in Fig. 5.3. The simple condition (Fig. 5.3, panel A) did not include any additional or alternative antecedents and reflects the standard pattern of results (see Fig. 5.2). Figure 5.3 shows clearly that alternative antecedents (panel B) suppress DA and AC but not MP or MT, whereas additional antecedents suppress MP and MT but not DA or AC (panel C).

The further information provided in the second conditional premise should directly influence the relevant probabilities, $P_0(q|p)$, $P_0(p)$ and $P_0(q)$. Additional antecedents suggest that there are other conditions that need to be fulfilled for turning the key to start the car, i.e. they raise the probability that the car will not start given the key is turned, i.e. $P_0(q|p)$ falls. If $P_0(q|p)$ falls, then so will the probabilities of drawing the MP and MT inferences (see 5.24). Alternative antecedent suggest there are other ways to start cars and

Table 5.1 Byrne's (1989) explicit suppression procedure

Additional Antecedents (MP)	Alternative Antecedents (AC)
If the key is turned the car starts	If the key is turned the car starts
If there is fuel in the tank the car starts	If it is hot-wired the car starts
The key is turned	The car starts
The car starts?	The key was turned?

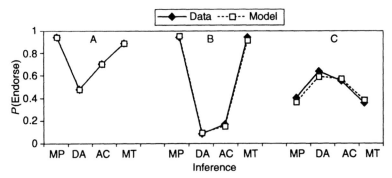

Fig. 5.3 The results of Byrne's (1989) experiment 1 in the simple condition (panel A); the additional antecedents condition (panel B); and the alternative antecedents condition (panel C) showing the fit of the conditional probability model in each condition.

so $P_0(q|\neg p)$ rises. If $P_0(q|\neg p)$ rises, then the probability of drawing the DA inference, $P_0(\neg q|\neg p)$, falls (see 5.22), as will the probability of drawing AC inferences (see 5.23).[9]

Figure 5.3 shows the overall fit of the model to Byrne's (1989) data. Panel A shows the results of Byrne's simple condition, which provided the baseline in which there was no manipulation of alternative or additional antecedents. Panel B shows the results of the alternative antecedent condition, where participants were provided with an alternative rule, e.g. if hot-wired, the car starts. Panel C shows the results of the additional antecedent condition, where participants were provided with an additional rule, e.g. if there is petrol in the tank, the car starts. As Fig. 5.3 shows, the overall fit was very good.

Implicit presentation

Cummins *et al.* (1991; see also: Cummins 1995) and Thompson (1994) report results that were very similar to Byrne (1989). However, they left information about additional and alternative antecedents implicit. That is, unlike Byrne (1989), these authors pre-tested rules for how many alternative and additional antecedents they allowed and used these rules in the experimental task

---

[9] $P_0(q|\neg p)$ is related to the other parameters, $P_0(q|p)$, $P_0(p)$ and $P_0(q)$, via 5.22, i.e. it is 1 minus the probability of the DA inference. This means that with $P_0(q|p)$ constant, for $P_0(q|\neg p)$ to rise, $P_0(p)$ must be low and $P_0(q)$ high. Oaksford and Chater (2003d) argue that these changes make intuitive sense.

with no further explicit cueing concerning the relevance of alternative and additional antecedents. Cummins *et al.*'s (1991) results are shown in Fig. 5.4 together with the fits obtained by the conditional probability model.

These results seem to directly contradict Byrne *et al.* (1999, p. 369), who have recently argued that people do *not* have 'a general insight into the idea that there may be alternatives or additional background conditions that are relevant to inferences'. Byrne *et al.* (1999) appear to argue that, in the absence of explicitly provided information about alternative or additional antecedents, people do not retrieve it from long-term memory for world knowledge to decide whether to draw an inference. This view is not consistent with Cummins *et al.* (1991) or Thompson (1994), where even when such information was left implicit, suppression effects were still observed. Consequently, participants must be accessing appropriate world knowledge to determine the likelihood that an inference can be drawn. This conclusion is further supported by the recent results of Liu *et al.* (1996). In their 'reduced' inference condition they presented participants with contentful material but without an explicit conditional premise, e.g. *knowing that the key has been turned, how probable is it that the car starts?* They found similar suppression effects as when an explicit conditional premise was provided. As Liu *et al.* (1996) argue, in the reduced inference condition, participants *must* be basing their inferences on accessing prior knowledge. Contrary to Byrne *et al.* (1999), that similar suppression effects were observed means that information about additional and alternative antecedents was being implicitly accessed.

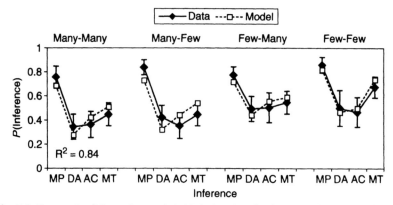

Fig. 5.4 The result of Cummins *et al.* (1991) showing the four conditions used: few or many alternatives, few or many additionals, and the fit of the conditional probability model.

Facilitating DA and AC

Byrne (1989) also showed that suppression effects can be removed by providing more information in the categorical premise. For example, given, *if p then q* and *if r then q*, participants would be given the categorical premise, *p and r*. In Byrne's experiment 2, she found that using materials of this kind this removed all suppression effects. Indeed using this manipulation produced a facilitation effect for DA and AC with respect to the simple condition (Fig. 5.3, panel A).

This effect can be explained by the different ways additional and alternative antecedents affect the appropriate conditional probabilities. Only the number of alternative antecedents independently affects these probabilities, whereas the number of additional antecedents does not. For example, take the rule *if the key is turned the car starts*. There are many exceptions to this rule: *the car will not start, if there is no petrol* (if there is petrol in the tank the car starts), *if the battery is flat* (if the battery is charged the car starts), and so on. To make the MP inference in the first place one must assume that all these possible additional conditions are *jointly* satisfied. Consequently being told that *the key is turned and the battery is charged* is not going to affect someone's estimate of the probability of MP, nor by parity of reasoning that of MT, as they have already assumed that this jointly necessary condition applies. In terms of Oaksford *et al.*'s model, this means that this manipulation does not affect people's estimates of $P_0(q|p)$. Conversely, there are other ways to start cars, such as hot-wiring (if hot-wired, the car starts), jump-starting (if jump-started, the car starts). Each is individually sufficient to start the car, consequently the more that are ruled out, the less likely the car is to start. Consequently, being told that *the key was not turned and the car was not hot-wired*, will increase someone's estimate of the probability of DA conclusion, *the car does not start*, and by parity of reasoning that of AC. In terms of Oaksford *et al.*'s model, this means that this manipulation decreases the probability that the car starts even though the key has not been turned. This explanation accounts for the facilitation effect for DA and AC that Byrne (1989) observed in her experiment 2. These considerations parallel discussion of the different ways multiple causes can interact, in the artificial intelligence literature (e.g. Pearl 1988).

Graded suppression of MP and MT

Stevenson and Over (1995) have shown variation in MP and MT inferences by concentrating, not on the number of additional antecedents but on their likelihood. So participants could be told that:

if the key is turned the car starts; (5.34)

if the battery is charged the car starts; and that (5.35)

the battery is always (almost always, sometimes, rarely, very rarely) charged. (5.36)

Participants are then given the categorical premise *the key is turned*. The manipulation in the third premise (5.36) directly manipulates $P(q|p)$. Participants' willingness to endorse MP and MT tracked this manipulation. From equation 5.21 for MP, as $P_0(q|p)$ decreases, so the probability of MP decreases. Equation 5.24 predicts a similar effect for MT, although if $P_0(p)$ and $P_0(q)$ are kept constant, the slope for MT will be steeper than for MP. In Stevenson and Over's data, using the *always* instruction leads to a facilitation effect compared to the condition in which premise 5.36 is absent. This is because, although in premise 5.35 participants are told that further conditions need to apply to make the inference in premise 5.34, they are then told in premise 5.36 that these conditions always apply!

Chan and Chua (1994) used a similar manipulation to Stevenson and Over (1995) to reveal graded suppression of MP and MT. However, rather than use a further premise, like 5.36 above, they used different additional antecedents that varied in their relative salience for achieving the conclusion. For example, 5.35′ is quite salient to whether the car starts or not. However, other less salient conditions can be imagined (5.35″):

> If the engine has not been removed overnight the car will start; or   (5.35′)
>
> If it was not foggy last night, the car will start (damp points can   (5.35″)
>   prevent ignition).

Chan and Chua (1994) observed similar graded suppression of MP and MT as observed by Stevenson and Over (1995).

George (1997) has also investigated graded suppression effects in conditional inference by directly introducing information in the conditional about the probability of the consequent given the antecedent. For example, he used rules like, *if Pierre is in the kitchen, then it is (not) very probable that Marie is in the garden*. This manipulation directly effects $P_0(q|p)$: when the consequent includes 'very probable', $P_0(q|p)$ is high; and when it includes 'not very probable', $P_0(q|p)$ is low. Predictably, in his experiment 1 there were more MP inferences in the very probable than in the not very probable condition.

Sufficiency and suppressing DA and AC

George (1997) also found suppression effects for DA and AC when perceived sufficiency was reduced (for 'valid arguments', see George 1997, table 1), i.e. when $P_0(q|p)$ is low. These effects are not predicted by a simple model based on the effects of additional and alternative antecedents. However, they are predicted by our probabilistic model. Examining equations 5.22 and 5.23, for DA and AC, reveals that decreasing $P_0(q|p)$, while keeping $P_0(p)$ and $P_0(q)$ constant, will also lead to reductions in the relevant conditional probabilities. These reductions also make intuitive sense because the number of exceptions and the number of alternatives are related. For example, the rule *if the key is turned the car starts* captures the *normal* and *most reliable* way ($P_0(q|p)$ is as high as it can get) of starting cars. Alternative methods of starting cars are generally less reliable, e.g. *if the car is bump started, the car starts*, relies on further factors like the speed being sufficiently high when you take your foot off the clutch and so on. So this alternative way of starting a car is also a less reliable way of starting a car, i.e. $P_0(q|p)$ is lower. Our probabilistic model captures this intuition and so can explain the suppression of DA and AC when perceived sufficiency is low.

Summary

Oaksford *et al.*'s (2000) simple probabilistic model appears capable of accounting for a wide range of suppression and facilitation effects in conditional inference. The key factor is that people's prior knowledge can be interpreted as affecting the subjective probabilities in the conditional probability model. Our arguments for how 5.21–5.24 can explain these effects are based on showing why, intuitively, a particular manipulation should affect the relevant probabilities. In the next section we extend this pattern of explanation to the phenomenon of polarity biases in conditional inference.

Polarity biases

Polarity biases in conditional inference occur when negations are used in the antecedent and consequent clauses of conditional rules. People seem biased to endorse inferences with negated conclusions (Evans 1993). There is also a suggestion in the literature (Evans 1993) that, according to mental models theory, people should show a complementary bias towards endorsing the conclusions of inferences with affirmative categorical premises. Oaksford *et al.*'s (2000) account of polarity biases suggests that negations provide cues to the probabilities of the antecedent ($P[p]$) and consequent ($P[q]$). It relies on Oaksford and Stenning's (1992) processing negations theory (Evans 1998), in which identifying contrast sets is one important function of negations. For example, the interpretation of 'Johnny didn't serve *coffee*' (where 'coffee' is the focus) is that he served a drink other than coffee. The superordinate category 'drinks' provides the universe of discourse and the contrast set is defined by the operation of set difference, i.e. it is the set of drinks Johnny could serve, less coffee. This account is called the 'otherness' theory of negation, which goes back to Plato (see also: Apostel 1972; Horn 1989; Ryle 1929). The set of drinks less coffee is likely to be much larger than the set of coffee drinks. Consequently, Oaksford and Chater (1994) suggested that negated categories are treated as high probability contrast sets (higher at least than their un-negated counterparts). The following equivalences were therefore suggested for the rules in the conditional-inference task: *if p, then q* ⇔LL; *if p, then ¬q* ⇔LH; *if ¬p, then q* ⇔HL; *if ¬p, then ¬q* ⇔HH (where H = high and L = low and the pair, e.g. HL, is ordered to indicate a high $P(p)$ and low $P(q)$ rule). These equivalences allow polarity biases to be re-interpreted. Negative conclusion bias can be regarded as a preference for high probability conclusions and affirmative premise bias can be regarded as a preference for low probability (categorical) premises.

As we discussed in outlining the conditional probability model, it predicts that people should endorse inferences with high probability conclusions for DA, AC, and for MT. However, it only unequivocally predicts that people should endorse inferences with low probability premises for AC. What does this model behaviour predict for people's behaviour? The model is defined at Marr's (1982) computational level, it concerns *what* computational problem the mind is trying to solve. Oaksford *et al.* (2000) did not consider *how* people actually solve the computational problem in any depth. However, a cursory look at how the cognitive system may implement their computational-level model allowed them to make some further predictions for people's behaviour on the task. They assumed that the algorithms or heuristics that people use, differentially weight the sources of information relevant to finding a solution. Because a high probability conclusion is always an unambiguous cue to endorse an inference, they concluded that people would weight this information heavily. In contrast, because a low probability premise is equivocal they concluded that people would not weight premise information heavily, and certainly a lot less than conclusion information. Consequently they predicted no premise effects.

The negations paradigm

We now show how well the model accounts for the data on the negations paradigm, where conditional rules apply to antecedents and/or consequents that may be negated. This will have two parts. We first describe the results of a meta-analysis carried out by Oaksford *et al.* (2000). Second, we describe the actual fit of the model to these data.

Oaksford *et al.* (2000) conducted a meta-analysis (Wolf 1986) of the conditional reasoning tasks that had used the negations paradigm (Evans 1977; Evans, *et al.* 1995: experiments 1 2, 3 (no scenario) and 3 (with scenario); Pollard and Evans 1980; Wildman and Fletcher 1977). There were seven studies in all. The relevant means computed across studies are shown in Fig. 5.5. With one exception this analysis revealed the pattern of predictions we have just discussed. There was a significant negative conclusion effect for DA, AC,

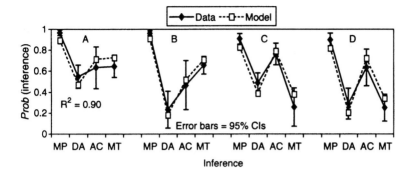

Fig. 5.5 The results of Oaksford *et al.*'s (2000) meta-analysis for the four rules used in the negations paradigm: *if p then q* (panel A); *if p then ¬q* (panel B); *if ¬p then q* (panel C); and *if ¬p then ¬q* (panel D) showing the fit of the conditional probability model. CI = confidence interval.

and for MT. So, for example, AC is endorsed more often for negative antecedent rules (panels C and D) than for affirmative antecedent rules (panels A and B). However, the only significant premise effect was an affirmative premise effect for AC. This pattern of results is consistent with our probabilistic model apart from the AC premise effect. In the next section we describe how Oaksford *et al.*'s experiments indicate that this premise effect may be an artefact.

Figure 5.5 also shows the fit of 5.21–5.24 to these data. The overall fit between the model and the data was very good, $R^2 = 0.90$. Importantly the best-fitting parameter values followed the pattern predicted by the model. In looking at these values we deal with the *if ¬p, then q* rule separately for reasons we discuss in the next paragraph. For the other rules, the mean of the best-fit values, when the antecedent or consequent was affirmative, was 0.57; while, when they were negative, it was 0.79. That is, negated constituents corresponded to higher probability categories, as predicted.

The HL or *if not-p, then q* rule is pragmatically infelicitous (Oaksford 1998; Oaksford and Chater 1994). For example, it is like asserting that *if something is black it is a raven*, which is known to be false, because there are far more black things than ravens. That is, the probability of the antecedent is much greater than the probability of the consequent $(P[p] > P[q])$. As we discuss further when looking at Wason's selection task in the next chapter, to make sense of this rule people must adjust the relevant probabilities so that the probability of the consequent is greater than the probability of the antecedent $(P[p] < P[q])$. However, in the conditional probability model, some exceptions are allowed, i.e. $P_0(q|p)$ can be less than 1. Consequently, the actual constraint imposed by the model is that $P_0(q|p)P_0(p) < P_0(q)$. The best-fit parameter values for the

HL rule were $P(p) = 0.86$ and $P(q) = 0.82$, which is consistent with an HH rule. That is, our model suggests that people adjust the probability of the consequent ($P[q]$) upwards to resolve the infelicity of asserting an *if $\neg p$, then q* rule.

A simple probabilistic model would appear to be able to account for the pattern of results that has been taken to show that people have a bias towards negative conclusions. The conditional probability model shows that far from representing biased behaviour, participants in the negations paradigm conditional-inference task are actually showing a rational preference for high probability conclusions.

Manipulating probabilities

The conditional probability model makes predictions for experiments where the probabilities of the antecedent and the consequent of a conditional are varied, rather than varying the presence or absence of negations. The main predictions, which can be derived directly from equations 5.21–5.24, are that a high-probability conclusion effect should be observed and that endorsements of the 'converse' inferences should be anti-correlated with endorsements of the standard inferences. The converse of, for example, the MP inference replaces the conclusion by its negation, i.e. *if p, then q, p, therefore not-q*. Equations 5.21–5.24 show that the probability of endorsing these converse inferences is simply 1 minus the probability of drawing the standard inference, hence the prediction of an anti-correlation. According to logic-based accounts, the converse inferences should never be drawn at all. Oaksford *et al.* tested these predictions in a series of three experiments, which we now describe concentrating on their experiment 1.

Oaksford *et al.* (2000) manipulated probabilities in a similar way to Kirby (1994) and to Sperber *et al.* (1995; see also: Oaksford *et al.* 1999). People were told that a machine prints cards with coloured shapes on them and that the quality controllers believe that there is a fault. In defining task rules relating shapes and colours, a range of possible shapes (6) and colours (5) were used. For example, for the LL rule (low $P[p]$, low, $P[q]$), participants were told that the machine was supposed to print equal numbers of shapes of different colours. So, out of every 60 cards printed, roughly there should be 60/6 = 10 of each shape, and roughly 60/5 = 12 cards of each colour, overall. The participants were also told that in a certain batch, the quality controllers thought they had detected a problem. They believed that all the triangles were blue, but that all the other shapes had the full range of colours printed on them. The structure of this problem meant that the probability of the antecedent ($P[p]$) was low, i.e. 1/6, as was the probability of the consequent ($P[q]$), i.e. 1/3. In this imaginary scenario, the machine sorted the cards into 11 bins labelled either with a shape (the 'shapes bins') or a colour (the 'colours bins'). It sorted cards by shape or by colour alternately, so if a card was sorted by shape, the next was sorted by colour, the next by shape, and so on. Participants were then told that one of the quality controllers was trying to predict what might be found in the bins. Assuming that all the triangles are blue, he looks at a shapes bin that is *not* labelled 'triangles' and predicts that if he picks a card out of this bin it will *not* be blue. This is an example of a DA inference. Participants' task was to rate how likely they thought the quality controller was to be right. They had to do this for all the standard and converse inferences for all possible rules (LL, LH, HL, and HH).

Figure 5.6(a) and (b) show the results of this experiment for the standard inferences (Fig. 5.6a) and the converse inferences (Fig. 5.6b). The most important feature of the results is the clear high-probability conclusion effect for DA,

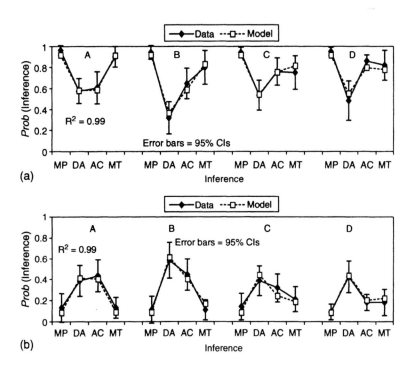

Fig. 5.6 The result of Oaksford *et al.*'s (2000) experiment 1 for the four rules used: Low $P(p)$, Low $P(q)$ (panel A); Low $P(p)$, High $P(q)$ (panel B); High $P(p)$, Low $P(q)$ (panel C); and High $P(p)$, High $P(q)$ (panel D) showing the fit of the conditional probability model for the standard condition (a) and the converse condition (b). CI = confidence interval.

AC, and for MT. So, for example, AC is endorsed more often for high-probability antecedent rules (Fig. 5.6a, panels C and D) than for low-probability antecedent rules (Fig. 5.6a, panels A and B). Consistent with the contrast-class account of negation, this pattern is directly analogous to a pattern of results observed in the negations paradigm task (Fig. 5.5). Furthermore, consistent with Oaksford *et al.*'s model, there were no significant premise effects observed in this experiment. There was a highly significant anti-correlation, $r(14) = -0.95, p < 0.0001$, between the standard and converse inferences, which is uniquely predicted by Oaksford *et al.*'s probabilistic model.

Figure 5.6(a) and (b) also show the fit between the model and the data. There were 32 data points in these experiments. $P_0(q|p)$ was kept constant across the four rules, but separate $P_0(p)$ and $P_0(q)$ values were fitted for each rule. This meant that there were nine free parameters to model the 32 data points, i.e. there were 23 degrees of freedom. Each converse inference was predicted to take the value of 1 minus the predicted value of its corresponding standard inference. The model fit the data very well, $R^2 = 0.99$. Importantly, the best-fitting parameter values followed the pattern predicted by the model. Excluding the HL rule (see above), the mean of the best-fit values, when the antecedent or consequent had a low probability, was 0.49; while, when they had a high probability, it was 0.70. Even including the HL rule, the difference between these values was highly significant (Oaksford *et al.* also estimated these parameters for each participant allowing them to test this statistically). That is, to account for the experimental results, the parameters of the model took on the values predicted by the conditional probability model and the contrast set account of negations (Oaksford and Stenning 1992). Oaksford *et al.*'s experiments 2 and 3 essentially replicated these effects while showing that they still occur when the task is framed using *if...then* rules, rather than the universal quantifier (experiment 2), and when participants are given no explicit cues that probabilistic information is relevant (experiment 3) by using contentful materials pre-tested for probability of occurrence, as in Cummins *et al.* (1991).

Fitting the conditional probability model to the data allowed Oaksford *et al.* (2000) to investigate the relationship between the best-fitting parameter values and the task probabilities that participants are given. In most cases these values are significantly correlated. However, the low values are over-estimated and the high values are underestimated. As Hattori (2002; see also: Oaksford and Chater 2003e) has commented, this pattern mirrors the pi-function for decision weights in *Prospect theory* (Kahneman and Tversky 1979) and is not necessarily irrational. As other authors have observed, this pattern may simply be a reflection of error variance in a regressive environment (Budescu *et al.* 1997; Dawes and Mulford 1996; Erev *et al.* 1994; Juslin *et al.* 2000). That is, as probabilities are bounded in the 0–1 interval, error can only pull towards the mean. Recently, Oaksford and Wakefield (2003) and Oaksford and Moussakowski (2004) have also demonstrated this relationship between participants' own direct estimates of task probabilities and those obtained by a more indirect method (see Chapter 6).

Implicit negations

Evans and Handley (1999) introduced *implicit* negations into the conditional-inference task (similar materials were used in experiment 2, Oaksford *et al.* 2000). For example, an MT inference on the rule *if A then 2*, would normally be presented as: *if A then 2*, $\neg 2$, therefore $\neg A$, but using implicit negation it would be presented as: *if A then 2, 7*, therefore $\neg A$. Implicitly negated premises can be used whenever the categorical premise would normally contain a negation, i.e. whenever the conditional probability model would designate a premise as a high-probability premise. Using this manipulation, Evans and Handley consistently found a strong affirmative premise bias, i.e. people withheld endorsing inferences from implicitly negated categorical premises (some caution is required in this interpretation because, with implicit negation, every categorical premise is now, in a sense, affirmative). Evans (1998) re-interpreted this effect as continuous with matching effects in other reasoning tasks (e.g. Evans 1972; Evans and Lynch 1973; see Chapter 7). This phenomenon occurs when cases match items named in the rule, regardless of the negation, e.g. the explicitly negated, categorical premise $\neg A$, matches the antecedent of *if A, then 2*, whereas the implicitly negated categorical premise, e.g. *K*, does not. All implicitly negated premises fail to match an item mentioned in the rule, whereas all affirmative premises match items mentioned in the rule.

These results do not seem consistent with Oaksford *et al.*'s explanation of negative conclusion biases. They found no evidence for low-probability premise effects. Consequently, Evans and Handley's results seem to contradict the probabilistic account of polarity biases we outlined in the last section. However, we now show that the results of this manipulation are consistent with, and indeed are predicted by, our interpretation of negations as identifying contrast sets.

We begin by introducing an example that shows that the effects of this manipulation conform to intuition. Consider the following DA inference on the rule, *if a bird is a raven, then it is not white*, using an implicit negation:

If a bird is a raven then it is not white;	(P1)	
This bird is a magpie ($\subseteq \neg$raven); therefore	(P2)	(5.36)
this bird is white OR not white?	(C).	

Note that an implicit negation involves selecting a member of the appropriate contrast set, i.e. a bird other than a raven, in this example *magpie*. If all someone was told in the categorical premise (P2) was that this bird is not a raven, then they might be inclined to infer that this bird is white by DA on P1. However, their knowledge of non-white, non-ravens, may mean their confidence would be low. What if, instead, they are told that this bird is a magpie? Although magpies are included in the contrast set for ravens, the intuition seems clear that P1 is irrelevant to whether magpies are white or not. This inference depends on what someone knows about magpies, not on what they know about ravens. Consequently, they would be even less confident in endorsing this inference if it were presented in implicit form.

Examples like this can be understood from a probabilistic perspective, once contrast sets are taken to represent negated categories. On a probabilistic interpretation, it is consistent to believe that one conclusion should be drawn when a negated categorical premise is presented in explicit form, and that the *opposite* conclusion should be drawn when that same premise is presented in implicit form. Consider the two contingency tables in Table 5.2. Table 5.2 (panel A) represents a dependency between two classes p and a, i.e. if p then;. p can be thought of as the set of ravens and a as the set of black birds. Table 5.2 (panel A) also represents the dependency that if $\neg p$ then $\neg a$. Table 5.2 (panel B) represents this same information but now using contrast set members to encode the negatives. The sets $P = \{p, q, r\}$ and $A = \{a, b, c\}$ are exhaustive. P can be thought of as the set of birds and A as the set of colours. So now if x is not a, then it is either b or c (e.g. if a bird is not a raven then it is either a crow or a robin). Now suppose someone were asked to assess the following alternative inferences:

$$\begin{array}{ccc} \text{if } \neg p \text{ then } \neg a & \text{if } \neg p \text{ then } \neg a & \\ \neg p & \neg p & (5.37) \\ \text{therefore } a? & \text{therefore } \neg a? & \end{array}$$

Table 5.2. Illustrative examples of contingency tables for a conditional rule using (A) explicit negations and (B) implicit negations where, e.g. $\neg a = \{b, c\}$

	A		B		A		
	a	¬a			a	b	c
p	0.3	0.1		p	0.3	0.05	0.05
¬p	0.1	0.5	P	q	0.1	0.025	0.025
				r	0	0.225	0.225

According to our probabilistic model, which conclusion is chosen will depend on the probabilities of the different conclusions, given the categorical premise. In this case, $P(\neg a|\neg p) > P(a|\neg p)$. Whether these probabilities are calculated over Table 5.2 (panel A) or Table 5.2 (panel B), the same answer results: $P(\neg a|\neg p) = 0.833$ and $P(a|\neg p) = 0.167$. According to the model, people should therefore pick $\neg a$ as the conclusion. Now suppose someone is asked to assess the same inferences using a contrast set member as the premise, i.e. using an implicit negation:

$$\begin{array}{ll} \text{if} \neg p \text{ then} \neg a & \text{if} \neg p \text{ then} \neg a \\ q(\subseteq \neg p) & q(\subseteq \neg p) \\ \text{therefore } a? & \text{therefore} \neg a? \end{array} \qquad (5.38)$$

Again, according to the probabilistic model, the conclusion that is preferred will depend on the probabilities of the different conclusions, given the categorical premise. In this case, Table 5.2 (panel B) indicates that $P(a|q) > P(\neg a|q)$: $P(a|q) = 0.667$ and $P(\neg a|q) = 0.333$. According to the model, people should therefore pick a as the conclusion, i.e. the opposite conclusion to that suggested when using an explicit negation. Consequently the introduction of implicit negations may reduce confidence in an inference because it creates the possibility that the opposite conclusion could be endorsed.

Using contrast set members to represent negated categories raises the issue of the nature of the joint probability distribution over the extra cells in the expanded contingency table. It could be argued that in the face of ignorance about this distribution, a reasoner should make a uniformity assumption. However, world knowledge indicates that natural taxonomies are not arranged like this. So for example, letting q = crow and r = robin and a = black, makes sense of the distribution in Table 5.2 (panel B): most crows are black, but no robins are black.

This approach to implicit negations suggests it is related to the problem of reasoning from partial information, where, although there may be some known constraints on a probability distribution, the precise distribution is unknown (Osherson et al. 1993; Over and Jessop 1998). One way of resolving this problem is too assume the distribution is uniform, as we suggested above. Another possibility is to apply the maximum entropy formalism (Jaynes 1978; see also: Oaksford and Chater 1998a, chapter 16). The idea is to adopt a distribution over the unknown cell values that maximizes uncertainty. This is reasonable because it reflects the fact that a reasoner is uncertain about the distribution and so they should not adopt any assumptions that may place more structure in the distribution than is justified by that uncertainty. This approach has been adopted by Over and Jessop (1998) in constructing models for Wason's selection task, which we discuss in the next chapter. An interesting line of future research on conditional inference will be to see if maximum entropy can predict people's inferences when using implicit negations. However, it seems, in Evans and Handley's (1999) experiments, that the effect has been to suppress inferences because a distribution is possible that could lead to the opposite conclusion.

Evans and Handley's (1999) results are, overall, consistent with the probabilistic interpretation of conditional inference. The affirmative premise bias they observe when using implicit negations does not reflect a low-probability premise effect. It is an artefact of the use of contrast set members to encode negations. Moreover, the high-probability conclusion effect and affirmative premise bias work against each other—they disagree on two rules for each inference. Consequently, Evans and Handley (1999) found little evidence for negative conclusion bias because it has been over-ridden by the effects of the implicit negations, which produced a very large affirmative premise bias, especially in their experiment 3.

Recently, Schroyens and Schaeken (2003) argued that Oaksford *et al.*'s (2000) model of the implicit negation effect, just outlined, appears to predict that the following two AC inferences should be endorsed equally often: *if A, then ¬2, 7, therefore A* (implicitly negated categorical premise), and *if A, then 7, 7, therefore A*. This is because both inferences should be drawn in proportion to $P(A|7)$. However, in Schroyens *et al.*'s (2000) experiment 1, the AC inference for the implicit, *if A, then ¬2*, rule was endorsed by 16%, 28.6%, and 7.4% of participants, across three conditions. However, the same inference for the explicit, *if A, then 7* rule, was endorsed by 76%, 95.2%, and 70.4% of participants, respectively. A similar pattern was observed in Evans and Handley's (1999) experiment 3 (6% versus 89%, respectively).

The force of these results depends on the fact that the very same lexical content is used as the categorical premise and conclusion, so that each inference seems to depend on the very same conditional probability. However, in these experiments, either (i) the lexical content is randomly varied or (ii) just two letters and two numbers are used with the same letter/number in the antecedent and consequent of each rule. In the latter case (ii), the actual inferences participants would see are: *if A, then ¬2, 7, therefore A*, and *if A, then 2 2, therefore A*. That is, a different conditional probability is being assessed in each case. Why this matters can be seen when we substitute real world content for the alphanumeric stimuli used in these experiments. First, we look at the two inferences that Schroyens and Schaeken present:

> If you are in Paris, then you are in France.
>
> You are in France. (5.39)
>
> Therefore, you are in Paris.

> If you are in Paris, then you are not in England.
>
> You are in France. (5.40)
>
> Therefore, you are in Paris.

Schroyens and Schaeken suggest that the relevant conditional probability is exactly the same in 5.39 and 5.40. With respect to the conditional probability model in 5.21–5.24, this suggestion is not strictly true. The probability of you being in Paris is surely higher given that you are in France than given that you are not in England. But 5.40 is intuitively a case where the categorical premise, *you are in France*, might lead to an adjustment of the conditional probability against which the inference is assessed, i.e. from $P(\text{Paris}|\neg\text{England})$ to $P(\text{Paris}|\text{France})$. Intuitively this seems fine for the conditional probability model because then 5.39 and 5.40 provide as much warrant for the conclusion as each other. However, as we said, the lexical content often remains fixed. In case (ii) the rule 5.40 would therefore be as follows:

> If you are in Paris, then you are not in France.
>
> You are in England. (5.40a)
>
> Therefore, you are in Paris.

Although in 5.39 $P(\text{Paris}|\text{France})$ will take on some positive value (most visitors to France go to Paris), in 5.40a, $P(\text{Paris}|\neg\text{France}) = 0$. That is, in 5.40a where the implicit negation is used, according to the conditional probability model, people should not draw this AC inference, which is exactly the result Schroyens and Schaeken describe.

We now turn to what happens in case (i):

> If you are in Berlin, then you are not in France.
>
> You are in England. (5.40b)
>
> Therefore, you are in Berlin.

In 5.40b, whether $P(\text{Berlin}|\neg\text{France}) = 0$ or is greater than 0 depends on which contrast class member for $\neg$France is used as the implicitly negated categorical premise. If, as in 5.40b, it is England then $P(\text{Berlin}|\neg\text{France}) = 0$, However, if it is Germany, then $P(\text{Berlin}|\neg\text{France}) > 0$. These examples show that for the cases that participants normally see, the conditional probability model predicts exactly the behaviour noted by Schroyens and Schaeken as a consequence of using implicitly negated categorical premises. In 5.40a you should not draw the AC inference, and in 5.40b only one member of the contrast class for the consequent will allow the inference to be drawn. The rest do not.

One effect of implicit negations may be to call to mind alternative antecedents. There are many ways of not being in France. For example, if you are in Dublin, then you are not in France. Being provided with such an alternative in the categorical premise, i.e. being in England, may bring these to mind. This may connect the effects of implicit negations to the effects of additional antecedents, which just so happen to suppress AC and DA inferences (see 'Suppression effects').

In sum, the conditional probability model can only be construed as making the counter-evidential predictions suggested by Schroyens and Schaeken (2003) when the lexical content is exactly the same in the categorical premise and conclusion of these two inferences (5.39 and 5.40). However, this is rarely the case in the actual experiments and, in the light of examples 5.39 and 5.40, it would appear that the data in this particular case violate strong intuitions that participants should draw these inferences in equal proportion. Once the lexical content varies as it normally does in these experiments (5.40a, 5.40b), intuition and the conditional probability model converge on the observed response pattern.

Summary

There are other results in the literature that are broadly consistent with this account and the contrast class account of negations in particular (Schroyens *et al.* 2000a, 2000b, 2001a,b). Schroyens and Schaeken (2003) provided a meta-analysis of these results and past results on the negations paradigm conditional-inference task. They showed that the original conditional probability model could account for five out of the six effects observed. Oaksford and Chater (2003a) observed that this was pretty good for the simple probabilistic model initially presented by Oaksford *et al.* (2000). Moreover, with respect to polarity biases, it can also be shown that the validating search model (Schroyens and Schaeken 2003), which we evaluated in 'Mental models and validating search', does not provide as good an account of the data. For example, it fails to predict the magnitude of the affirmative premise bias for the DA inference (Oaksford and Chater 2003).

In sum, in this section we have shown how Oaksford *et al.*'s simple probabilistic model can explain polarity biases in conditional inference as a rational effect of high probability categories. As we have argued, it appears that many apparently irrational patterns of inference seen in the laboratory make rational sense when compared to a probabilistic standard.

Order effects

Another important determinant of performance on conditional inference is the order of clauses within the conditional premise, i.e. the difference between, *if p, then q* and *q only if p*, and the order of presentation of the premises and conclusion of a conditional inference. These manipulations are important and interesting and we argue that they may also be amenable to a probabilistic treatment.

Clause order

There are two consistent effects of the change of clause order. First, *the car starts only if the key is turned* leads to more AC and MT inferences and fewer MP and DA inferences than, *if the key is turned the car starts* (Evans 1977; Evans and Beck 1981; Roberge 1978). Second, it has been found that paraphrasing a rule, *if p, then q*, using *only if* depends on two factors: temporal precedence, i.e. which of *p* and *q* occurs first, and perceived necessity, i.e. is *p* necessary for *q* or *q* necessary for *p*? (Evans 1977; Evans and Beck 1981; Evans and Newstead 1977; Thompson and Mann 1995). Note that in our example, turning the key (*p*) both precedes, and is causally necessary for, the car to start, and hence is best paraphrased as *q only if p*; the opposite paraphrase *the key is turned only if the car starts* seems pragmatically infelicitous. Thompson and Mann (1995) have also observed that these effects seem independent of content domain, i.e. they occur for conditionals expressing causes, permissions, definitions or co-occurrence relations.

The conditional probability model, as described above, clearly does not address the psycholinguistic findings on paraphrasing. However, we can look to see whether the principle effect of the *q only if p* rule revealed by these results, to emphasize the necessity of *p* for *q*, is amenable to a probabilistic treatment. Probabilistically this effect seems to correspond to a situation where the probability of the consequent given that the antecedent has not occurred $(P[q|not\text{-}p])$ is lowered, i.e. there are fewer alternative ways of achieving the effect. This immediately gives rise to the problem that if this probability decreases, then the probability of the DA inference increases. But the observation in this literature is that DA and MP inferences decrease while AC and MT increase (Evans 1977; Evans and Beck 1981). However, an alternative interpretation is that the *q only if p* rule lowers the joint probability of *q* and *not-p*$(P[q, not\text{-}p])$. Under these circumstances it is possible to re-arrange the marginals, i.e. $P(p)$ and $P(q)$, so that the probability of DA falls and the probability of AC rises. However, to model the increase in MT then requires a rise in $P(q|p)$. This predicts an increase in MP inferences. But in the data, the move to the *q only if p* rule leads to decreases in the frequency of MP endorsements, not increases. Consequently, however one tries to capture the effect of the *q only if p* rule, it seems that the model is bound to get the direction of change wrong for at least one inference. This is further borne out in fitting the model to Evans (1977) results. The fits to both rules were quite good, $R^2 = 0.87$ for the *if p then q* rule and $R^2 = 0.86$ for the *q only if p* rule. Moreover, although the predicted proportion of endorsements minimised the differences between rules, the direction of change was correct for MP, AC, and MT. However, the model predicted an increase in DA inferences for the *q only if p* rule where either no change (Evans 1977) or decreases are found (Evans and Beck 1981).

Clause order, utilities, and conversational pragmatics

No straightforward probabilistic account of clause order effects is available in our simple model. However, we believe that this may be because order manipulations have pragmatic functions that may be better captured via changes in utilities rather than probabilities. Oaksford *et al.* (1999) made a similar argument in the selection task. Order effects are usually discussed in terms of their direct effect on the construction of mental representations for the premises (Evans *et al.* 1998; Girotto *et al.* 1997; Johnson-Laird and Byrne 1991). However, ordering of information may have pragmatic effects other than affecting the order in which a discourse representation is assembled. For example, order typically encodes the *topic* or focus of a discourse. For example, in an active sentence the subject is the topic, hence the subject is mentioned first, whereas in a passive sentence the object is the topic, hence the object is mentioned first. Consequently, in interpreting even the relatively restricted discourse provided by a conditional syllogism, it is important to understand the normal communicative function of different sentential and clausal orderings.

Ordering manipulations may change the topic of a discourse. Changing the clausal ordering from, *if p, then q*, to *q only if p*, switches the topic from *p* to *q*. Communicative functions can be revealed by posing questions, where one or the other linguistic form would be the most appropriate reply. For example, in response to the query, 'what happens if I turn the key?' one might respond 'if you turn the key, the car starts'. However, in response to the query, 'why did the car start at that moment?' or for that matter 'why didn't the car start' one might reply, 'Well the car starts only if you turn the key'. Switching responses to these two queries would be pragmatically infelicitous. These examples suggest that the pragmatic function of, *if p, then q* is to focus attention on what can be predicted, given that *p* is known, whereas the pragmatic function of *q only if p* is to focus attention on explaining why *q* happened. Assuming that *p* temporally precedes *q*, as is normal (Comrie 1986), MP and DA are the predictive inferences that are suppressed for the *q only if p* form, and AC and MT are the explanatory inferences that are facilitated for this form. This pattern of suppression and facilitation is consistent with the explanatory function of the *q only if p* form of the rule. The effect here is not to alter the relevant probabilities, but rather to alter the importance attached to the different inferences. Consequently, we argue that the utility to a reasoner of the different classes of inference is altered by the clause order manipulation. For the *q only if p* rule people assign higher utility to the explanatory, AC and MT, inferences and a lower utility to the predictive, MP and DA inferences.

Premise and conclusion order

A further manipulation of order involves altering the order of premises and conclusion (Evans *et al.* 1998; Girotto *et al.* 1997). Girotto *et al.* (1997) showed that people are more willing to draw MT when the premises are presented in order (PCR) rather than in the standard order (PCS):

(PCR)	The car has not started.	(PCS)	If the key is turned the car starts.
	If the key is turned the car starts.		The car has not started.
	(The key was not turned (C).)		(The key was not turned (C).)

(The labels derive from Evans *et al.* (1998); 'PC' means the conclusion (C) comes after the premises (P), 'S' means that the premises are in standard order, conditional before categorical premise, and 'R' means that this premise order is reversed). The conclusion (in parentheses) was not presented in Girotto *et al.* (1997) as they used a production task where participants must spontaneously produce a conclusion rather than evaluate the validity of particular conclusions provided by the experimenter. Girotto *et al.* (1997) found no affect of this manipulation on MP, DA or AC, and neither does it affect *q only if p* conditionals or bi-conditionals.

Evans *et al.* (1998) used a similar manipulation but also varied the position of the conclusion. They used the orders in PCR and PCS (including the conclusion because Evans *et al.* used an evaluation task) and the following orders:

(CPR)	The key was not turned (C).	(CPS)	The key was not turned (C).
	The car has not started.		If the key is turned the car starts.
	If the key is turned the car starts.		The car has not started.

Evans *et al.* (1998) failed to replicate Girotto's *et al.*'s (1997) finding of increases in MT inferences with premise order reversals (PCR and PCS). What they did find was that both presenting the conclusion first (CPR and CPS vs. PCS) and reversing the premises (PCR and CPR vs. PCS) led to a reduction in negative conclusion bias, which we discussed in 'Polarity biases'. It was possible for Evans *et al.* (1998) to discover this because they used all the four conditions fully crossed with Evans' (1972) negations paradigm, where the four rules are presented: *if p, then q; if p, then not-q; if not-p, then q;* and *if not-p, then not-q.* Evans *et al.*'s (1998) failure to replicate Girotto *et al.* (1997) suggests that it may be too simplistic to attempt an interpretation that concentrates only on variation in MT inferences. We therefore concentrate on the effects described by Evans *et al.*

Probabilities and conversational pragmatics

Oaksford and Chater (1995a) suggested that conversational pragmatics may influence reasoning by affecting subjective probabilities. In that paper, we were concerned with accounting for the effects of relevance manipulations in Wason's selection task (Sperber *et al.* 1995), the topic of the next chapter. We suggested that increasing the relevance of particular instances of a rule may result in increasing the degree of belief that such instances exist. Consequently, order effects, which alter the topic of a sentence, may also serve to increase the relevance and hence the subjective probability of a described property or event. This viewpoint suggests investigating the probabilistic effects of ordering manipulations. We have done this by fitting our probabilistic model to the results from Evans *et al.*'s (1998) experiment 2, which used the fully crossed design outlined in PCR to CPS. We fitted the model to the mean data for each individual rule in the negations paradigm (4) in each condition (4). We allowed all three parameters $(P_0(p), P_0(q), P_0(q|p))$ of the model to vary. The best fits were obtained by minimizing the residual sum of squares between the model's predictions and the data. The average level of fit (averaged over the rules) between data and the model was very good (mean $R^2 = 0.93$, SD $= 0.08$).

According to the conditional probability model of the negations paradigm, negated clauses should correspond to high-probability categories. For example, our model predicts that $P_0(q)$ should be higher for the rule, *if p, then not-q* than for, *if p, then q*. Consequently, we should see an effect of negation: negated clauses should correspond to higher probabilities. For the best-fit parameter values, this effect was observed. However, the best-fit values of $P_0(p)$ and $P_0(q)$ were significantly higher when they corresponded to a negated rather than an affirmative clause, only for the PCS condition. This analysis just re-describes Evans *et al.*'s (1998) finding, that these order manipulations remove negative conclusion bias, in terms of the conditional probability model. However, why this happens in terms of the parameter values in the model is interesting.

The difference between affirmative and negated clauses narrowed for the non-standard orders mainly because the probabilities of the affirmative clauses *increased*. All the non-standard conditions had affirmative clauses that had significantly higher probabilities than the standard PCS condition but there were no other differences. A very different pattern of results was found for the negated clauses. There were no significant differences between the PCS, PCR, and CPS conditions, i.e. the probabilities of the negated clauses remained high. However, all three of these conditions had negated clauses that had significantly higher probabilities than the CPR condition.

How could these order manipulations lead to these changes in subjective probability? We have suggested that making some piece of information relevant (Sperber *et al.* 1995) may increase the subjective probability of an event (Oaksford and Chater 1995a), and that making something the topic of a discourse, may have the same effect. We should not be surprised at such changes in our subjective probabilities because in inference they are all relative to context. So, for example, the probability of encountering a lama on the streets of Cardiff is extremely low by our estimation. However, the probability of such an encounter at London zoo is far higher. In all but the standard PCS condition, one of the antecedent or consequent clauses is the first sentence of the limited discourse provided by these argument forms, rather than the rule. That is, rather than the rule, one of the antecedent or consequent clauses acts as the topic of the discourse. This explains why the probabilities of the affirmative clause rise. No corresponding increases in the probabilities of negated clauses occur because they are already high. This seems to make sense. For example, the probability that someone is *not* going to encounter a lama on the streets of Cardiff is already very high. And telling them that they are not going to encounter one, i.e. making *not* encountering lamas the topic of some discourse, is unlikely to increase their subjective estimate of this event.

Another aspect of the ordering manipulation concerns the coherence of the resulting discourse. PCS, PCR, and CPS all seem to be coherent, whereas CPR does not. We illustrate this point by providing discourse examples of these different orders. We use the MP argument form throughout.

PCS'　When there is heavy rain in the Welsh Marches, there are often floods along the river Severn. In summer 1999, there was heavy rain in the Welsh Marches. Towns along the river Severn were flooded for days.

Here the causal relation between rain in the Welsh Marches and flooding on the Severn is the topic. After the second sentence, the invited inference is clearly what is stated in the final sentence, i.e. the conclusion. So the function of this ordering seems to be to consider the consequences of the truth of the relationship described in the conditional.

PCR'　In summer 1999, there was heavy rain in the Welsh Marches. When there is heavy rain in the Welsh Marches, there are often floods along the river Severn. That year towns along the river Severn were flooded for days.

Here the topic is the heavy rain in the Welsh Marches in the summer of 1999. Introducing the causal relation in the second sentence clearly invites the reader to consider the consequences of this fact. So the function of this ordering seems to be to consider the consequences of the fact described in the first sentence, i.e. of the topic of the discourse.

> CPS'   In Summer 1999, towns along the river Severn were flooded for days. When there is heavy rain in the Welsh Marches, there are often floods along the river Severn. There was heavy rain in the Welsh Marches that year.

Here the topic is clearly the flooding along the river Severn in the summer of 1999. Introducing the causal relation in the second sentence clearly invites the reader to consider possible explanations of this fact. So the function of this ordering seems to be to consider possible explanations of the fact described in the first sentence, i.e. of the topic of the discourse.

Note that PCR' and CPS' are interchangeable, e.g. if we presented AC in CPS form, the resulting discourse would be identical to MP in PCR form. This correspondence predicts that MP and AC inferences in both PCR' and CPS' should be endorsed at similar levels, whereas normally MP inferences are endorsed much more strongly. In Evans *et al.*'s (1998) results, the difference between endorsements of MP and AC was 21% in the PCS condition, whereas in the PCR and CPS conditions it was only 5% and 6%, respectively (DA and MT inferences were at similar levels overall in all conditions).

> ?CPR'   In Summer 1999, towns along the river Severn were flooded for days. There was heavy rain in the Welsh Marches that year. When there is heavy rain in the Welsh Marches, there are often floods along the river Severn.

There is a question mark by CPR' because although the discourse is not nonsensical it is not wholly coherent. The first sentence introduces a fact. For the second sentence to be coherent, it must be regarded as relevant to this fact. The only way it seems this can come about is when the fact in the second sentence is explanatory of (or can be predicted from) the first. That is, the second sentence is a tentative attempt to suggest a causal relation between the facts described in these juxtaposed sentences (on the use of sentential juxtaposition to suggest causation, see: Comrie 1986). The final conditional sentence then states that there is such a relation. This seems to violate the pragmatic maxim of quantity (Levinson 1983): a statement should be as informative as is required for the current discourse. The problem here is that the first two sentences in CPR' suggest only that there *may* be a causal relation between these two facts. However, the final sentence makes the more informational statement that there actually is such a relationship. According to the maxim of quantity if someone knew that such a relationship existed then there was no point in just suggesting that did it in the first two sentences.

What effects might be predicted from this apparent violation of the maxim of quantity? The most obvious effect of stating only that a causal relation *may* exist in the first two sentences is to weaken participants' belief in the conditional describing that relation in the final sentence. This interpretation suggests that the effect of CPR′ should be to increase the probability of exceptions, i.e. $P_0(q|p)$ should fall in the CPR′ condition. At 0.79 (SD = 0.08), $P_0(q|p)$ was significantly lower in the CPR condition than the other three conditions: PCS, mean = 0.92, SD = 0.02; PCR, mean = 0.92, SD = 0.03; CPS, mean = 0.90, SD = 0.03 (Oaksford and Chater 2003d). Consequently, it would seem that Evans *et al.*'s (1998) results are consistent with the likely probabilistic effects of a pragmatic account of the premise-conclusion ordering manipulation.

Summary

We have argued that the pragmatic effects of ordering manipulations are compatible with Oaksford *et al.*'s (2000) probabilistic account of conditional inference. In the case of premise and conclusion order effects (Evan *et al.* 1998; Girotto *et al.* 1997), the explanation is mediated by the pragmatic effects of these manipulations. This is consistent with Oaksford and Chater's (1995) arguments about the probabilistic effects of pragmatic phenomena. In explaining the effect of clause order changes (e.g. Evans 1977; Evans and Beck 1981; Roberge 1978), we argued that a decision theoretic perspective may be required to capture the different explanatory and predictive functions of the *if p then q* and *q only if p* rule forms.

Further theoretical issues and future directions

We conclude this section on conditional inference by addressing three further theoretical issues that have arisen in the recent literature on conditional inference surrounding the probabilistic approach. First, we look at the theoretical differences between the probabilistic approach and recent accounts of conditional reasoning that preserve the logical approach but supplement it with a search for counter-examples in long-term memory (Markovits and Barrouillet 2002; Markovits and Quinn 2002; Markovits *et al.* 1998; Quinn and Markovits 1998, 2002; Schroyens *et al.* 2001a, b). Second, we look at Liu's (2003) recent *two-step conditionalization* model and whether it differs significantly from the account outlined above. Finally, we suggest the future direction of conditional reasoning research, focusing on the algorithmic level.

Logic and long-term memory search

The definition of conditional probability in Adams's (1998) and Oaksford *et al.*'s (2000) accounts is based on the subjective definition provided by the Ramsey Test (Ramsey 1931). That is, the antecedent is added to one's stock of beliefs, appropriate revisions are made, and the resulting degree of belief in the consequent is the conditional probability. The Ramsey test clearly relies on an account of how knowledge is stored and accessed. Moreover, as Oaksford and Chater (2003a; see also: Sellen *et al.* 2005) observed, this reliance means that the probabilistic approach to the MP–MT and DA–AC asymmetries is very similar to approaches like Schroyens and Schaeken's (2003) and that of Markovits and colleagues (see references above). These approaches suggest that people search long-term memory for counter-examples and, if they find them, reduce the ratings they assign to an inference or do not endorse it at all. According to our account (see Chapter 6, 'The negations paradigm selection task'), counter-examples are often suggested to DA, AC, and MT inferences because of possible rigidity violations (Sobel 2004). This results in revising the conditional probability for these inferences. One difference is that the probabilistic approach provides a normatively consistent account of what people do when they consider a counter-example, i.e. they revise down $P(q|p)$ by Bayesian revision. As we now show, these other approaches seem to be logically inconsistent in this respect.

The problem centres on the continued adherence of these approaches to a truth-functional view of the conditional embodied in theories like mental models (e.g. Schroyens and Schaeken 2003). These accounts suggest that people initially interpret the conditional as true, i.e. they must assume there can be no counter-examples. On this assumption they draw the appropriate logical inference. Then, *in violation of their initial assumption*, people then search for counter-examples to the conclusion and conclude the conditional is false if they find one. Consider the following example. Given the non-logical axiom, *if x is a bird, x flys*, and the claim that *Tweety is a bird*, we conclude validly that *Tweety can fly*, but when we retrieve from long-term memory the proposition that *Tweety is an ostrich*, we conclude that, *if x is a bird, x flies* is false (presumably because I also know that *if x is an ostrich, x cannot fly*). This has the consequence that most conditional knowledge is strictly false.

This conclusion is unproblematic from a probabilistic point of view because probability theory is *non-monotonic*, as we have discussed throughout Chapters 1 to 4 of this book. However, it does mean that people cannot have a deductive reasoning system of the kind proposed by mental models. If, on learning that, *if x is a bird, x flies* is false, it is nonetheless retained as an axiom, then contradictions will result. For example, on subsequently learning that *Chirpy is a bird and an ostrich*, given the axioms about birds and ostriches above, the conclusion can be derived that *Chirpy can fly and Chirpy cannot fly*, i.e. a logical contradiction results. Moreover, given that logically one counter-example is enough to reject as false any item of everyday conditional knowledge, reaching logical contradictions should be endemic in everyday human reasoning.[10]

And, given this state of affairs, it would seem pointless for the cognitive system to attempt to assess the strength any conclusion by the attempt to search for counter-examples; because it is inevitably true, in any non-monotonic reasoning system, that such counter-examples exist.

These problems seem to stem from the conviction that it makes sense to have an isolated deductive reasoning module that simply picks information out of the bin of long-term memory for world knowledge, the organization of which is completely independent of this module. However, the issue of monotonicity precisely relates to the management and organization of this knowledge-base, such that reasoning about that knowledge can be characterized logically. The contents of world knowledge just are the non-logical axioms of the system that encode knowledge as logical theories of a knowledge domain. Maintaining the consistency of that knowledge-base, so that contradictions are not possible, means that the cognitive system cannot simply conclude that a false conclusion means that the conditional premise is false, because in that case it must be expunged from the knowledge-base and it is therefore no longer available to draw reasonable inferences about the world.

Two-step conditionalization

One intriguing result in the psychology of conditionals is that people's pattern of reasoning performance is pretty much the same, even if they are not provided with a conditional premise, as long as it can access appropriate world knowledge. So for example, in one condition, participants might be asked, *if I tell you this is a rock, would you infer it is hard* (a *reduced* problem), which contains no conditional premise (Liu 2003; Liu *et al.* 1996). In another condition they would be asked, *if I tell you that if something is a rock it is hard and that this is a rock, would you infer that it is hard* (a *complete* problem). Studies show that while the general pattern of responding is unchanged, adding the conditional premise leads to systematic increases in the endorsement of inferences. This could be because people engage a logical reasoning mechanism when

---

[10] This may sound odd in terms of the standard rhetoric of mental models theory, which is appealed to by, for example, Schroyens and Schaeken (2003). But note that in mental models one looks for counter-examples to a stated conclusion, *while preserving the truth of the premises*. In the case we are considering here, if a counter-example is found in LTM, then the conditional must logically be false, i.e. these counter-examples *deny the (classical) truth of the premises*.

explicit premises are provided. However, Liu (2003) favours a probabilistic interpretation involving two steps of conditionalization. So, for MP, people first update their probability that q is true by conditionalizing on the truth of p, i.e. the categorical premise, to arrive at $P(q|p)$. This is what Liu (2003) calls the 'proportionality hypothesis', which he attributes to Oaksford *et al.* (2000). According to this hypothesis, people totally disregard the conditional premise. In the second step of conditionalization, people take the conditional premise in to account to evaluate $P(q|p, if\ p\ then\ q)$. This second step of conditionalization explains the differences observed between the two conditions of Liu's (2003) experiments where the conditional premise is either present or absent.

A problem for the two-step conditionalization approach is that the second step seems redundant. The first step conditionalizes on the categorical premise. To do this, an estimate of $P(q|p)$ is derived from long-term memory for world knowledge, for $P(p) = 1$ to conditionalize on. This is estimated, according to the Ramsey test, by adding p to world knowledge, adjusting, and reading off the degree of belief in q. But then the second step seems unnecessary. The second premise is, *if p then q* and $P(if\ p\ then\ q) = P(q|p)$, which must be estimated *in exactly the same way as in the first step*. So it seems unclear how the second step conditionalization could alter the results of the first step.

Pragmatically it could be that the act of asserting the conditional for a complete problem provides further evidence that p is sufficient for q, i.e. $P(q|p)$ is higher than just considering one's own world knowledge would suggest. However, this would seem to violate the constraints on Jeffrey conditionalization, which works by keeping the relationships between cells in the joint probability distribution constant, i.e. the conditional probabilities do not change. As we have seen, this is called the rigidity condition on Jeffrey conditionalization, i.e. $P_0(q|p) = P_1(q|p)$. Liu's second step argues that the conditionalizing on the conditional premise leads to an increase in this conditional probability, i.e. $P_2(q|p) > P_1(q|p)$. But by Jeffrey conditionalization these should remain the same, i..e. $P_0(q|p) = P_1(q|p) = P_2(q|p)$.

It seems that the only effect the assertion of the conditional premise could have is to provide additional *evidence* that q and p are related, which increases the assessment of $P_2(q|p)$ *because people now know more than they did before*, although this violates the rigidity condition. That is, Liu's (2003) second step cannot be described as just another application of Jeffrey conditionalization. We therefore see no advantage in Liu's (2003) two-step approach. Our original account (Oaksford *et al.* 2000) did not disregard the conditional premise but assumed that people conditionalize on it. Consequently, people were assumed to take into account the extra knowledge that in this context the conditional premise is asserted..Therefore $P(q|p)$ is higher than their prior world knowledge would predict. That is, this additional knowledge is assimilated to world knowledge before the Ramsey test is carried out to evaluate $P(q|p)$. When reduced problems are presented, participants are not provided with the extra knowledge that the dependency described in the conditional rule holds in this context.

Future directions: the Ramsey test

The analysis provided here, and by probability logic (e.g. Adams 1998), shows that the principle effort in the psychology of conditional inference should be directed at delineating the cognitive processes underlying the Ramsey test. Currently, the best philosophical understanding of conditional probability is given by this test, which essentially invokes a currently unarticulated mental process (Bennett 2003). Moreover, recent appeals to the Ramsey test (Evans and Over 2004) treat it as a primitive mental operation and deals only with the mental representations that may result from having performed one.

In contrast, Oaksford (2004) presented an algorithmic account of conditional inference based on the probability conditional using a simple constraint satisfaction neural network (McClelland 1998; Rumelhart *et al.* 1986). In such a framework, performing a Ramsey test amounts to clamping on (or off) the node corresponding to the categorical premise and reading off the activation level of the node corresponding to the conclusion. Given certain constraints (McClelland 1998), for MP this operation corresponds to computing the real posterior probability, i.e. $P_0(q|p,K)$, where K stands for the other knowledge embedded in the connections between nodes. K will also include $P_0(p)$ and $P_0(q)$ which are represented as bias terms.

This framework may also capture the contrast between MP and MT. For MP people may simply perform the Ramsey test without considering other possibilities. However, as it has been argued, the conditions under which the categorical premise of MT can be asserted suggests a counter-example. Consequently, people may not just clamp off the q-node to perform the Ramsey test, but may also consider the possibility where the q-node is clamped off and the p-node is clamped on. This can lead to updating of the connection weight by local learning (which would need to be reversible as people are only *supposing*, after all). The q-node is then clamped off and the posterior probability, $P_0(\neg p|\neg q,K)$ (with the revised $P_0(q|p,K)$), read off. The results of these operations would also need to be stored in working memory, perhaps as 'mental models'. While the constraints that guarantee this probabilistic interpretation of the network's operation may be unrealistic (McCllelland 1998), this seems at least a promising avenue to pursue to provide an algorithmic level account of inference based on probability logic and the Ramsey test.

This account of the Ramsey test suggests that future theorizing in the psychology of reasoning must address the storage and representation of world knowledge and how this interacts with the reasoning process (Chater and Oaksford 1993; Oaksford and Chater 1991, 1998a). However, with the advent of probabilistic approaches with their emphasis on the Ramsey test (see also, Evans and Over 2004) and the interpretation of neural networks as Bayesian statistical analysers (McClelland 1998), how this can be achieved is perhaps clearer than it once was.

Conclusion

In this chapter we have argued that a probabilistic approach can resolve many of the problems for logic-based approaches to non-monotonic or defeasible reasoning. These problems are revealed by phenomena like the failure of strengthening of the antecedent for everyday conditionals. Adopting a probabilistic approach leads naturally to the expectation of suppression effects in conditional inference. We also showed how the same model accounts for a variety of other suppression and facilitation effects. We also showed that this model explains polarity biases as a rational, high-probability conclusion effect; and we described some of Oaksford *et al.*'s (2000) experiments confirming this account. Finally we examined two other effects: suppression of negative conclusion bias by implicit negations and order effects. We argued that these phenomena can also be explained within a rational probabilistic framework. We also explored some more recent theoretical developments and possible future directions. In sum, the major effects in the psychology of conditional inference all seem to be captured by a rational probabilistic model. This is important because previous commentators on this research have seen these data as providing evidence of systematic bias or of the operation of sub-optimal algorithms for conditional reasoning. In the next chapter we extend the probabilistic programme to a more complex form of inference: data selection in Wason's selection task.

Chapter 6

Being economical with the evidence: collecting data and testing hypotheses

Our goal in this chapter is to show how the probabilistic treatment of the conditional, introduced in Chapter 5, can be used to explain people's behaviour on the Wason selection task. This task is the most discussed task in philosophical debates about rationality (Cohen 1981; Stein 1996; Stich 1985 1990). It is a laboratory version of the problem of choosing the best experiments to test scientific laws. Popper's (1959) method of falsification suggested that, logically, experiments can only falsify general laws. Accordingly, the rational strategy is to seek counter-examples to our hypotheses. On finding such a counter-example, or falsifying instance, then we at least know that our putative rule is false.

In the selection task, participants are presented with four cards, each of which has a number on one side and a letter on the other. They can only see one side of each of the four cards, which are arranged to reveal an A, a K, a 2 and a 7. Participants are asked to indicate which card or cards they want to turn over to determine whether a rule, e.g. *if there is an A on one side then there is a 2 on the other side*, is true or false. According to the logical standard provided by falsification, participants should select the cards that potentially falsify the rule. The rule is only false if an instance can be found that conforms to the antecedent of the rule (A) but not to the consequent (2). By convention, the card showing the true antecedent case (A) is labelled p, the false antecedent case (K) $\neg p$, the true consequent case (2) q, and the false consequent case (7) $\neg q$. Thus, for the example rule, a card with an A on one side but without a 2 on the other side is a falsifying p, $\neg q$ instance. Only the A (p) and 7 ($\neg q$) cards are potentially of this type and consequently these are the only cards that participants should ask to be turned over. However, they typically select just the A card or the A and the 2 card. Only as few as 4% of people select just the p card and the *not-q* card. That is, compared to the logical standard provided by falsification, participants' behaviour seems irrational.

However, as we now argue, this lack of fit between normative strategy and actual behaviour in the reasoning laboratory is matched by a lack of fit between Popper's method of falsification and actual scientific practice.

Logicism and the philosophy of science

Contemporary philosophers of science have rejected falsificationism as unfaithful to the history of science (Kuhn 1962; Lakatos 1970) and to be anyway unworkable (Churchland 1986; Duhem 1914; Putnam 1974; Quine 1953). As Kuhn (1962) and Lakatos (1970) showed, the history of science is replete with examples where falsification was clearly not the rational strategy. Interestingly, there is a tight relationship between the reasons why falsification is often irrational and the suppression effects observed in human reasoning that we discussed in the last chapter. We illustrate the connection using an example discussed by Putnam (1974). Newton's theory of Universal Gravitation (UG) was held as unquestionably true for over 200 years. However, observations available at the time indicated that it was false. The orbit of Uranus revealed perturbations that could not be explained by UG. However, rather than regard the theory as falsified, Leverrier in France and Adams in England hypothesized that there was another planet influencing Uranus' orbit. The predictions from UG that got the orbit wrong relied on the auxiliary assumption that there were only seven planets, which were all that had been observed at that time. Consequently, rather than view the theory as falsified, it was more rational to suppose that one of the auxiliary assumptions had failed, i.e. there were more than seven planets. It also turned out that physicists were right to ignore this apparently falsifying evidence. In 1848 the eighth planet, Neptune, was observed.

The case of scientific laws, and people's attitudes towards them, are directly reflected in their common-sense use of conditional claims. When someone turns the key, presumably in the expectation that the car will start, they make the auxiliary assumption that there is petrol in the tank, the points are not welded, the fuel lines are clear, and so on. If the car does not start, it would not be rational for them to believe that the rule, *if you turn the key, the car starts*, is falsified. Following the eminent physicists of the seventeenth and eighteenth centuries, it makes far more sense to believe that one of the auxiliary assumptions has failed: there is no petrol in the tank, or the points are welded, or the fuel lines are blocked.

The force of examples like these, for contemporary debate in the psychology of reasoning, should not be underestimated. For Johnson-Laird, for example, searching for counter-examples to an argument (which is exactly what a prediction is according to the hypothetico-deductive method; Hempel 1965) defines rationality. However, the history of science reveals clear instances of falsifying cases simply not being allowed to falsify a hypothesis. Science is our paradigm case of a rational activity (Brown 1988), but here there is clearly an issue about whether it is rational or not to allow falsification. Consequently, rationality cannot inhere in searching for counter-examples, but only in the decision as to how to proceed if one is found. Moreover, as Kuhn (1962) argued, in periods of normal science there may be a general decision not even to seek counter-examples at all, as this would block the development of the theoretical paradigm.

In sum, close attention to the history and philosophy of science can directly inform the study of human reasoning in the psychological laboratory (Oaksford 1989). Popperian falsification provided an alternative given the apparent failure of confirmation theory (see: Goodman 1954) to provide a coherent account of when evidence confirms a theory. However, in more recent accounts of scientific inference, many of these problems have been resolved by taking a Bayesian probabilistic approach to confirmation (Earman 1992; Horwich 1982; Howson and Urbach 1993; Mackie 1963). In particular, the Bayesian theory of optimal data selection (Federov 1972; MacKay 1992) offers a different account of how scientists should choose experiments, which does not place an exclusive emphasis on falsification. Oaksford and Chater (1994b) used this theory to show that we can view behaviour in the selection task as optimizing the expected amount of information gained by turning each card.

The organization of this chapter is as follows. In the first section, we develop our rational analysis. In the following sections, we apply this analysis to the experimental results. We then review the more recent literature on the selection task. We argue that Oaksford and Chater's (1994b) information-gain model still provides an excellent account of the selection task. However, there are now a range of other similarly detailed probabilistic models that may account for people's behaviour, where the information-gain model does not apply (e.g. Klauer 1999). We briefly review and evaluate these theories. Finally, we turn to a detailed set of criticisms of the probabilistic approach to data selection and reply to each one.

The information-gain model

Oaksford and Chater (1994b) characterized a participant's job in the selection task as selecting data to discriminate between two hypotheses. In one of the hypotheses there is a dependency between the antecedent p and the consequent q of a conditional rule, *if p then q*. This hypothesis, which we call the dependence model (M_D), is represented by the contingency table in Table 5.2. In the other hypothesis, p and q are independent. This hypothesis, which we call the independence model (M_I), is represented by a similar contingency table, where each cell value is simply the product of the marginal probabilities. Participants want to know which hypothesis truly describes the disposition of letters and numbers on the cards, and their task is to select the data that will provide the most information about making this discrimination.

To determine the most informative data to select, Oaksford and Chater (1994b) argued that people want to select the data that will produce the greatest reduction in their uncertainty about which hypothesis is true. This goal first requires calculating how uncertain someone is about which hypothesis is true before they select any data. Uncertainty is measured using Shannon–Wiener information:

$$I(M_i) = \sum_i P(M_i) \log_2 \left(\frac{1}{P(M_i)} \right),$$
(6.1)

where $P(M_i)$ indicates the prior probability that M_D or M_I truly describe the relationship between the letters and numbers on the cards. The uncertainty before selecting any data will be at a maximum when $P(M_D) = P(M_I) = 0.5$, i.e. maximal uncertainty arises when M_D and M_I are equally likely.

To determine the amount of information someone gains by turning over a card requires working out how uncertain they are after they select some data. The difference between this uncertainty and the prior uncertainty, calculated in the last paragraph, indicates the gain in information provided by a piece of data (i.e. what is on the other side of a card). To calculate the new uncertainty requires calculating the probability of each model given some data, i.e. $P(M_i|D)$, and these values can be calculated using Bayes' Theorem:

$$P(M_i | D) = \frac{P(D|M_i)P(M_i)}{\sum_j P(D|M_i)P(M_j)}.$$
(6.2)

To use 6.2, the likelihoods, $P(D|M_i)$, are needed (we already have $P(M_D) = P(M_I) = 0.5$) and these can all be calculated directly from the contingency tables in Table 5.2 and the independence model. For example, suppose someone is contemplating turning the p card because they think there is a q on the back. The probability of finding this piece of data (q) given the dependence model, $P(q|p, M_D)$, is given by equation 5.21 (MP), i.e. $P(q|p)$ or a. In the independence model, this probability, $P(q|p, M_I) = P(q|M_I) = c$. Putting these values in to Bayes' theorem (6.2) means that the probability that the dependence model is true, given someone finds a q on the back of the p card, $P(M_D|q, p)$, is $a/(a + c)$. And of course, $P(M_I|q, p) = 1 - P(M_D|q, p)$. To determine how uncertain someone is after finding a q on the back of the p card requires using these posterior probabilities in equation 6.1. We can then calculate the information gain (I_g) associated with turning the p card to find a q (p_q):

$$I_g(p_q) = I(M_i) - I(M_i | p_q). \qquad (6.3)$$

However, in the selection task, participants never actually get to turn over the cards to see what is on the other side, i.e. they never actually get to see the data. Consequently, they must make their decision on whether to turn a card on the information gain they might *expect* to find by turning a card. This requires calculating the probability of the different data outcomes, and how much they would learn from each of them. For example, for the p card, the posterior information must be calculated, not only for when a q is found but also, for when a *not-q* is found. The latter is calculated in exactly the same way as we have already outlined. To calculate the gain in information we can expect from turning the p card, means that these two posterior information values must be weighted by the probability of finding each of these two possible outcomes: q or a *not-q*. These probabilities are the expected values of either $P(q|p)$ or $P(not-q|p)$, calculated over both models, e.g.

$$P(q | p) = P(M_D)P(q | p, M_D) + P(M_I)P(q | p, M_I). \qquad (6.4)$$

The expected uncertainty associated with turning the p card ($EI(p)$) is then:

$$EI(p) = P(q | p)I_g(P_q) + P(\neg q | p)I_g(p_{not-q}) \qquad (6.5)$$

and the expected information gain associated with turning the p card is:

$$EI_g(p) = I(M_i) - EI(p). \qquad (6.6)$$

Similar calculations can be performed for the other three cards.

Card choice in the selection task is competitive. So the information gains associated with each card were scaled by the total information available, i.e. the information gain summed over the four cards (see: Oaksford and Chater 1998a). So scaled expected information gain associated with card x is defined as:

$$SEI_g(x) = \frac{EI_g(x)}{\sum_{x_i \in \{p, not-p, q, not-q\}} EI_g(x_i)}. \tag{6.7}$$

Hattori (1999, 2002) derived a 'selection tendency function' (STF) that maps scaled expected information gain on to the predicted probability that a card will be selected. Such a function allows a better comparison of the models predictions with the actual data. The STF that Hattori chose was a logistic that has also been used to map the outputs of neural networks on to a probability of responding (e.g. Gluck and Bower 1988). The probability that any particular card x will be selected to be turned over, $P(T_x)$, is:

$$P(T_x) = \frac{1}{1 + e^{2.37 - 9.06 SEI_g(x)}}. \tag{6.8}$$

Hattori estimated the two parameters in the exponent (2.37 and 9.06) directly from past data on the selection task.

We show the behaviour of the model in Fig. 6.1. Each panel represents a card using a density plot with the probability of the antecedent ($P(p)$) on the x-axis and the probability of the consequent ($P(q)$) on the y-axis. The third dimension, shown by shading, corresponds to the probability that the card should be selected, $P(T_x)$, according to the information-gain model. The lighter the shading, the higher the probability that a card should be selected. As in Oaksford and Chater (1994b), the prior probabilities do not influence the ordering of the probabilities that each card should be selected, so we set $P(M_D) = P(M_I) = 0.5$. $P(q|p)$ was set to 0.9. Points in the lower triangular region in black violate the assumption of the dependence model that $P(q) > P(p)P(q|p)$.

In modelling performance on the selection task, perhaps the most important point to observe from these density plots is that, when $P(p)$ and $P(q)$ are both small, there is a region where the probability that the q card should be selected is greater than the probability that the not-q card should be selected,

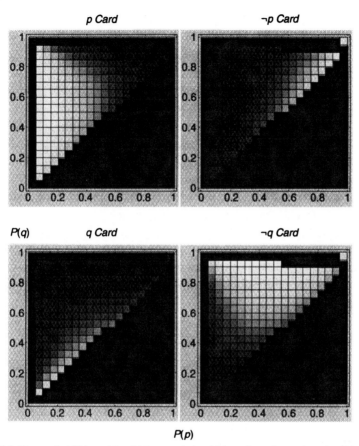

Fig. 6.1 The probabilities with which a card should be selected as a function of the probabilities of the antecedent ($P(p)$, x-axes) and the consequent ($P(q)$, y-axes) according to the revised information-gain model. The lighter the region, the greater the probability that a card should be selected. These probabilities were calculated by transforming the information gains using a logistic selection tendency function. The prior probabilities ($P(M_I)$ and $P(M_D)$) were set to 0.5 and the exceptions parameter (ε) was set to 0.1. Points in the lower triangular region in black violate the assumptions of the dependence model that $P(q) > P(p)P(q\,|\,p)$.

i.e. $P(T_q) > P(T_{not\text{-}q})$. In the selection task, the most frequent response is to select the p and the q cards only. This behaviour is usually regarded as irrational. However, according to the information-gain model, if people normally regard the probabilities of the antecedent and consequent as being quite small, then this selection of cards is the rational selection: these two cards are more informative about which hypothesis is true relative to the other cards. That the probabilities of the antecedent and consequent should be low is consistent with the observation that the categories of natural language cut the world up quite finely. So, for example, very few things are tables, cars, or gorillas. This is because broad categories like, for example, 'thing' that have a high probability of applying to an object in the world, are not very useful for telling us what to expect this object to do or how to interact with it. In contrast, knowing that an object is a chair tells us just about everything we need to know. This is the 'rarity assumption', that we discussed in Chapter 5. As we shall see, this assumption seems to explain the experimental results very well.

We now turn to showing how the information-gain model can explain the evidence on the selection task. The model presented above is a revised version of the model presented by Oaksford and Chater (1994b). Oaksford and Chater (1994b) showed how the model accounted for a variety of pre-1994 data on the selection task. Here we concentrate primarily on showing how well it accounts for the data that has emerged more recently; but we begin with the standard findings.

The standard abstract results

Oaksford and Chater (1994b) conducted a meta-analysis (Wolf 1986) of the abstract data, which included 13 studies reporting 34 standard abstract-selection tasks (i.e. using standard alpha-numeric stimuli) involving a total of 845 participants. The results are shown in Fig. 6.2. They are averaged over the 34 studies in the meta-analysis. Oaksford and Chater (2003e) fitted the model

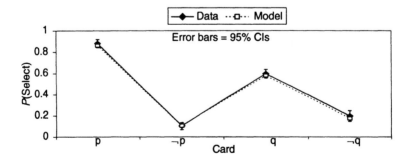

Fig. 6.2 Results of Oaksford and Chater's (1994a) meta-analysis of the selection task showing the fit of the information gain model.

to these data. In these fits, $P(M_D)$ and $P(M_I)$ were kept constant at 0.5 and $P(q|p)$ was set to 0.9, i.e. these parameters were not varied to capture the data. Similarly, the parameters of the selection tendency function (Hattori 1999, 2002) were kept at the values estimated by Hattori. The model was fitted to the results from each study individually, by comparing the best-fitting predicted values to a 'saturated' model consisting of the actual probabilities of selecting the cards. The fit is satisfactory if the predicted values do not differ significantly from the actual values. Across all 34 studies, the model provided very good fits of the data and could not be rejected (G^2 (68) = 88.37, $p > 0.05$). Fig. 6.2 show the fit of the model to data.

Over the studies in Oaksford and Chater's (1994b) meta-analysis, the mean value of the probability of the p card, $P(p)$, was 0.22 (SE = 0.019) and the mean value of the probability of the q card, $P(q)$, was 0.27 (SE = 0.022). These values were very close to the expected prior probability of a cause (0.25) and of an effect (0.27) found by Anderson (1990) when modelling causal estimation tasks (Schustack and Sternberg 1981). This raises the possibility that participants bring very similar prior expectations to bear in both tasks.

The negations paradigm selection task

Evans' negations paradigm, which we met in the last chapter on conditional inference (Chapter 5, 'The negations paradigm'), was originally used in the selection task (Evans and Lynch 1973). Exactly the same four rules are used—AA, AN, NA, and NN—which produces changes in card selections more consistent with falsification (Evans 1983, 1984, 1989; Evans and Lynch 1973). This happens for rules with a negated consequent: *if p, then ¬q*, and *if ¬p, then ¬q*. For these rules, participants select more consequent cards that can make the rule false (i.e. false consequent, or FC, cards) than consequent cards that can make it true (i.e. true consequent, or TC, cards). For example, for the *if p, then ¬q* rule, participants typically select the q card (FC). Evans (e.g. 1998) explains this finding by people 'matching', i.e. they display a *matching bias*. Participants are hypothesized to ignore the negations and match the items named in the rule to the corresponding cards, rather than carry out any logical, or for that matter, probabilistic, reasoning. Because the cards that falsify or confirm vary between rules, the convention has been adopted of referring to the cards in the negations paradigm using the labels: true antecedent (TA), false antecedent (FA), true consequent (TC), and false consequent (FC). For example, for the *if ¬p, then ¬q* rule, TA is the ¬p card, FA is the p card, TC is the ¬q card, and FC is the q card.

Meta-analysis and model fits

Just as for the conditional-inference task, Oaksford and Chater (1994b; see also: Oaksford 2002a) argued the effects in the negations paradigm can be rationally explained on the assumption that negations define higher probability contrast classes (Oaksford and Stenning 1992). Recently, Oaksford and Chater (2003e) fitted the information-gain model to Oaksford and Chater's (1994b) meta-analysis of results on the negations paradigm selection task. The fits when the model was fitted on a rule by rule basis are shown in Fig. 6.3. Across 24 rules, the model could not be rejected (G^2 (48) = 62.69, $p > 0.05$). They also fitted a mental models account of these results and found very similar fits. However, as Oaksford and Chater (2003e) argued, the information-gain model explains why people behave as they do. In their normal environment where properties are rare, selecting confirming evidence is more likely to be informative. People are also sensitive to the fact that negations define higher probability contrast sets, which alters the probabilities of the antecedent and consequent. According to this viewpoint, whatever the conditional in the negations paradigm people are always looking for the rare evidence, i.e. the p and q cards.

The $if \neg p$, then q rule is anomalous. The reason is that, if the contrast set account of negation is correct, then the set of things that are $\neg p$, e.g. non-white cars, is far larger than the set of things that are q, e.g. Fords. Consequently, a hypothesis like 'all non-white cars are Fords' is known at the

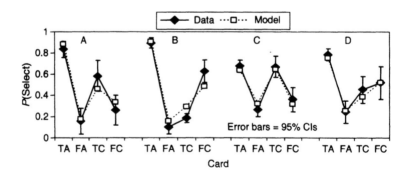

Fig. 6.3 The results of Oaksford and Chater's (1994b) meta-analysis of the negations paradigm selection task for each rule: if p then q (panel A); if p then $\neg q$ (panel B); if $\neg p$ then q (panel C); and if $\neg p$ then $\neg q$ (panel D) shoing the fit of the optimal data selection model. CI = confidence interval.

outset to be false because of people's experience of non-white Nissans, BMWs, Peugeots, and so on (Oaksford 1998, 2002a; Oaksford and Chater 1994b). In the model fits, the best-fit parameter values for this rule were similar to the *if p, then q* rule. As in Chapter 5, we adopt the convention that rules are described using ordered pairs $<P(p), P(q)>$ so that, for example, 'LH' means a low-probability antecedent and high-probability consequent rule. So, in the selection task, the HL rule appears to be treated like an LL rule. We have argued that people tend to revise the probability of the antecedent, $P(p)$, down for the HL rule (Oaksford and Chater 1994b, 1998a). Later on, we discuss some empirical evidence (Oaksford and Wakefield 2003) that suggests that we were mistaken and that people seem to compensate for this rule by revising down $P(q|p)$. However, for the purpose of fitting the model to the data, we keep $P(q|p)$ fixed at 0.9, as for the other rules, because not doing so would amount to introducing a further free parameter.

Contrast classes or matching?

Recently, Yama (2001) pitted the matching bias explanation of the matching effect against the contrast class approach. He did this by using rules like, *if p, then q* and *if p, then ¬q*, where the *q* category was binary and related to the blood types, Rh+ and Rh–. People were told that one of these categories, Rh–, was rare. Therefore, by the contrast-class account, the rule, *if p, then ¬Rh+*, should lead to selecting the rare Rh– card but, according to matching, they should select the Rh+ card. In four experiments, the predictions of optimal data selection *and* matching were confirmed, although as Oaksford (2002a) argued, there was most support for optimal data selection.

In a recent experiment, Oaksford and Moussakowski (2004) repeated Yama's (2001) experiment 4, which provided most evidence for the matching account, but used a *natural sampling* method (which we introduce more fully later on in discussing Oaksford and Wakefield 2003) to convey the probability information. In this experiment, the detailed predictions of the optimal data selection and contrast-class account were strongly confirmed. The results of fitting the optimal data selection model to the data are shown in Fig. 6.4. Four rules were used in this experiment with Rh– introduced as a rare category. These are indexed in Table 6.1 to the panels in Fig. 6.4, where 'high' and 'low' probabilities refer to the probability of the true consequent case, e.g. for negative high, the probability of ¬Rh–, i.e. the probability of *Rh+* (Table 6.1).

According to optimal data selection there should be more false consequent (FC) selections for the the high rules (B and D) than for the low rules (A and C);

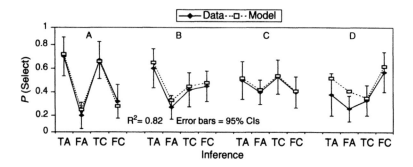

Fig. 6.4 The results of Oaksford and Moussakowski's (2004) experiment 2 for each rule identified in Table 6.1

and there should be more true consequent (TC) selections for the low rules than for the high rules. Both predictions were significantly confirmed (see Fig. 6.4). However, matching predicts that participants should make more FC selections for the negative rules (C and D), than for the affirmative rules (A and B); and that they should make more TC selections for affirmative rules, than for the negative rules. Neither effect was significantly in evidence in Oaksford and Moussakowski's (2004) results.

Manipulating probabilities

The main novel prediction of the information-gain model is that probability manipulations should affect selection task performance. Moreover, according to the contrast-class account (Oaksford and Stenning 1992), using high-probability categories in the antecedent and consequent should produce effects similar to varying negations.

Table 6.1 The Rules used Yama (2001) indexed to the panels in Fig. 6.4

(A)	Affirmative-low rule (AL):	*if p then Rh-*
(B)	Affirmative-high rule (AH):	*if p then Rh+*
(C)	Negative-low rule (NL):	*if p then ¬Rh+*
(D)	Negative-high rule (NH):	*if p then ¬Rh-*

Probabilities of fictional outcomes

Kirby (1994) developed a signal-detection model of the selection task that predicted that, as the probability of the antecedent, $P(p)$, increases, so the likelihood that participants select the $\neg q$ card also increases. In three experiments, Kirby had participants check whether a computer had made a mistake in generating cards with integers between 0 and a 1000 (or 0 and 100 in experiments 2 and 3) on one side and either a '+' or '−' on the other side. In experiment 1 they were told that the computer had an error rate of 0.01 ($P(q|p) = 0.99$), and in experiment 2, 0.1 ($P(q|p) = 0.9$). In experiment 1 the rules were: *if there is a 0 on one side, there is a + on the other side* (small P set condition), and *if there is a number between 1 and a 1000 on one side, there is a + on the other side* (large P set condition). If each number is equally probable, then when 0 is the antecedent, $P(p)$ is 1/1001; and when any number between 1 and 1000 is the antecedent $P(p)$ is 1000/1001. In his experiments 2 and 3, Kirby used three values, so that $P(p) =$ 1/100, 50/100, or 90/100. Kirby observed increases in $\neg q$, as $P(p)$ rose.

However, Kirby's model failed to predict the systematic changes in selections of the other cards that occurred in his data. As $P(p)$ was increased, $\neg p$ card selections increased and p card selections decreased (in experiment 1, there was some evidence that q card selections also decreased, but this was not replicated in experiments 2 and 3). The revised information-gain model can account for these results. In these experiments, only $P(p)$ was manipulated. However, it would violate the constraints on a probability model that the probability of q cannot be less than the joint probability of p and q, i.e. $P(q) > P(p)P(q|p)$. When $P(q|p)$ is high (as here, where it is 0.99 or 0.9), this means that, as $P(p)$, increases, so must $P(q)$. Figure 6.1 shows that therefore increasing $P(p)$ will increase the probability that the $\neg p$ and $\neg q$ cards will be selected and decreases the probability that the p and q cards will be selected. That is, the information-gain model is consistent with the observed pattern of effects. This is important because, according to Kirby's model, people try to detect falsifying, p and *not-q* instances. However, these instances are not available for the *not-p* or the q cards and so Kirby's model cannot explain why these cards are chosen.

As for the negations paradigm, we fitted the model to the data from each of the eight conditions in Kirby's experiments 1–3. In Kirby's experiment 1, there were two conditions: a small and large $P(p)$ condition. In his experiments 2 and 3, there were three conditions: a small, medium, and large $P(p)$ condition. For six out of the eight conditions, the model could not be rejected (mean G^2 (2) = 4.36 (SD = 1.29), $p > 0.10$). Across these six conditions the model could also not be rejected at the 1% level (G^2 (12) = 26.18). By experiment, the model could not be rejected for experiment 1 (G^2 (4) = 7.36, $p > 0.10$) or for experiment 3 (G^2 (6) = 14.26, $p > 0.02$). Both conditions for which the model could be rejected were in experiment 2, the medium and large conditions. In both cases the saturated model provided a significantly better fit to the data.

It would be premature to reject the information-gain model on the basis of these two failures to fit the data for several reasons. First, we report other results using probabilistic manipulations that reveal good fits. Second, later on we discuss the kind of probability manipulation that would be expected to move people away from their default rarity values. Moreover, we describe a recent experiment using an alternative and much more effective manipulation. Finally, only the information-gain model or other probabilistic accounts (see below) predict the observed pattern of effects in Kirby's data.

It is also important that the best-fit parameter values follow expectation, i.e. they are low when they should be low and high when they should be high. Generally this is the case when fitting the information-gain model. However, when probabilities are manipulated, the question arises as to the relationship between the manipulated probabilities (or 'given' probabilities) and the best-fit parameter values. What we have found in modelling Kirby's data, and in the other results we report in this section, is that this relationship follows Kahneman and Tversky's (1979) pi-function relating given probabilities to subjective probabilities. That is, people's subjective probabilities (best-fit values) over-estimate low, given probabilities, but underestimate high, given probabilities. We will not discuss this issue further in reporting the results of experiments manipulating probabilities. This is because later on we report the results of an experiment that seems to confirm that the subjective probabilities used to compute information gain do seem related to given probabilities as a p-function.

The reduced array selection task (RAST)

In the reduced array selection task (RAST), participants choose only between the q and *not-q* options (hence 'reduced array') and, moreover, they are given the opportunity to see the data. For example, they might be told that they must test the rule that *all the circles are black* by picking out shapes from two boxes, one labelled 'black shapes' and the other labelled 'white shapes.' Participants typically select shapes from both boxes but on average they select more shapes from the box containing white shapes. That is, far more falsificatory responding is observed (Johnson-Laird and Wason 1970; Wason and Green 1984). Oaksford and Chater (1994b) argued that this is because the RAST makes explicit that the rule applies to a limited domain of cards and participants are told that there are equal numbers of q and *not-q* instances. It follows that the probability of the consequent, $P(q)$, is 0.5, violating the rarity assumption. When rarity is violated the information gain of the *not-q* card is higher than the *q* card (Fig. 6.1), and hence the revised information-gain model predicts more *not-q* card selections than *q* card selections.

Oaksford *et al.* (1997) tested this explanation of the reduced array selection task by systematically varying the probability of the consequent, $P(q)$. They used stacks of cards depicting coloured shapes on one side, rather than boxes of coloured shapes. The numbers of cards in each stack was varied to achieve the probability manipulation. By varying these probabilities, Oaksford *et al.* (1997) showed that the proportions of *q* and *not-q* cards selected varied in accordance with the information-gain model, i.e. as $P(q)$ fell, *q* card selections rose and *not-q* card selections fell.

Figure 6.5 shows the results of Oaksford *et al.*'s (1997) experiment 1. As can be seen, trends for the *q* and the *not-q* cards as the probability of the consequent, $P(q)$, varied were in line with the predictions of the information-gain model. As $P(q)$ rose there was a significant increase in the proportion of *not-q* cards selected; and a significant decrease in the proportion of *q* cards selected.

A possible alternative explanation for these effects is that participants were selecting cards from the smallest stack or were selecting cards at random. In the low $P(q)$ condition, the smallest stack corresponded to the *q* card. In the high $P(q)$, the smallest stack corresponded to the *not-q* card. Consequently, a small stack bias could explain the pattern of selections in Oaksford *et al.*'s (1997) experiment 1. Oaksford *et al.* (1997, experiment 3) therefore repeated that experiment but now participants selected cards from equal-sized stacks of cards. This was achieved by having the experimenter deal ten cards from

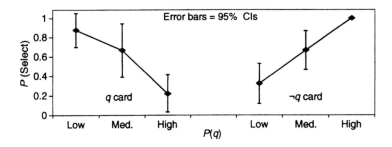

Fig. 6.5 The result of Oaksford *et al.*'s (1997) experiment 1 showing the probability of selecting the *q* and ¬*q* cards in the low, medium (Med.), and high *p*(*q*) conditions.

different-sized packs, so although the probability information was available, the stack sizes were the same. The results of this experiment replicated their experiment 1, confirming that the effects were indeed due to the probability manipulation.

Probabilities and the standard selection task

Oaksford et al. (1999) conducted a series of four experiments on the original four-card task, systematically varying the probabilities of the antecedent and consequent of the conditional rule. According to the information-gain model, if high- and low-probability categories are varied systematically between the antecedent and consequent, the high-probability categories should produce results very similar to negated terms in the negations paradigm (see 'The negations paradigm selection task'). This is exactly what they observed.

We fitted the revised information-gain model to each of Oaksford et al.'s (1999) experiments. In their experiments 1 and 2, participant's belief in the rule ($P(M_D)$), high or low) was also manipulated. In experiment 3, an 'effects' manipulation (high or low) was included. Cognitive 'effects' manipulations were proposed by Sperber et al. (1995) to overcome habitual responses in the selection task by emphasizing the falsificatory p, not-q cases. Given these additional manipulations, there were eight conditions in each of Oaksford et al.'s experiments 1 to 3. There were four in experiment 4. The model could not be rejected for any of the 28 conditions in these experiments (mean G^2 (2) = 3.15 (SD = 2.31), $p > 0.20$). To assess the model across all conditions, the four high-effect conditions in experiment 3 were removed because Oaksford et al. (1999) argued that these were better explained by other probabilistic models that make explicit appeal to utilities (see below). Overall, the model could also not be rejected (G^2 (48) = 65.45, $p > 0.02$). By experiment, the model could not be rejected for experiment 1 (G^2 (16) = 24.84, $p > 0.05$), for experiment 2 (G^2 (16) = 22.67, $p > 0.10$), for experiment 3 (G^2 (8) = 11.35, $p > 0.10$), or for experiment 4 (G^2 (8) = 6.69, $p > 0.20$). In sum, the model provided good fits to these data.

However, as Oaksford et al. (1999) concede, their attempts to manipulate probabilities were not entirely successful. Experiments 1 and 2 used real-world contents, e.g. *if a person is a politician, then they are privately educated*, that were pre-tested for probability of occurrence. This raised the possibility that these materials may cue other relevant prior knowledge. In experiment 1, although all the trends were in the right direction, the frequency of *not-q* card selections never exceeded that of *q* card selections. Oaksford et al. (1999) argued that this was because these materials did not provide a sufficiently powerful manipulation to overcome the default rarity assumption in data selection.

In experiment 2, the high-probability antecedent rules reversed roles. That is, the HL rule produced results like the HH rule and vice versa. Following other researchers in the area (Green and Over 1998; Green *et al.* 1997; Over and Jessop 1998), Oaksford *et al.* (1999) suggested that this might be because participants were comparing the dependence model against different foils, i.e. other than an independence model. To achieve the probability manipulation, they used rules such as, *if an MP is a Conservative, then s/he votes Labour in the General election*, which was an unbelievable, high-probability antecedent (high $P(p)$) and high-probability consequent (high $P(q)$) rule. The rule is unbelievable because it violates the strong belief that Conservative MPs vote anything but Labour in the general election. When Oaksford *et al.* (1999) used the opposite to the dependence model as a foil hypothesis, instead of the independence model (i.e. the dependency is between being a Conservative MP and *not* voting Labour), they found good fits to the data. It is the fit using this foil model in the revised information-gain account that we reported above. To avoid the effects of prior beliefs like this, Oaksford *et al.* (1999) used abstract material in their experiments 3 and 4 and found results much more in line with the probabilistic model.

Causal selection tasks

Further evidence consistent with the revised information-gain model has recently been presented by Green and Over (1997, 2000; see also: Over and Jessop 1998). Green and Over (1997) tested the Bayesian account of data selection by having participants test the causal relation, *if a person has Zav's disease, then they have a raised temperature*. They would be asked, for example, 'how many out of a 100 patients already diagnosed with Zav's disease do you want to take the temperature of?' (*p* card selections). This manipulation provided data for the first time on within-participant selection tendencies. According to mental models (Johnson-Laird and Byrne 1991) only four selection patterns are possible. Recall that if models for the conditional or bi-conditional interpretation are not fleshed out, then participants must select either only the *p* card or the *p* and the *q* cards, respectively. If these models are fleshed out, then on the conditional interpretation participants should select the *p* and the *not-q* cards and on the bi-conditional interpretation they should select all four cards. None of these interpretations are consistent with Green and Over's (1997) results. Around 70% of participants wanted to examine some of all four classes of patient but wanted to see more patients that corresponded to the *p* and *q* cards than to the *not-p* and *not-q* cards. As Green and Over (1997) observe, this finding is only consistent with Bayesian probabilistic accounts like information gain.

Green and Over's (1997) response procedure allows participants to reveal the underlying probabilistic basis of their selection decisions. These are continuous data and so we cannot really model them in the same way as we have until now. However, we can think of each participant's response to each card, i.e. 'x out of a hundred', as a response frequency as if they had experienced a hundred trials. This of course vastly inflates the value of N, the number of responses, which increases the probability of a poor fit (Read and Cressie 1980). Nonetheless, when fitted to Green and Over's (1997) experiment 1 (mild condition data, see below), the revised information-gain model could not be rejected at the 1% level (G^2 (2) = 7.61, $p > 0.02$). If people are generating an analogue of the probabilities calculated in the revised information-gain model, then it is straightforward to convert these to frequencies of patients they wish to look at. It is much harder to envisage how a consistent logical interpretation of the conditional, as embodied in mental logic and mental models theory, could account for these within-participant preferences.

Green and Over (1997) also manipulated the utility of finding out whether a raised temperature is diagnostic of Zav's disease by providing information about whether the disease is life-threatening (serious condition) or not (mild condition). The information-gain model does not incorporate utilities, so we do not attempt to model this manipulation.

Green and Over (2000) used a very similar scenario to Green and Over (1997), but with cholera as the disease. However, participants were only asked whether they wanted to see, for example, 'villagers already diagnosed as having cholera' (p card) rather than how many they wanted to see. Consequently the task yielded binary response data as in the standard selection task. The rule used was, *if you drink from the well, then you will get cholera*. The main experimental manipulation involved telling participants that either *most* villagers have cholera and *most* drink from the well, which corresponds to a high-probability antecedent (high $P(p)$) and high-probability consequent (high $P(q)$) condition; or that *few* villagers have cholera and *few* drink from the well, which corresponds to a low $P(p)$ and low $P(q)$ condition. The fit of the information-gain model to Green and Over's data (category condition) was very good: in the *few* condition (G^2 (2) = 0.88, $p > 0.20$) and in the *most* condition (G^2 (2) = 0.14, $p > 0.20$). In the *few* condition $P(p) = 0.42$ and $P(q) = 0.40$ and in the *most* condition $P(p) = 0.61$ and $P(q) = 0.59$. In both cases $P(p) \approx P(q)$. According to our model this entails that participants were treating the dependence model as a bi-conditional (i.e. most of the probability is located in the *p,q* and the *not-p, not-q* cells, indeed if $P(p) = P(q)$ and $P(q|p) = 1$, then all the probability is located in these two cells). That is, they were testing a model in which drinking well water was both necessary and sufficient for catching cholera. This may be a typical feature of causal selection tasks, where the rule describes a putative causal regularity.

The results reported in this section seem to support the view that, '... no account of the selection task is sufficiently general if it cannot take account of the set size of p and the set size of q or the probability judgements which reflect these' (Green and Over 2000, p. 66). That is, any explanation of the selection task must take a probabilistic approach as embodied in the information-gain model. However, there have been some apparent failures to replicate these probabilistic effects.

Probabilities or coherence bias?

Oberauer et al. (1999) carried out three experiments that they argue all failed to replicate the effects we reviewed above. These findings led them to the conclusion that, 'optimal data selection does not explain the selection task' (Oberauer et al. 1999, p. 141). It is of course always difficult to interpret such failures to replicate. However, in this case the failure was only partial. In their experiment 1, they found trends that were consistent with optimal data selection. Oberauer et al.'s main argument hinges on the poor fits they obtained using the values of $P(p)$ and $P(q)$ that participants were given experimentally. However, as we mentioned earlier in 'Probabilities of fictional outcomes', it is unlikely that experimental manipulations will affect people's subjective probabilities so directly (see also: Evans and Over 1996b; Hattori, 2002; McKenzie and Mikkelsen 2000, McKenzie et al., 2001).

We therefore fitted the model to the data from Oberauer et al.'s (1999) experiment 1 as in this chapter: by seeking the parameter values that provided the best fit. The fit of the model to the data was comparable to, if not better than, the fits we have already reported (mean $G^2 (2) = 0.84, p > 0.20$), across all four conditions ($G^2 (8) = 3.38, p > 0.20$). Moreover, when the parameters were supposed to be high (mean = 0.44, SD = 0.02) they were higher than when they were supposed to be low (mean = 0.28, SD = 0.12), $t (5) = 2.88, p < 0.025$. Consequently, contrary to Oberauer et al., the revised information-gain model can provide very good fits to their data.

How do Oberauer et al. explain the results of their experiment 1, which as we have shown would appear to provide good evidence for the information-gain model? They suggest that the categories they used, e.g. numbers between 1 and 10 or between 10 and 1000, lack *coherence* in that they do not all share some common property. Oberauer et al. therefore suggest that lacking such a coherent basis, a more coherent category will be one with fewer members. They then argue that people are demonstrating a *coherence bias*, i.e. they are selecting the cards that correspond to a lower prior probability. They argue that if coherence is restored, then the putative probability effects observed in their experiment 1 should disappear. They achieved this manipulation by using categories such as vowel and consonant in their experiment 2 and A (or B) and 1 (or 2) in their experiment 3. Probabilities were manipulated by indicating that a certain number of cards had vowels or As, etc., on them. Neither experiment revealed any effects of the probability manipulation.

However, Oaksford *et al.* (1999) used coherent real-world categories in their experiments 1 and 2, and coherent abstract materials in their experiment 4, and observed many of the probabilistic effects predicted by optimal data selection accounts. Consequently, coherence bias is unlikely to be the explanation of Oberauer *et al.*'s experiment 1 results. Moreover, there is a factor that was present in Oberauer *et al.*'s experiments 2 and 3 that was not present in their experiment 1 or in Oaksford *et al.*'s experiments. These experiments involved two sample-selection phases. First, participants were given probability information about a large pack of cards (1000) from which they were told a smaller sample was selected at random (50 or 52). Second, the four selection task cards were then drawn from this smaller sample. Consequently, for this manipulation to work, it must be assumed that participants treated the smaller random sample as *representative* of the larger pack of cards from which it was drawn. However, participants' understanding of the probability manipulation was only assessed with respect to the larger pack and not the smaller sample. Therefore, there is no evidence that Oberauer *et al.*'s participants treated the smaller sample as representative of the larger pack. Indeed to preserve the known probability distribution of the larger pack in the sample, representative as opposed to random sampling is required. Because of the distribution in the larger packs, in Oberauer *et al.*'s experiments 2 and 3, it was possible for $P(p)$ and $P(q)$ (in the sample), to take on any value between 0 and 1. Given this uncertainty, we suggest that people have simply made the default rarity assumption for all four rules. This hypothesis has been tested recently by Oaksford and Wakefield (2003), who used a natural sampling paradigm to manipulate probabilities.

Probabilities and natural sampling

Oaksford and Wakefield (2003) used the same materials as in Oberauer *et al.*'s (1999) experiment 3, but without the second sample-selection phase. The main purpose of this experiment was to test two hypotheses. First, they argued that providing probability information via 'natural sampling'

(Gigerenzer and Hoffrage 1995) should lead to a stronger manipulation. According to Gigerenzer and Hoffrage (1995), manipulating probability information experimentally is best achieved by manipulations that simulate the way people normally acquire this information in their natural environment, i.e. by experiencing instances one at a time. For example, people presumably estimate the probability of a bird being black, at least partly based on their observations of many individual birds and storing information about sample size and the number of black birds (although frequency estimates may also rely on background knowledge). Such 'natural sampling' was implemented in Oaksford and Wakefield's experiment by showing participants 40 cards, one at a time. The proportion of *p*, *not-p*, *q*, and *not-q* cards reflected the probability information participants were given before performing the selection task. Second, Oaksford and Wakefield (2003) argued that obtaining probability estimates from participants indirectly should more accurately reflect the values they use in data selection. Therefore, after the selection task, participants were asked to classify 50 cards 'drawn' from the pack into the four possible card types: *p* and *q*, *p* and *not-q*, *not-p* and *q*, and *not-p* and *not-q*. The proportions of each card type provided estimates of the four cells in the joint probability distribution for *p* and *q*, from which all the parameters of the model could be calculated.

The results (see Fig. 6.6) showed all the probability effects predicted by the information-gain model. This was impressive given that the materials were identical to those used by Oberauer *et al.* (1999) who failed to find any effects of manipulating probabilities. There were also some other interesting effects observed. First, the indirect estimates of the parameters of the model overestimated the low probabilities and underestimated the high probabilities given in the experimental set up. This directly mirrors a pi-function relating the experimentally given probabilities and the best-fit estimates (see 'Probabilities of fictional outcomes'). Importantly the best-fit parameter values were higher when they were predicted to be high than when they were predicted to be low, t (6) = 5.10, $p < 0.0025$, and they were highly significantly correlated with the given probabilities, r (6) = 0.89, $p < 0.005$.

Second, when the indirect estimates of the parameter values were weighted for prior knowledge of rarity (by averaging with the indirect estimates for the LL rule), they provided good fits to the data. Oaksford and Wakefield (2003) also showed that the information-gain model provided better fits than a *post hoc* model of probability effects proposed by Oberauer *et al.* to explain the results of their experiment 1. That is, contrary to Oberauer *et al.* (1999), experimentally derived values of the parameters of the information-gain

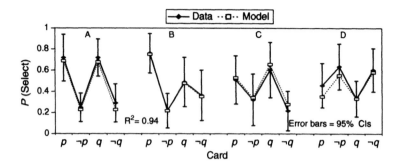

Fig. 6.6 The results of Oaksford and Wakefield's (2003) experiment for the Low $P(p)$, Low $P(q)$ condition (panel A); the Low $P(p)$, High $P(q)$ condition (panel B); the High $P(p)$, Low $P(q)$ condition (panel C); and the High $P(q)$, High $P(p)$ condition. CI = confidence interval.

model can show good fits to the data. However, indirect estimates (reflecting a pi-function) corrected for the effects of prior knowledge must be used. Consequently, contrary to Oberauer *et al.*'s conclusion, optimal data selection does explain the selection task.

Alternative probabilistic models

There are now a variety of other probabilistic accounts of the selection task (Evans and Over 1996a, b; Klauer 1999; Nickerson 1996; Over and Evans 1994, Over and Jessop 1998). Oaksford *et al.* (1999) reviewed these accounts, which can all be encompassed within the optimal experimental design approach (Berger 1985; Fedorov 1972) and consequently they all share the basic underlying structure of the information-gain model. The main theoretical difference is how each model formalizes the notion of informativeness. The critical difference concerns whether a 'disinterested observer' or a 'decision-theoretic' approach is taken to inquiry (Chater and Oaksford 1999a; Chater *et al.* 1998). On the disinterested observer approach (Nickerson 1996; Oaksford and Chater 1994b), it is assumed that participants are not biased towards any particular type of evidence by their current goals. Consequently their data-selection behaviour is influenced only by the relevant probabilities. On the other hand, someone might be seeking evidence that, for example, drinking water from the well makes you ill. With this goal in mind they will place greater value on finding evidence of someone being ill after drinking the well water. This is because the costs of erroneously rejecting this hypothesis are very great: many people will continue to get ill. This is an example of a decision-theoretic approach (Evans and Over 1996a, b; Klauer 1999; Over and Evans 1994; Over and Jessop 1998). People are inquiring into their world with a particular decision problem in mind: should you drink the well water or not? The important costs and benefits relate to accepting or rejecting a hypothesis, i.e. the Type I and Type II errors in standard hypothesis testing.

These other models point to a convergence of opinion that a probabilistic approach is the right way to explain the indicative and the causal selection task. However, there is a clear disagreement about whether a disinterested or decision-theoretic framework should be adopted. We think that each is equally valid, but that care must be taken about when each should be applied. It seems to us that, unless the experimental set up can provide clear-cut utilities for making Type I or Type II errors, a disinterested approach is clearly more appropriate. For example, Oaksford et al. (1999) argued that Sperber et al.'s (1995) 'effects' manipulation can be explained better by decision-theoretic approaches, such as Evans and Over (1996a) and Klauer (1999). The effects manipulation involved making the p, not-q instance salient by creating a context where it indicates a fault, e.g. a machine that is supposed to be printing cards such that, *if there is a circle, then the card is blue*, starts printing red circles. This manipulation can be regarded as raising the costs of failing to reject a hypothesis when it is false (i.e. failing to detect a fault). A decision-theoretic perspective may also be more appropriate to explaining some of the results of Green and Over (1997), who also manipulated the seriousness of an illness and thereby the costs associated with failing to detect the illness. Moreover, as we will see, Oaksford and Chater (1994b) also suggested that a decision-theoretic account was most appropriate to explain the results on *deontic* selection tasks, where the rule is about what one must and must not do (see 'The deontic-selection task'). Nonetheless, in most selection-task experiments that use abstract material or use contentful indicative rules without a context introducing explicit utilities, a disinterested model seems more appropriate.

However, these approaches are often represented as in competition rather than as complementary (Evans 1999; Evans and Over 1996a; Green 2000; Klauer 1999). That is, it is argued that the decision-theoretic approach should be seen as an alternative, and descriptively more adequate, way of explaining the data. The key empirical issue concerns the effect of believability where the disinterested and decision-theoretic approaches diverge. Whereas the decision-theoretic approach predicts that if people disbelieve the rule they should select more *not-q* cards than *q* cards, disinterested approaches predict no effect of believability. Klauer cites several studies that seem to show results consistent with the decision-theoretic approach (Fiedler and Hertel 1994; Love and Kessler 1995; Pollard and Evans 1983). However, Chater and Oaksford (1999a) argued that in all these studies, only exceptions were manipulated, i.e. the incidence of *p, not-q* instances, and not believability *per se*. As they point out, it is possible to believe a rule strongly that has many exceptions. For example, many people believe quite strongly that allowing children to walk home from school increases their chance of being abducted, although the probability of being abducted while walking home from school is tiny. That is, the probability of exceptions and the degree of belief in a rule can be independent.

Only two studies have explicitly manipulated believability in the selection task: Green and Over (1997) and Oaksford *et al.* (1999). In their experiment 2, Green and Over found that an almost identical proportion of participants turned the *not-q* card in the believed true (55.3%) and in the believed false (54.9%) conditions. Similar results were obtained in Oaksford *et al.'s* (1999) experiment 1 (high-belief condition: 29.7% *not-q* card selections; low-belief condition: 25%) and experiment 2 (high-belief condition: 33.1%; low-belief condition: 33.4%). Consequently, it seems that the best interpretation of these models is that they apply in different situations. The challenge for proponents of the decision-theoretic approach is to demonstrate believability effects in contexts where the utilities are well-defined.

Recently, Nelson (2005) has tested a variety of putative data selection norms that have been appealed to in the psychological literature, including Bayesian diagnosticity (Evans and Over 1996a; McKenzie and Mikkelsen, in press), information gain (mutual information) (Oaksford and Chater 1994b, 1996, 2003e; Hattori 2002), Kullback–Liebler distance (Klauer 1999; Oaksford and Chater 1996), probability gain (error minimization) (Baron 1981, 1985), and impact (absolute change) (Nickerson 1996). He used a combination of computer simulation and experiment to assess the theoretical and empirical adequacy of these norms. First, he showed that they disagree on the best data to select under certain circumstances. For example, diagnosticity differs from all the other sampling norms when the probabilities of evidence are very low and so diagnosticity approaches infinity. Nelson then took a range of cases where the norms differ on the ordering in the informativeness of data and conducted an experiment to see what order people would adopt. He found the strongest correlations with information gain (0.78) and probability gain (0.69), which is the same as impact (Nickerson 1996). Correlations with diagnosticity (–0.22) and log diagnosticity (–0.41) were actually *negative*, strongly contradicting the view that people's data-selection behaviour can be modelled using these norms, *pace*, e.g. Evans and Over (1996a). The agreement between information gain and impact mirrored Oaksford *et al.'s* (1999) experimental results on the selection task, which failed to discriminate between these measures, while being able to reject the alternative measures proposed by Evans and Over (1996a) and Klauer (1999).

We have now seen that the information-gain model seems to account for the existing data better than other theoretical proposals. It also appears to be well-supported by data confirming its novel predictions. It is also accounts well for data with which it has been argued to be inconsistent. Finally, as we have just seen, it provides better explanations than closely related probabilistic theories. In the next section, we show how a probabilisitic or decision-theoretic approach can be extended to the deontic-selection task.

The deontic-selection task

In the deontic-selection task participants might be told that their job is to enforce the regulation that, *if someone is allowed to enter the country (p), then they must be inoculated against cholera (q)* (Cheng and Holyoak 1985). They are presented with four cards and told that each card describes whether a specific person is allowed to enter on one side, and their inoculations on the other. Four cards are presented showing, for example, *enter (p* card), *denied (not-p* card), *inoculated against cholera (q* card), and *not inoculated against cholera (not-q* card) (in the actual experiment, for the *q* cards participants saw a list of inoculations including cholera, *q* card, or not including cholera, *not-q* card). Participants' task was to indicate which cards must be turned over to determine if the person is cheating or violating the rule. Participants predominantly select the *p* and the *not-q* cards, which is the correct selection to identify cheaters but is also the logical response. This contrasts with standard abstract versions of this task, where as few as 4% of participants make this response (Johnson Laird and Wason 1970).

These deontic rules can also be reversed: *if you have an inoculation against cholera (p), then you may be allowed to enter the country (q)*. With respect to this rule, a cheater is a *not-p, q* instance, i.e. as before, a cheater is a person who enters the country without being inoculated against cholera. Cosmides (1989) showed that people do make the *not-p, q* response for these reversed problems. This switch in the pattern of card selections would not appear to be predictable from a purely logical interpretation of the conditional. Moreover, a similar switch can be achieved by another manipulation.

Manktelow and Over (1991) showed that the perspective participants adopt, can also affect responses. When acting as the enforcer of a regulation, participants are concerned to detect cheaters who are trying to take the benefit without meeting the requirement (the *enforcer's* perspective). However, someone trying to enter the country will have different concerns (the *actor's* perspective). They will feel cheated if, although they have an inoculation against cholera, they are still denied entry into the country. From this new perspective, with respect to the original regulation, people will pick the card showing *denied* (*not-p*) and the card with *cholera* on it (*q*). With respect to the reversed rule they will pick the card showing *denied* (*not-q*) and the card with *cholera* on it (*p*). Notice that in both perspectives people are looking for the cases where someone is being cheated. However, what counts as a cheater and who is doing the cheating, switches between perspectives.

A decision-theoretic model

In this section we outline a simplified version of the model of the deontic-selection task presented in Oaksford and Chater (1994b), that can account for the same range of effects and which was used recently by Perham and Oaksford (2005). Oaksford and Chater (1994b) argued that the deontic-selection task required re-focusing their existing probabilistic model away from rule-*testing* and on to rule-*use*. In modelling rule testing, the probability model, defined by the dependence and independence matrices, was used to calculate expected information gain. In modelling rule use, these probability models were used to calculate expected utilities and it was argued that participants use the rules to maximize expected utility. However, in modelling rule use, there is no need to include an independence model. In Oaksford and Chater (1994b), it was included to provide an indication of the probability that someone is disobeying the rule. That is, the probability that they were a *p*, *not-q* case, assuming either, an obligation rule and the enforcer's perspective, or a permission rule and the actor's perspective. In the dependence model, $P(p, not\text{-}q) = 0$, whereas in the independence model $P(p, not\text{-}q) = P(p).P(not\text{-}q)$. Hence, the higher $P(M_I)$, the higher the probability of an exception. Consequently, in modelling the deontic task, $P(M_I)$ no longer indicated how likely two alternative hypotheses about the world were to be true, but simply how likely an exception to the rule (assumed to be in force) was to be found. However, with the assumption that $P(q|p)$ could be less than 1 in the dependence model, this expedient is no longer required. We simply model the probabilistic component with the dependence model.

This modification is consistent with the contention that, in the deontic-selection task, people are *using* the rule and are not *testing* it. As in the conditional inference paradigm (see Chapter 5), the truth or falsity of the rule is not in question. Indeed, as Manktelow and Over (1987) observed, it makes no sense to ask whether a deontic rule is true or false. It may or may not be in force, but no number of counter-examples stops it being in force. For example, however many times someone jumps a red light, the law that they should not do so is still in force. This means that the deontic task bears more relation to the conditional-inference task than the abstract-selection task. People use the rule to predict what might be on the other side of a card, but need not compare these predictions to an alternative hypothesis about the disposition of information on the card sides. Consequently, as in the conditional-inference paradigm, we only require the probabilistic model of the rule given in the dependence model.

To calculate the expected utilities associated with acts of detecting cheaters by turning over cards requires specifying the utilities associated with the four possible combinations, i.e. $U(p, q)$, $U(p, \neg q)$, $U(\neg p, q)$, and $U(\neg p, \neg q)$. The expected utilities for each card are then calculated as follows:

$$
\begin{aligned}
EU(p) &= U(p,q)P(q\,|\,p) + U(p,\neg q)P(\neg q\,|\,p) \\
EU(\neg p) &= U(\neg p,q)P(q\,|\,\neg p) + U(\neg p,\neg q)P(\neg q\,|\,\neg p) \\
EU(q) &= U(p,q)P(p\,|\,q) + U(p,\neg q)P(\neg p\,|\,q) \\
EU(\neg q) &= U(p,\neg q)P(p\,|\,\neg q) + U(\neg p,\neg q)P(\neg p\,|\,\neg q).
\end{aligned}
\tag{6.9}
$$

Consider the original rule that, *if someone is allowed to enter the country (p), then they must be inoculated against cholera (q)*, from the enforcer's perspective. Here a cheater is a $p, \neg q$ case and so a benefit, i.e. a high, positive utility, would be assigned to $U(p, \neg q)$. Any other outcome is assigned a cost, i.e. a small, negative utility, as from this perspective these cases do not satisfy the goal of detecting teachers. It is relatively straightforward to see that because benefits, i.e. $U(p, \neg q)$, only arise in calculating the expected utility for the p and the $\neg q$ cards in the equations in 6.8, only these cards can have a positive expected utility. Consequently, if participants are maximizing expected utility, then these are the only two with a chance of being selected. If some participants take the actor's perspective, then a cheater will be defined by the $\neg p, q$ case and so a benefit, i.e. a high, positive utility, would be assigned to $U(\neg p, q)$ rather than to $U(p, \neg q)$. Maximizing expected utility would now be associated with selecting the $\neg p$ and q cards, thus explaining perspective shifts. Obviously, the precise fits to the data depends on the relative values of the utilities assigned and the conditional probabilities (all of which can be calculated from the standard set of parameters, $P(p)$, $P(q)$, and $P(q|p)$).

When modelling the standard selection task, Oaksford and Chater (1994b) exploited the rarity assumption, i.e. the probabilities of the antecedent, $P(p)$, and of the consequent, $P(q)$, were both low. However, they also argued that, for deontic rules, it is not reasonable to prejudge rarity (Oaksford and Chater 1994b).

This is because many deontic rules provide information that suggests that rarity need not be the default. For example, the cholera rule is usually used in the context of passengers disembarking from a plane. Clearly different assumptions about where the plane has come from, and whether it is going on to another destination, will lead to different estimates of the probability that someone will seek entry to the country. To model deontic effects, Oaksford and Chater (1994b) averaged expected utilities over the the joint distribution of $P(p)$ and $P(q)$.

Modelling Kirby (1994)

This model can explain the results of Kirby's (1994) experiment 4, where probabilities and utilities were both manipulated for an enforcer's perspective. Kirby varied the probability that someone may be breaking the under-age drinking law, *if you are drinking beer, you must be over 21*, by varying the ages of the cases presented on the cards. For example, a 19-year-old is more likely to be breaking the law than a 4-year-old. We model this manipulation by varying $P(q|p)$. As long as $P(p)$ and $P(q)$ remain fixed, $P(q|p)$ and $P(\neg q|\neg p)$ rise and fall together. So, the lower the probability that someone does not drink, given they are not over 21, the lower the probability that someone is over 21 years, given they drink. Consequently, to model the case where the card indicates that someone is 19 years old, the value of the $P(q|p)$ was lower than for someone who is 4 years old. Kirby also varied the utilities associated with detecting violators, either with instructions emphasizing the need not to upset customers (*do not check*) or the need not to miss potential violators (*do not miss*). With respect to a baseline condition (*baseline*), the *do not check* condition should increase the cost associated with turning a card; and the *do not miss* condition should increase the benefit associated with detecting a cheater. To model Kirby's (1994) results, we used the same utilities and probabilities as Oaksford and Chater (1994b). In the baseline condition, the cost = –0.1 and the benefit = 5. $P(q|p)$ was set to 0.6 for the 4-year-old, 0.5 for the 12-year-old, and 0.4 for the 19-year-old. For the *do not check* condition, the cost was increased to –0.5 and in the *do not miss* condition the benefit was increased to 6. The results are shown in Fig. 6.7, which plots the expected utility of a card on the x-axis against the results of Kirby's experiment 4, i.e. the probabilities of selecting the cards. As usual, we kept $P(p) = P(q) = 0.5$ throughout. However, the same general pattern of results is observed if we averaged over the whole parameter space defined by $P(p)$ and $P(q)$. Although we made no attempt to optimize the fit to the data, the product moment correlation was high, $r(16) = 0.97$, i.e. our simple model accounted for 94% of the variance in the results.

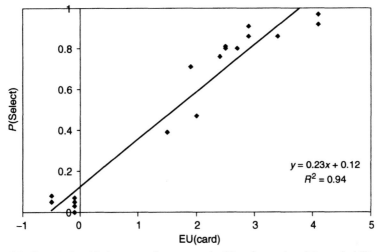

Fig. 6.7 The relationship between the expected utility of a card and its probability of being selected for Kirby's (1994) experiment 4.

Modelling Manktelow *et al.* (1995)

Like Kirby (1994), Manktelow *et al.* (1995) manipulated the probability of exceptions using the enforcer's perspective on an obligation rule. Unlike Kirby, they presented extra cards, not only for the *q* card (experiment 4) but also for the *p* card (experiment 1). They used the rule, *if you want to enter the country, then you must be inoculated against cholera*. The four cards represented different individuals trying to enter the country, with information about whether they were trying to enter or were in transit on one side, and information about their inoculations on the other side. To achieve the probability manipulation additional *p* (entering) or *not-q* cards (no inoculation against cholera) were presented, each of which also indicated whether the individual came from a European or a Tropical country. It was predicted that, because the probability of having cholera given an individual comes from a Tropical country is higher than the probability of having cholera given an individual comes from a European country, participants would select more *p* and *not-q* cards marked 'Tropical' than marked 'European.' This is what Manktelow *et al.* (1995) found in their experiments 1 and 4.

Manktelow *et al.*'s manipulation clearly involves varying $P(q|p)$. To model their data, we therefore kept the costs and benefits at the same baseline levels assumed above (cost = −0.1, benefit = 5). We then computed two sets of expected utilities for each card by averaging over the whole parameter space defined by $P(p)$ and $P(q)$ for two different levels of $P(q|p)$ corresponding to whether an individual came from a Tropical country ($P(q|p) = 0.2$) or a European country ($P(q|p) = 0.5$). In Manktelow *et al.*'s experiment 1, only p cards were marked Tropical or European, whereas in their experiment 4 only the q and the *not-q* cards were marked Tropical or European. This meant that in experiment 1, for example, although participants knew that individuals could come from either a Tropical or a European country, for the individuals represented by *not-q* cards, they did not know which. For experiment 4, they were in the same position with respect to the p card. We assumed that participants made a *worst case* assumption. That is, the *not-q* cases in experiment 1 and the p cases in experiment 4 represent individuals from a Tropical country. On this assumption, when a card is not marked for a Tropical or a European country, we assigned the expected utilities predicted for a Tropical country (see Fig. 6.8). Again, although we made no attempt to optimize the fit to the data, the product moment correlation was high, $r(9) = 0.98$, i.e. our simple model accounted for 96% of the variance in the results.

Emotions and deontic reasoning

More recently this decision-theoretic model of the deontic-selection task has been applied to situations where the emotional content of a deontic rule varies

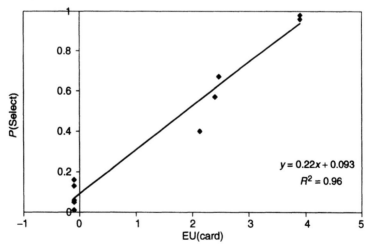

Fig. 6.8 The relationship between the expected utility of a card and its probability of being selected for Manktelow *et al.*'s (1995) experiments 1 and 4.

(Perham and Oaksford 2005). For example, participants could be given rules like, *if you are in pain, then you must stop working for a break* or *if you work for 90 minutes, then you must stop working for a break*. The former has the threatening word 'pain' in the antecedent. The reason for using material like this was to distinguish between the decision-theoretic account and the *evolutionary-psychology* account (e.g. Cosmides and Tooby 1997; Fiddick *et al.* 2000) of deontic reasoning. These rules relate to managing hazards, in this case avoiding pain or fatigue. Fiddick *et al.* (2000) point out that if your goal is manage this hazard, then you will be interested in detecting people who are in pain but are not taking a break, i.e. the $p, \neg q$ case. However, Perham and Oaksford (2005) observed that these rules could also be embedded in a situation where the reversed deontic response is predicted. So, if someone is told, not that they are managing a hazard, but rather that they are monitoring that workers are not cheating, then they will be interested in $\neg p, q$ cases, i.e. people who are taking a break although they are not in pain.

By embedding a hazard-management rule in a situation that engages what Cosimides (1989) called a 'social contract', either of these two response patterns may be observed. This is because according to the evolutionary-psychology account, there are domain-specific innate modules for each type of reasoning, i.e. social-contract reasoning or hazard-management reasoning. Which response is made will depend on which module is most activated. Given a reasonably rich context defining the social-contract situation, one might expect more $\neg p, q$ responses than $p, \neg q$ responses. This should also be modulated by emotional content. According to Cosmides and Tooby (2000), threatening situations serve to activate the appropriate hazard-management module. So the rule containing the threatening word 'pain' should activate this module more than the other rule. Consequently there should be more $p, \neg q$ hazard management responses for the threat rule.

The decision-theoretic account makes the opposite prediction. On this account, when a hazard-management rule is embedded in a social contract, there is potentially a benefit associated with detecting both cheaters, $\neg p, q$, and people at risk, $p, \neg q$, i.e. $U(p, \neg q) = B_H$ and $U(p, \neg q) = B_S$. The other two cases will be associated with costs. People's acts of detection also bring about a *state of the world* that people may find threatening. People have an innate fear reaction to threatening stimuli like spiders, snakes, or blood (Davidson 1993; Mineka and Oehman 2002; Oehman and Mineka 2001). Such stimuli invoke an avoidance response (Davidson 1993). Such a fear and flight response may also be innate, as it made adaptive sense in our ancestral environment (Mineka and Oehman 2002; Oehman and Mineka 2001). Given the work-injury rule, the threatening stimuli 'pain' (p) may be found for either of the states of the world described by p, q or p, *not-q*. In calculating *generalized expected utility* (Zeelenberg *et al.* 2000), a *regret* term is subtracted from the expected utility of the act of detection, if a state of the world is anticipated that leads to a negative emotion such as fear. Consequently, the cost associated with the p, q case should increase and/or the benefit, B_H, associated with the p, $\neg q$ case should decrease. The upshot will be that rather than increases in selections of the p and the $\neg q$ cards, there should be decreases because, assuming the probabilities remain constant, their expected utilities will fall.

Perham and Oaksford (2005) tested these predictions using several sets of materials. They assessed participants' performance using the Pollard Index (Pollard and Evans 1987), computed as $(\neg p + q) - (p + \neg q)$, where 1 is assigned if the corresponding card is turned and 0 if it is not. If a participant makes a pure social-contract response they score 2 and if they make a pure hazard-management response they score –2. According to the evolutionary-psychology account, this index should be lower in the threat condition, whereas the decision-theoretic model makes the opposite prediction. Consistent with decision theory, in two experiments the Pollard index was higher for the threat rule (i.e. 'pain' in the antecedent) than for the no-threat rule (see Fig. 6.9). This prediction is not made by any other theory of deontic reasoning (Perham and Oaksford 2005).

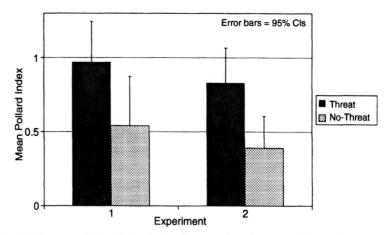

Fig. 6.9 The mean Pollard index in the threat and no-threat conditions of Perham and Oaksford's (2005) experiments 1 and 2. CI = confidence interval of the data.

Falsifications of the information-gain model?

We now review some results on data selection that have been claimed to be inconsistent with the information-gain model. Most of these results involve 'facilitating' the logical response without manipulating probabilities.

Group reasoning

In a single experiment, Moshman and Geil (1998) showed that solving the selection task in groups leads to higher rates of the falsificiation p, $\neg q$ solution. This result is very interesting but stands in need of replication and further study. An aspect of the results that is interesting is that in nearly all groups at least one person initially chose the $\neg q$ card. Consequently there was always someone who needed to account for why they had done this. The question is what changes peoples' minds? One answer is that they develop true logical insight into the falsificationist nature of hypothesis testing (Moshman and Geil 1998). As we have argued elsewhere (Oaksford and Chater 1994b), since it is philosophically debatable whether hypothesis testing is best regarded as logical (e.g. Howson and Urbach 1993), this is a dubious argument. It seems more likely that people come to adopt an interpretation of the rule in which p, $\neg q$ instances definitely make the rule false and where prior knowledge is irrelevant. The former happens even in our probabilistic model when $P(q|p) = 1$. The latter occurs when people realize that the rule applies only to the four cards. Under this interpretation, prior knowledge, which affects the probabilities of the antecedent and consequent, is irrelevant. What would be interesting is to probe the participants' understanding of the rule before and after the group discussion, in addition to indexing such changes simply on the basis of changes in responses patterns on the selection task.

Getting the right interpretation

Gebauer and Laming (1997; see also: Osman and Laming 2001) argue that performance in their experiments was logical when participants' interpretations of the task rule were taken into account. In their experiment 1, although most participants failed to give the logical response, it seemed that this was because they misinterpreted the rule. For example, 'one side … other side' may be conflated with 'front...back'. When these interpretations were taken into account, performance could be interpreted as logical. This interesting result is not consistent with the attempts to encourage a logical interpretation in the early literature on the selection task, which focused on exactly the same possible misinterpretations (Wason and Johnson-Laird 1970, 1972). These earlier attempts to remove these possible misinterpretations completely failed to improve performance. Neither Gebauer and Laming (1997) nor Osman and Laming, (2001) attempt to explain this apparent inconsistency.

Moreover, if they are right, then their findings do not only threaten probabilistic accounts. Gebauer and Laming argue that their misinterpretation account is consistent with formal rule theories and mental models. However, according to these accounts, the rules are not misinterpreted in the way that 'one side...other side' may be conflated with 'front...back'. Rather, the rules are interpreted as either conditionals or bi-conditionals *assuming the 'one side...other side' interpretation*. However, in mental models theory, people normally only represent part of the meaning of the original conditional, i.e. one line of the corresponding truth table. It is this *partial* interpretation that explains performance not any *mis*-interpretation of the rules. This is absolutely clear from the fact that this partial interpretation is taken to apply to all conditionals, whether they appear in selection tasks that introduce 'one side...other side' ambiguities, or not. Consequently, logicist accounts, like mental models and mental logic, are as much at risk if Gebauer and Laming (1997) are correct as probabilistic accounts. Thus, although at present we offer no explanation of these findings, it should be borne in mind that they potentially invalidate essentially all explanations of the selection task. Clearly, more research will be required before it will be possible to clarify the implications of these intriguing and puzzling results.

Facilitation without probabilities

Almor and Sloman (1996) presented evidence that certain conditional rules reliably produced the logical response, although probabilities were not manipulated. However, Oaksford and Chater (1996) argued that these rules fell into two categories, which meant that the information-gain model did not apply. First, some of the rules were analytic truths, e.g. 'if a large object is stored then a large container must be used', for which evidence is irrelevant. It is part of the meaning of 'large object' that if it is stored, a large container must be used. As this has to be true, there is no uncertainty to be reduced. Second, the remaining rules were deontic regulations, 'if a product gets a prestigious prize, then it must have a distinctive quality'. Oaksford and Chater (1994b) dealt with deontic regulations in a separate theory in which people were argued to maximize expected utility rather than information gain. Consequently, these apparent displays of logicality do not impugn the claim that when participants construe their task as selecting data to test a hypothesis, they choose cards that maximize information gain.

Varying the card array

Hardman (1998) introduced an interesting manipulation where certain cards were removed from the four-card array and substituted by an additional copy of one of the other cards. He argues that this manipulation should affect the predictions of the information-gain model because card choice is competitive, i.e. card informativeness is scaled by the total amount of information available (see equation 6.7). Thus, if a highly informative card, e.g. p, is replaced by an uninformative card, e.g. $\neg p$, then the informativeness of the two $\neg p$ cards should rise, as they now represent a greater proportion of the information available. Hardman presented three experiments using different replacement strategies and different rules, either a standard affirmative rule, *if,p then q*, or a negated consequent rule, *if p, then $\neg q$*. In each experiment he argues that his results are not consistent with the information-gain model. For example, suppose that the p card has an information gain of 0.45 bits, the q card 0.35 bits, the $\neg p$ card, 0.05 bits and the $\neg q$ card, 0.15 bits. Then, according to the scaling procedure with the standard $<p, \neg p, q, \neg q>$ card array, the scaled informativeness values would be unchanged at $<0.45, 0.05, 0.35, 0.15>$. But given the array $<\neg p, \neg p, \neg p, \neg q>$, the scaled informativeness values would be $<0.17, 0.17, 0.17, 0.50>$, which predicts that there should be considerable increases in $\neg p$ and $\neg q$ card selections compared to the standard array. Hardman did not observe these predicted changes in card selections. For example, in his experiment 3, although he observed the change for the $\neg q$ card in our example, he observed no similar changes for the $\neg p$ cards.

As Hardman (1998) observed, this problem does not arise if the information gains are not re-scaled according to equation 6.7. We originally scaled the information gain in this way by analogy to foraging models of food-patch selection (Myerson and Miezen 1980; Oaksford and Chater 1998a; Pirolli and Card 1999), where animals disperse their foraging activities between food patches depending on the total food available. Of course, before deciding how to disperse its time between patches, an animal must decide which patches it is worth dispersing its time between. Suppose this decision is made pair-wise by first comparing the amount of food in the largest patch with the next largest; if the ratio of the smaller to the larger patch is greater than 0.5, then forage at this smaller site as well, and so on. If we do this calculation, then for the standard card array the process will stop at the q card that is more than half as informative as the p card but is more than twice as informative as the $\neg q$ card. However, in the $<\neg p, \neg p, \neg p, \neg q>$ array, the $\neg q$ card is more than twice as informative as any individual $\neg p$ card, so the latter are not chosen which may explain Hardman's (1998) results. This process determines the number of cards selected before re-scaling to determine the strength of conviction that the card should be turned, as suggested by Chater and Oaksford (1999a).

Null effects

Another category of results claimed to be inconsistent with optimal data selection are those that have attempted to explicitly manipulate probabilities and failed to find effects (Feeney *et al.* 2002, 2003; Oberauer *et al.* 1999, 2004). The first observation to make is that these apparent failures to replicate have to confront the accumulated evidence, listed above, showing that probabilistic manipulations do affect data-selection performance on Wason's task. Against this background, it is difficult to interpret failures to replicate. None of these studies offer a critical experiment, where one theory makes one prediction and optimal data selection makes the opposite prediction. Rather they are all null results. A series of null results is convincing only to the extent that the researchers have tried hard to find the predicted effects by, for example, using many different ways of trying to produce the effect. However, these experiments either use one method several times (Handley *et al.* 2002) or one method with a large sample size (Oberauer *et al.* 1999, 2004). We now look at the work of Feeney and colleagues before turning to the work of Oberauer and colleagues.

Feeney and Handley's (2000) original experiment did not explicitly vary probabilities but introduced an alternative rule in to the selection task. This was the same as Byrne's (1989) suppression manipulation in the conditional-inference task. Byrne also used alternative rules, i.e. alternative ways of starting cars, e.g. *if the key is hot-wired it will start*. Feeney and Handley argued that this manipulation should suppress $\neg p$ and q card selections for the same reason it suppresses DA and AC inferences. Their account assumes that people are attempting to draw deductive inferences about what might be on the other side of these cards. Thus Feeney and Handley interpret their finding, that $\neg p$ and q card selections are reduced, as evidence for a deductive construal of the selection task. They also pointed out that this result does not seem consistent with Oaksford and Chater's (1994b) original model in which the $\neg p$ card was always uninformative. However, Oaksford (2002b) pointed out that a model using a contingency table as in table 5.18 (introduced by Oaksford *et al.* 2000), could explain this result because using this table $\neg p$ can be informative and this manipulation should increase the joint probability of $\neg p$ and q cases. Oaksford (2002b) therefore fitted the model to Feeney and Handley's (2000) results and found very good fits.

Handley *et al.* (2002) repeated these experiments and also manipulated $P(q)$. Feeney *et al.* (2003) also fitted the optimal data-selection model to these data and showed poor fits. However, by the same standards adopted in Oaksford and Chater (2003e), the model could not be rejected for 13 out of the 18 conditions in Handley *et al.* (2002). But when participants estimates of $P(q)$ were used rather than allowing this to be a free parameter, the model could be rejected for all 18 conditions.

Feeney and colleagues did not attempt to show that their own theory provided better fits to these data. This runs counter to the standard logic of model fitting: the idea is to do better than the competition. Our original model-fitting exercise responded to an explicit claim that optimal data selection could not explain Feeney and Handley's (2000) data, and showed that it could. However, advocates of alternative models need to show that such models provides better fits. In a proper comparison between models, Oaksford and Chater (2003e) have shown that the optimal data selection provided better fits to the standard results on the selection task than a parameterized version of the mental models theory which Feeney *et al.* (2003) endorse. Moreover, the parameters of that model are the probabilities that people adopt the various interpretations of the conditional predicted by the mental models theory. These parameters cannot be manipulated experimentally and hence it is difficult to see how direct parameter free model comparisons could be made.[1]

There is also recent evidence contradicting Feeney *et al.*'s main claim that their evidence supports deductive processing in the selection task (Lucas and Ball 2005). Feeney *et al.*'s explanation of reductions of, for example, $\neg p$ card selections is that when participants select this card, they assume a bi-conditional interpretation and infer there is $\neg q$ on the other side. So given the rule *if A, then 2*, participants who turn the *L* card infer that the hidden face is, for example, a 7. However, when told that it is also the case that, *if L, then 2*, then they tend not to turn this card because they now know that there is very likely to be a 2 on the other side, i.e. they now know that the presence of an A is not necessary for there to be a 2 on the other side. This explanation means that when people select this card, they do so because they contemplate that the hidden side should be a number that does not match the number in the rule, i.e. a number other than 2. However, using protocol analysis, Lucas and Ball (2005) found that for all selected cards, the hidden sides participants mention, match those stated in the rule. That is, rather than consider the 7 on the hidden face, as Feeney and Handly (2000; Feeney *et al.* 2003; Handley *et al.* 2002) predict, they consider the 2. Lucas and Ball (2005) observe that while this 'secondary matching' effect (Wason and Evans 1975) is inconsistent with Feeney and Handley (2000), it is consistent with the optimal data-selection model. This is because optimal data selection predicts that people should be seeking the rare cases that are always the matching cases. So this model explains the cases people actually consider on the hidden face as a rational consequence of seeking

---

[1] When alternative rules are considered it is also difficult to determine how to appropriately parameterize the mental models theory to derive quantitative fits. In these cases, mental models 'wins by vagueness'. That is, the representations it proposes are claimed to explain some qualitative feature of the evidence but it is impossible to quantitatively evaluate this claim.

the most informative data. In contrast, Feeney and Handley's theory of what is happening in their experiments seems to lack support.

In sum, there may be various factors at work in these experiments, but there is no demonstration that the theory invoked to explain them does a better job than optimal data selection. Moreover, the alternative theory's predictions for what people think may be on the other sides of the cards are inconsistent with Lucas and Ball's (2005) results. It would be premature to speculate further on what these experiments reveal about human reasoning, partly because some of the probability manipulations may not be sufficiently strong.

This latter concern was also raised by Oaksford and Wakefield (2003) about some experiments reported by Oberauer *et al.* (1999), which we have already discussed (see 'Probabilities or coherence bias' and 'Probabilities and natural sampling'). However, more recently, Oberauer *et al.* (2004) have carried out a 'comprehensive test' of the probabilistic approach, in which they tested predictions for conditional inference, the selection task, and syllogistic reasoning (see Chapter 7). Using a single probability manipulation, they failed to replicate the large number of findings showing probabilistic effects in the conditional-inference task and in the selection task that we have reviewed in this book. Again, given the number of results confirming probabilistic effects from a variety of labs around the world, for both conditional inference and the selection task, it is difficult to interpret a null result like Oberaruer *et al.*'s (2004). Importantly, it has been possible to provide good, close to parameter-free fits to the data (Oaksford and Wakefield 2003). However, researchers must use more indirect methods to obtain estimates of these parameters, by, for example, asking for estimates of joint probabilities (Over *et al.* 2005) or by the similar methods used in Oaksford and Moussakowski (2004) and Oaksford and Wakefield (2003).

Objections and replies

In the final section of this chapter, we consider the objections that have been raised to our probabilistic model of the selection task and reply to each one in turn. These objections all relate to the model of the standard task and not to the decision-theoretic model, which has been the focus of 'The deontic-selection task'.

Model fits

Laming (1996) argued that the original optimal data-selection model (Oaksford and Chater 1994b) was only able to provide ordinal fits to the data, i.e. we only modelled the rank order in participants' card selections. However, Oaksford and Chater (2003e) showed that the optimal data-selection model can provide excellent fits not only to the ordinal trend in the data but also to frequencies of card selections.

Information gain vs. other information measures

Some critics have been concerned that we narrowly focused our account on only one particular measure of information, Shannon–Wiener information (Shannon and Weaver 1949; Wiener 1948), although there are other possibilities (Evans and Over 1996a; Klauer 1999; Laming 1996; Oberauer *et al.* 1999). The review of other measures ('Alternative probabilistic models') showed a general feature of the optimal data-selection models. That is, although they all propose different measures of informativeness, given the rarity assumption, they all make similar predictions (with the exception of the believability predictions we discussed 'Alternative probabilistic models'). That is, given the rarity assumption, the optimal data-selection approach can quite robustly predict the main findings, even under changes of the particular information measure used.

Sequential sampling

Laming (1996) criticized the original model because a Bayesian account should involve sequential sampling, i.e. participants should turn the most informative card, revise their priors, re-assess the informativeness of the cards, pick the next most informative card, and so on. Of course this is not what happens in the selection task because participants never actually turn the cards over. The main point to make here (but see also: Oaksford and Chater 1998a) is that Klauer (1999) has modelled the selection task using both sequential and *non-sequential* Bayesian models. The predictions agreed with the information-gain model. Consequently, a non-sequential Bayesian account not only makes sense (see: Chater and Oaksford 1999a) but also makes similar predictions to a sequential account.

Alternative models

In Oaksford and Chater's (1994b, 2003e) specific application of optimal data selection, participants compare the rule, i.e. the dependence model, to an independence model. Various authors have criticized this choice on varying grounds (Green and Over 1997, 1998; Green *et al.* 1997; Laming 1996; Oberauer *et al.* 1999; Over and Jessop 1998). First, we have been criticized for proposing that participants are testing a particular dependence model against just the possibility that there is no dependency between p and q, rather than against every other possible dependency between p and q (Laming 1996; Oberauer *et al.* 1999). However, without any prior knowledge about other possible relationships between p and q, it seems psychologically plausible that the only alternative considered is no relationship. Moreover, the dependency between p and q that we always had in mind was *causal* sufficiency. In most recent models of causal judgement, the independence model is always the foil against which the presence of a causal dependency is assessed (e.g. Cheng and

Novick 1991, 1992). In these models, a causal dependency (however weak) is taken to exist between p and q if $P(q|p) > P(q)$ (positive causal relationship) or if $P(q|p) < P(q)$ (negative causal relationship). Thus, in attempting to construct a theory of data selection, the independence model seemed to be the most natural. The real question is the nature of the infinite number of possible causal dependencies that might exist between p and q. However, it turns out that the nature of the dependency between p and q, and the data one should select, are relatively independent. That is, variation in $P(q|p)$ has little effect on the data people should select. For example, it never affects the rank order of informativeness over the four cards when $P(p)$ and $P(q)$ are kept constant. Moreover, other prior knowledge constrains the relevant probabilities. First, the conditional statement *if p, then q* clearly suggests a positive, causal dependency, which indicates that $P(q|p)$ is high, which is why we set it to 0.9 in all the model fits we report. Second, causal sufficiency suggests that $P(q) > P(p)$. Finally, the rarity assumption indicates that $P(p)$ and $P(q)$ are low.

Second, other authors have pointed out that prior knowledge may suggest better foil models or indeed more than one such model (Green and Over 1997, 1998; Green *et al.* 1997; Over and Jessop 1998). The information-gain model can incorporate these possibilities. Indeed Oaksford *et al.* (1999) invoked just such an alternative foil in modelling the results of their experiment 2 (see 'Probabilities and the standard selection task'). Moreover, in contrast to the log–likelihood ratio (Evans and Over 1996a), the information gain measure can incorporate many different hypotheses.

Exceptions

Evans and Over (1996a) argued that the original dependence model (Oakford and Chater, 1994b) was incapable of explaining data from Kirby (1994) or from Pollard and Evans (1983). Oaksford and Chater (1998b) argued that this was because the original dependence model did not allow exceptions. Kirby told his participants that a machine printing cards had made an error, i.e. it produced a p, *not-q* instance. Consequently, an exceptionless generalization was already known to be impossible and therefore the independence model had to be true. Oaksford and Chater (1998a) conceded this problem with the original model, and so modified it to allow $P(q|p)$ to be less than 1. This new model, see 5.18, showed good fits to most of Kirby's data, as we have shown.

Parameter alignment

The original model and (Oakford and chater, 1994b) has been criticized (Green and Over 1997, 1998; Green *et al.* 1997; Laming 1996; McKenzie and Mikkelsen 2000) on the grounds that the particular form of the dependence model was only used to explain the data. In particular, it has been argued that this model was used simply to guarantee that the $\neg p$ card, which is rarely selected, would be completely uninformative (Laming 1996). This selection of models also had the odd consequence, noted by Green and Over (1998), that the probability of the consequent varied between models. Green and Over (1997) also pointed out that, contrary to the predictions of the original model, the $\neg p$ card can provide useful information (see also: McKenzie and Mikkelsen 2000). All of these problems have been resolved in the dependence hypothesis used in the revised information-gain model, see 5.18. In that model, the $\neg p$ card can be informative, the probability of the consequent is the same in both models and yet, contrary to what one might expect from Laming's (1996) argument, the revised model still provided good fits to the data.

Bi-conditional interpretation

The revised model i.e. 5.18 also resolves a problem raised by Oberauer *et al.* (1999) for Oaksford and Chater's (1994b) account of the Kirby's (1994) data, where probabilities were manipulated in an abstract-selection task for the first time. To model these data we assumed that $P(p) = P(q)$ (although Oaksford and Chater (1998a) relaxed this assumption and still showed good fits to the data). Oberauer *et al.* (1999) objected to this assumption on the grounds that for the q and $\neg q$ cards, participants were always told that either a '+' or a '−' is printed on a card. However, as Over and Evans (1994) pointed out, Kirby did not tell participants that these symbols were printed at random, so this fact does not license any particular value for the probability of finding one of these symbols on a card. So, contrary to Oberauer *et al.*'s suggestion, it is certainly not incoherent to propose that these probabilities vary with $P(p)$.

Oberauer *et al.* (1999) also argue that we should have used a bi-conditional dependence model, because simply equating the probability of the antecedent and consequent does not achieve this interpretation in the original dependence model. They introduce a bi-conditional model, where $P(p, \neg q) = P(\neg p, q) = 0$, and show poor fits to Kirby's results. However, a revised dependence model, when $P(p) = P(q)$ and $P(q|p) = 1$, implies that $P(p, \neg q) = P(\neg p, q) = 0$, i.e. in the revised model, the bi-conditional interpretation and the assumption that $P(p) = P(q)$ go hand in glove (see also: Hattori, 2002). Of course, it was the revised-dependence model that Oaksford and Chater (2003e) used to model Kirby's data (see 'Probabilities of fictional outcomes'), and they showed good fits to most of the data without making any of the assumptions that Oberauer *et al.* (1999) criticize.

Rarity assumption

Some authors object to the rarity assumption (Laming 1996; Oberauer *et al.* 1999); that is, to explain the data it must be assumed that $P(p)$ and $P(q)$ are small.

Recently, it has been shown that rarity is the default when people are testing (Anderson and Sheu 1995; McKenzie and Mikklesen 2000) or framing hypotheses (McKenzie *et al*. 2001). McKenzie and Mikkelsen (2000) showed that people regard rare evidence as more relevant to supporting a hypothesis than common evidence. So, for example, logically both black ravens and non-black non-ravens (e.g. pink flamingos) confirm the hypothesis that *if it is a raven, then it is black*. However, people regard black ravens as more supportive of this hypothesis (see also: Oaksford and Chater 1996). Moreover, rare observations were often selected even when they were not mentioned in the hypothesis.

It could be argued that people are simply matching the salient named items (see: Evans 1998). However, McKenzie *et al*. (2001) showed that hypotheses are normally phrased in terms of rare events, so that such a matching strategy is invariably rational. They showed participants data about a group of students' SAT scores and whether these students were admitted to a select university. Only one student was admitted and this was the only student with a high SAT score. When asked to fill in a sentence frame describing this situation, 'if … then …', participants strongly preferred the phrasing 'if applicants have high SAT scores, they will be accepted' over 'if applicants have low SAT scores, they will be rejected', even though both are equally legitimate ways to complete the statement. Crucially, when given the information that most students were accepted, and that few applicants had low SAT scores, this finding reversed, i.e. they now preferred the second phrasing. In both cases, participants preferred to frame a hypothesis in terms of rare rather than common events. In sum, the rarity assumption not only makes conceptual sense of the literature in the philosophy of science (see: Mackie 1963; Oaksford and Chater 1996), it is also a part of people's normal expectations about the hypotheses they formulate and test about their everyday world.

An important observation made by McKenzie (2000, p. C7) is that the rarity assumption 'is presumed to exist because of lifelong learning that presence is rarer than absence'. Consequently, experimental manipulations that violate rarity are unlikely to totally eliminate the tendency to select the *p* and *q* cards in the selection task (for a similar argument, see: Oaksford *et al*. 1997, 1999). This is because 'violations of rarity move participants' behaviour in the appropriate direction, but not by as much as the normative theory (unencumbered by strong priors about how the world usually works) would predict' (McKenzie 2000, p. C7). This argument is consistent with our findings that, although our probability manipulations had a large effect on the best-fit parameter values, calibration was not perfect, i.e. it followed a pi-function. That is, the observed behaviour was consistent with the probability manipulation but the changes were not as extreme as the model would predict if the experimentally given values were simply plugged in to the model.

Revising $P(p)$

Several authors (Green and Over 1998; Oberauer *et al.* 1999) have questioned the revision strategy for the, *if ¬p, then q* rule (or, assuming the contrast set account of negations, the high $P(p)$ and low $P(q)$ rule (HL)). Indeed Green and Over (1998) provide an example for which it would be incoherent to adopt this strategy. However, the example relies on allowing $P(q)$ to vary between models, which is no longer possible in the revised model (see 'Parameter alignment'). However, when there are exceptions, i.e. $P(q|p) < 1$, the only constraint is that $P(p)P(q|p) < P(q)$. Consequently, $P(p)$ can be greater than $P(q)$, as long as participants are willing to countenance sufficiently low values of $P(q|p)$. So, HL rules can make sense without making any revisions to $P(p)$ and $P(q)$. The question is: do people revise down $P(p)$ or $P(q|p)$? Oaksford and Wakefield's (2003) data addressed this issue (see 'Probabilities and natural sampling'). In the indirect estimates for the HL rule, participants provided very low values of $P(q|p)$ of, on average, 0.16, a finding replicated by Oaksford and Moussakowski (2004). This result suggests that our earlier proposal about the revision strategy may have been an unnecessary carry-over from when we did not allow for exceptions in the original dependence model, as noted by Evans and Over (1996). However, Oaksford and Moussakowski (2004) also observed significant reductions in indirect estimates of $P(p)$ when $P(q)$ was low. This result suggests that both revision strategies may be used in response to an aberrant HL rule.

Mentioning the relevance of probabilities

Oberauer *et al.* (1999) raises the possible concern that, in Oaksford *et al.*'s (1997) experiments (see 'The reduced array selection task' (RAST)), selections may have been affected because some participants were cued to the relevance of frequency information for card choice. In Oaksford *et al.*'s (1999) experiments 1 and 2, half of the participants were cued to the relevance of probability information, by being asked to assess $P(p)$ and $P(q)$ prior to the selection task. The remaining participants were not cued, because they provided this information only after they had performed the selection task. In Oaksford *et al.* (1999), we presented no analyses of this order manipulation because there were no effects that indicated that it was a confounding factor. To test Oberauer *et al.*'s hypothesis, we looked at each significant effect of the probability manipulations in each subgroup of participants.

More participants selected the ¬q card when $P(p)$ was high than when it was low. This was significant for participants who performed the probability check before, χ^2 (1, $N = 64$) = 4.22, $p < 0.025$ (all tests were one-tailed), and after the selection task, χ^2 (1, $N = 64$) = 4.00, $p < 0.025$. More participants selected the $\neg q$ card when $P(q)$ was high than when it was low. This difference was *not* significant for participants who performed the probability check before the selection task, χ^2 (1, $N = 64$) = 0.67, *ns*, but it was significant for those who performed it afterwards, χ^2 (1, $N = 64$) = 8.33, $p < 0.005$. More participants selected the q card when $P(q)$ was low than when it was high (this was significant only for the comparison between the LL and LH rules). This difference was *not* significant for participants who performed the probability check before the selection task, χ^2 (1, $N = 32$) = 1.17, $p = 0.14$, but it was significant for those who performed it afterwards, χ^2 (1, $N = 32$) = 3.14, $p < 0.025$. In summary, Oberauer *et al.*'s concern can be put aside. If anything, cueing participants to the relevance of probability manipulations would appear to suppress, rather than facilitate, their effects on people's card selections.

Sample from a larger population

A further criticism of the model is that it assumes that people regard the four cards as a sample from a larger population (Laming 1996; Oberauer *et al.* 1999; Peter Wason, personal communication). However, it is only on this assumption that considerations from the philosophy of science (e.g. Popper 1959) bear on the task: no meaningful scientific hypothesis has ever been stated over a domain of only four objects. In the summary of early work in this area (Wason and Johnson-Laird 1972, p. 172), the selection task was introduced as bearing on 'how, psychologically, science is possible', and it was concluded that, 'one contributory cause must be a pre-eminent ability to generalize and to test generalizations'. Despite the immediate inference that participants were originally intended to view the cards as a sample from a larger population, they may not. If they do not, then whether they were seeking falsificatory or confirmatory evidence, logically they should turn the p, and the $\neg q$ cards. As participants conspicuously refrain from this selection of cards, it seems reasonable to assume that they do not spontaneously interpret the rule in this way. Moreover, as Oaksford *et al.* (1999) pointed out, when Legrenzi (1971) presented participants with the four cards, so that they could look at both sides, only 1 participant out of 30 described the situation using a conditional. That is, with such a limited domain, the conditional is not the most natural description of the situation.

However, some authors nonetheless insist that people *should* interpret the rule as applying only to the four cards. Oberauer *et al.* (1999), for example, argue that conditionals can be both general and specific, e.g. 'if it rains tomorrow, the game will be cancelled' is an example of a specific, conditional claim.

However, to construct a selection task with these rules, the cards can no longer be interpreted as instances, i.e. as individual people or objects. Rather they must be interpreted as possible states of affairs concerning what happens tomorrow. Moreover, just like the corresponding counter-factual, 'if it had rained yesterday, the game would have been cancelled', whether you should believe such a rule seems to depend on the existence of a law or social convention that games of this kind do not take place if it rains (Goodman 1954). Consequently whether you should believe it or not depends on the evidence you have for the generalization, 'if it rains, then games of this kind are cancelled'. And this need not involve looking at data, but may simply involve remembering the laws of the game, e.g. if the game in question is grass-court tennis, then you will be strongly inclined to believe the claim. In sum, the mere fact that conditionals can be used to make specific claims, does not mean it would be at all natural to interpret the rules in a selection task as specific. Moreover, even if they were so interpreted, whether one believes specific conditionals of this form may rely on the truth or falsity of a related generalization that may be assumed to be the real rule under test.

Individual differences

Green (2000) and Evans (1999) both question whether the probabilistic approach is sufficient as an explanation of human-reasoning performance. Both commentators argue that there is clear evidence of deductive competence. For example, Green (2000) notes that, although people are sensitive to the believability of conclusions (see also: Oaksford *et al.* 2000), these effects are far stronger on invalid than valid conclusions. Moreover, Green (1995a, b; Green and Larking 1995) has shown that some participants do construe the selection task logically, and Stanovich and West (1998) have shown that a subgroup (around 10%) of participants with high intelligence are capable of logical performance. That is, it appears that people have some sensitivity to the notion of logical validity.

However, as Stanovich and West's (1998) results show, this may be as few as 10% of students at a top rank university (their research was conducted at the University of Toronto). That is, assuming only the top 1% of the population ever attends such institutions (and this is a very liberal estimate), logical performance may be very rare in the population. Moreover, even the behaviour of this élite band does not necessarily implicate an underlying innate logical competence. It could simply reflect an accumulation of experience showing that these particular inferences seem to work in the real world more often than others. Or it could reflect a learned ability acquired at school while learning, e.g. mathematics or IT, which may account for its association with IQ as measured by the scholastic aptitude test (Stanovich and West 1998).

Summary

The information-gain model has been subject to intense scrutiny since it first appeared, as is attested by the number of theoretical criticisms of its adequacy that we have just reviewed. In the last section, we have argued either that the revised model addresses these criticisms, that new data confirms our original assumptions, or that the criticism does not stand up under analysis. As we have seen, many of the criticisms of the original model were well-founded and could be easily incorporated into the revised model (Oaksford and chater, 1994b) presented here and in Oaksford and Chater (2003e). The selection task was the first task to which the probabilistic approach was applied and in terms of complexity it is perhaps intermediate between conditional inference and quantified syllogistic reasoning to which we turn to in Chapter 7.

Chapter 7

An uncertain quantity: how people reason with syllogisms

Although the accounts of conditional inference and the selection task reported in the last two chapters appear encouraging for a probabilistic account of reasoning, it may be thought that this apparent success would not carry over to more complex, and perhaps more central, logical-reasoning tasks. After all, some proponents of logical approaches have argued that participants do not interpret the selection task as a logical-reasoning task (e.g. Rips 1990) and hence would not see the results of the previous chapter as raising broader doubts about the logicist programme in the psychology of reasoning. Moreover, it can perhaps be argued that probabilistic accounts are only really applicable to conditional inference when one premise is regarded as uncertain (of course, we would argue that this is all the time!). So it might credibly be argued that probabilistic and logical approaches may apply to disjointed sets of phenomena and hence do not stand in genuine competition. Consequently, in order to assess the general hypothesis that human everyday reasoning is uncertain, and hence that probabilistic reasoning strategies will be imported into the laboratory, we must look to laboratory tasks that are regarded as unequivocally logical. If the probabilistic approach is to provide a general account of human reasoning, then it should also explain performance in such core logical reasoning tasks.

Aside from the selection task, perhaps the most intensively researched and theoretically important task in the study of logical reasoning is the centrepiece of Aristotelian logic, syllogistic reasoning (Dickstein 1978; Ford 1994; Guyote and Sternberg 1981; Johnson-Laird 1983; Newstead 1989; Newstead and Griggs 1983; Polk and Newell 1995; Rips 1994; Stenning and Oberlander 1995; Stenning and Yule 1997; Woodworth and Sells 1935). Syllogisms involve two quantified premises, each of which can have the forms: *All X are Y, Some X are Y, No X are Y,* or *Some X are not Y,* where *X* is the subject term, and *Y* is the predicate term, e.g:

all beekeepers are artists;
all chemists are beekeepers;
therefore, all chemists are artists.

In this argument, 'beekeepers' forms the 'middle term', which occurs in both premises, and the conclusion relates the 'end terms', artists and chemists, which occur in only one premise.

The main empirical finding is that performance is good on the logically valid syllogisms, but people systematically and erroneously assert conclusions for syllogisms with no valid conclusion. Syllogisms are unequivocally logical—indeed, from Aristotle until the beginnings of modern logic in the nineteenth century, syllogisms formed almost the whole of logic. Moreover, the major logic-based theories of reasoning either were first applied to syllogistic reasoning (mental models; Johnson-Laird 1983), or have treated explaining syllogistic reasoning as a major theoretical goal (mental logic; Rips 1994). Syllogistic reasoning therefore provides an ideal case study for the probabilistic approach. It is unequivocally logical; there are strong theoretical alternatives against which a probabilistic account can be compared; and there is a large body of empirical data, against which these theoretical proposals can be evaluated.

Chater and Oaksford (1999b) developed both computational- and algorithmic-level analyses of syllogistic reasoning, based on a probabilistic approach. The resulting model was called the probability heuristics model (PHM). In this chapter we first outline PHM. We then show how it can account for the existing data and compare it with alternative theories. Finally, we look at the empirical results that have emerged since the model's appearance and address some of the arguments that have been levelled against it. An important feature of PHM is that it extends directly to syllogisms involving generalized quantifiers such as *most* and *few* (Barwise and Cooper 1981; Moxey and Sanford 1991). The crucial feature of these syllogisms is that they cannot be explained logically and hence they fall outside the scope of theories like mental logic and mental models (although see, Johnson-Laird 1983) that assume standard logic as their computational-level theory.

The probability heuristics model

We first introduce the terminology associated with syllogisms. Syllogisms involves two quantified premises; these are: *All X are Y*, *Some X are Y*, *No X are Y*; and *Some X are not Y*. We deal with two further premise types, *Most* (M) and *Few* (F). These premises can occur in one of four 'figures' shown in Fig. 7.1.

Figure 7.1 shows the traditional figure numbering in parentheses. Syllogistic conclusions relate the end terms, X and Z, of the premises. There are traditionally (i.e. using just *All*, *Some*, *Some ... not*, and *None* as premises) 64 possible forms of syllogistic premises (four quantifier combinations for the each

X - Y	Y - X	X - Y	Y - X
Y - Z	Z - Y	Z - Y	Y - Z
[4]	[1]	[2]	[3]

Fig. 7.1 Syllogistic figures.

of the two premises × four figures). Each syllogism will be identified by the quantifiers it contains and its figure, e.g. *All-None*[4]: first premise: *All X are Y*, second premise: *No Y are Z* (when no figure is specified, e.g. *All-None*, the type of syllogism, generalizing over all four figures, is being referred to). Using the standard logical interpretation of the quantifiers, there are 22 syllogisms with a logically valid conclusion. Aristotle also assumed that *All X are Y* and *No X are Y* presuppose that there are some *X*s, which allows five more valid syllogisms (see Table 7.1). Conclusions that are valid by making such an 'existential presupposition' are denoted by '∃p'.

Having introduced the necessary terminology, we now outline the computational- and algorithmic-level theories that together make up Chater and Oaksford's (1999b) probability heuristics model of syllogistic reasoning. We begin by outlining the algorithmic-level heuristics from which the empirical predictions of PHM are derived. We then show how these heuristics provide an efficient way of drawing probabilistically valid inferences (*p*-valid, see below; this notion of validity is stronger, and distinct, from that used in probability logic and discussed in Chapter 5).

The algorithmic level

Chater and Oaksford (1999b) propose an algorithmic-level analysis consisting of a set of 'fast and frugal' heuristics (Gigerenzer and Goldstein 1996), which *generate* likely syllogistic conclusions. They assume that people may also employ test processes for assessing whether generated conclusions are valid. However, in PHM it is assumed that for most people these are not well-developed, which explains why many people frequently produce conclusions that are not logically valid. Moreover, these test procedures might very well involve the kinds of processes discussed by other theories, that can account for logical performance, such as mental models (e.g. Johnson-Laird and Byrne 1991), mental logic (Rips 1994), or reasoning with Euler circles (Stenning and Oberlander 1995). PHM focuses on generation heuristics, and includes only two simple test heuristics that are used across participants. These heuristic processes of generation closely approximate the prescriptions of a probabilistic computational-level analysis (see below), while imposing minimal computational overheads—they provide

Table 7.1 The valid syllogisms showing those conclusions that are valid according to (i) Aristotle, where the conclusion type is in a fixed order and ∃p is allowed; (ii) Johnson-Laird, where the conclusion type is in free order and ∃p is allowed; and (iii) first order predicate logic where the conclusion type is in free order but ∃p is not allowed

Syllogism	(i) Aristotle (Fixed + ∃p) D1&2	(ii) Johnson-Laird (Free + ∃p) J-LS&B	(iii) Frege (Free − ∃p)
AA1	A(I)	A(I)	A
AA3	I	I	
AA4	I	A(I)	A
AE1		E	
EA1	E	E	E
AE2	E	E	E
EA2	E	E	E
AE3		O	
EA3	O	O	
AE4	E	E	E
EA4	O	O	
IA4	I	I	I
IA3	I	I	I
AI3	I	I	I
AI1	I	I	I
EI1	O	O	O
IE1		O	O
OA2		O	O
EI2	O	O	O
IE2		O	O
AO2	O	O	O
OA3	O	O	O
EI3	O	O	O
IE3		O	O
AO3		O	O
EI4	O	O	O
IE4		O	O

'fast and frugal' heuristics, in the sense of Gigerenzer and Goldstein (1996). These simple heuristics account for a great deal of the data, without the need to appeal to the elaborate test processes which are the focus of other accounts.

All the heuristics rely on an ordering in the informativeness of quantified statements that serve as premises of syllogistic arguments. Intuitively informative statements are the ones that surprise us the most, if they turn out to be true. Chater and Oaksford's (1999b) computational level analysis specifies the following ordering: *All* > *Most* > *Few* > *Some* > *None* >> *Some...not* (where '>' stands for 'more informative than'). There are three generation heuristics, discussed below.

> (G1) The *min*-heuristic: choose the quantifier of the conclusion to be the same as the quantifier in the least informative premise (the *min-premise*).

The most informative conclusions that can validly follow from a pair of syllogistic premises almost always follow this rule. Furthermore, some conclusions probabilistically entail ('*p*-entail') other conclusions. For example, if *All X are Y*, then it is probable that *Some X are Y* (this will follow as long as there are some *X*s). These additional conclusions are called '*p*-entailments.' Thus the second heuristic is:

> (G2) *P*-entailments: the next most preferred conclusion will be the *p*-entailment of the conclusion predicted by the *min*-heuristic (the '*min*-conclusion').

The *p*-entailments include a family of heuristics corresponding to the probabilistic relationships between the various quantified statements that make up the premises of a syllogism. Heuristics (G1) and (G2) specify the quantifier of the conclusion. The third heuristic, the *attachment*-heuristic, specifies the order of end terms in the conclusion:

> (G3) *Attachment*-heuristic: if just one of the possible conclusion subject noun phrases matches the subject noun phrase of just one premise, then the conclusion has that subject noun phrase.[1]

We illustrate these heuristics with some examples. Consider *All-Some*[1]:

All Y are X	(*max*-premise).
Some Z are Y	(*min*-premise).
Therefore, *Some*-type conclusion	(by *min*).
Some Z are X	(by *attachment*).

By the *min*-heuristic, the conclusion is *Some*. The *min*-premise has an end term (*Z*) as its subject. Therefore, by *attachment*, the conclusion will have

---

[1] We thank Geoff Goodwin (Brisbane University, Australia; personal communication) for pointing out an error in the original formulation of G3. Although the examples are consistent with the definition we provide here, the original definition was too narrow.

Z as its subject term, and the form *Some Z are X*. In contrast, consider *All-Some*[4], where the order of terms in both premises is reversed, and the *min*-heuristic also specifies a *Some* conclusion. But now the *Some* premise does not have an end term (neither X nor Z) as its subject. Therefore, the end term of the *max*-premise (i.e. *All X are Y*) is used as the subject in the conclusion, giving the form *Some X are Z*.

Now consider the following syllogism, *Some-None*[2]:

	Some X are Y	(*max*-premise)
	No Z are Y	(*min*-premise)
Therefore,	*Some...not*-type conclusion	(by *p*-validity or logic, or by *p*-entailments).
	Some X are not Z	(by *attachment*)
	None-type conclusion	(by *min*)
	No Z are X	(by *attachment*)

This is a *Some-None* syllogism, where the *min*-heuristic does not give the type of the *p*-valid conclusion. The logical and *p*-valid conclusion is of type *Some...not*. Here the conclusion order varies depending on whether the *min*-heuristic conclusion or the *p*-valid conclusion is chosen. Both logical and *p*-validity specify that the conclusion is of type *Some...not*, whereas the *min*-heuristic specifies a conclusion of type *None*.

Logical validity and *p*-validity license a *Some...not* conclusion, which contains the quantifier *Some*. The statements *Some ϕ are ψ* and *Some ϕ are not ψ* have the same subject noun phrase (*Some ϕ*), which contains the same quantifier *Some*. More generally, the subject terms of *Some...not* and *Some* statements (whether as premises or conclusions) will attach or fail to attach in the same way. In this example, the quantifier in the conclusion is *Some*, which attaches to the quantifier of only one premise (the *max*-premise); moreover, the subject term of this premise is an end term (X), and so X is used as the subject term of the conclusion, leading to the conclusion *Some X are not-Z*. The *min*-heuristic licenses a *None* conclusion, which attaches directly to the second premise, producing the *No Z are X* conclusion. This makes the novel prediction that, in these cases, conclusion order will depend on conclusion type.

G1–G3 generate syllogistic conclusions. As noted above, Chater and Oaksford (1999b) assume that people are generally unable to test these conclusions for *p*-validity (or, for that matter, logical validity). However, they assume that people employ two test heuristics that provide a fast and frugal estimate of how likely the conclusion generated by G1-G3 is to be informative and *p*-valid.

(T1) The *max*-heuristic: be confident in the conclusion generated by G1–G3 in proportion to the informativeness of the most informative premise (the *max*-premise).

(T2) The *Some...not*-heuristic: avoid producing or accepting *Some...not* conclusions, because they are so uninformative relative to other conclusions.

T1 gives a fast and frugal estimate of the likelihood that a syllogism has an the informative, valid conclusion. T2 gives a fast and frugal heuristic for focusing on informative conclusions. Chater and Oaksford (1999b) also show how these algorithmic-level heuristics can be justified at the computational level.

Computational level

Their computational-level analysis has three parts. Given the uncertainty of everyday reasoning, they first interpret quantified statements as probabilistic statements. Second, they use this probabilistic semantics to derive an analysis of informativeness, which justifies the informativeness ordering over which the heuristics above were defined. They use Shannon's notion of 'surprisal' (see (7.1) below) as the measure of information (Shannon and Weaver 1949). The third part of the computational-level analysis consists of an account of validity, which is defined over probabilistic statements (distinct, as noted above, from the notion of probabilistic validity in probability logic, and described in Chapter 5). This probabilistic notion of validity (*p*-validity) has the advantage of allowing a definition of valid syllogistic inferences involving *Most* and *Few*, in a way that is uniform with a definition of validity for the standard quantifiers. Thus, Chater and Oaksford (1999) assume that people do not treat even syllogistic reasoning as a logical task, but assimilate it to people's everyday probabilistic reasoning strategies. The notion of *p*-validity is crucial to generalizing the account to reasoning with *Most* and *Few*, because without a notion such as *p*-validity, there is no way of defining the correct answers to these generalized syllogisms. This explains why experimental studies of syllogistic reasoning with *Most* and *Few* have not previously been conducted, despite the fact that in, for example, mental models theory, there has been considerable theoretical interest in these quantifiers (e.g. Johnson-Laird 1983, 1994).

Probabilistic semantics for the quantifiers

Quantified statements can be given intuitively natural meanings in terms of constraints on the conditional probability of the predicate (*Y*) given the subject (*X*). *All X are Y* means that the probability of *Y* given *X* is 1 ($P(Y|X) = 1$). *Most X are Y* means that the probability of *Y* given *X* is high but less than 1 ($1 - \Delta \leq P(Y|X) < 1$, where Δ is small). *Few X are Y* means that the probability of Y given X is small but greater than 0 $(0 < P(Y|X) \leq \Delta)$. *Some X are Y* means that the probability of Y given X is greater than 1 and that there are some things that are both Xs and Ys $(P(Y|X) > 0, \exists X, Y)$. *No X are Y* means that the probability of Y given X is 0 $(P(Y|X) = 0)$. *Some X are not Y* means that the probability of Y given X is less than 1 and that there some things that are Xs but not Ys $(P(Y|X) < 1, \exists X, not\text{-}Y)$.

This probabilistic account immediately provides the justification for the G2 heuristic. There are inclusion relationships between the intervals associated with the different quantified statements (see Fig. 7.2). These inclusion relationships license the inferences that we call *p*-entailments in the G2 heuristic. *All* is included in *Some*, i.e. *All* $\subset$ *Some*, which licenses the inference that if *All X are Y*, then *Some X are Y* (which holds just as long as there are some Xs), i.e. *All* $\Rightarrow$ *Some*. Similarly, *Most* $\Rightarrow$ *Some*; *Few* $\Rightarrow$ *Some*; *Most* $\Rightarrow$ *Some...not*; *Few* $\Rightarrow$ *Some...not*, and *None* $\Rightarrow$ *Some...not*. *Some...not* and *Some* overlap almost completely, aside from the endpoints, i.e. *Some...not* $\Rightarrow$ *Some* and *Some* $\Rightarrow$ *Some...not*. Finally, there are weak relations such that *Some* and *Some...not* are both compatible with *Most* or *Few* (although they do not imply them). These relations depends on the size of Δ and the particular presumed values of $P(Y|X)$, giving, *Some* $\Rightarrow$ *most, few*; and *Some...not* $\Rightarrow$ *most, few* (where the lower case initial letter denotes a weak *p*-entailment). Although some of these relationships can be motivated on pragmatic grounds, all those involving *Most* and *Few* constitute novel predictions of Chater and Oaksford's probabilistic semantics.

Informativeness

Chater and Oaksford (1999b) apply this probabilistic semantics in deriving an informativeness ordering over quantified statements that justifies the *Some...not*-heuristic (T2), and underlies the other heuristics. In information

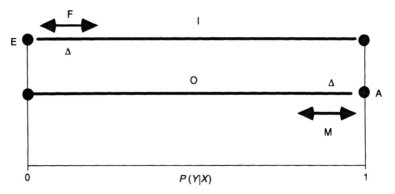

Fig. 7.2 The probabilistic semantics for the quantifers AMFIEO, where A = *All*, M = *Most*, F = *Few*, I = *Some*, E = *None*, and O = *Some...not*.

theory (Shannon and Weaver 1949) the informativeness $I(s)$ of a statement, s, is inversely related to its probability, $P(s)$:

$$I(s) = \log_2 \left[\frac{1}{P(s)} \right].$$

(7.1)

On the above semantics for quantified statements, some relationships between informational strengths can be inferred directly, i.e. if $\Theta \Rightarrow \Phi$ then $I(\Phi) < I(\Theta)$, providing a partial order corresponding to the p-entailments: $I(All) > I(Some)$; $I(Most) > I(Some)$; $I(Few) > I(Some)$; $I(Most) > I(Some...not)$; $I(Few) > I(Some...not)$; $I(None) > I(Some...not)$. But applying the min-heuristic requires a total order.

Oaksford and Chater (1994b) made a 'rarity' assumption (see Chapter 6), i.e. the properties referred to in natural language typically apply to a small proportion of possible objects. Rarity affects the frequency with which different quantified statements will be true and hence their informativeness. Intuitively, rarity is important because most natural language predicates are mutually exclusive, e.g. *toupee* and *table* do not cross classify objects in the world, i.e., no object is both a toupee and a table. Therefore, the joint probability of being a toupee and a table is 0, i.e. the *None* statement *No toupees are tables* is true. Because of rarity, this holds in general, i.e. a *None* statement will typically describe the relationship between any two natural language properties. Therefore *None* statements are almost always true and are hence fairly uninformative. If most predicates applied to more than half the objects in the world, then their extensions would *have* to overlap and *None* statements would hence be very surprising and informative. Chater and Oaksford (1999b, appendix A) prove how a general rarity assumption enforces the total order $I(All) > I(Most) > I(Few) > I(Some) > I(None) \gg I(Some...not)$.

The *Some...not*-heuristic is justified because *Some...not* statements are so uninformative. This is because, for almost all pairs of predicates X and Y, the statement *Some X are not Y* will be true (e.g. *Some toupees are not tables*). Chater and Oaksford's formal analysis shows that *Some...not* statements are very much less informative than all other types of quantified statement.

Probabilistic validity

To justify the min-hueristic (G1), the *attachment*-heuristic (G3), and the max-heuristic (T1), requires a notion of validity that applies to probabilistic statements. Whether these heuristics favour p-valid conclusions can then be assessed.

Syllogistic reasoning relates two end terms X and Z via a common middle term Y. According to the probabilistic interpretation of the quantifiers, the two premises correspond to constraints on the conditional probabilities between the end terms and the middle term. Chater and Oaksford make the standard assumption (Pearl 1988) of conditional independence between the end terms, given the middle term (i.e. the end terms are only related by the middle term). A p-valid conclusion follows if the premises place sufficient constraints on the conditional probability of one end term given the other (i.e. either $P(Z|X)$ or $P(X|Z)$). For example, if one of these probabilities is constrained to be 1, an *All* conclusion follows; if the conditional probabilities are constrained to be greater than 0, then a *Some* conclusion follows, and so on. Chater and Oaksford formally derived the p-valid conclusion for all 144 syllogisms involving the quantifiers *All, Most, Few, Some, None*, and *Some...not*. Table 7.2 shows the p-valid syllogisms involving the quantifiers *All, Some, None*, and *Some...not*, and Table 7.3 shows the additional p-valid syllogisms involving *Most* and *Few*.

Notice that the conditional independence assumption in this notion of p-validity allows valid inferences that are not valid according to the stricter criterion of probabilistic validity, from probability logic (Chapter 5). Probabilistic validity in probability logic requires that uncertainties of the conclusion cannot exceed the summed uncertainties of the premises (where uncertainty of a statement is the probability that it is not true). And, as we noted, this is a more stringent criterion than logical validity, which drops out as a special case when the uncertainties of the premises are 0. Thus, from *Some A are B*, and *Some B are C*, it does not follow by standard logical validity that *Some A are C*, because it clearly does not follow, for example, that *Some poodles are dachshunds*, from the premises *Some poodles are dogs*; and *Some dogs are dachshunds*. And hence this syllogism is therefore clearly not valid, using the more stringent notion of validity in probability logic. And here, of course, the relevant independence assumptions clearly fail: $P(dachshund, dog)$ is not equal to $P(dachshund, dog, poodle)$. By contrast, we are here concerned with what conclusions can be drawn if we make default independence assumptions (see Fig. 7.3) (Pearl 1988), where we have no reason not to do so (this notion of validity will of course be non-montononic, because it will be overturned by any reasons that undercut such independence assumptions). To say that the relations between *As* and *Bs*, and between *Cs* and *Bs*, are independent is to require that $P(A, B, C) = P(B)P(A|B)P(C|B) = 1/P(B)[P(A, B)P(C, B)]$. If *Some A are B*, then $P(A, B) > 0$; If *Some B are C*, then $P(B, C) > 0$. Hence $P(A, B, C) > 0$, which implies that $P(A, C) = P(A, B, C) > 0$. And if $P(A, C) > 0$, according to our probabilistic interpretation of quantified statements, this means that *Some A are C*.

Table 7.2 The p-valid syllogisms using the standard AIEO quantifiers, showing the p-valid conclusion, the p-valid response available in the forced choice task (Dickstein 1974), and the conclusion predicted by the min-heuristic

Syllogism	p-Valid conc.	Valid conc available response	min-heuristic
AA1	A	A	A
AA4	A	A	A
AI1	I	I	I
AI3	I	I	I
AE2	E	E	E
AE4	E	E	E
AO2	O	O	O
AO3	O		O
IA3	I	I	I
IA4	I	I	I
II1	I	I	I
II2	I	I	I
II3	I	I	I
II4	I	I	I
IE1	O		E
IE2	O		E
IE3	O		E
IE4	O		E
IO4	O		O
EA1	E	E	E
EA2	E	E	E
EI1	O		E
EI2	O		E
EI3	O		E
EI4	O		E
OA2	O		O
OA3	O	O	O
OI1	O	O	O
OO1	O	O	O
OO2	I	I	O
OO4	O		O

Table 7.3 The additional p-valid syllogisms when the standard AIEO quantifiers are supplemented by M and F, showing the p-valid conclusion, the p-valid response available in the forced choice task used in our experiments, and the conclusion predicted by the min-heuristic

Syllogism	Valid conc.	Valid conc available response	*min*-heuristic
AM1	MΔA	MΔA	M
MA1	M	M	M
MM1	M	M	M
AM2	O	O	M
MA2	O		M
MM4	M		M
AM4	M		M
MA4	MΔA		M
FA1	F	F	F
FM1	F	F	F
AF2	FΔE	FΔE	F
FA2	FΔE		F
MF4	F		F
AF4	F		F
MF1	O	O^{AMFO}	F
MO1	O	O	O
FF1	O	O^{AMFO}	F
FO1	O	O	O
OM1	O	O	O
OM3	O	O	O
OF1	O	O	O
OF3	O	O	O
FO3	O	O	O
FO4	O	O	O
MO3	O	O	O
MO4	O	O	O
OF4	O	O	O
FF4	O		F
OM4	O		O
FM4	O		F

Table 7.3 (Continued)

Syllogism	Valid conc.	Valid conc available response	*min*-heuristic
MI1	I, O	I	I
MI3	I, O	I	I
IM3	I, O	I	I
IM4	I, O	I	I
FI1	I, O	I	I
FI3	I, O	I	I
IF3	I, O	I	I
IF4	I, O	I	I

Note: The notation 'MΔA' indicates the constraint on the relevant conditional probability is that it must be greater than 1–Δ, and consequently that either M or A follow. Similarly, 'FΔE' indicates that the relevant conditional probability must be less than Δ, and consequently that either F or E follow. The notation I, O indicates that the conditional probability must be greater than 0 and less than 1, and therefore that both conclusions can follow. The superscript AMFO indicates that this syllogism occurs in both our subsequent experiments but that this response option is only available in the experiment using just the AMFO quantifiers

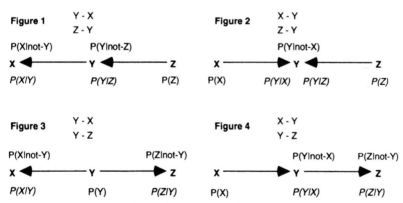

Fig. 7.3 Probability models for the four syllogistic figures, and their parameters, showing the independence relations between premises. For each syllogistic figure, arrows indicate dependencies between terms. The direction of the arrow corresponds to the appropriate conditional probability (i.e., $P(Y|X)$ corresponds to $X \longrightarrow Y$). The nodes correspond to the end terms are not directly connected, which means they are conditionally independent, given the middle term. The probabilities shown are the parameters for each model. Nodes which do not receive an arrow from other nodes are associated with unconditional probabilities (e.g., $P(X)$).

Thus, probability logic seeks a more stringest criterion of validity than standard logic; *p*-validity, as developed here, aims to capture how people can make reasonably assumptions about what is likely to follow from the available premises, by assuming independence between relationships as a default. It is an interesting technical question for future work to explore whether or how these notions might be fused into a single model of *p*-validity.

Chater and Oaksford compared their heuristics (G1, G3, T1) with *p*-validity, to establish that they reliably predict the *p*-valid conclusion when there is one, thereby justifying the heuristics as a way to draw *p*-valid syllogistic conclusions. Tables 7.2 and 7.3 reveal that 54 of the 69 *p*-valid syllogisms conform exactly to the *min*-heuristic, 14 have less informative *p*-valid conclusions, and only 1 violates the *min*-heuristic. Thus *p*-validity confirms that the *min*-heuristic is reliable. In assessing the *attachment*-heuristic, the only relevant syllogisms are those with asymmetric conclusions, where conclusion order matters. Attachment correctly predicts 44 of the 48 syllogisms with asymmetric *p*-valid conclusions (the exceptions are *Most-Few*[1], *Few-Most*[4], *All-Most*[2] and *Most-All*[2]). Therefore, *attachment* reliably gives the logically or *p*-valid conclusion order, where one exists. There are a small number of syllogisms where *attachment* does not apply. Where the conclusion type either attaches to both or neither premise (i.e. for figures 2 and 3), *attachment* decides the conclusion order from the most informative premise. But this criterion does not apply if the premises are of the *same* type (e.g. *All-All*, *Most-Most*, etc.), and so neither conclusion is preferred. With respect to the *min* conclusion, this arises for 12 syllogisms, of which 8 have asymmetrical conclusions (*All-All*[2, 3]; *Most-Most*[2, 3]; *Few-Few*[2, 3]; *Some...not-Some...not*[2, 3]). With respect to conclusions recommended by *p-entailment*, this arises for all 24 syllogisms where the premises are of the same type, irrespective of figure, leading to 14 asymmetric cases (*Most-Most*[1-4]; *Few-Few*[1-4]; *None-None*[1-4]; *Some-Some*[2, 3]). Although *attachment* does not apply to all syllogisms it makes predictions for figures 2 and 3 syllogisms made by no other theory. Moreover, it provides a reliable way of determining conclusion order for most syllogisms.

The *max*-heuristic is based on the *most* informative (i.e. the *max*) premise and suggests that confidence is proportional to the average informativeness of the conclusions of syllogisms with that *max*-premise. For example, consider *All-Some...not* and *None-Some...not*, which both generate a *Some...not* conclusion. However, the *max* premise type for *All-Some...not* is *All*, which has high average informativeness; while for *None-Some...not*, it is *None*, which has low average informativeness. Thus confidence that *Some...not* follows validly from *All-Some...not* should be higher than from *None-Some...not*. Consequently, according to the *max*-heuristic

Some...not should be selected in far higher proportion for *All-Some...not* than for *None-Some...not* syllogisms. Chater and Oaksford (1999) calculated the expected informativeness of the syllogisms with the different *max* premise types, which predicted that confidence in the *min*-conclusion should follow the following order in *max*-premise types: *All > Most > Few > Some > Some-not ≈ None.*

Summary

This section has shown how Chater and Oaksford (1999) introduced and justified PHM. The *min*- and *attachment*-heuristics almost always yield a correct informative conclusion, if there is one. Because these strategies can be applied to all syllogisms, whether there is a *p*-valid conclusion or not, systematic errors will arise for those syllogisms that do not have a valid conclusion. Test procedures, which lie outside the scope of PHM, may be able to distinguish valid from invalid syllogisms to some degree. However, these are complex processes likely to be subject to large individual variation. The *max*-heuristic provides a 'fast and frugal' (Gigerenzer and Goldstein 1996) estimate of the likely validity and potential informativeness of a syllogistic conclusion. In conclusion, according to PHM although people are poor at distinguishing valid from invalid syllogisms, they can get the valid conclusion, if any. Overgeneralization according to the *min*-heuristic is extremely widespread in laboratory tasks.

   The heuristics of PHM are consistent with work showing that simple heuristics can be highly adaptive, insofar as they approximate optimal solutions (Gigerenzer and Goldstein 1996; McKenzie 1994). These heuristics are used in place of complex and sometimes computationally intractable optimal strategies, which are therefore denied any cognitive role. The role of the optimal solution is to explain why the heuristic is adaptive. Chater and Oaksford's theory of syllogisms follows this pattern of reasoning. The principal difference is simply that they develop the optimal theory and processing heuristics in tandem, rather than seeking a post hoc explanation of the success of processing principles observed in human performance. In the next three sections, we look at how PHM explains the data on syllogistic reasoning.

Explaining the data

Chater and Oaksford (1999) assessed PHM against the empirical evidence in three ways. First, they conducted a meta-analysis over the past data on syllogistic reasoning that had only used the quantifiers *All, Some, None,* and *Some...not.* Second, they compared PHM to other theories, looking for past data discriminating between these accounts. Finally, they conducted two experiments to test the novel predictions of PHM when the generalized quantifiers, *Most* and *Few* are introduced in to syllogistic arguments. In this section we provide some illustrations of the results of these analyses.

Meta-analysis

Chater and Oaksford (1999) performed a meta-analysis over the five experiments then available that used all 64 syllogisms (Dickstein 1978, experiments 1 and 2; Johnson-Laird and Steedman 1978, experiments 1 and 2; Johnson-Laird and Bara 1984, experiment 3). They first looked at this data ignoring over conclusion order, to get an overall impression of how well the heuristics fit the data. We illustrate the results of these analyses in Figs 7.4 and 7.5. These figures illustrate the proportion of conclusions chosen for syllogisms with an *All max*-premise (Fig. 7.4) and a *Some max*-premise (Fig. 7.5). Similar figures can be calculated for the syllogisms with a *None* and a *Some-not max*-premise. However, Figs 7.4 and 7.5 are sufficient to illustrate most of the important effects. In these diagrams, syllogism-type generalizes over figure and premise order.

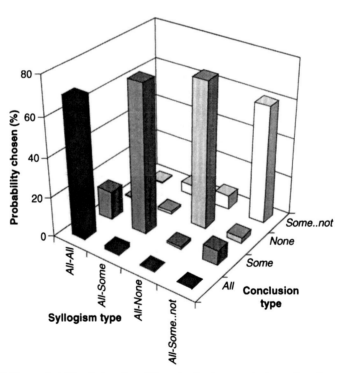

Fig. 7.4 The probability of choosing different syllogism conclusions when the *max*-premise = *All* in Chater and Oaksford's (1999b) meta-analysis.

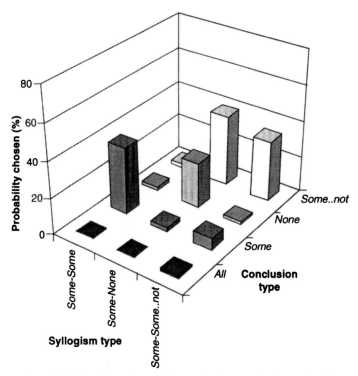

Fig. 7.5 The probability of choosing different syllogism conclusions when the *max*-premise = *Some* in Chater and Oaksford's (1999b) meta-analysis.

So, for example, *All-Some* refers to *All-Some*[1-4] plus *Some-All*[1-4]. This is because the *min*-heuristic, the *p*-entailments, the *max*-heuristic, and the *Some...not*-heuristic, make the same predictions for both orders, i.e. premise order only affects the *attachment*-heuristic. Figures 7.4 and 7.5 show that the two modal conclusions for each type of syllogism, either have the same type as the *min*-premise or the same type as its *p*-entailment. For example, for *All-None*, the modal conclusion is *None*, and the next most selected conclusion is *Some...not*, the *p*-entailment of *None*. Thus the *min*-heuristic and the *p*-entailments seem to accurately account for participants' behaviour. However, in these data there are far more conclusions predicted by the *min*-heuristic than by its *p*-entailment because only one response was elicited to each syllogism. Figures 7.4 and 7.5 also illustrate a clear order in the frequency of responding by *max*-premise type, such that the *min*-conclusion is endorsed more for *All max*-premise type syllogisms (Fig. 7.4) than for *Some max*-premise type syllogisms (Fig. 7.5). This behaviour is consistent with the *max*-heuristic.

Chater and Oaksford assessed the quantitative fit between data and model by adding some parameters to PHM that attached specific numerical values to the degrees of confidence suggested by the *max*-heuristic. Each parameter indicated the percentage of choices according to the *min*-heuristic for each *max*-premise type: *All* = 70.14, *Some* = 31.11, *None* = 18.78, *Some...not* = 18.04. They assumed that participants draw *p*-entailments on a fixed proportion of syllogisms, which is the same for all types. Consequently, they introduced a parameter indicating the percentage of *p*-entailment responses averaged over all syllogism types (10.76). Finally, an error parameter (1.22) was introduced indicating the percentage of responses not predicted by the *min*-heuristic including *p*-entailments. Best-fit estimates of these six parameters were obtained directly from the mean values of the relevant quantities in the data. The product moment correlation between the 320 observed and predicted values was good, r (318) = 0.90. Thus PHM accounts for over 80% of the variance and so provides good overall fits to the empirical data on syllogistic reasoning.

Having assessed the overall fit to the data, Chater and Oaksford went on to assess how well their meta-analysis supported other more fine-grained predictions of PHM. In the following sections we describe some of the results of their analyses.

The *min*- and *Some...not*-heuristics

Chater and Oaksford checked the predictions of these two heuristics for the valid and invalid syllogisms separately. According to the *Some...not*-heuristic, *Some...not* conclusions are much less informative than *All*, *Some*, and *None* conclusions. Consequently, for the valid syllogisms there should be more correct solutions for *All*, *Some*, and *None* conclusions than for *Some...not* conclusions. For the 22 valid syllogisms, *all* the *All*, *Some*, and *None* conclusions were drawn more frequently than *all* the *Some...not* conclusions. This difference was reliable both by study, t (4) = 6.11, $p < 0.005$ (means: *All*, *Some*, and *None* = 86.33% (SD = 4.41); *Some...not* = 47.07% (SD = 18.17)), and by materials, t (20) = 7.34, $p < 0.0001$ (means: *All*, *Some*, and *None* = 86.33% (SD = 4.47); *Some...not* = 47.07% (SD = 16.36)). For valid syllogisms with *All*, *Some*, and *None* conclusions the *min*-heuristic works perfectly. For valid syllogisms with *Some...not* conclusions the *min*-heuristic works for the *All-Some...not* (and *Some...not-All*) syllogisms. However, it only captures the *Some...not* response for the *None-Some* (or *Some-None*) syllogisms via *p*-entailments. The *min*-heuristic therefore predicts that participants should find the *All-Some...not* syllogisms easier than the *None-Some* syllogisms. Except for *None-Some*[1], the valid *Some...not* conclusion was drawn more frequently for *all* the *All-Some...not* syllogisms than for *all* the *None-Some* syllogisms. This difference was reliable both by study, t (4) = 4.76, $p < 0.01$

(means: *All-Some...not* = 61.26 (SD = 20.83); *None-Some* = 39.97 (SD = 17.66)), and by materials, t (10) = 2.64, $p < 0.025$ (means: *All-Some...not* = 61.26 (SD = 6.23); *None-Some* = 39.97 (SD = 15.21)). As we show later on, this analysis is important because it shows that PHM can account for exactly the same distinctions in the data on the valid syllogisms explained by mental models.

For the invalid syllogisms, if people over-generalize from the valid syllogisms, as Chater and Oaksford suggest, then retaining the parameter values derived from the overall data should provide as good a fit to the data on the invalid syllogisms alone. The correlation co-efficient, at r (208) = 0.90 (rms error = 0.29), produced the same level of fit as for the overall data. Consequently, the same informational strategy accounts for the valid and for the invalid syllogisms.

The *max*-heuristic

The *max*-heuristic predicts that there should be a linear order in the frequency of the *min*-heuristic response dependent on the *max*-premise such that *All* > *Some* > *Some...not* > *None*. A one-way ANOVA with *max*-premise type (A, I, E, O) as the within-studies factor and the percentage of responses that the *min*-heuristic predicts as the dependent variable, revealed a highly significant linear contrast in the predicted direction, $F(1, 12) = 120.39$, $MSe = 59.62$, $p < 0.0001$, confirming that confidence in the *min*-response is determined by the *max*-heuristic as PHM predicts.

P-entailments

PHM predicts that: (1) there should be more *min*-heuristic responses that do not rely on *p*-entailments than do rely on *p*-entailments; and (2) there should be more *min*-heuristic responses that do rely on *p*-entailments than responses that the *min*-heuristic does not predict. To test prediction (1), within each study, Chater and Oaksford counted the number of syllogisms for which more participants selected the *min*-heuristic response than selected its *p*-entailment. This number was compared to the number of syllogisms for which more participants selected the *p*-entailment of the *min*-heuristic response than the *min*-heuristic response (ties were excluded). There were far more of the former (across the five studies the range was 50 to 56) than the latter (across the five studies the range was 5 to 13). This analysis confirmed that for most syllogisms, participants preferred the *min*-heuristic response over its *p*-entailment, as Chater and Oaksford predicted. They performed similar analyses for the second prediction. Here they counted those syllogisms where the *p*-entailment response was preferred to the response not predicted by the *min*-heuristic and those syllogisms for which the reverse was true. There were far more of the former (across the five studies the range was 22 to 36) than the latter (across the five studies the range was 0 to 16). This analysis confirmed that, for most syllogisms, participants pre-ferred the p-entailment response over the responses not predicted by the *min*-heuristic, as Chater and Oaksford predicted. Overall these analyses showed that, even though there was little opportunity in these experiments to observe p-entailment responses (as only one response was allowed), they were still signif-icantly more common than other responses not predicted by PHM.

The *attachment*-heuristic

To test the predictions of the *attachment*-heuristic, Chater and Oaksford consid-ered each syllogism in turn and compared the number of participants produc-ing the *min* conclusion in the order predicted by attachment with the number of participants producing the opposite conclusion order. There are 56 conclusions for which attachment makes a prediction. Of these, 54 syllogisms conformed to attachment, i.e., more participants selected a conclusion order, e.g. X-Y, pre-dicted by attachments than the opposite order, e.g. Y-X. 1 violated attachment, and there was 1 tie. There are 52 conclusions for which attachment makes a pre-diction for the p-entailments. Of these, 34 syllogisms conformed to attachment 1 violated attachment, and there were 17 ties. Removing the logically valid syllo-gisms did not affect this result. Interestingly, the result was also unchanged when focusing on symmetric conclusions, i.e. where the *min*-response is *None* or *Some*. Attachment still predicts a systematic bias towards a particular conclusion order for all figures. These results confirm that conclusion order is determined by the conclusion type as the *attachment*-heuristic suggests.

The *min*- and *attachment*-heuristics also explain a well-known descriptive generalization about conclusion order: the 'figural effect'. This is the tendency to select the end term that is the subject of one of the premises (if there is exactly one) as the subject of the conclusion. For example, for figure 1, Y-X, Z-Y, the end term Z is the only end term in subject position so by the figural effect, Z should be selected as the subject of the conclusion, which therefore has the order Z-X. Conversely, in figure 4, X-Y, Y-Z, the end term X is the only end term in subject position so the conclusion order is X-Z. The figural effect does not apply to figures 2 and 3 because either both or neither of the possible end-terms in the conclusion are in subject position in the premises. The fig-ural effect is purely descriptive—it has not been proposed to have any rational basis. However, mental models theory (Johnson-Laird 1983; Johnson-Laird and Bara 1984) attempts to explain the figural effect, in terms of the process-ing characteristics of working memory (see below).

For all 32 syllogisms in figures 1 and 4, the predictions of the *min*- and *attachment*-heuristics are exactly in agreement with the figural effect. Moreover, in figures 2 and 3, of the 24 syllogisms for which the *attachment*-heuristic makes predictions, 22 conformed to attachment, one violated attachment, and there was one tie. Removing the logically valid syllogisms does not alter this result. In sum, in accounting for the data on conclusion order, the *attachment*-heuristic goes beyond a combination of the figural effect and logic.

Chater and Oaksford also re-modelled the data including conclusion order in the same way as they modelled conclusion type. Although this required an additional parameter, the number of data points to be modelled also considerably increased. Nonetheless, the fit was still very good, $r(510) = 0.86$ (rms error = 7.56), the model accounting for 74% of the variance in the data. This was a good fit given that just seven parameters are capturing 512 data points.

In summary, the *attachment*-heuristic seems to account accurately for the data on conclusion order. Previous accounts rely on the figure of the premises to explain the observed biases. These accounts only work for figures 1 and 4. One of the virtues of mental models was it could explain the effects for these figures by the presumed 'first-in-first-out' characteristics of a putative working memory store (Johnson-Laird 1983; Johnson-Laird and Bara 1984). The *attachment*-heuristic not only explains the data on figures 1 and 4 but also the complex pattern of data from figures 2 and 3.

These analyses confirmed the main predictions of PHM using past data on the selection task. Each component heuristic seems to capture some important aspect of people's syllogistic reasoning behaviour. Chater and Oaksford (1999) also discuss some limitations of the model. For example, there appears to be a residual effect of logical validity. Thus, taking two syllogisms like *All-All*[4], which is logically valid, and *All-All*[2], which is logically invalid, PHM would predict equal rates of endorsement. However, people endorse the *min*-conclusion for *All-All*[4] (75.32%) more than for *All-All*[2] (58.23%). These are both very high rates of endorsement compared to chance (11.1%). Chater and Oaksford (1999) argue that this indicates that some people do have rudimentary learned test procedures, possibly based on mental logic or mental models. Moreover, for the syllogisms where the *attachment*-heuristic does not predict a preferred conclusion order, there is a systematic pattern. For nearly all these syllogisms, the end-term of the first premise is used as the subject term of the conclusion. Chater and Oaksford (1999) argued that this pattern may reflect the operation of a first-in-first-out principle in working memory, like that proposed in mental models theory. Finally, in apparent violation of PHM, participants sometimes select the *None* conclusion for *None-Some...not* syllogisms. However, as Chater and Oaksford point out, syllogisms of this type uniquely predict a different *p*-entailment conclusion if *p*-entailments are derived for premises as well as for conclusions. Applying the *min*-heuristic to the *p*-entailments of the premises yields a *None* conclusion. In sum, although, PHM has some limitations, the generate processes it embodies explain a great deal of the data on syllogistic reasoning. In the next section, we consider whether it explains more of the data than other theories of syllogistic reasoning.

Comparison with other theories

Chater and Oaksford (1999) compared PHM with the leading alternative theories of syllogistic reasoning: mental logic (Rips 1994), mental models (Johnson-Laird 1983; Johnson-Laird and Byrne 1991), the deduction as verbal reasoning framework (Polk and Newell 1988, 1995), and the atmosphere (Woodworth and Sells 1935), matching (Wetherick 1989), and conversion hypotheses (Chapman and Chapman 1959).

Mental logics: the evaluation task

The mental logic view is that people reason logically using formal rules like those of a natural deduction system (Braine 1978; Galotti *et al.* 1986; Rips 1983). Rips (1994) provided such an account of syllogistic reasoning, PSY-COP, and modelled his own data in a new task where participants *evaluated* syllogisms, given both premises *and* the conclusion. With a fixed order of terms in the conclusion, this led to 256 problems in total. Participants indicated whether the conclusion was 'necessarily true' or 'not necessarily true', given the truth of the premises, i.e. whether the conclusion did or not did follow. The crucial novelty of the evaluation task is that it allows participants to endorse more than one possible conclusion, given the same premises. Chater and Oaksford (1999) argued that, according to PHM, this procedure predicts that the *p*-entailments should now be endorsed as frequently as the *min*-heuristic response. Fig. 7.6 shows that for the *All max*-premise type syllogisms in the Rips (1994) study, this was indeed the case (compare this figure with Fig. 7.4). Over all syllogisms there was no difference between the frequency of endorsing the *min*-heuristic conclusion (mean = 29.84, SD = 24.43) and the frequency of the endorsing its *p*-entailment (mean = 25.31, SD = 8.85).

Chater and Oaksford compared the fit of PHM to Rips' data, to the fit provided by PSYCOP and obtained a very good fit, r (254) = 0.81, rms error = 0.44. Computing the same comparison for PSYCOP's predictions they obtained a comparable fit, r (254) = 0.82, rms error = 0.45. Thus, PHM achieved as good a fit to these data as PSYCOP. However, in fitting PSYCOP to the data Rips (1994) used nine parameters compared to PHM's five. Consequently, Chater and Oaksford argued that PHM provides a far more parsimonious account of these data than PSYCOP.

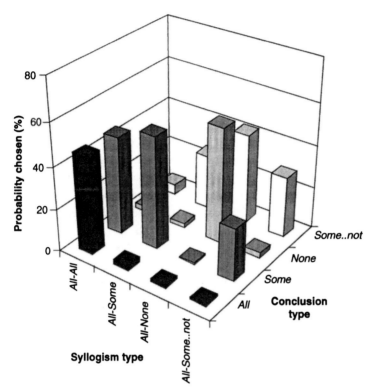

Fig. 7.6 The probability of choosing different syllogism conclusions when the *max*-premise = *All* in Rips' (1994) evaluation task.

Mental models

Chater and Oaksford (1999) compared PHM with mental models theory with respect to several aspects of the data from their meta-analysis.

First, for the valid syllogisms, the distinction between one-, two-, and three-model syllogisms in mental models, maps directly onto distinctions in PHM. All one-model syllogisms have *informative* (*All*, *Some*, or *None*) conclusions. Multiple-model syllogisms have an uninformative (*Some...not*) conclusion. Moreover, the distinction between two- and three-model syllogisms mirrors the distinction between syllogisms for which the *min*-heuristic does (*All-Some...not* and *Some...not-All*: 2 model syllogisms) or does not (*Some-None* and *None-Some*: 3 model syllogisms) work. As we discussed above, all these differences were highly significant thus PHM captures the distinctions in difficulty between the valid syllogisms as well as MMT.

Second, Chater and Oaksford argued that the *Some-None* (and *None-Some*) syllogisms, and those that require an existential pre-supposition (∃p, see 'The probability heuristics model'), provide a critical test of the mental models theory. Apart from *All-All*[3], these are all three-model syllogisms and hence, according to mental models theory, they are all equally difficult. However, when they analysed the results for these syllogisms, Chater and Oaksford found a highly significant crossover interaction: for the *Some-None* (and *None-Some*) syllogisms, participants preferred the logically valid conclusion; whereas for the $\exists p$ syllogisms, they preferred the logically invalid conclusion. However, although there were no significant differences for the *Some-None* (and *None-Some*) syllogisms, there were significantly more responses predicted by PHM than by validity for the $\exists p$ syllogisms. Consequently, while mental models must explain away the significant effects for the $\exists p$ syllogisms, PHM only has to allow that for *Some-None* (and *None-Some*) syllogisms, there is a non-significant tendency to prefer the conclusion type that coincides with validity.

Third, according to mental models theory, participants should respond 'no valid conclusion' if no conclusion is found to be true in all possible models. Erroneous 'no valid conclusion' responses arise when they do not construct all the possible models. Thus, mental models theory predicts that participants should be equally likely to make the 'no valid conclusion' response for all syllogisms requiring the same number of models. Chater and Oaksford focused on two-model syllogisms, for which each *max*-premise type occurs. PHM predicts *max*-premise type will affect 'no valid conclusion' responses, whereas MMT predicts no difference. Chater and Oaksford found a highly significant linear contrast such that 'no valid conclusion' responses increased as the informativeness of the *max*-premise type decreased. Although consistent with PHM this finding is not consistent mental models theory.

Finally, Johnson-Laird and Bara (1984) argued that mental models theory predicts the order 4 > 1 > 2 > 3 over the syllogistic figures in the ease with which participants draw valid inferences. Chater and Oaksford failed to confirm this prediction in their meta-analysis. Thus a key prediction of mental models theory is not borne out in the data and therefore PHM requires no modification to account for putative effects of figure on syllogism difficulty. Chater and Oaksford concluded that PHM captures the data explained by mental models, but also provides a more accurate and detailed account of that data.

Deduction as verbal reasoning

Polk and Newell (1988, 1995) account for syllogistic reasoning within their framework of 'deduction as verbal reasoning'. They derive 14 predictions from this model. Chater and Oaksford argue that some of these also follow very straightforwardly from PHM. For example, Polk and Newell's model predicts that errors on valid syllogisms (excluding 'no valid conclusion' responses) are typically logically *consistent* with the premises. PHM also predicts this, because errors arise from the use of implicatures, which are always logically consistent with the valid conclusion.

The deduction as verbal reasoning framework also predicts more 'no valid conclusion' responses in figures 2 and 3 than in figures 1 and 4. Polk and Newell consider four pairwise comparisons (1 vs. 2, 1 vs. 3, 4 vs. 2, and 4 vs. 3), for all 64 syllogisms, for the 27 Aristotelian valid syllogisms, and for the 37 invalid syllogisms, giving 12 predictions in all. Chater and Oaksford tested these predictions meta-analytically. For all syllogisms, there was a mixed picture, but when divided by valid or invalid syllogisms, a very sharp division was revealed. For the valid syllogisms, *no* pairwise comparison was significant, whereas for the invalid syllogisms, *all* comparisons were significant. Thus only 6 of the 12 predictions were confirmed, providing equivocal support for the deduction as verbal reasoning framework.

Chater and Oaksford argued that, by contrast, PHM can explain these effects. The poor performance on figures 2 and 3 arises because these figures contain all eight syllogisms, where the *attachment*-heuristic fails (*All-All*[2, 3], *Some-Some*[2, 3], *None-None*[2, 3], and *Some...not-Some...not*[2, 3]). If attachment fails, participants may balk in attempting to produce a conclusion, and hence respond 'no valid conclusion'. All these syllogisms are invalid, correctly predicting that differences between figures will occur only for the invalid syllogisms. To confirm this, Chater and Oaksford re-analysed the above pairwise comparisons with these syllogisms removed, and, as PHM predicts, there were no significant differences. Thus, PHM would appear to provide a more accurate account of the effects of figure than the deduction as verbal reasoning framework.

Atmosphere, matching, and conversion

Atmosphere, matching, and conversion are non-logical accounts of syllogistic reasoning, with similar predictions to PHM.

The atmosphere hypothesis (Begg and Denny 1969; Woodworth and Sells 1935) has two parts: *the principle of quality*, that if one or both premises are negative (*None* or *Some...not*), the conclusion should be negative, otherwise it is positive (*All* or *Some*); and *the principle of quantity*, that if one or both premises are particular (*Some* or *Some...not*), then the conclusion will be particular, otherwise it is universal (*All* or *None*). Although its predictions are well confirmed experimentally (Begg and Denny 1969; Jackson 1982), atmosphere has attracted relatively little attention, presumably because it seems theoretically unmotivated.

Chater and Oaksford (1999) argued that PHM explains why atmosphere provides good data fits: the predictions of atmosphere and the *min*-heuristic are almost identical. They only disagree for the *None-Some* (*Some-None*) syllogisms, where atmosphere predicts an *Some...not* conclusion, and *min* predicts a *None* conclusion with a *Some...not* conclusion as a *p*-entailment. In the meta-analysis reported above, there were no significant differences between the frequencies with which *None* and *Some...not* conclusions were drawn for the *None-Some* (*Some-None*) syllogisms, although the trend favours atmosphere. However, PHM is more comprehensive than atmosphere. For example, it explains the second most frequently chosen conclusion (in terms of the *p*-entailments), where atmosphere makes no predictions. This is particularly serious for Rips' (1994) data, where these responses are as frequent as those predicted by the *min*-heuristic. Moreover, atmosphere does not apply to the generalized quantifiers, *Most* and *Few*, whereas PHM generalizes straightforwardly to these cases.

Matching (Wetherick 1989, 1993; Wetherick and Gilhooly 1990) resembles the *min*-heuristic, but relies on 'conservatism' rather than informativeness. A quantified statement is *conservative* to the extent that it commits the speaker to a small number of objects. Thus, *None*-statements are the most conservative, because they do not presuppose any objects, *All*-statements are the least conservative, and *Some-* and *Some...not*-statements are in between, i.e. C(*All*) < C(*Some*) = C(*Some...not*) < C(*None*). The matching hypothesis is that people select conclusions of the same type as the *most* conservative premise. Matching gives good empirical fits (Wetherick 1993).

Some predictions of matching conflict with PHM. For *Some-Some...not* syllogisms, matching predicts no differences between *Some* and *Some...not* conclusions, because conservatism does not differentiate between these. In contrast PHM, via the *min*-heuristic, predicts more *Some...not* responses. For *None-Some...not* syllogisms, matching predicts a preference for *None* over *Some...not* conclusions, whereas PHM, again via the *min*-heuristic, predicts the opposite. As Chater and Oaksford show where matching and PHM diverge, the evidence significantly favours PHM.

A classic explanation of syllogistic reasoning errors is that people erroneously 'convert' one or more premises, e.g. representing *All A are B* as *All B are A* (e.g. Ceraso and Provitera 1971; Chapman and Chapman 1959; Revlis 1975a, b) and then draw a logically valid conclusion from these incorrect premises. Conversion allows, for example, an *All-All*[2] syllogism to be 'converted' into an *All-All*[1], *All-All*[3] and *All-All*[4] syllogism. Consequently conversion effectively ignores figure. Thus, if any syllogism with the given premise types has a valid conclusion, then it is assumed to be a possible response, whatever the figure.

Chater and Oaksford argued that PHM captures the predictions of conversion, but also accounts for many additional effects. For example, PHM correctly predicts the conclusions for syllogisms that are invalid in every figure (*Some-Some...not, Some...not-Some, None-None, None-Some...not, Some...*

not-None) by the *p*-entailments, where conversion does not apply. This is particularly problematic for conversion in Rips' (1994) evaluation task, where responses for conclusions licensed by PHM, but not conversion, are as frequent as responses predicted by both accounts.

Generalized quantifiers

Chater and Oaksford also conducted two experiments to test PHM. They introduced the generalized quantifiers *Most* and *Few* in to syllogistic arguments with the other logical quantifiers. In their experiment 1 they used the quantifiers, *All*, *Most*, *Few*, and *Some...not* and in their experiment 2 they used the quantifiers, *Most*, *Few*, *Some*, and *None*. They did this to ensure that participants were not overburdened with the sheer number of inferences and to make the experiments as much like the standard syllogistic reasoning experiment as possible. No other theory of syllogistic reasoning task performance makes any predictions for the extra 80 syllogisms introduced by this manipulation. However, PHM predicts business as usual, i.e. given the informational ordering, *All* > *Most* > *Few* > *Some* > *None* > *Some...not*, participants should simply apply the heuristics as we have seen they do for the logical quantifiers.

The results of Chater and Oaksford's (1999b) experiment 1, for the *All max*-premise type syllogisms are shown in Fig. 7.7. This figure shows a very similar pattern of performance to their meta-analysis of the data for the logical quantifiers (see Fig. 7.4). For each syllogism type, the modal response is that predicted by the *min*-heuristic, and the next most frequent response is its *p*-entailment (s). So, for example, for *All-Few* the modal response was *Few* and the next most frequent response was *Some...not*. Moreover, for *All-Some...not*, the weak *p*-entailments of *Some...not*, *most* and *few*, are both endorsed more frequently than *All*. This pattern confirms the predictions of PHM's probabilistic semantics for the quantifiers. Chater and Oaksford also provided model fits for these data. The fit was even better than to the meta-analysis reported above, $r(254) = 0.94$ (rms error = 0.16). Thus the model accounts for over 88% of the variance in the overall data. Any theory aimed at explaining logical reasoning, such as mental models or mental logic, does not appear to be well-placed to explain this pattern of performance for the *All-Most* and the *All-Few* syllogisms.

Fig. 7.8 shows the results of Chater and Oaksford's (1999b) experiment 2 for the *Most max*-premise type syllogisms. The first thing to note is that, consistent with the *max*-heuristic, people are less confident in their conclusions than for the *All max*-premise type syllogisms in Fig. 7.7. Nonetheless, the pattern of endorsements is the same: for each syllogism type, the modal response is that predicted by the *min*-heuristic and the next most frequent response (s) is its *p*-entailment (s). The one exception here is that *Few* was as frequent

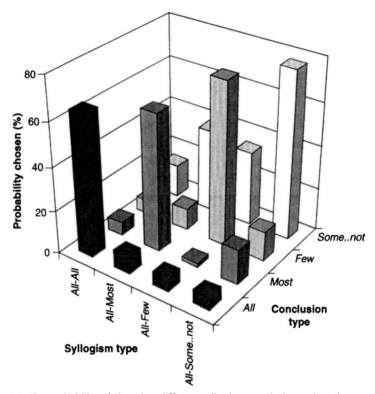

Fig. 7.7 The probability of choosing different syllogism conclusions when the *max*-premise = *All* in Chater and Oaksford's (1999b) experiment 1.

a response for the *Most-None* syllogisms as the *min*-heuristic response, although it is not a *p*-entailment. However, like *None-Some...not* syllogisms, if premise *p*-entailments are taken, then *Few* is a *p*-entailment of the resulting *Some...not* conclusion. *Some...not* was not an available response in experiment 2, so people may have responded with its weak *p*-entailment, *Few*. However, in that case one would predict similar levels of endorsement of *Most*, which is also a weak *p*-entailment of *Some...not*, which was not observed. There is a relatively straightforward explanation of this result that also explains some of the other anomalies observed in experiment 2, which we discuss in the next section. These anomalies are probably responsible for the fact that the overall fit of the model to experiment 2 was less good than to experiment 1, r (254) = 0.65 (rms error = .26).

Chater and Oaksford (1999b) argued that these experiments show that PHM applies successfully across all 144 possible syllogisms involving the quantifiers, *All*, *Most*, *Few*, *Some*, *None*, *Some...not* (although not with all

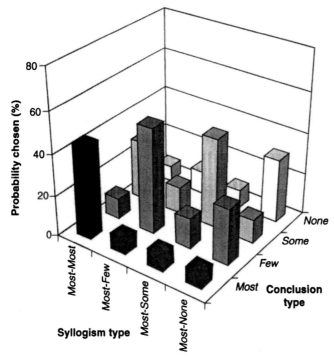

Fig. 7.8 The probability of choosing different syllogism conclusions when the *max*-premise = *Most* in Chater and Oaksford's (1999b) experiment 2.

possible conclusion types). The uniform pattern in these data across the generalized and the standard logical quantifiers challenges other theories of syllogistic reasoning, which currently apply only to the logical quantifiers, to generalize to these data.

Further evidence for PHM

Further recent work on syllogistic reasoning has produced results consistent with PHM.

Strong and weak possible conclusions

Evans *et al.* (1999) showed that the *min*-heuristic captures an important novel distinction between strong and weak possible conclusions. A conclusion can be necessarily true, possibly true, or impossible. For example, take the syllogism *All-Some*[1]. The conclusion *Some Z are X*, follows *necessarily* from these premises. Moreover, with respect to these premises, the conclusion *No Z are X*, is *impossible*. However, the conclusion *Some Z are not X* is *possible* given these premises, but it is not necessary, because the premises do not rule out the possibility that *All Z are X*, which is the contrary of this conclusion. Evans *et al.* (1999) observed that some of the possible conclusions were endorsed by as many participants as the necessary conclusions. Moreover, they observed that some of the possible conclusions were endorsed by as few participants as the impossible conclusions. As they observed, possible strong conclusions (as in the example) all conform to the *min*-heuristic, i.e. they either match the *min*-premise or are less informative than the *min*-premise. Possible weak conclusions all violate the *min*-heuristic (with one exception), i.e. they have conclusions that are more informative than the *min*-premise. Thus PHM explains this important novel finding.

Prima facie, mental models theory also explains this result. A conclusion is necessarily true if it is true in all models of the premises, a conclusion is possibly true if it is true in at least one model of the premises, and a conclusion is impossible if it is not true in any model of the premises. Strong possible conclusions are those that are licensed in the initial model constructed but not in subsequent models. Moreover, weak possible conclusions are those that are only licensed in non-initial models. This explanation means that the conclusions licensed by initial mental models correspond to those recommended by the *min*-heuristic. However, other than the suggestion that this is an 'emergent property' of the computer program embodying the mental models theory, no account of the principles underlying initial model construction that could explain this fit are provided by Evans *et al.* (1999), or elsewhere. Consequently it would seem that PHM currently provides a more principled account of this important new finding.

Alternative conclusions

In a series of experiments designed to test the claim that syllogism difficulty is determined by the number of alternative mental models constructed, Newstead *et al.* (1999) found evidence consistent with PHM. Participants were asked to indicate the alternative conclusions they considered for different syllogisms or were asked to draw diagrams consistent with the premises. According to mental models theory, more alternative conclusions and more diagrams should be produced for multiple-model syllogisms than for single-model syllogisms. However, Newstead *et al.* found no relationship between the number of models a syllogism requires for its solution and the number of conclusions or diagrams participants produced. This is consistent with PHM, where it is argued that test procedures are rarely invoked. In all Newstead *et al.*'s experiments, participants' responses also agreed with those predicted by the *min*- and *attachment*-heuristics. Furthermore, according to PHM, there should be no differences in task difficulty dependent on figure, a prediction that is inconsistent with mental models theory. Consistent with PHM, in two of Newstead *et al'*.s experiments where figure was an independent variable, they found no effect of figure on syllogism difficulty. As they point out, their findings clearly favour PHM over mental models.

However, Newstead *et al.* (1999) argue that two other aspects of their results sit less well with PHM. First, they argue that PHM predicts that people would consider more conclusions when they are less confident in the *min*-conclusion. Consequently, they argue there should be a linear trend in the number of alternative conclusions considered such that *All < Some < Some-not ≈ None*. However, they found no such result. We are unsure how Newstead *et al.* derived this prediction. The only way that PHM allows alternative conclusions to be generated is via *p*-entailments. However, in modelling the data from their meta-analysis, Chater and Oaksford (1999) argued that *p*-entailments were endorsed in a fixed proportion across all syllogisms. In their meta-analysis this proportion was 0.09. Thus for each *max*-premise type, PHM predicts one conclusion predicted by the *min*-heuristic to be considered plus this small proportion of *p*-entailments, leading to approximately 1.09 conclusions considered. For *All max*-premise type syllogisms, Newstead *et al.* observed an average of 1.05 and for the other *max*-premise type syllogisms they observed an average of 1.13. Thus their findings seem completely consistent with PHM.

An illuminating comparison would be to check whether the alternatives produced (although rare) were consistent with the *p*-entailment of the *min*-conclusion or with other conclusions licensed by the initial mental model of particular syllogisms (where these disagree). But given that so few alternatives were generated, only very sparse data is presumably available to test this prediction. However, Rips' (1994) data does allow a comparison. In his data, *p*-entailment conclusions were as frequent as those predicted by the *min*-heuristic. This was because Rips presented each possible conclusion alone with the premises, thus eliminating response competition. Given that people rarely construct more than one model, it seems that mental models must predict that the *p*-entailment response is always a possible conclusion in the initial mental model as well as the *min*-heuristic response. However, checking this prediction is complicated by the problem that we mentioned above in discussing Evans *et al.* (1999): the principles by which initial models are generated are opaque.

Newstead *et al.* (1999) also argue that the close correspondence between the diagrams people produce and the conclusions that they draw suggests that, contrary to PHM, representational processes are involved in reasoning. Again we are unsure of why this correspondence should be thought inconsistent with PHM. According to PHM, the heuristics apply to *representations* of the premises to generate *representations* of the conclusion. We conceive of the representations more linguistically than diagrammatically. So perhaps the disagreement concerns people's apparent ability to use diagrams. However, that people are capable of drawing external diagrammatic representations of those conclusions does not entail that that is how they are mentally represented. For example, it is easy to draw a picture representing the sentence that 'the cat is on the mat'. However, this ability hardly counts as evidence for a diagrammatic or imagistic account of mental representation over a propositional account (Pylyshyn 1973).

Working memory and syllogistic reasoning

Copeland and Radvanksy (2004) have recently observed that there have been few experiments directly relating memory-span measures to syllogistic-reasoning performance. They therefore took a variety of working memory-span measures and then had participants perform a computerized version of the standard syllogistic-reasoning task. They also compared the predictions of the mental models theory and PHM. PHM makes similar predictions to mental models theory because it can account for the difference in accuracy on the one-, two-, and three-model syllogisms. Getting the valid conclusion requires the use of different numbers of heuristics. For one-model syllogisms, just the *min*-heuristic and attachment is required. For two-model syllogisms, the *min*-heuristic, attachment and the *Some...not*-heuristic are invoked (because the conclusion is always *Some...not*, so the *Some...not*-heuristic is invoked, leading to fewer correct selections). For three-model syllogisms a *p*-entailment has to be drawn, the *min*-heuristic and attachment applied and the *Some...not*-heuristic invoked. Thus, for one-model syllogisms, two heuristics are invoked; for two-model syllogisms, three are invoked; and for three-model syllogisms, four are invoked. The generation heuristics operate over a mental representation of the premises to generate a conclusion, the test heuristics determine confidence that will be related to RTs. The more mental operations that need to be performed, the more complex the inference. People with high IQs are likely to be better at more complex processes and WM span and IQ are highly correlated. Thus it seems that the analyses in terms of the number mental models are consistent with PHM.

Consistent with this analysis, Copeland and Radvansky (2004) found significant correlations between working memory span and strategy use, for both mental models and PHM. Moreover there were no differences between mental models and PHM on the percentage of responses made that agreed with the predictions of each model. Consequently although these data did not discriminate between theories, they confirmed the predictions that each theory

independently makes for the complexity of syllogistic reasoning and its relation to working memory span.

Few⁺ and *few⁻*

Oaksford *et al.* (2002) pointed out that some of the results of Chater and
Oaksford's (1999) experiments were unexpected from the perspective of their
theory. In particular, the results seemed to question a core assumption of the
model concerning the ordering in the informativeness of the quantifiers. For
example, for *Few-Some...not (Some...not-Few)* syllogisms, the *min*-heuristic
predicts a *Some...not* conclusion. However, in Chater and Oaksford's experiment 1, there was no significant difference in mean percentage endorsements
of *Few* (mean = 51.9, SD = 8.4) and *Some...not* (mean = 54.4, SD = 9.4). They
were, however, both endorsed significantly more often than the other possible
response options: *All* (mean = 0, SD = 0) and *Most* (mean = 2.5, SD = 2.7).
Moreover, for *Few-Some (Some-Few)* syllogisms, the *min*-heuristic predicts a
Some conclusion. However, in Chater and Oaksford's experiment 2, there was
no significant difference in mean percentage endorsements of *Few* (mean =
37.5, SD = 8.9) and *Some* (mean = 26.9, SD = 10.0), although they were both
endorsed significantly more often than the other possible response options:
Most (mean = 3.75, SD = 5.2) and *None* (mean = 12.5, SD = 7.1). These results
suggest that in Chater and Oaksford's experiment 1, *Few* was regarded as having the same informativeness as *Some...not*, whereas in their experiment 2, *Few*
was regarded as having the same informativeness as *Some*.

Oaksford *et al.* (2002) argued that there are two factors contributing to these
effects. The first factor concerns a possible pragmatic ambiguity in the interpretation of *Few*. Take for example, 'a few staff attended the meeting'. It makes
sense here to extend this to, 'a few staff attended the meeting, and perhaps they
all did'. Thus 'a few' does not rule out the possibility that an *All* statement
is true. 'A few' is a positive quantifier, which Oaksford *et al.* designate by *Few⁺*
(Moxey and Sanford 1987, 1991; Paterson *et al.* 1998; Sanford *et al.* 1994,
1996). However, it makes no sense to say, 'few staff attended the meeting, and
perhaps they all did'. By contrast, it does make sense to say, 'few staff attended
the meeting, and perhaps none at all'. Thus 'few' does not rule out the possibility that a *None* statement is true. 'Few' is a negative quantifier, which Oaksford
et al. designate by *Few⁻*. Oaksford *et al.* argue that these two interpretations of
Few are always in play, and that they can both be captured probabilistically.
Few⁻ means that $P(Y|X) < \Delta$. Note that this now means that if Δ is small then
Few⁻ and *None* almost perfectly overlap creating new *p*-entailments: *Few⁻* $\Leftrightarrow$
None. *Few⁺* means that $P(Y|X) \geq \Delta$. Oaksford *et al.* point out that these adjust-
ments mean that if Δ is small *Few⁺* will have the same informativeness as

Some, and that if Δ is high *Few⁻* will be close to the informativeness of *Some...not*. Oaksford *et al.* conducted four experiments that confirmed the ordering in informativeness predicted by these new definitions.

The second factor concerns a difference in the quantifiers used between Chater and Oaksford's experiments, that provides good reasons to believe that *Few* was interpreted differently in each of Chater and Oaksford's (1999) experiments. It is well-established that whether a particular quantifier is considered appropriate to describe a situation may be dependent on the other quantifiers available (Brownell and Caramazza 1978; Moxey and Sanford 1991). For example, suppose that 10 out of 100 squares are white. One might choose to describe this state of affairs by *Few squares are white*. But if *Few* is unavailable, then *Some squares are white* may do perfectly well. In Chater and Oaksford (1999), only the quantifiers *All, Most, Few*, and *Some...not* were used in experiment 1, and only the quantifiers *Most, Few, Some*, and *None* were used in experiment 2. This was to keep the total number of syllogisms in a single experiment at manageable levels. In Chater and Oaksford's experiments we suspect that the change in the quantifiers used has led participants to interpret 'few' as *Few⁻* in experiment 1 and as *Few⁺* in experiment 2. This is because in experiment 1, using *All, Most, Few*, and *Some...not*, *Few* is not needed to express the possibility of *All* or *Most*, because these quantifiers are available. Consequently 'few' was interpreted as *Few⁻*, i.e. as applying only to the bottom end of the probability scale. The reverse was true for experiment 2 that used *Most, Few, Some*, and *None*. Here *Few* is not needed to express *None* as this quantifier is available. Consequently, 'few' was interpreted as *Few⁺*, i.e. as applying to top end of the probability scale. So, the apparent anomaly in Chater and Oaksford's (1999) results may be resolved by taking account of some of the pragmatic properties of these quantifiers that can be easily incorporated in to the probabilistic semantics of PHM.

In sum, much of the evidence that has emerged since PHM was published seems to be consistent with that model. Importantly it accounts for an important novel distinction discovered by Evans *et al.* (1999) between strong and weak possible conclusions. Moreover, PHM's prediction of the figural independence of syllogism difficulty, which is inconsistent with mental models theory, has been confirmed. In the next section we look at recent objections to PHM as a theory of syllogistic reasoning.

Summary

PHM provides a set of 'fast and frugal' heuristics for syllogistic reasoning, which approximate a rational standard for reasoning with quantifiers under a probabilistic interpretation. These heuristics reliably *generate* the *p*-valid conclusion, if there is one (the *min*- and *attachment*-heuristics). They also provide a relatively crude measure to *test* whether a syllogism is valid or not (the *max*-heuristic). However, this means that people are likely to generate and propose conclusions for the invalid syllogisms as well. PHM accounts for this pattern of errors, not only for the standard logical quantifiers but also for syllogisms involving the generalized quantifiers *Most* and *Few*. Importantly, to apply to these quantifiers, other theories of syllogistic reasoning must either adopt Chater and Oaksford's notion of *p*-validity, or develop an alternative notion of validity. That is, they must define some computational-level theory of the inferences people should draw with generalized syllogisms. Only then can they differentiate correct from incorrect performance when people reason with these syllogisms. Moreover, Chater and Oaksford's experiments using generalized quantifiers show a pattern of performance apparently uniform with performance using the standard quantifiers. People typically choose the correct conclusion if there is one, but are relatively poor at distinguishing *p*-valid from *p*-invalid conclusions. *Independently of PHM, all other theories of syllogistic reasoning must show how to generalize to this pattern of performance.*

Mental logic approaches seem to be in worst shape in this respect, because they rely only on logical machinery that could not generalize to Most and Few. Mental models seems to be in better shape here because, as Johnson-Laird (1983, 1994) has urged, one main advantage of the mental models formalism is that it can naturally represent generalized quantifiers (such as *Most* and *Few*), and moreover, deal with certain kinds of probabilistic reasoning (Johnson-Laird *et al.* 1999). However, merely representing generalized quantifiers does not define a proof procedure for deriving conclusions from premises containing quantifiers like *Most* and *Few*. In particular, with these quantifiers the guiding principle of mental models, that people search for counter-examples, will be of no use—with probabilistic relations counter-examples will always be available and so finding one tells you little about the *p*-validity of an inference. Whatever the outcome, it is clear that mental logic and mental model theories must face the central challenge of accounting for generalized quantifiers and for the pattern of inferences revealed in Chater and Oaksford's experiments 1 and 2. With respect to this challenge PHM presently has the advantage over the other main theories of syllogistic reasoning.

Objections and replies

In this section, we tackle some possible objections to PHM that may appear to question its plausibility as a general model of syllogistic reasoning.

Generality

The heuristics Chater and Oaksford proposed to explain syllogistic reasoning, although providing good fits to the existing data and generalized quantifiers, may seem very domain-specific. This may be felt to contrast with other accounts like mental logics and mental models that, although failing to generalize to generalized quantifiers, have been shown to account for a broad range of data from other reasoning tasks.

The first thing to note is that similar strategies apply and are in evidence in other areas of reasoning. For example, a heuristic similar to the *max*-heuristic is used in well-known AI systems for medical diagnosis such as MYCIN and EMYCIN to compute the believability of conclusions (Gordon and Shortliffe 1985). Moreover, George (1997) argues that a similar heuristic to the *max*-heuristic is evident in human data on conditional inference with uncertain premises. Note that, given our probabilistic semantics, the conditional premise can be characterized as a quantified statement. George (1997) used three levels of probability: certain (C), very probable (VP) and not very probable (NVP), e.g. *if A, then certainly B*. According to our probabilistic semantics, we can interpret conditional premises containing these terms as corresponding to quantified premises using *All*, *Most* and *Few* respectively. According to probability theory, it has to be the case that the probability of the conclusion is on average higher for *All* than for *Most* and higher for *Most* than for *Few*. That is, on average, our confidence in a conclusion should be proportional to the informativeness of the conditional premise. So if you do not know the precise probabilities, then a good heuristic for how confident you should be in the conclusion is to follow the $A > M > F$ order, as we have recommended in syllogistic reasoning. George's (1997) experiment 2 confirms that people conform to this average ordering: the average rated probability of a conclusion when the conditional premise contained 'certainly' (*All*) was .70, when it contained 'very probable' (*Most*) it was .60, and when it contained 'not very probable' (*Few*) it was .36 (these expected values were calculated by re-scaling George's (1997) rating scale into the 0–1 probability scale).

Acquisition

How would naïve participants acquire the heuristics we propose in this paper? Although the *min* and *max*-heuristics may have analogues in other areas of reasoning, we believe that their specific application in syllogistic reasoning is acquired from the ubiquity of various forms of implicit syllogistic reasoning that people must carry out routinely. We also believe that this is how the *attachment*-heuristic is learned; before outlining the forms of implicit syllogistic reasoning that we believe underpin our explicit abilities in syllogistic reasoning tasks, we first outline just how simple attachment is to master.

Attachment is the most task-specific heuristic in PHM. However, on our assumption that *min* only generates a conclusion type, participants must have a way of making the simple binary choice concerning the ordering of end terms in the conclusion. The first point worth making is that attachment is a very simple pattern-matching strategy that it is very easy for participants to apply despite its somewhat cumbersome definition. The second point worth making is that attachment generally has an even simpler characterization: go with the order of end terms dictated by the premise most similar to the generated conclusion type, but if tied for similarity, leave the order of terms as they appear in the premises (this is very similar to the description of the figural effect in Stenning and Yule 1997). This works for the *min*-responses by definition. So, for example, the conclusion of *All-Some*[1] is *Some Z are X*, because *Z* is in subject position in the *Some* premise, whereas the conclusion of *All-Some*[3] is *Some X are Z*, because *Z* is now in the predicate position in the *Some* premise. This definition also works for the *p*-entailments: because the *p*-entailment of *Some* is *Some...not*, the same ordering of end terms as found in the *min* conclusion is predicted for both *All-Some*[1] and *All-Some*[3]. The point we wish to emphasize is that the simplicity of the strategy means that acquiring it requires only minimal experience of reasoning syllogistically. However, this is clearly not a strategy that can be generalized from other modes of reasoning where the problem simply does not arise. Moreover, if you agree with Russell (and disagree with Johnson-Laird) then one might question whether even this minimal level of experience is available before people enter the reasoning lab.

However, many psychological processes involve implicit syllogistic reasoning, which must be going on from a very early age as more knowledge is slowly acquired about the world. The purpose of acquiring world knowledge is to guide expectations. Most often that knowledge will be acquired in many different contexts. Hence, to derive the appropriate expectations, this information will need to be combined somehow. Combining stereotypical information is a paradigm case. As people meet other people throughout their lives, in the flesh and in fiction, they develop stereotypical information very early on. So, for example, you may come to believe that *Few skydivers are boring* but that *All accountants are boring*. If the issue of the occupations of skydivers arose, you could use this information rapidly to form the expectation that *Few skydivers are accountants*. You are likely to perform this inference rapidly and implicitly and even be able to justify your conclusion: in general, accountants are boring and skydivers are not. However, you may only become aware that you are implicitly committed to this expectation when you are surprised on being told that the skydiver you just met was an accountant. People must be drawing implicit inferences of this form, in order to generate their expectations about other people all the time. Rarely do these inferences receive an explicit formulation. Nonetheless, we suggest that they provide a rich backdrop of implicit experience from which people acquire their short cut heuristics for deriving syllogistic conclusions.

Representation

The heuristics in PHM do not, at least on the face of it, involve manipulating people's representations of the meanings of the premises of a syllogistic argument. This, it may be argued, contrasts with other accounts of syllogistic reasoning that account for the derivation of syllogistic conclusions by manipulating these internal representations. This fact may be felt to argue that accounts such as mental logics and mental models are, a priori, more plausible than PHM. However, as our discussion of implicit syllogistic reasoning reveals, applying these heuristics does presuppose that people represent the meanings of the premises that enter into syllogistic arguments. To identify the *min*-premise (and therefore the *max*-premise) requires that their probabilities, which according to our account provide the meanings of these premises, are represented in the cognitive system (although they may be represented in a more coarse grained way than required by probability theory; see: Pearl 1988). Moreover, the cognitive system must be able to convert these probabilities into structured representations containing the quantifier dictated by our probabilistic semantics and the arrangement of end and middle terms. Only then can the heuristics that make up PHM be applied to implicitly derive syllogistic conclusions. Consequently PHM does require semantic representations that capture people's understanding of syllogistic premises. All that PHM denies is that people need to perform complex derivations over these representations to derive syllogistic conclusions.

Individual differences

Ford (1994) argues from protocol data that some people use *verbal*, and others use *spatial*, representations of syllogistic arguments. We should expect different strategies to show up in different patterns of normal performance in syllogistic reasoning. It might therefore seem surprising that PHM can provide such an accurate overall data fit. One explanation is that the apparent *verbal/spatial* difference does not arise in the standard data, because people are forced to change their reasoning strategy when a protocol must be generated. Thus, in terms of PHM, the difference would be located in the test procedure.

An alternative possibility is some correlate of the *verbal/spatial* difference may arise from individual differences in the generate procedures, which PHM does not currently allow. For example, there could be subtle differences in the heuristics people use, in the weightings given to *max*, or in the sophistication of the *attachment*-heuristic and so on. Indeed, assumptions about domain size could even affect the very informational ordering that people adopt. Consequently, there seems just as much scope for explaining individual differences in PHM as in other accounts. Finally, as we noted in discussing Polk and Newell (1995) above, modelling data from individual participants presents an important future direction for PHM.

A logical account of figural effects?

Stenning and Yule (1997, see also Stenning and Oberlander 1995) have shown how algorithms for syllogistic reasoning based on both mental logic and mental models are both instances of *individual identification algorithms*. These algorithms rely on the *case identifiability property* of syllogisms, whereby a valid conclusion specifies a unique type of individual that must exist. In particular, Stenning and Yule have shown a novel way of predicting figural effects at the computational level without relying on the limitations of a putative working memory store. They identify the *source* premise as the source of the existential force of a valid conclusion. They suggest that the end term of the source premise will invariably be chosen as the subject term of the conclusion. Importantly this hypothesis also makes predictions for figures 2 and 3. Stenning and Yule (1997) report important evidence from a novel version of the syllogistic reasoning task that is consistent with the source premise hypothesis. Although this is a very interesting development, there appear to be some limitations on the scope of these proposals. First, the concept of a source premise only applies to the valid syllogisms, 'the source premise for some valid individual conclusion is any premise which makes an existential assertion, from which the existence of that individual can be inferred', (see: Stenning and Yule 1997, pp. 126–7). Consequently, figural effects cannot be predicted for the invalid syllogisms. But recall that out of 56 syllogisms for which the *attachment*-heuristic makes a prediction, 54 conformed to attachment, and yet only 27 of these are logically valid (Stenning and Yule allow existential presupposition). This leaves 27 syllogisms for which Chater and Oaksford's meta-analysis revealed a figural preference that is unexplained by the 'source-founding hypothesis'. Second, this explanation of figural effects could not account for the figural effects observed for the *p*-entailments, which, when there is no response competition, are drawn as frequently as the standard inferences, as Rips (1994) data reveals. Of course, the *p*-entailments (or indeed the Gricean implicatures; Grice 1975) are not the product of deductive inferences, and so by definition identify the existence of individuals that cannot be deductively inferred. Third, the concept of case identifiability, on which Stenning and Yule's (1997) analysis relies, does not apply to syllogisms containing generalized quantifiers, where according to PHM, the existence of particular individuals is not certain, just more or less likely. Yet we have suggested above that the behavioural data on how people reason with conventional and generalized quantifiers invites a single, uniform, explanation.

Belief bias

Belief bias occurs when the believability of the materials influence reasoning performance. Although first demonstrated in syllogistic reasoning (Henle and Michael 1956; Morgan and Morton 1944), belief bias effects arise in a wide range of experimental tasks (e.g. Cheng and Holyoak 1985; Griggs and Cox 1982; Griggs and Newstead 1982; Wason and Brooks 1979; Wason and Shapiro 1971). A natural explanation is that, in everyday reasoning, people use all their knowledge to arrive at the most plausible conclusions. But in experimental reasoning tasks, participants must reason only from the given premises, ignoring background knowledge. Therefore, belief bias may simply reflect the inability of participants to disengage their everyday reasoning strategies in any reasoning context (Fodor 1983; Oaksford and Chater 1991; Pylyshyn 1987) and therefore does not distinguish between alternative accounts of syllogistic reasoning.

Multiply quantified sentences

Johnson-Laird et al. (1989) provide another line of related work. Consider the argument: 'None of the Princeton letters is in the same place as any of the Cambridge letters', 'All of the Cambridge letters are in the same place as all of the Dublin letters', therefore 'None of the Princeton letters is in the same place as any of the Dublin letters'. Such reasoning appears similar to syllogistic reasoning. However, each premise and the conclusion contains (1) two quantifiers and (2) a relation (in the example, 'is in the same place as'), which increases the logical complexity significantly. We have no general theory of the representation of relations over which we could compute informativeness. In this respect, MMT does better than PHM, because Johnson-Laird et al. (1989) have extended mental models to handle problem such as that above, arguing that the number of mental models predicts problem difficulty. However, they deal with only one equivalence relation: 'in the same place as' rather than giving a general account of quantified relational reasoning. Further, an observation of Greene (1992) points to a possible informational account of these data. Greene (1992) observed that, as we have found for syllogisms, conclusion type reflects the distinction between one and multiple model problems—the only valid conclusion for multiple-model problems was of the form, 'none of the X are related to some of the Y'. Intuitively, such conclusions seem particularly uninformative. This observation may be a starting point for an informational account, but presently these data provide most support for mental models.

'Only' reasoning

Johnson-Laird and Byrne (1989) have used *Only*, which is equivalent to *All* (i.e. *Only X are Y ≡ All Y are X*), in syllogistic reasoning. A critical finding is that *Only-Only* syllogisms tend to lead to *All* conclusions, i.e. the conclusion quantifier is not of the same type as either premise. This cannot, of course, be explained by *min*. However, *p*-entailments do allow this possibility. They are typically less common, because *p*-entailments do not imply perfect logical entailment, but only that the *p*-entailment follows with some probability (or that it is less informative than the standard conclusion, and hence it is less likely to be picked). According to PHM, logical equivalence between different quantifiers, e.g. *All* and *Only*, can be regarded as an especially strong *p*-entailment. A crucial asymmetry between *All* and *Only* is that *All* is much more frequently used to express class inclusion. Therefore a strong bias would be expected for people to give conclusions using the familiar *All* form rather than the less familiar *Only* form. So, although the *p*-entailment here is bi-directional, it will occur much more frequently in one direction than the other. This is a matter of experience with natural language usage, rather than arising from logical factors. This explanation gives rise to the pattern of data in Johnson-Laird and Byrne (1989).

Do people draw *p*-entailments?

That people draw the *p*-entailments is an important novel prediction of PHM. Moreover, in their meta-analysis of the past literature on syllogistic reasoning, Chater and Oaksford (1999b) found considerable evidence for the *p*-entailments. The *p*-entailments are closely related to the Gricean implicatures. But recently Newstead (1995) has argued that the implicatures are not in evidence either in the past literature on syllogistic reasoning or in his experiments. This apparent inconsistency is easily resolved. First, Newstead looked only at the valid syllogisms. However, *min*-heuristic conclusions can be drawn for all syllogisms. Consequently, Chater and Oaksford checked whether participants occasionally responded with a *p*-entailment of the *min*-heuristic conclusion across all syllogisms.

Second, Newstead regarded an implicature response as only in evidence if it had a greater than chance probability of being made. This criterion seems inappropriate when other possible responses are being made at significantly less than chance levels, where this is defined as arising from entirely random responding. For example, in Chater and Oaksford's meta-analysis, for the *All-All*[4] syllogism, 75.32% selected the logically correct or *min*-heuristic *All* conclusion; 16.46% the implicature or *p*-entailment *Some* conclusion; and 1.27% selected the *None* and 0.63% selected the *Some...not* conclusion. According to the chance criterion, although *Some* was selected significantly more often than either *None* or *Some...not*, this does not count as evidence that implicatures or *p*-entailments are being drawn! However, it is clear that people are responding non-randomly and close to zero on responses that PHM predicts should not be made. Consequently, it is simply not appropriate to assess the occurrence of responses that PHM predicts should be made with respect to chance. Chater and Oaksford (1999b) argued that it was good evidence that the implicatures or *p*-entailments are drawn if there are more syllogisms where more participants select the *p*-entailment response than the remaining two responses combined. As they show, on this criterion the past literature reveals considerable evidence for the implicatures or *p*-entailments.

Third, the experiments that Newstead (1995) considers, and his own experiments, all involved selecting or producing a single conclusion. That is, even if participants consider more than one possible conclusion, only one can be used. According to PHM, in these circumstances this will always be the *min*-heuristic conclusion, which is why the *p*-entailments are less in evidence. However, if response competition were eliminated, then people should respond as readily with the *p*-entailment conclusion as with the *min*-heuristic conclusion. In Rips' (1994) experiment, where each pair of premises was presented with a single possible conclusion (making 256 syllogisms in all) this is exactly what happened. For most syllogisms, the implicature or *p*-entailment conclusion was drawn as often as the *min*-heuristic conclusion (Chater and Oaksford 1999b). Consequently, it appears that implicatures or *p*-entailments may substantially affect syllogistic reasoning in the way that both Rips (1994) and Chater and Oaksford (1999b) argue, albeit from very different perspectives.

Activation of end terms

Espino *et al.* (2000) reported innovative studies investigating the time to respond to a probe word that has or has not occurred in the premises of a syllogistic argument. They derived predictions from mental models theory that they compared to the predictions of the other leading theories in this area, including PHM. In their experiments 2 to 5, they claimed to have found conclusive evidence for the mental models account of syllogistic reasoning and against all these contenders.

Three results are important. First, in their experiments 2 to 4, Espino *et al.* found that for figure 4 syllogisms (e.g. *All the X are Y, All the Y are Z*), responses were faster when the end term *Z* was used as the probe, than when the end term *X* was used as the probe. However, this reversed for figure 1 syllogisms (e.g. *All the Y are X, All the Z are Y*). Espino *et al.* argued that this finding is consistent with mental models theory because the end term responded to the fastest is the last item in the mental model. And in theories of language comprehension, during comprehension the last mentioned item in an integrated representation of a multi-clausal sentence is the most active. This is because this item is where further information must be attached. Espino *et al.* argued that PHM must predict the opposite finding because the *attachment*-heuristic, which determines the order of end terms in the conclusion, must attach to the end term in subject position in either premise, i.e. *X* for figure 4 and *Z* for figure 1.

Second, in experiments 2 to 4, Espino *et al.* consistently found that responses to the probe words in figure 4 were faster than in figure 1. They took this to indicate that figure 4 syllogisms are easier than figure 1 syllogisms, which is consistent with mental models theory but not with PHM which predicts no differences in difficulty with figure.

Third, in their experiment 5, Espino *et al.* showed that after people had performed the reasoning task the pattern of RTs switched. Now, for figure 4, syllogism responses were faster when the end term *X* was used as the probe, than when the end term *Z* was used as the probe, and this reversed for figure 1 syllogisms. Espino *et al.* argued that this finding is consistent with mental models theory because the end term responded to the fastest is now the first item in the mental model. And in theories of language comprehension, after a sentence has been heard, the first-mentioned item in an integrated representation of a multi-clausal sentence is the most active. This is because, with no further information to attach to the representation, the first clause is the item to which all other items are attached. Although now consistent with the predictions of PHM, Espino *et al.* would presumably argue that PHM cannot explain why the switch occurs.

We now consider each finding in turn. To derive their predictions, Espino *et al.* assume that the heuristics of PHM are applied to the premises during the comprehension stage. The heuristics of PHM operate over representations of the premises (see: Chater and Oaksford 1999, p. 236) to build a representation of the conclusion. For example, take the figure 4 syllogism, *All the X are Y, All the Y are Z*, the *min*-heuristic selects the frame *All _ are _* as the form of the conclusion with place holders for the end terms. The *attachment*-heuristic selects the subject term of the *min*-premise (as long as it is an end term) as the subject term of the conclusion: *All X are _*. This representation is of course incomplete. The final operation of the attachment heuristic is to place the other end term in the remaining place holder: *All X are Z*. That is, the last item to enter the representation in figure 4 is *Z*. Consequently, consistent with existing accounts of language comprehension, PHM makes exactly the same predictions as mental models. Therefore, PHM is consistent with Espino *et al*.'s first and most robust finding.

It could be argued that in specifying the *attachment*-heuristic, Chater and Oaksford (1999) left the final step of selecting the remaining end term as the predicate term of the conclusion implicit. Consequently it was reasonable for Espino *et al.* to derive the predictions they did. However, once the subject term is fixed, there is no other choice for the predicate term. Therefore, it follows straightforwardly on this viewpoint that the remaining end term would enter the conclusion representation last.

The reaction time differences between figures reported by Espino *et al.* concern differences in the activation level of a representation of the end terms. They do not necessarily reflect differences in processing difficulty in creating an integrated representation of the premises. Indeed, it seems perfectly reasonable that the relation between the activation level of items in a representation and the difficulty experienced in constructing that representation should go in precisely the opposite direction to that exploited by Espino *et al.* It could be argued that the more processing effort required to construct a representation, the more attention will be paid to the items in it, and so the more active they will be. This of course would predict the opposite result to that found by Espino *et al.* In sum, the reaction time differences they describe do not necessarily relate to processing difficulty; and there is good reason to think they should be making the opposite prediction in any case. Consequently, PHM is consistent with Espino *et al*.'s second finding, because PHM's prediction concerns differences in processing difficulty not in the activation of end terms. As far as we can see, Espino *et al*.'s finding is not predicted by any current theory of syllogistic reasoning.

Finally, in their experiment 5, Espino *et al.* provided their participants with the valid conclusion to the syllogism and then asked them to make a validity judgement, before being tested on the probe words. Consequently the single sentence the participants saw immediately prior to being presented with the probe word, always contained the end term now responded to fastest as its subject term. So, for the figure 4 syllogism (*All the X are Y, All the Y are Z, Are All the X, Z?*) *X* is the subject term of the conclusion sentence and this term is responded to faster than *Z* when presented as a post-conclusion probe. This could happen if the conclusion is represented separately. No further information need attach to this conclusion representation. Therefore, according to Espino *et al.*, the first term will be more active because it is the term to which other information is attached. Representing the conclusion sentence separately makes sense in PHM (and in a variety of other accounts). This is because this allows the results of applying PHM's heuristics (or other inferential processes) to the premises to be compared to the conclusion. In sum, placing the probe word after the conclusion can lead to a response switch, because now the conclusion representation is being probed not the premise representation. However, with two representations, one might predict that the effects would be weaker because of the potential ambiguity over which representation is being probed. And in Espino *et al.*'s experiment 5 the interaction effect was far weaker than in their experiments 2 to 4. Consequently Espino *et al.*'s third finding is consistent with PHM (and with most other approaches).

In summary, to explain Espino *et al.*'s most robust finding in experiments 2 to 4, requires considering the details of PHM, i.e. no *ad hoc* proposals are required to see how PHM can explain this result. Their second finding does not address the issue of processing difficulty, so it is difficult to see how it bears on PHM's prediction of no differences in processing difficulty between figures. Moreover, as we pointed out above, Newstead *et al.*'s (1999) results confirm this prediction of PHM. Finally Espino *et al.*'s third and less robust finding can be explained by the simple proposal that people represent the conclusion sentence to compare with the results of whatever operations they perform on the premises. This latter proposal may appear *ad hoc*, but it is implicit in almost any theory of syllogistic reasoning. For example, PSYCOP(Rips 1994), as in all natural deduction systems, normally requires a potential conclusion representation to work towards before a syllogistic deduction can even begin. Consequently, this is a proposal that Espino *et al.* should have considered in deriving their predictions. Finally, it is important that in arguing for alternative explanations of Espino *et al.*'s results we have appealed to exactly the same psycholinguistic phenomena, i.e. both explanations are consistent with the known psycholinguistic effects. In conclusion, Espino *et al.*'s (2000) experiments may provide an interesting addition to the techniques used to explore the mental processes involved in human reasoning. However, their experiments do not discriminate between theoretical proposals to anything like the extent argued in their paper.

Dispelling the atmosphere effect

Shaw and Johnson-Laird (1998) provide evidence and arguments that they take to conclusively dispel accounts of syllogistic reasoning such as atmosphere, matching, and PHM, which argue that the conclusion will be affected by the surface form of the premises. They present five points that we deal with in turn.

First, they argue that there have always been results that refuted the idea that the form of the conclusion will match one of the premises. For example, they point out that in Sells' (1936) original study participants were more willing to endorse a conclusion if it was valid. So for the *All-All*[1] syllogism, participants endorse the valid conclusion *All Z are X* (94%) far more than the invalid *All X are Z* (45%). However, although atmosphere predicts that both conclusions should be drawn in equal proportion, PHM does not. Only the *All Z are X* conclusion conforms to the *attachment*-heuristic, so it should be selected more often. Consequently, this finding does not question PHM.

Second, Shaw and Johnson-Laird (1998) argue that some conclusions do not fit any form of the atmosphere effect. For example, in Johnson-Laird and Steedman (1978), the most frequent response to the *All-None*[3] syllogism was *Some X are not Z* (which is logically valid, assuming an existential presupposition is made in the *All* premise). This conclusion does not violate the *min*-heuristic because this conclusion is less informative than the *min*-conclusion (*None*). Moreover, Shaw and Johnson-Laird's (1998) reporting of this result is an example of picking the result to suit the argument. Although *Some...not* may have been the most frequent response in Johnson-Laird and Steedman (1978), in our meta-analysis (which included this study), the *None* conclusion, licensed by the *min*-heuristic, was endorsed by 61.39% of participants versus only 13.29% who endorsed *Some...not*. Consequently, this finding does not question PHM.

Third, they argue that similar atmosphere effects should be observed for other argument forms. This critique does not apply to PHM, as the heuristics are motivated by an informational analysis of the premises, not just their surface form. However, Shaw and Johnson-Laird also argue that the finding that *All* is a frequent response to *Only-Only* syllogisms counts against PHM. We discussed this argument above where we dismissed it as linguistic-frequency effect. Consequently, this finding does not question PHM.

Fourth, Shaw and Johnson-Laird argued that for every syllogism there is a conclusion that is consistent with atmosphere and so there should be no 'no valid conclusion' responses. However, although there are fewer of these responses than there should be according to logic, they are nonetheless very frequent. Of course in PHM this response will be more likely as the informativeness of the *max*-premise decreases, in accordance with the *max*-heuristic. So PHM does predict 'no valid conclusion' responses. Shaw and Johnson-Laird also argued that for some syllogisms a 'no valid conclusion' response is given even though there is a logically valid response. For example, for the *None-Some* (*Some-None*) syllogisms, participants are more likely to say 'no valid conclusion' than that there is a *Some...not* conclusion. As we have argued, in PHM this happens because the conclusion is not captured by the *min*-heuristic (although it does not violate it) and is particularly uninformative (*Some...not*-heuristic). Shaw and Johnson-Laird report results on multiply quantified sentences (see 'Multiply quantified sentences'), where a similar result occurs for conclusions of the form *None of the X is in the same place as some of the Z*. We argued above that these cases seem to mirror the more simple *Some...not* cases for singly quantified sentences in being particularly uninformative. Consequently, this finding also seems consistent with PHM.

Finally, Shaw and Johnson-Laird report an experiment on multiply quantified sentences (see 'Multiply quantified sentences'), which appeared to show that responses matching one of the premises reduces for multiple model syllogisms. They argue that mental models always generates an initial model where a conclusion can be read off that matches one of the premises, i.e. where there is a conclusion consistent with the *min*-heuristic. This conclusion cannot be refuted in one-model syllogisms, but it can be in multiple-model syllogisms, where people can seek alternative models. However, the balance of evidence (Evans *et al.* 1999; Klauer *et al.* 2000; Newstead *et al.* 1999; Schroyens *et al.* 2000a) appears to indicate that people rarely, if ever, construct more than one model (see 'Further evidence for PHM' on 'Alternative conclusions'). Consequently this explanation of the apparent reduction in matching responses seems improbable. PHM would explain these results in terms of multiple model syllogisms leading to less informative conclusions, and consequently an increase in no valid conclusion responses. PHM has not been extended to multiply quantified sentences but this seems to provide a promising avenue to explore (see 'Multiply quantified sentences').

In sum, Shaw and Johnson-Laird's attempt to dispel the atmosphere hypothesis may succeed; but it does nothing to cast doubt on PHM. Indeed, their explanation's reliance on the processes that construct initial mental models and the subsequent search for alternative models makes their account look particularly untenable. The processes of initial model construction are opaque in mental models theory; and this is particularly crucial, if people rarely, if ever, construct alternative models.

Cardinal quantifiers

Geurts (2003) pointed out that the notion of a generalized quantifier is more general than Chater and Oaksford (1999) allow. Not only are there *proportional* quantifiers, like *Most* and *Few* (and a whole range of others), there are also *cardinal* quantifiers, e.g. *exactly three* artists are beekeepers. The reason that generalized quantifiers are important to a psychological theory is that they take reasoning out of the realm of *first-order* logic, where quantification is only allowed over objects. Indeed, Johnson-Laird (1983) initially argued that one of the principle virtues of mental models was that proportional quantifiers could be represented. However, what was lacking was an account of how mental models allowed valid inferences with these quantifiers according to some normative account. That is, Johnson-Laird (1983) provided a theory of how these quantifiers could be represented but not of the inferences that could and should be made.

Proportional quantifiers require quantification over sets, i.e. it requires a *second-order* logic. So to say *Most A are B* could be interpreted as the set of things that are A and B is larger than the set of things that are A but not B. Such an account can extend naturally to cardinal quantifiers. For example, *Exactly three As are B* is interepreted as the number of things that are A and $B = 3$. Geurts makes the point that these cardinal quantifiers do not seem to have a probabilistic interpretation. The meaning of *Exactly three As are B* seems unaffected by the number of As, i.e. by sample size (N). So $P(B|A)$ could vary from close to 0 to 1, without affecting the meaning of the statement.

While we make no claims that our probabilistic interpretation directly extends to cardinal quantifiers, there are several problems for Geurts' proposal. While monadic second-order logic has a decidable proof procedure, in general, second-order logic does not have a complete proof theory. Monadic second-order logic quantifies over *monadic* predicates, those taking a single argument, e.g. beekeeper (x) (x is a beekeeper). More generally one can quantify over relations, which take more than one argument, e.g. loves (x, y) (x loves y). However, one cannot prove mechanically what conclusions follow. If people find reasoning in this logical domain at all natural and provide systematic responses, then it is not at all clear what proof procedures standard mental logic approaches (e.g. Rips 1994) might employ.

Apart from these deep logical and process issues, there is another problem. Although the meaning of these statements using cardinal quantifiers may seem independent of probabilities, what they entail would seem to depend on probabilities and hence on N. For example, suppose there are 10 As, i.e. $N = 10$, then the following entailments seem intuitively clear:

Exactly 3 As are B	$\Rightarrow$	Some As are B, Few As are B, Most As are not B.
Exactly 7 As are B	$\Rightarrow$	Most As are B, Few As are not B.
Exactly 10 As are B	$\Rightarrow$	All As are B, No As are not B.

That is, the cardinals have direct relationships with the proportional and logical quantifiers that do depend on probabilities.

Exact cardinal quantifiers seem only to be relevant to domains where it is possible to make precise counts. However, in people's normal experience of the world, they are rarely in this position. Thus, normally they have to express their knowledge using vaguer terms. So we are rarely able to assert *Exactly n As are B*, where *n* is a definite number. Moreover, it is not clear, in general, why making such precise assertions is that inferentially useful. Geurts (2003) describes the inferences that such statements permit when sample size is not included. However, even if people do not have precise counts, it seems that they will have sufficient information to make a statement using a proportional quantifier. For example, looking into the aviary, you may see that there are many birds, but you only see three or four ravens. One assertion this situation licenses is: *at least 3 of the birds are ravens*. However, this is not a very informative assertion, especially when, by taking sample size into account (you know there a lot of birds in the aviary) you are in a position to assert: *few of the birds in the aviary are ravens*. Armed with this information, on being told that Tweety is a bird in the aviary, you can infer that Tweety is unlikely to be a raven. This seems like an interesting inference to be able to make. So, on pragmatic grounds, it always seems sensible to use whatever background knowledge one has about sample size in order to make a more informative statement using a proportional quantifier. One need not deny that the cardinal quantifiers cannot have a directly probabilistic interpretation. However, they may only be interesting to the extent that they entail a proportionally quantified claim that can be given a probabilistic interpretation. Thus it may be premature to abandon a general probabilistic approach purely on the argument that it does not immediately generalize to cardinal quantifiers.

A further problem for Geurts (2003) is that he only models the meta-analytic data reported by Chater and Oaksford (1999) using the standard logical quantifiers. He does not attempt to show how his account applies to the two experiments of Chater and Oaksford (1999), where the proportional quantifiers, *most* and *few*, where combined with the logical quantifiers. This would seem an obvious next step. That is, having shown theoretically that his second-order logic approach applies to the standard logical quantifiers and that it captures the data using these quantifiers, Geurts (2003) needs to show that his approach generalizes empirically in the same way as the probabilistic approach. Otherwise one is left with the concern that it may not and consequently that there may already be evidence in the literature that disconfirms Geurt's (2003) account.

Summary

Most human reasoning must deal with the uncertainty of the world in which we live. Consequently we have argued that probability theory rather than logic provides a more appropriate computational-level theory of human reasoning.

In this chapter we have shown that it is possible to extend the probabilistic approach to a core area of research on deductive reasoning, the syllogism. PHM provides a probabilistic, rather than a deductive, framework for syllogistic inference, and a set of fast and frugal heuristics that are justified by this probabilistic framework. There may be other sets of heuristics that may provide a better approximation to probabilistic validity, and thus a richer model of human syllogistic reasoning. Searching for alternative sets of heuristics, both for empirical adequacy and for approximation to probabilistic norms (e.g. Gigerenzer and Goldstein 1996; McKenzie 1994) is an important direction for future research. Currently, PHM provides more comprehensive fits to past data than alternative accounts, and is confirmed by two experiments with syllogisms involving *Most* and *Few*, which are beyond the scope of other accounts. Moreover, a range of possible objections to PHM appear to miss the mark and may indeed be more challenging for alternative theories. We believe that fast, frugal and rational probabilistic heuristics will be important in explaining apparent biases in performance on laboratory reasoning tasks in other domains of reasoning. When confronted with a laboratory reasoning task people are simply applying the strategies that they have learned to deal with their uncertain world.

Chapter 8

The rational analysis of mind: a dialogue

In this book, we hope to have convinced the reader that the project of developing a rational analysis of human reasoning based on probability theory has been fruitful, and that it has considerable promise in the future. But, in pursuit of a clear presentation of our main theses, we have left a range of puzzles and concerns outstanding. The final chapter takes the form of a dialogue between a sceptic and an advocate of the approach. The aim is to give an intuitive sense of the thinking underlying this book, and its broader intellectual context, as well as stressing challenges for, and assumptions of, the approach. We hope some readers may be intrigued enough to take part in the on-going academic dialogue on rational analysis and human reasoning.

The sceptic: After seven chapters, I'm bound to say that this all looks very plausible on the surface. Taking things at face value, the approach appears have deep theoretical roots; and it appears to capture a lot of psychological data.

But this whole strategy leaves me feeling extremely uneasy. I've got a lot of concerns, but perhaps I should start with the most basic. It just seems to me that rational analysis is just not psychological explanation, in any way I'm familiar with it. Psychological explanation, at least from the point of view of cognitive psychology, is surely all about explain in terms of algorithms and representations—and this is the bit that rational analysis leaves out.

The advocate: It's quite true that this style of explanation is relatively unusual in cognitive psychology—hence the significance of Anderson's (1990, 1991a) work in developing an explicit methodology for this approach. But the general idea that we have to explain *why* cognitive processes work, as well as explaining the computational mechanisms that allow them to function, has, of course, been around for a long time. Marr's computational-level analysis of vision is one example, discussed above. Shepard (1992) has also attempted to explain various aspects of visual processing by virtue of their adaptiveness to the environment. For example, he argues that three classes of cone cells are all that is needed to discriminate the naturally occurring light intensities in nature. If sunlight had a different composition, or the range of surfaces in the natural environment were different, then a different number of cones would be required—indeed, in the unconstrained case, an infinite number of classes of cone would be required for perfect discrimination. And, in practice, any psychologist attempting to build a mechanistic theory of anything typically finds considerations of adapativeness creeping in to their thinking, even if in quite a covert way.

For example, think about the influence of AI in cognitive psychology (lets use AI as a general catch-all for computational research not primarily directly towards explaining empirical data). A lot of the flow of influence has arisen because AI researchers have been able to suggest some potential ways in which a cognitively relevant problem might be solved reasonably effectively; and then the question naturally arises—does the mind solve this problem in the same way? But in solving the original AI problem, the guiding principle will typically be purely normative—the goal is to get a system that does some particular job as well as possible. In the mind of the AI researcher, questions concerning why the system works a particular way will seem entirely natural and appropriate. Deciding how to construct a system is to face a continual stream of 'why' questions—concerning how to make the system perform the specified job effectively. But when the theoretical output of this relatively a priori activity is taken up by psychology, these questions concerning why the system works successfully are very much in the background. The emphasis instead is on producing testable empirical predictions from the system. So, frequently, the system is viewed in psychology purely as a mechanism.

Now this is to exaggerate things rather drastically of course, in particular because there is typically a good deal of two-way interaction between artificial intelligence ideas and psychology, so that information flows from the empirical data to inform the construction of the AI system, as well as in the opposite direction. And this is true to the extent that many of the people designing novel computational systems might just as much be viewed as theoretical psychologists as artificial intelligence researchers. But the general picture is right—by the time that a theory is being considered for empirical testing, which is the heart of standard cognitive psychology, questions of adaptive funtion are typically very much out of view. Examples abound, including research on knowledge representation (semantic networks, scripts, frames), connectionist networks, computational models of vision, examplar models of classification, and so on. All of these have been tested by empirical psychological research which has downplayed the adaptive story behind these computational models.

The sceptic: Well, there probably is not much point arguing about how broadly we use 'psychological' explanation. But there is a substantive issue concerning the degree to which this 'adaptive' style of explanation is really relevant

to constructing standard cognitive psychological accounts in terms of algorithms and representations—in short, in terms of cognitive mechanisms. If
I'm interested in explaining how a person draws an inference, mental logic
theory and mental models theory tell me what calculations a person goes
through to draw that inference (although one might quibble about the level of
detail of such explanations, and the scope of the inferences they can deal
with). But the probabilistic rational analysis does not—it focuses instead on
developing some (possibly rather non-standard) 'rational' account; and it
leaves the mechanism vague. So if I'm a good old-fashioned cognitive psychologist, and I care about cognitive mechanism, why should I care about rational
analysis at all? Can't I just ignore it?

The advocate: I'd argue that, to the contrary, even if the only thing you care
about is mechanism, you have to pay close attention to rational analysis.
Imagine attempting to understand the algorithms underlying the performance
of a cash register, if one didn't know the laws of arithmetic. The task would be
hopeless! But once you know what the cash register is doing—once you have a
rational analysis for its performance, then, first, you have immediately placed
a very strong constraint on the possible algorithms that must be considered
(you only have to consider those that approximate, to some reasonable degree,
the correct answers to arithmetic problems); and, second, you can narrow
things down further by paying close attention to the cases in which the system
'breaks down'—where its output diverges from the 'correct' answer. These will
tell you something about the specifics of the algorithm, memory limitations,
the nature of the internal representations of numbers, and so on. Even
so, the problem of pinning down the algorithm is still immensely hard; so
hard indeed that some theorists argue that it is impossible (e.g. Anderson
1978; Hahn and Chater 1998). But one thing is clear—if the process of
finding algorithms on the basis of the observation of behavioural data is
doable at all, it will be enormously easier given an appropriate rational analysis
for the task.

A good example of the point, in this book, is in the theory of syllogisms,
outlined in Chapter 7. Here, the detailed model that matches the psychological
data is algorithmic—specifically, it takes the form of a set of simple heuristics
for syllogistic reasoning. But note that this model could not even be defined at
all, without the probabilistic interpretation of the quantifiers and the probabilistic rational analysis of syllogistic reasoning that can be framed in terms of
these. Now there are no doubt other sets of heuristics, aside from *min, max*,
and the rest that approximate the *p*-valid syllogisms, as specified by the
rational analysis. And it may be that one of these provides an even closer fit
with the empirical data than the set of heuristics so far identified. But the

important point is that the search for a mechanistic account of syllogistic reasoning has been crucially underpinned by the rational analysis.

Note that, of course, this is also true from the point of view of logic-based theories of reasoning—the processes involved in mental logic and mental models theory are very strongly constrained by the need for the algorithms to match up with the dictates of classical logic; i.e. to get the right answers. So for these accounts too, issues of rational explanation are fundamental in driving mechanistic explanation.

The sceptic: The syllogistic reasoning case is all very well. But in other areas of reasoning (and in other areas of cognitive science where the rational analysis approach has been used), there is often only the most cursory discussion of process-based issues.

The advocate: I'd like to stress the complementarity of rational and mechanistic explanation. Ideally, we would like to have both. In some cases, this may be possible. In others, though, there is simply not enough relevant empirical data to tie a rational explanation down in terms of a specific mechanistic story. So the answer is to collect more data. In the original rational analysis of the selection task, for example, Oaksford and Chater (1994b) explicitly noted that the rational analysis could be implemented to different degrees of approximation (from, at one extreme, all the detailed probabilistic calculations being calculated on-line by each experimental participant, to, at the other extreme, responses being completely pre-programmed and entirely inflexible to the specific circumstances in which the task in carried out). As we noted in Chapters 5 to 7, recent research has attempted to distinguish where along this spectrum of possibilities human reasoning lies. The answer appears to be that it is somewhere between the two. The probabilistic structure of the materials used in the task has a robust and systematic effect on responding (which would not be predicted by non-probabilistic analyses of the selection task). But this effect does not amount to a perfect embodiment of the probabilistic calculations involved in the rational analysis—the implementation is in clearly an approximation, and probably quite a crude one. But a complementary project to rational analysis is trying to implement particular approximations computationally. For example, Oaksford (2004) describe a connectionist approximation of the Ramsey Test in conditional inference (described in Chapter 5); a similar approach could be developed using Bayesian networks rather than connectionism as a computational framework.

The sceptic: Well, let's leave this issue—I'll take it that traditional cognitive psychology, both in terms of its theoretical structure and its empirical method, is very much still in business, and are not supplanted by the rational analysis approach. But as to whether rational considerations are really so helpful, let me turn to a rather different tack—the question of the utility (or otherwise) of rational explanations across the board.

Perhaps the place to start is in thinking about the economic style of explanation of human behaviour embodied in what has become known as 'rational choice' theory. According to this viewpoint, much of human behaviour can be understood by assuming that people optimally use the information available to them and choose their actions in order to maximize their expected 'utility'. The methodology works by building a formal model of the social or economic situation in which a decision is made. Then appropriate mathematical machinery is used to work out what a 'rational' agent will choose—where the mathematical machinery includes probability theory, decision theory, game theory and their extensions.

Rational choice explanation has certainly been on the offensive over the last few decades. One example of this is the provision of an increasingly rich game-theoretic foundation for micro-economics (e.g. Kreps 1992), and sophisticated attempts to absorb aspects of apparently non-rational behaviour of individual managers or entire organizations into a rational choice framework (Tirole 1986; Williamson 1964, 1985). Moreover, where Keynes put a considerable emphasis on 'animal spirits' (1936/1973) as drivers of key aspects of business thinking and behaviour, modern macro-economic theory has increasingly used what might term 'hyper-rationality' assumptions as its starting point. This transition is embodied in its most extreme form in the rational expectations movement, which dominated much macro-economic thinking in the 1970s and 1980s (Lucas 1972). Advocates of the rational expectations approach assume that each individual has an unbiased model of the macro-economy, and can work through all the implications of this putative knowledge with perfect fluidity and precision. And rational choice theory has, more broadly, been on the offensive throughout the rest of the social sciences, attempting to set questions of family structure, addictive behaviour, racial discrimination, criminal behaviour, class structure, political structures, and much more besides on a rational footing (Becker, 1957, 1991, 1996; Downs 1957, Elster 1983).

Now the rational choice approach has come under some heavy attacks from a number of quarters in economics and the social sciences (e.g. Frank 1988; Green and Shapiro 1996; Nelson and Winter 1982). But, from the point of view of psychology—and also from the perspective of many researchers in other areas of the social sciences—this growth of rational choice theory has always been fatally undercut by the psychological (and perhaps intuitively) obvious fact that people just don't carry out calculations of anything like this complexity.

People have difficulty with the most elementary probabilistic and decision-theoretic calculations, as Kahneman and Tversky and their colleagues have shown (e.g. Kahneman and Tversky 1979; Kahneman *et al.* 1982; Tversky and Kahneman 1974). They are, indeed, arguably just as bad at calculations involving probability theory as they are at deductive reasoning, as discussed in this book. So the whole edifice of rational choice explanation is doomed from the start; and the programme of the rational analysis of human reasoning and cognition more generally seems to be doomed from the start also, and for just the same reason.

The advocate: This sounds worrying; but the concern is actually based on a misunderstanding of the nature of rational analysis. Recall that the purpose of rational analysis is to help explain *why* certain behaviours are successful. Doing this requires developing an account of the optimal behaviour—and showing that actual behaviour approximates this to some degree. But, to stress again, there is no assumption that the cognitive system itself must actually make these calculations. Rational analysis has the same role with respect to the understanding of mental structure that analysis in terms of engineering principles might have with respect to, say, the structure of the skeleton. Many aspects of the skeleton can, presumably, be explained on the basis that they amount to 'good design'—and cashing this out requires talk of stress and strain tensors, and much complex mathematics; but there is no requirement that skeletons themselves make such calculations! The difference with respect to cognition is that there is at least the possibility that *some* relevant calculations are made on line by the agent, to respond in a flexible way to changing circumstances.

The probabilistic approach to reasoning may be open to misinterpretation here. It is not intended to imply that the brain is a probabilistic calculating engine; rather, it is intended to imply that a probabilistic framework is crucial to understanding the nature of the computations that the cognitive system performs (to some approximation). On the other hand, it would be a mistake to rule out the possibility that the brain may be a fantastically powerful probabilistic calculating machine. It may just be that the interface with probabilistic problems phrased in natural language and symbolic numerical representations is sufficiently poor that verbal reasoning tasks about probability are completely unable to harness this machinery; or that the machinery is only available for a narrow range of specialised cognitive tasks (e.g. aspects of perception, language processing, and motor control). But this is an issue about *mechanisms* for probabilistic inference. What is at issue in this book is something different— whether the rational analysis for (many aspects of) human reasoning, including some areas that are traditionally viewed as involving deduction, should be framed in terms of probability, rather than logic. As it happens, one of us has been interested in models of how people explicitly reason with verbally stated probability and decision-making problems, which starts from a mechanistic and ecological point of view (Stewart *et al.* 2006).

So there simply is no contradiction in this with the fact that people are not very good at probabilistic calculations. Moreover, there is no contradiction with the claim, which is increasingly gaining ground, that rational choice explanation should be substantially modified, to take account of cognitive factors (Bacharach 1999; Kacelnik and Bateson 1997).

The sceptic: Yes, but this seems a bit slippery. Once you allow that rational analysis is only to some (unspecified degree of) approximation, then isn't it just 'anything goes?' Indeed, does not this just exacerbate the problem with rational choice explanation in social science—that by fiddling around with beliefs, desires, discount rates, and a myriad of other factors, one can always find a rational model that has any predictions—it exacerbates the problem because it allows a myriad of 'performance limitations' to be drawn in, wherever appropriate, to capture the data. Indeed, the whole assumption that the system being explained is rational at all is, by these lights, unfalsiable, and is hence meaningless, or at least, lacking in any practical significance.

The advocate: But this is not as worrying as it sounds. First, it is just the normal case that theoretical proposals cannot be falsified by any empirical data—because *ad hoc* adjustments to other beliefs can always be made, in order to save them. This is just the Quine–Duhem thesis, and is widely held to apply to Newtonian mechanics, general relativity, and, indeed, any other theory in science. So there is no *special* problem for rational explanation here, at the general level. Second, at the specific level, yes, there is a lot of scope for hanging on to rational explanation by a series of increasingly implausible theoretical epicycles. But such theorizing should be attacked according to the normal canons of scientific explanation—parsimony, generality, precision of fit with the empirical data, conservatism, and so on. Theories involving rational explanation, including the accounts of aspects of human reasoning discussed in this book, have to compete with accounts of other forms. There will clearly be aspects of cognition for which a rational explanation is not appropriate—the detailed cognitive effect of brain lesion can hardly be predicted from rational principles alone, after all—knowledge of the algorithms that the brain uses and their neural implementation will, of course, be crucial here. The opponent of rational explanation will insist that this is the general case—that rational explanations are never any good. But this is just the normal scientific debate. In practice, rational explanation seems to be able to explain a lot of data in a parsimonious and general way.

The sceptic: I take the point that rational explanation should be assessed according to the same criteria as any other scientific explanation. But I wonder if this is really what occurs in practice. After all, isn't creating rational explanations just as easy as creating evolutionary 'just-so' stories? One can always think up some rational model according to which any behaviour makes sense—that was my previous point—and, moreover, it's usually possible to make the rational explanation sound reasonably plausible. But then it's possible to simply downplay all the myriad choices that led to the particular rational explanation, and to end up giving the spurious impression that the data fall out quite naturally from principles of rationality, and a few additional assumptions concerning goals, environment, and cognitive limitations. But it would be equally possible to provide a plausible sounding explanation for the opposite pattern of data, and to then suppress all the myriad of assumptions that went in to that explanation. In the context of the rational models in this book, one might decide, for example, to use a different measure of information gain in the account of the selection task; or one might have parameterized the dependence and independence models differently; or one might have integrated over possible parameter values, rather than just choosing particular parameter values; or one might have added in various alternative hypotheses, which might compete alongside the dependence and independence models. But in presenting a particular model, these choices, and a host of others, are not really made explicit—the account flows out with an apparent inevitable logic. But it's an illusion, of course.

The parallel with evolutionary 'just-so' stories seems rather apt. Again, it's always possible to make up some plausible-sounding explanation for why an animal has a particular feature (why the giraffe has a long neck). But it would be equally possible to give a 'just-so' story explaining that the animal had to the opposite feature. One might argue that giraffes should be selected to have short necks, because long necks are more prone to damage, or make the animal less fleet of foot, or any number of alternatives.

The advocate: The point that possible alternatives are often hidden from view in rational explanations in a good one—but it's important to realize that it is precisely as appropriate when considering scientific explanations of any kind. This is why it is very difficult to even qualitatively gauge the number of 'degrees of freedom' in a particular explanation of some set of data. It is always a tendency to present a theory as providing a terribly constrained explanation of the data, when it has actually been chosen from a large class of theories (not presented to the reader) most of which miserably fail to account for the data. The moral of this point is not, though, specific to rational explanation. It is, instead, to point out the crucial importance of novel predictions of a theory—because no amount of post-hoc fiddling about with a theory can magically make it produce the right novel predictions—because until those predictions have been tested, it is not clear what fiddling is appropriate.

In each of the domains discussed in this book, conditional inference, the selection task, and syllogistic reasoning, it has therefore been of crucial significance that each account generates novel predictions, which have since been experimentally confirmed. This does not, of course, mean that the rational analyses are right, but it does undercut the charge of being no more than 'just-so' stories. The reason that some areas of adaptive explanation in evolutionary theory (including many aspects of evolutionary explanation of the mind) are rightly criticized for being no more than speculation is just because novel empirical predictions can sometimes be hard to find.

The sceptic: So it seems that you are driving a wedge between rational explanation and evolutionary psychology. This is particularly important in the context of the psychology of reasoning, where there has been a great deal of argument that human reasoning (as evident, for example, in the difference between reasoning in deontic and nondeontic versions of the selection task) is explained by evolutionary considerations—roughly, the importance of certain kinds of aspects of social reasoning (e.g. Cosmides 1989; Gigerenzer and Hug 1992; though see the interchange between Cummins 1996 and Chater and Oaksford 1996). But this seems rather odd, particular in view of the fact that there would seem to be a natural alliance between rational explanation of human cognition and optimality-based explanation in behavioural ecology, where evolutionary considerations are almost invariably considered to be the fundamental guarantor that the system will be close to optimal (Krebs and Davies 1996).

The advocate: There is no necessary tension between rational and evolutionary explanation. But neither are the two indissolubly linked. To put the point as simply as possible, a rational analysis of a cognitive process aims to show that it is the way it is because it is adaptive—more particularly, the cognitive process approximates, to some degree, the optimal way of solving the problem. But it says nothing at all about the origin of that adaptiveness. It may be that the adaptive solution has been learned by the system in an individual's lifetime; it could equally well be that the adaptive solution has been wired in by evolution. So rational analysis is entirely neutral between nativism and empiricism. Of course, there are many sources of evidence that can be adduced to attempt to decide to what extent some aspect of cognition (e.g. a particular mode of inference) is genetically determined or learned (and there may also have been concerns expressed about the degree to which it is possible to untangle the two—e.g. Elman *et al.* 1996). But that means, essentially, that rational analysis, plus some evidence of the genetic basis for the aspect of cognition to be explained, amounts to evolutionary explanation. Given that for most aspects of cognition, the issue between nativism and empiricism is still very much alive, it would seem misguided to leap to interpret every successful rational explanation as, ipso facto, an evolutionary explanation.

It may be worth commenting that quite a lot of supposed evolutionary explanations for aspects of cognition do not really amount to anything more than (sometimes qualitative and often poorly specified) attempts at rational analysis. For example, suppose it were true that human reasoning were especially good in some domain (e.g. reasoning about social interactions, say); this does not imply that the explanation must lie in an evolutionary history that has selectively favoured people who are particularly good at such reasoning. It could equally well be the case that, because the relevant aspect of social reasoning is so important, children learn to pay special attention to it, get most practice at it, and so on, and hence that this special facility is learned rather than a product of evolution. Similarly, to show that some aspect of visual processing is very well adapted to the constraints of the actual world does not indicate that these constraints are built it by evolution—again, it is also possible that these constraints are learned during the life of an individual.

To make a rational analysis really have evolutionary bite (i.e. to really have implications for the genetic basis of the adaptiveness of the relevant aspect of the cognitive system), it seems to me that the following is required. We need to find cases where a current aspect of cognition is presently counter-adaptive, but would have been adaptive during some relevantly long period of evolutionary time. It is by no means clear that there are currently any convincing rational explanation meeting this criterion, at least in the domain of reasoning research.

The sceptic: Now this is all very well, but there is a fundamental flaw in the approach adopted in this book, which we have yet to consider. The aim is to specify rational optimal patterns of performance, according to some set of assumptions about goals, environment, and so on. But this approach fails disastrously to scale up to deal with any real-world reasoning problems—because, as has been conceded in this book, there are no viable rational theories about how real-world everyday reasoning should be conducted. As noted in Chapter 4, this point has become widely recognized in the light of the failure over the last thirty years of AI to successfully provide formal models of how people represent and use apparently mundane everyday knowledge.

This failure to scale-up is, if I may say so, a bit ironic, given the emphasis on relevance to common sense reasoning in the motivation for the probabilistic approach.

The advocate: Remember, though, that as was pointed out when discussing artificial intelligence research in Chapter 4, that the probabilistic approach is the most promising direction that we have for attacking the problem of mathematically and computationally dealing with everyday reasoning—this is back to the point that the inference system might turn out to be a probabilistic engine, after all. The reason that probabilistic approaches are being increasingly favoured over logic-based approaches is precisely that the former are naturally equipped to deal with the uncertain character of everyday inference, whereas the latter must be put through some unpleasant contortions, even to allow the possibility of uncertain inference. As we have mentioned, graphical models (Frey 1998; Pearl 1988, 2000; Spiegelhalter and Lauritzen 1990) seem an extremely promising direction in this research, and it may be hoped that such models may provide the basis for concrete cognitive psychological hypotheses and experimental tests concerning human-knowledge representation in the future. The assumption that a future computational model of everyday reasoning will be based on probabilistic rather than logical foundations may, of course, turn out to be incorrect. But it currently the best guess we have.

If this general viewpoint is right, then we would expect people to import everyday reasoning strategies with a probabilistic basis to solve laboratory tasks; and, this might even be true when the task is a supposedly 'deductive' reasoning task. In fact, this is a very strong test of the probabilistic approach, because probabilistic methods are being applied where one might least expect them. The rational analyses in this book aim to show that, indeed, much of the data on human 'deductive' reasoning can be explained from this probabilistic viewpoint.

In AI there are now many other accounts that introduce probabilities or other measures of uncertainty, as part of a computational account of argumentation and *defeasible* reasoning, i.e. reasoning in which conclusions can be *defeated* by subsequent argument. Moreover, it is the inclusion of these uncertainty measures that provides these systems with their nice default properties (see: Fox and Parsons 1998; Gabbay 1996; Pollock 2001; in particular, for a recent overview, see: Prakken and Vreeswijk 2002). Some of this discussion focuses on technical issues about how such an approach can provide solution to problems retractable reasoning (see the special issue of the *Journal of Logic and Computation*, vol. 13 (3), on computational dialectics). Further, there is a great deal of technical work looking at the relationship between probability and logic (see the special issue of the *Journal of Applied Logic*, vol. 1, on combining probability and logic). Here the debate seems to be between those who think *probability theory is logic* and address the issues involved in making good on this claim (e.g. Howson 2003; Kyburg 2003) and those who explore alternative formalisms to *interface between probability and logic* (e.g. Fox 2003). So, creating practical artificial reasoning systems that deal with defeasibility seems to require the introduction of probabilities or some measure of uncertainty. We simply argue that the natural reasoning system has evolved a similar solution.

There is no doubt that vast problems of scaling-up remain, but these problems arise for any approach to reasoning. To put it bluntly, the 'frame problem' and related problems still remain unsolved, and hence nobody has any technical proposals that are adequate to model human common-sense reasoning. This means that, *ipso facto*, there are no psychological proposals that can scale-up to produce a complete account of such common-sense inference. So, to a degree, the problem of scaling-up will inevitably bedevil any account of human reasoning, at present. But this does not mean that we cannot specify some qualitative features of human reasoning that may be in common between laboratory performance and common-sense reasoning. The best hope for the work outlined in this book is that some aspects of it survive, and perhaps may inform, a future account of everyday reasoning. The emphasis on the probabilistic interpretation of natural language conditionals (Chapter 5), the focus on measures of information gain (Chapter 6), the emphasis on 'cheap and dirty' reasoning heuristics that approximate probabilistic rational theories (Chapter 7), are among aspects of the present work that at least may be relevant to a full theory of common sense-inference.

The sceptic: Well, even if the probabilistic approach is in no worse shape than anyone else on the frame problem, it's still the case that the whole experimental basis for this work, and the psychology of reasoning more generally, is based on decontextualized lab-based reasoning, over a very narrow set of tasks. Surely a good psychology of reasoning should at least scale up to the informal patterns of reasoning that are standard in everyday argument—as you said in Chapter 3, there is not much deductive inference in everyday thought and argument; so surely the real test is applicability to informal argument.

The advocate: Well, to some degree, all theories of reasoning in psychology are in the same boat on this issue; and it's true that the real goal of a good theory of reasoning should presumably be to explain the patterns of everyday reasoning that we use in everyday life; and the patterns of informal argument that we use to explain the world to other, and persuade them of our points of view. We suggest, though, that the probabilistic approach has two advantages over approaches which take logic as their starting point.

The first, as we have emphasize in this book, is that everyday reasoning almost always is concerned with uncertainty; certain reasoning, if it occurs at all, may be viewed as a rather unusual special case. Hence it seems that the calculus of uncertain reasoning (probability) rather than the calculus of certain reasoning (logic), is the appropriate place to begin in building theories of informal reasoning. And, as we have argued in this book, it is interesting that probabilistic explanations of laboratory reasoning appear to be highly explanatory, even on tasks that were originally intended to tap human deductive reasoning. Moreover, the probabilistic turn in artificial intelligence and philosophy of science, that we noted in Chapter 4, is a further indication that attempts to understand non-deductive forms of argument appear to require probabilistic methods.

The second advantage is that probabilistic methods seem to provide a natural way in which to model informal patterns of argument directly—where these arguments are typically rejected simply as 'invalid' by logical analysis. Inference to the best explanation, known in artificial intelligence as abductive inference, is a ubiquitous pattern in informal reasoning, for example, and one that we have noted is naturally modelled using Bayes' theorem. But it is logically invalid, of course: there can be no deductive argument that alights on a particular explanation among many possible explanations—precisely because such an inference is inevitably uncertain and hence not logically valid. But a wide range of other informal argument forms, such as certain kinds of circular arguments, arguments from ignorance, and slippery slope arguments, may also be understood in probabilistic terms, despite their logical invalidity. Exploring such informal arguments in probabilistic terms is currently a key direction for future research (Hahn and Oaksford, 2006).

The sceptic: But, though one can point to upsurges of work in rational explanation, based on probabilistic ideas in order to bolster the case for a probabilistic rational analysis of the mind, it is equally possible to point to a range of research areas which are moving away from rational explanations altogether. For example, influential research in 'behaviour-based' robotics (Brooks 1991) moves away from a 'rational' decomposition and solution of the problems of perception and action—instead, the approach is to build a viable robot by overlaying relatively simple behaviours (such as a avoiding a looming object, approaching particular targets, and so on). There has been an increasing focus on building extremely simple systems that must survive in the real world—the emphasis has thus shifted from abstruse theory about optimality, to the cheap and dirty approach of engineering. A related set of ideas has been developed in the realm of software agents (Agre and Chapman 1987)—crude but effective strategies leading to good performance are derived without recourse to 'rational' explanation of any kind. Relatedly, in psychology, there has been increasing interest in the idea that cognition may be a rag-bag of heuristics, rather than embodying a coherent and rich theory of the world. In vision, some theorists have attacked Marr's paradigm for computational vision research as placing too great an emphasis on rational considerations (e.g. Churchland *et al.* 1994); in evolutionary psychology, several theorists have argued that the mind can be viewed as a very large system of innately specified modules, which work blindly and independently, rather than being synthesized together by some overall rational framework; and finally, there have been specific proposals that cognitive processes based on 'fast and frugal' heuristics could perform as well as a 'rational' approach in any case (Gigerenzer 2002; Gigerenzer *et al.* 1999).

Looking more generally, these viewpoints are consonant with similar moves away from rational explanations, not just in psychology, but also in the analysis of animal behaviour and in economics. For example, one of the most celebrated advocates of the optimal models of animal behaviour (e.g. McFarland and Houston 1981), David McFarland has notably abandoned this approach in favour of behaviour-based robotics, as mentioned above (McFarland and Bosser 1993). Similarly, the economist Reinhard Selten, who won a Nobel prize for economics for work on game theory, the fundamental rational framework used in many areas of modern micro-economics. Selten has, more recently, argued for understanding some economic phenomena by modelling cognitive agents as implementing simple decision heuristics, rather than following the dictates of game-theory, or any other rational account (e.g. Gigerenzer and Selten 2001).

The advocate: It's certainly true that there has recently been a reaction against 'rational' approaches to modelling the cognitive system. And equally, rational accounts have developed apace during recent years. But it is crucial to emphasize that there are two issues here that must be carefully distinguished.

The first issue is whether the cognitive system implements calculations, as specified by a rational theory. As we have stressed, the programme of rational analysis is neutral on this issue—indeed, in most rational models in psychology, the presumption is that the rational calculations is *not* carried out by the agent, as we noted above. The second issue is whether there is a rational account that explains why the cognitive system's performance is consistently successful (to the degree that it is). This is the question of whether a rational analysis is an appropriate style of explanation.

The real significance of the 'non-rational' approaches above is surely that, in many circumstances, relative crude heuristics may perform nearly as well as a full-blown implementation of rational calculations. For example, in an important and influential paper Gigerenzer and Goldstein (1996) consider a two-alternative forced-choice task concerning which of two German towns has the larger population, based on a set of nine binary 'features' of each town (e.g. 'has a soccer team', 'is a state capital', etc.). Gigerenzer and Goldstein consider the computational problem of learning how to predict which of two cities is the larger, from a 'training set' of cities, their features, and populations. From the point of view of conventional statistics, an 'obvious' way to proceed in such a task is to attempt to use some form of regression (e.g. linear regression) to assess the influence of each of the features on city size. When presented with a forced-choice test, the regression might then be used to intregrate all the features of the two cities, to come to an overall conclusion concerning which is likely to be the larger. Gigerenzer and Goldstein's Take-the-Best algorithm, however, takes a radically different approach. It has two steps. The first routine, the *recognition principle* states that, if a reasoner recognizes the name of one city but not the other, then the first city should be assumed to be the larger—no further memory search is carried out. If the recognition principle does not decide the issue, Take-the-Best moves to a second and more elaborate routine (on which we concentrate below). Features of the cities are considered in order, one-by-one, from the feature most diagnostic of city size to the feature that is least diagnostic of city size (where diagnosticity is calculated as the probability that the feature will correctly signal which is the larger of two randomly chosen cities which differ on this feature). As soon as a feature is found on which the cities differ (e.g. one city has a soccer team but the other does not), then the feature is used to decide which city is the larger (the city with the soccer team) and the calculation terminates. This means that the decision is based on a single feature, rather than attempting to 'integrate' all the different features of the two cities; and indeed many of the features of the cities are not even considered in the decision. Gigerenzer and Goldstein showed that, despite this apparently very 'frugal' use of information, Take-the-Best performs impressively. In a computational 'competition' using real features of German cities, Take-the-Best performs as well as linear regression and a range of approximations to linear regression.[1]

Results of this kind are extremely interesting. But even if this kind of approach can be developed more generally (and it is by no means clear that this is possible), it does not threaten rational analysis. Even where an aspect of cognition works by using a 'cheap trick', rather than by rational calculation,

---

[1] Whether multiple regression can really be viewed as an appropriate rational analysis for estimation problems of this kind is, though, open to question. Rather than get into the technicalities here, we merely note that multiple regression is an appropriate statistical tool, given some specific independence assumptions about the features of objects that are used in the estimation task.

the question still remains: why does that cheap trick consistently work? This requires understanding the goals being achieved, the structure of the environment, and the computational resources of the agent, and being able to analyse why this particular cheap trick is consistently close (or close enough) to the 'right' behaviour for consistently good performance to result. That is, explanation why the 'cheap trick' works requires formulating a rational analysis.

But it is worth putting this kind of result in perspective. No doubt the cognitive system uses such tricks where they are available—indeed, the account of syllogistic reasoning in Chapter 7 has exactly this character. But human everyday reasoning is fantastically flexible, and can deal with changing goals and changing knowledge about the world in an effective way. It seems highly unlikely that such flexibility can be achieved without human reasoning is purely a bag of precompiled tricks. Rather than try to develop a full-blown argument here, consider an analogy. In computer software, it is a standard observation that the problem with using highly specific procedural 'tricks' to solve a problem is that the solution cannot be modified easily to solve even slightly different problems. This is one source of the drive towards structured programming, object-oriented programming, declarative languages, and the like. So one might expect that the flexibility of human everyday reasoning is not compatible with the whole system consisting purely of tricks. Instead, there must be some explicit representations and general principles underlying reasoning over those representations.

Now of course the analogy is not exact—the modification of human reasoning processes by learning about new goals and new pieces of knowledge is, no doubt, very different from the modification of pieces of software by computer programmers. But, nonetheless, the onus is on the advocate of an across-the-board view that human reasoning is no more than a collection of reasoning heuristics to show how the flexibility of human reasoning is possible.

The sceptic: Well, what you are really saying is that we just can't imagine how a collection of heuristics might underlie the flexibility of human reasoning—this is just 'argument by failure of imagination'. And perhaps the reason that we can't imagine this is precisely because our intuitions are tied all to directly to conventional computer science, which we have reason to believe is a very poor model of mental computation. So just because we can't imagine heuristics underlying a flexible reasoning system does not mean that this is not how human reasoning works.

The advocate: This is all reasonable enough. But I'm quite happy with 'argument by failure of imagination', because it seems to be an inevitable and ubiquitous feature of scientific explanation. All we can ever do in science is to compare the best hypotheses that we can imagine, and decide which seem the most plausible. Whatever conclusion you draw, it can always be claimed that there is another hypothesis that is both true and goes against the conclusion— but that it just can't yet be imagined exactly how this hypothesis might work. Well, true enough, but this is just to say that science is always provisional— scientific inference is non-monotonic.

The sceptic: Well, let's leave this issue and consider a more basic challenge, on the same theme. The philosophical tradition of attempting to explain the mind in terms of inference, and then attempting to characterize the inferential principles that govern that inference, has a long and venerable history, of which Boole was a culmination. As we have pictured it, current psychology of reasoning and contemporary cognitive science more generally, still work, to a large extent, within this tradition. But is cognition really a matter of *inference* at all? Does the entire view of the mind as pervaded by principles whose rationality must be uncovered and explicated rest on a mistake?

The advocate: This is an important question. From my viewpoint, the answer is just an extension of the previous point—rational analysis has a role, whatever the nature of internal mental processes.

A wide range of theoretical viewpoints challenge the view of cognition as inference, and hence appear to eliminate a role for rational explanation of cognition. Let us focus on a single, paradigmatic, example: behaviourism—a view that is actually not that far from the behaviour-based robotics mentioned above, and even some, perhaps extreme, interpretations of connectionism. For the behaviourist, the units of psychological explanation are stimuli to which an agent is subjected, and the responses that the agent produces. The stimuli and responses are assumed to be characterized in purely physical terms—in terms of magnitudes such as energy, frequency, force, velocity. The substance of psychology then concerns the relationship between stimuli and responses; and how learning leads to specific connections between stimuli and responses being established. For the behaviourist, cognition is not a matter of inference over internal representations of knowledge about the world; hence, necessar- ily, it is not a matter of inference that might be justified either in logical or probabilistic terms. The question of the rational explanation of mind and behaviour does not, it seems, even arise. So, for the behaviourist, rational explanation appears, necessarily, to be beside the point.

But this conclusion would be too swift. Even a behaviourist must still face the question of why the particular rules by which associations between stimuli and responses (and between different stimuli) are formed happen to lead to successful behaviour, at least most of the time. It seems somehow more justifi- able to form an association between a tone and a shock, if the tone is reliably, rather than unreliably, paired with the shock. Equally, it seems more reasonable that the extinction of an association between the tone and shock should occur more quickly if the prior association was invariable, than if it were high unreliable. This is because in the case of a previously reliable relation, as soon as the pairing fails once, it is at least plausible that the environment has changed in some fundamental way. By contrast, if the relationship is always unreliable, then considerable data are likely to be needed to establish that the relationship has now ceased—because it is hard to distinguish the case where the stimulus and response are genuinely disconnected, from the case where the connection is noisy. In these, and hosts of other ways, rather specific properties of associative learning, which appear to be 'reasonable' on intuitive grounds are, indeed, empirically observed. This raises the question of whether these properties can actually be justified, not merely intuitively, but in some more rigorous and formal way—and, before we know it, we have entered into the process of the rational analysis of associative learning.

This project, under a variety of titles, is being vigorously pursued. In artificial intelligence, a mathematical theory of 'reinforcement learning' has been developed, which provides a rigorous analysis of various associative algorithms for relating actions to reinforcements (Sutton and Barto 1998). Much of this theory concerns the nature of the tasks and the structure of the task environment, that such methods are able to solve, thus providing reinforcement learning with a normative justification. Thus, the technical development of reinforcement learning, which can be viewed as a direct outgrowth of behaviourist theory, has led head-on into a rich and important area for rational analysis. Furthermore, results from this work have fed back directly into explanations of reinforcement learning in animals and people (Kakade and Dayan 2002; Sutton and Barto 1981). In psychology, associative learning processes have been viewed as implementing rationally justified methods for learning the causal structure of the world. While the focus has been on providing good characterizations of the algorithms that underly associative learning.[2]

A significant recent development has been connecting these accounts with normative theories of contingency learning and causal induction. For example, Cheng (1997) shows that a normatively motivated theory of causal inference

---

[2] In animal learning, the theories include the Rescorla–Wagner account (Rescorla and Wagner 1972), Pearce's configural model (Pearce 1994), and many others (e.g. Gallistel and Gibbon 2000; Kakade and Dayan 2002). There has also been a considerable body of research aiming to explain aspects of human contingency learning and judgement in the same terms (Dickinson et al. 1984; Gluck and Bower 1988; for a collection, see: Shanks et al. 1996).

defines, under certain circumstances, the asymptotic performance of the Rescorla–Wagner model of conditioning. Thus, Cheng's model can be viewed as part of a rational analysis that is complementary to the Rescorla–Wagner account. But while the rational theory and the Rescorla–Wagner algorithm agree at asymptote, they differ during the early stages of learning. Hence, just as with the models of inference in this book, the question arises: to what degree of precision is the rational theory followed? To answer this question requires collecting data concerning cases where the predictions of the rational and algorithmic accounts differ. To date, despite vigorous experimentation, the picture is unclear (e.g. Buehner and Cheng 1997; Cheng 1997; Courville *et al.* 2006; Griffiths and Tenenbaum 2005; Lober and Shanks 2000).

We have seen that, although the doctrine of behaviourism directly attacks the view that cognition is inference, nonetheless, the practical result of research in the behaviourist tradition has been theories of learning to which rational analysis can be naturally and fruitfully applied. This pattern is repeated across many theoretical perspectives that appear to challenge the view of cognition as inference, and hence threaten the role of rational explanation in psychology.

The sceptic: Well, for the sake of argument, suppose I accept all this. That is, suppose that, behind every successful cognitive process, there is a rational analysis waiting to explain that success. This does not mean that it will ever be possible to *formulate* such a rational analysis—might it not just be enormously and hopeless complex. Indeed, come to think of it, isn't this likely to be the standard case; because a realistic model of the real goals, environmental structure, and cognitive limitations will be enormously complex. This will mean, too, that the problem of finding the optimal behaviour (step 4 of the rational analysis) will typically be intractable; and hence we will not be able to carry through the rational analysis programme.

The advocate: Yes, this is quite right—and the same point applies to any kind of scientific explanation. No style of explanation works across the board—indeed, a good part of practical scientific knowledge involves having an intuition for which phenomena can be explained using which styles of explanation. So, with the gas laws, we aim to explain what happens to gases when they are heated or compressed. But we do not attempt to explain, say, atmospheric turbulence, using the gas laws—of course, the gas laws apply to this case—but using them is hopelessly intractable. Equally, Newtonian mechanics is, in principle, good at predicting how objects fall. Yet attempting to predict how something complicated, like a fainting person, or knocked plant, might fall is hopelessly beyond detailed analysis. It's easy to forget how general this is— despite the fantastic power of the physical sciences, the great bulk of everyday phenomena that we encounter are, at a detailed level, beyond tractable analysis using basic physical principles.

The really impressive thing about good scientific theories is that there are *any* identifiable classes of phenomena that they can explain well. But these are tiny islands in a sea of phenomena that presently have no tractable explanation. It's just the same for any kind of psychological explanation, including explanation using rational analysis. What is therefore impressive and surprising is that rational explanations, in psychology, animal behaviour, and economics, seem to be able to explain some useful and important things about mind and behaviour; and, specifically, that the probabilistic rational analyses seem to make useful inroads into the data on human reasoning.

The sceptic: And, of course, there will be many aspects of mind and behaviour that just aren't adaptive anyway—and hence the question why they succeed will be inappropriate, because they don't! There is a danger of slipping into a Panglossian 'best of all possible cognitive systems' state of mind, when considering rational analysis. It's just obvious that there are hosts of ways in which we persistently think and do the 'wrong' things in systematic ways across many cognitive domains.

The advocate: In general, I quite agree. But one of the lessons of the models in this book is that one can jump too rapidly to the conclusion that the cognitive system is not behaving in a rational way. From the point of view of the deductive interpretation of the reasoning tasks we have discussed, people appear to be doing badly. But from the point of view of a probabilistic rational analysis of those tasks, behaviour suddenly snaps into a different focus—the pattern of behaviour suddenly drops out of (different) rational assumptions. The key point is that the rational or adaptive standard against which thought and behaviour are measured cannot be taken as given a priori. Finding out what the cognitive system is adapted to do is an empirical project—and rational analysis provides a methodology for carrying out this empirical project.

The sceptic: I have a another concern about rational analysis—and it's a big one. The rational analysis methodology seems committed to comparing data on human behaviour directly against a putatively 'optimal' rational standard (step 4 in the rational analysis methodology). But there is a covert assumption here—that there is a single 'optimal' behaviour, and that behaviour will be optimal only insofar as it approximations this optimal behaviour. But it might equally well be that there are very large numbers of equally good by very different 'optimal' or close to optimal solutions. But if these solutions work in very different ways, then there may be few or no general conclusions that can be learned from a rational analysis—because all that we can reasonably conjecture is that the cognitive system is near one of this large set of very different solutions.

The advocate: Yes, the concern is a good one. It would be misguided confidently to reel off a string of predictions from an 'optimal' solution to a problem (i.e. from the output of a step 4 in a rational analysis), if a host of near optimal solutions, produced different predictions. Nonetheless, there will often be *aspects* of any close-to-optimal behaviour that can reliably be predicted—and this is typically all that can ever be experimentally tested anyway. To choose an analogy, there may be lots of near-optimal ways of playing chess (presumably any grandmaster level chess player has found one of these ways); and clearly these ways are, to some degree, different from each other. But, nonetheless, the play of good chess players share a lot of similarities—indeed, the fact that there is an agreed lore of the strategy and tactics of chess is a testimony to this. Principles such as 'control the centre', 'develop the pieces as rapidly as possible', 'do not advance the king in the middle game', and, more basically 'avoid having your pieces taken' apply, most of the time, to good chess, whoever is playing it. So just knowing about the rational structure of the problem (the game that is being played) is enough, in this case, to give a great deal by way of predictions concerning how it will be played.

The crucial differences in switching from considering game playing to real cognition is that, first, the problems to which the cognitive systems are adapted are much less clearly defined, more uncertain, more complex, and more open-ended than a formal game like chess; second, we must discover the nature of the problem of that being solved—what the cognitive system's goals are, and how its environment works. But there still seems reason to hope that, as in chess, the assumption of 'good play' in cognitive performance places a lot of restrictions on how the cognitive system can behave. The programme of rational analysis is based on this assumption.

The sceptic: So you are admitting, if this assumption is false, the rational analysis approach fails.

The advocate: Yes, but notice that if rational analysis proves not to be possible, then the implications for cognitive science as a whole are pretty disastrous. Because then we will be in the position of trying to understand the cognitive processes involved in playing chess, without knowing how to play chess! Or we will be in the position of someone trying to understand the functioning of a cash register, without knowing how to add and substract (or at least, without knowing that the cash register is a machine for adding and subtracting). Without knowing *what* a highly complex computational system is doing, our chances of establishing *how* it operates, at an algorithmic level, is negligible. So, according to this view, pursuing rational explanation has to be a central priority, not just in the psychology of reasoning, but in cognitive science more generally.

The sceptic: This sounds reasonable enough—but is it really all that new? Hasn't the attempt to understand the mind always involved an element of 'rational' explanation, though perhaps under a range of different guises.

The advocate: Quite true. At the most general level, one can distinguish two large and distinct traditions for explaining of the mind. One approach is causal. It explains why the mind works in a particular way by spelling out the mechanisms that cause it to work in this way. The approach applies at many different levels of detail, from the attempt to specify representations and algorithms in cognitive psychology, through to neuroscientific explanation.

The other approach is to use rational explanation. It explains why the mind works in a particular way by showing that this is a 'good', 'rational' way to work, from some point of view. Rational explanation includes common-sense folk psychological explanation (e.g. explaining why a person puts up an umbrella, because she believes it is going to rain, does not want to get wet, and so on—for discussion, see: Pickering and Chater 1995; Stich 1983). But it also includes evolutionary explanation, 'rational choice' theory in economics and the social sciences, and many aspects of psychological explanation, particularly in applied domains (e.g. cognitive therapy in clinical psychology is centred on this style of explanation). And the study of rational explanation has also been intense in disciplines which are fundamentally concerned with specifying normatively justified methods of reasoning—including philosophy, logic, probability theory, statistics, operations research and machine learning.

The distinction between causal and rational explanation is, of course, a venerable one. What is different about rational analysis is that it attempts to use rational explanation to capture detailed patterns of psychological data. It thus aims to encroach on ground that has previously been viewed as the domain of purely causal explanation in psychology—such as explaining patterns of supposed reasoning 'errors'. Moreover, the programme of rational analysis treats the construction of rational theories, not as a matter for a priori analysis, but as an aspect of empirical enquiry. The issue is therefore not primarily how rational people are, but what kind of rationality the cognitive system embodies.

The sceptic: Assuming, of course, that the cognitive system does embody some kind of rationality—otherwise the programme does not even get started.

The advocate: Yes, but to abandon the rationality assumption is not really a live option. We noted in Chapter 1, that to do so has drastic and rather horrifying intellectual consequences—undercutting rational explanation across the social and biological sciences, our everyday folk psychological explanations of each others behaviour (see Fodor 1987), the project of linguistic interpretation (Davidson 1984a; Quine 1960); and dooming to failure any attempt to distinguish good from bad argument, or intelligent from absurd behaviour. In short, to deny human rationality is to step into an intellectual void. Indeed, there is even the concern that scepticism about rationality is self-defeating—by undercutting the rational credentials of any arguments for this position, as well as undermining the rationality assumptions required to understand how natural language sentences are intelligible. Scepticism concerning human rationality, were it true, could not be argued for, or even expressed (Davidson 1984b).

But let's leave such potentially controversial philosophical arguments to one side. The consistent and phenomenal success of the cognitive system in dealing with an immensely complicated and partially understood world raises the question: how is this success achieved? This is one type of puzzle for cognitive science. The other type of puzzle is provided by the wealth of empirical data that has been amassed by psychological research. The two types of puzzle need to be solved simultaneously—a good theory of some aspect of cognitive science needs to explain why the system is consistently successful; and it needs to capture the empirical data. But, in practice, the two puzzles have been considered separately, for the most part. Cognitive psychologists have mainly been concerned with capturing the empirical data—but have often ended up with accounts of the mind as consisting of an eclectic jumble of processes and memory stores, with no obvious adaptive function. Philosophers, mathematicians, and computer scientists have, conversely, mainly been concerned with how to determine which thoughts, arguments, and behaviours are justified, and may be expected to lead to reliable success—but the resulting models typically have little immediate application to psychological data. Rational analysis attempts to bring these two traditions together—to explain why cognition works, at the same time as capturing data concerning how cognition works.

Like any other methodological approach, the only real test of the utility of rational analysis is whether it is scientifically fruitful. Across a range of areas of psychology, from memory to categorization, the rational approach appears to be highly promising—probabilistic rational models have provided normatively justified and descriptively successful accounts. The goal of this book is to argue that the approach is also promising in the domain of the psychology of reasoning. The challenge for future research is to chart the scope, and the limits, of probabilistic rational analysis of the mind.

Sceptic: Well, let's put these issues to one side, and instead focus on some questions of more traditional concern in the psychology of reasoning. I'm still not clear what your answer is on some pretty basic points. For a start: are you really claiming that logic has no role in understanding human reasoning, even on deductive reasoning tasks?

Advocate: That would be pushing things too far, at least on the present evidence. What we are claiming is that the human reasoning system is adapted to probabilistic problems; and that many laboratory tasks that are intended as tests of deductive reasoning actually engage mechanisms for probabilistic reasoning. That's what we have attempted to show in the empirical sections of this book—that in core areas in which human deductive reasoning has been studied, a probabilistic analysis nicely captures how people actually reason. Of course, there may be other domains where a logical analysis of how people reason is more appropriate than a probabilistic analysis—the message of this book is really that probability has unexpectedly large scope, and hence that the emphasis on logic in the psychology of reasoning, and for that matter in many areas of artificial intelligence, is misplaced.

In practice, anyone building a complex computational system will find it impossible to even get started if they attempt to implement unconstrained probabilistic reasoning. Structural constraints on how probabilities are interdependent are of crucial importance. Among these constraints will be the dependence and independence relations that are described by Bayesian graphical models (discussed in Chapter 4). But to manipulate and modify such models, as an intelligent reasoning system must do in the light of new information, requires the ability to *represent* these interdependencies explicitly— for example, people need to be able to reason about whether they think that one variable is causally relevant to another; and to adjust any putative probabilistic model appropriately in consequence.

The representation of these structural relationships is, clearly, not possible from inside the 'object-language' of probability theory itself, but need to be separately represented. One way of doing this is by representing probabilistic constraints directly, by representing them in a language, as is exemplified by Bayesian knowledge-bases (Rosen *et al.* 2004), in artificial intelligence. Moreover, the apparent separation between probability and logical reasoning in mathematics is, to some degree, an artefact of the limited range of probabilistic problems that are typically analysed. Typically, it is possible to work with a fixed set of variables, each of which has some set of values, over which a probability distribution may be defined. But as soon as we turn to the types of reasoning relevant in human everyday thought, it becomes clear that we need to be able to talk about degrees of uncertainty about how many variables there are; whether two variables are actually identical, and so on, in a way that is difficult to represent, except by *ad hoc* manoeuvres in traditional probabilistic terms. To adapt up an example from the artificial intelligence researcher

Stuart Russell, suppose you have a set of coloured blocks in a box and you sample these with replacement. Then interesting questions will include: were the first and fourth green blocks actually instances of the very same block; how many green blocks are in the box, given that we have sampled two after one-hundred trials and so on; and many more. Suppose that the blocks also vary in weight; then we can also ask, given certain observations, how probable is it that all the green blocks are the same weight; or whether all the green blocks are heavier than all the blue blocks? But clearly, to even represent these claims, we need to machinery for first-order logic (i.e. quantification over objects); and more-over, to assess probabilities concerning such claims, requires a probabilistic calculus that can be defined over first-order statements. Thus, logic *and* prob-ability are required to provide a model of even quite simple plausible argu-ments—it seems entirely inappropriate to argue that probability sweeps away any role for logic (or vice versa). This viewpoint is embodied in a range of artificial intelligence formalisms for sophisticated everyday reasoning, includ-ing Bayesian knowledge-bases (Rosen, *et al.* 2004), argumentation approaches to defeasible reasoning (Prakken and Vreeswijk 2002), and Bayesian logic (Milch *et al.* 2005).

We take this viewpoint to somewhat undercut recent experimental attempts to demonstrate that the probabilistic approach will not provide a complete account of human reasoning, and that, in particular, there will be aspects of human reasoning that are better understood in logical terms (e.g. Rips 2001). This viewpoint also contrasts with some previous remarks by proponents of this view (e.g. Oaksford and Chater 2001, 2002), which appear to support a purely probabilistic approach to the rational analysis of human reasoning, despite a long-standing commitment both to the importance of structured representations (Chater and Oaksford 1990) and advocacy of Bayesian net-work approach (Oaksford and Chater 1994b, 1998b). The present point of view is that structured representations are indeed critical to human knowl-edge representation, for reasons that have been widely discussed in the classi-cal symbolic cognitive science tradition (Fodor 1975). But of course structured representations are only useful, given the ability to reason over structures—and logic, after all, is the project of understanding what follows from a state-ment in virtue of its structure (Fodor and Pylyshyn 1988). But the mistake of the logicist viewpoint in cognitive science is to assume that no probabilistic flesh about the contingent, uncertain, real world, need be put on the logical bones. However, it is only when this is done that inferences that makes sense in the real world are possible.

Sceptic: But surely it's just obvious that some people are using logical strate-gies in reasoning. After all, some people do choose the 'logical' solution in the selection task; and some people can apply more or less well-remembered logical and mathematical methods to solve reasoning problems.

Advocate: This is, of course, quite right. Given suitable education, people can, of course, learn logic and apply it in reasoning problems. That's pretty uncontroversial. To the extent that relevant bits of such education impact performance in reasoning tasks, then it's pretty clear that we need to take logic into account.

Sceptic: So how does this relate to a dual process account of reasoning (e.g. Evans and Over 1996b, 2004; Sloman 1996; Stanovich and West 2000). At the non-conscious, implicit, level, the cognitive system is presumed to work according to probabilistic principles. Yet at the level of conscious reasoning, logic may play a role—for example, to the extent that the reasoner deliberately draws on learned logical strategies. The balance between these two forces in determining a person's performance in a particular reasoning task might go a long way to explaining patterns of individual differences in reasoning behaviour (e.g. Stanovich and West 2000).

Advocate: First, the previous discussion on the relationship between logic and probability should make clear it is not necessarily appropriate to think of there being two systems of reasoning, one of which uses probability whereas the other uses logic. Instead, we would assume that the basic processes of human knowledge representation and common sense are likely to use both logical and probabilistic machinery in an integrated way.

It is nonetheless clearly the case that people may differ substantially, however, in relation to how effectively they can introspect on, reflect, and criticize, their own, or other's, patterns of reasoning. Hence, we might well expect differences in people's level of ability to explicitly formulate and employ the principles of reasoning that they use. This is analogous to the fact that people clearly differ considerably in relation to how well they can explicitly describe their knowledge of their language. The fact that people differ in relation to their explicit grammatical knowledge is not typically used by cognitive scientists to argue that people differ profoundly over how the core linguistic knowledge that underlies their ability to use language is represented. Similarly, we assume that differences in ability to explicitly employ logical or probabilistic reasoning strategies is not indicative of individual differences in the nature of the fundamental principles of human reasoning.

By contrast, some areas of the literature appear to assume that individual differences in explicit reasoning ability do connect to the contribution of two distinct types of cognitive mechanism. For example, Stanovich and West (2000) suggest that individual reasoning differences are partly driven by the differential development of a System 2, analytical reasoning system, which carries out deductive reasoning, in relation to a more primitive System 1 heuristic reasoning process. Their evidence is primarily through correlational studies, showing associations between high IQ and 'normative' (logical) performance in a variety of reasoning tasks. They conclude that high IQ individuals, who have large working memory capacity, are more reliant on the analytical System 2.

The present viewpoint is relatively neutral on the question of whether there are one or more systems for reasoning—but our previous arguments strongly suggest that any basic system for commonsense reasoning (a 'System 1') will involve logical and probabilistic aspects. Hence, a view in which logic, and other normative reasoning methods, is restricted to a rarefied explicit reasoning system only fully available to the highly intelligent seems to be implausible.

Sceptic: You mentioned mental models and mental logics—where do you stand, if anywhere, in the controversy between them?

Advocate: The account that we have described does not directly address this kind of controversy at all. We have been arguing for a probabilistic rational analysis for the tasks that form the principle battleground between the mental logic and mental models approaches, both of which presuppose logical rational analyses of these same tasks. So, in these contexts, at least, the probabilistic approach is a rival to both approaches, rather than taking a stand with one against the other.

I would assume that the same point applies in the context of everyday, rather than laboratory, reasoning, where conclusions almost never follow certainly from premises (see Chapter 3) and hence where, I would argue, a probabilistic approach is particularly plausible.

This isn't a direct answer to the question concerning mental logics vs. mental models, because that question is a question concerning the algorithmic level of analysis—specifically, are logical operations determined by the algorithmic operations carrying out logical inference (in the jargon, 'mechanized proof theory'), or are they determined by constructing and reading off from mental models?

Sceptic: But while we're on the subject of mental models, isn't it the case that recent mental models theory has directly addressed how people reason with probability? Does that mean that mental model theory can adopt any useful insights from the probabilistic approach, but maintain its additional computational assumptions?

Advocate: In reality, though, mental models theory does not really deal with probability in a natural way—only by counting distinct models, or tagging models with probability values. Thus, the ability to reason about uncertainty is marginal to the account—and the scope of probabilistic reasoning in the framework is very limited. If the argument of this book is correct, though, almost all reasoning involves dealing with uncertainty; and hence we might expect the cognitive processes underlying everyday reasoning, and indeed much of the rest of cognition, to be specifically designed to carry out uncertain inference. This does not, of course, imply, as we have noted that people will be good at explicit numerical reasoning problems, as typically studied in psychological experiments. But it does imply that the rational analysis of human inference should take a probabilistic form.

Sceptic: Finally, let me ask how far you think the programme of probabilistic models of reasoning can go. Isn't it likely that, to understand human reasoning at any depth, the field will inevitably need to focus on process-level constraints on reasoning? And if so, does not the probabilistic approach give us no more than a crude first approximation; and to do better than this approximation, we will end up with just the kinds of process-based models that the present approach appears to try to avoid.

Advocate: It may be useful to think about the scope of the probabilistic approach as having two relevant dimensions. One dimension concerns how precisely patterns of reasoning data within a domain can be captured: can the probabilistic approach capture, not merely the typical patterns of responses across a range of task variants, but individual differences, also reaction times, protocols, data from imaging studies, and so on. The other dimension concerns the scope of the approach in terms of the range of cognitive processes to which it applies, potentially broadening out from the narrow range of classical reasoning tasks, to everyday reasoning, pragmatics, and cognitive processes more generally.

Along the first dimension, we suggest that the boundaries of the rational approach are not currently clear—but clearly the approach must be supplemented with information about the information processing capacities and limits of the brain. Yet this need not detract from the utility of the probabilistic account. Note, on the one hand, that it might turn out that reaction time is inversely proportional to task difficulty in some specific task; and task difficulty might itself be a function of the accuracy with which a certain probability can be estimated (if a very crude estimate of a probability suffices to make a judgement, for example, responding might be faster). So, in this caricatured scenario, we might, in principle, be able to predict reaction times quite well, from a probabilistic perspective alone. But even, as seems more likely, predicting reaction times would require reference to specific heuristics that the cognitive system might use (as might be predicted from, for example, the heuristics described in Chapter 7 on syllogistic reasoning), it might nonetheless turn out that without a clear sense of the computational job that the heuristics are supposed to solve, the search for such heuristics is likely to be severely unconstrained. In short, even if we are interested in departures from rationality; or on phenomena (like reaction times) that appear not directly to be in the scope of rational explanation at all, having an appropriate rational theory concerning the objectives of the cognitive system may nonetheless be of critical importance— both in providing indirect accounts of non-rational phenomena (i.e. explaining reaction time in terms of task difficulty, as above); as defining a standard against which departures from purely rational performance can be thrown into relief; and as providing a standard to which particular heuristic mechanisms may approximate. Following Marr (1982), we strongly believe that understanding the computational-level task in which the cognitive system is engaged is fundamental. And the argument of this book is that probability theory provides the framework for formulating a computational-level theory of reasoning.

The second dimension of scope, concerning the range of topics, seems to present large and exciting challenges for the future. Even within the relatively narrow field of reasoning tasks, extensions of the probabilistic approach to handle inductive reasoning tasks, such as the 2–4–6 task (Wason 1960) and property induction (Kemp and Tenenbaum 2003) seem tractable. Causal reasoning also provides a rich domain for probabilistic reasoning—indeed, it may be that causal relations provide the structure over which everyday probabilistic reasoning is defined (Chater and Oaksford 2006; Fiedler and Juslin 2006; Pearl 2000). Equally, pragmatics, rhetoric, and informal argument provide rich territory for probabilistic analysis (Hahn and Oaksford, 2006; McKenzie 2004; Sher and McKenzie, in press); and the wider questions of how human common-sense reasoning operates also provide fascinating challenges—although challenges that may require substantial progress in the technical literatures in statistics, computer science, and artificial intelligence, to provide a firm foundation for psychological models. More broadly, as we have touched on, though not explored, in this book, almost all cognitive processes, from categorization and memory, to learning and motor control, seems to crucially involve dealing with uncertainty. Indeed, probabilistic methods are also being viewed as providing crucial insights into the coding and processing of information at a neural level (e.g. Rieke *et al.* 1999).

Almost every aspect of cognition involves uncertainty; and the spectacular success of human reasoning suggests that the brain has developed remarkably effective methods for dealing with uncertainty. Understanding how this is possible requires understanding how human cognition can be provided with a rational analysis: and the only machinery that we have to think effectively about this problem is, we suggest, probability theory. But the task of understanding the mind in probabilistic terms is not merely a challenge for psychology; it is a challenge for probability—to provide a rich and deep enough calculus and set of conceptual tools to help capture the laws of thought.

References

Ackley, D. H., Hinton, G. E., and Sejnowski, T. J. (1985). A learning algorithm for Boltzmann machines. *Cognitive Science, 9*, 147–169

Adams, E. W. (1966). On the nature and purpose of measurement. *Synthese, 16*, 225–269.

Adams, E. (1975). *The logic of conditionals: an application of probability to deductive logic.* Dordrecht: Reidel.

Adams, E. W. (1998). *A primer of probability logic.* Stanford: CLSI Publications.

Adelson, E. H. and Pentland, A. P. (1996). The perception of shading and reflectance in perception as Bayesian inference. In D.Knill and W. Richards (ed.), *Perception as Bayesian inferences* (pp. 409–423).Cambridge: University Press.

Agre, P. and Chapman, D. (1987). PENGI: an implementation of a theory of activity. In *Proceedings of the Sixth National Conference on Artificial Intelligence (AAAI-87)*, pp. 268–272, Seattle, WA.

Allais, M. (1953). Le comportement de l'homme rationnel devant le risque: critique des postulats et axiomes de l'école américaine. *Econometrica, 21*, 503–546.

Alloy, L. B. and Abramson, L. Y. (1979). Judgement of contingency in depressed and nondepressed students: sadder but wiser? *Journal of Experimental Psychology: General, 108*, 441–485.

Almor, A. and Sloman, S. A. (1996). Is deontic reasoning special? *Psychological Review. 103*, 374–338.

Anderson, J. R. (1978). Arguments concerning representations for mental imagery. *Psychological Review, 85*, 249–277.

Anderson, J. R. (1983). *The architecture of cognition.* Cambridge, MA: Harvard University Press.

Anderson, J. R. (1990). *The adaptive character of thought.* Hillsdale, NJ: Lawrence Erlbaum Associates.

Anderson, J. R. (1991a). Is human cognition adaptive? *Behavioral and Brain Sciences, 14*, 471–517.

Anderson, J. R. (1991b). The adaptive nature of human categorization. *Psychological Review, 98*, 409–429.

Anderson, J. R. (1993). *Rules of the mind*, Erlbaum, Hillsdale, NJ: Lawrence.

Anderson, J. R. (1995). *Learning and memory.* New York: Wiley.

Anderson, A. R. and Belnap, N. D. (1975). *Entailment: the logic of relevance and necessity* (vol. I). Princeton, NJ: Princeton University Press.

Anderson, J. R. and Matessa, M. (1998). The rational analysis of categorization and the ACT-R architecture. In M. Oaksford and N. Chater (ed.), *Rational models of cognition* (pp.197–217). Oxford, England: Oxford University Press.

Anderson, J. R. and Milson, R. (1989). Human memory: an adaptive perspective. *Psychological Review, 96*, 703–719.

Anderson, J. R. and Schooler, L. J. (1991). Reflections of the environment in memory. *Psychological Science, 2*, 396–408.

Anderson, J. R. and Sheu, C. F. (1995). Causal inferences as perceptual judgments. *Memory and Cognition, 23*, 510–524.

Apostel, L. (1972). Negation: the tension between ontological positivity and anthropological negativity. *Logique et Analyse, XV*, 209–317.

Aristotle (1995). *The Nicomachean ethics* (trans., W. D., Ross). Oxford: Clarendon Press.

Arrow, K. J., Colombatto, E., Perlman, M., and Schmidt, C. (ed.) (1996). *The rational foundations of economic behavior*. London: Macmillan.

Ashby, F. G. and Gott, R. E. (1988). Decision rules in the perception and categorization of multidimensional stimuli. *Journal of Experimental Psychology: Learning, Memory, and Cognition. 14*, 33–53.

Ashby, F. G. and Townsend, J. T. (1986). Varieties of perceptual independence. *Psychological Review, 93*, 154–179.

Attneave, F. (1954). Some informational aspects of visual perception. *Psychological Review, 61*, 183–193.

Ayer, A. J. (1936). *Language, truth and logic*. London: Gollancz.

Bach, K. and Harnish, R. M. (1979). *Linguistic communication and speech acts*. Cambridge, MA: MIT Press.

Bacharach, M. (1999). Interactive team reasoning: a contribution to the theory of cooperation. *Research in Economics, 53*, 117–147.

Barlow, H. B. (1959a). Possible principles underlying the transformation of sensory messages. In W. Rosenblith (ed.), *Sensory communication* (pp. 217–234). Cambridge MA: MIT Press.

Barlow, H. B. (1959b). Sensory mechanisms, the reduction of redundancy, and intelligence. In *The mechanisation of thought processes* (pp. 535–539). London: Her Majesty's Stationery Office.

Baron, J. (1981). *An analysis of confirmation bias*. Paper presented at 1981 Psychonomic Society meeting.

Baron, J. (1985). *Rationality and intelligence*. Cambridge, England: Cambridge University Press.

Baron, J. (2000). *Thinking and deciding*, (3rd edn). Cambridge, England: Cambridge University Press.

Barsalou, L. W. (1987). The instability of graded structure: implications for the nature of concepts. In U. Neisser (ed.), *Emory symposia in cognition 1, concepts and conceptual development: ecological and intellectual factors in categorisation*. Cambridge: Cambridge University Press.

Barwise, J. and Cooper, R. (1981). Generalized quantifiers and natural language. *Linguistics and Philosophy, 4*, 159–219.

Barwise, J. and J. Perry. (1983). *Situations and attitudes*. Cambridge, MA: MIT Press.

Batchelder, W. H. and Riefer, D. M. (1999). Theoretical and empirical review of multinomial processing tree modeling. *Psychonomic Bulletin and Review, 6*, 57–86.

Beck, A. T., Rush, A. J., Shaw, B. F., and Emery, G. (1979). *Cognitive therapy of depression*. New York: Guilford Press.

Becker, G. (1957). *The economics of discrimination*. Chicago: University of Chicago Press.

Becker, G. (1976). *The economic approach to human behavior*. Chicago: University of Chicago Press.

Becker, G. (1991). *A treatise on the family*. Boston, MA: Harvard University Press.

Becker, G. (1996). *Accounting for tastes*. Cambridge, MA: Harvard University Press.

Begg, I. and Denny, J. P. (1969). Empirical reconciliation of atmosphere and conversion interpretations of syllogistic reasoning errors. *Journal of Experimental Psychology, 81,* 351–354.

Belnap, N. (1970). Conditional assertion and restricted quantification. *Noûs, 4,* 1–12.

Bennett, J. (2003). *A philosophical guide to conditionals*. Oxford England: Oxford University Press.

Bernado, J. M. and Smith, A. F. (1994). *Bayesian theory*. New York: Wiley

Bernoulli, J. (1713/2005). *Ars conjectandi, the art of conjecture,* (trans. and notes by E. Dudley Sylla). John Hopkins University Press.

Berger, J. (1985). *Statistical decision theory and Bayesian analysis*. New York: Springer–Verlag.

Birnbaum, M. H. (2004). Causes of Allais common consequence paradoxes: an experimental dissection. *Journal of Mathematical Psychology, 48,* 87–106.

Blake, A., Bulthoff, H. H., and Sheinberg, D. (1996). Shape from texture: ideal observers and human psychophysics. In D. Knill, and W. Richards, (ed.), *Perception as Bayesian inference,* (pp 287–321), Cambridge, England: Cambridge University Press.

Boolos, G. S. and Jeffrey, R. C. (1980). *Computability and logic,* (2nd edn). Cambridge: Cambridge University Press.

Bovens, L. and Hartmann, S. (2003). *Bayesian epistemology*. Oxford: Clarendon Press.

Brachman, R. J. and Levesque, H. J. (ed.), (1985). *Readings in knowledge representation*. Los Altos, CA: Morgan Kaufmann.

Braine, M. D. S. (1978). On the relation between the natural logic of reasoning and standard logic. *Psychological Review, 85,* 1–21.

Braine, M. D. S. and O'Brien, D. P. (1991). A theory of if: a lexical entry, reasoning program, and pragmatic principles. *Psychological Review, 98,* 182–203.

Brooks, R. A. (1991). New approaches to robotics, *Science, 253,* 1227–1232.

Brown, H. I. (1988). *Rationality*. London: Routledge.

Brownell, H. H. and Caramazza, A. (1978). Categorizing with overlapping categories. *Memory and Cognition, 6,* 481–490.

Budescu, D. V., Wallsten, T. S., and Au, W. (1997). On the importance of random error in the study of probability judgment. Part II: Using the stochastic judgment model to detect systematic trends. *Journal of Behavioral Decision Making, 10,* 173–188.

Buehner, M. J. and Cheng, P. W. (1997). Causal induction: The power PC theory versus the Rescorla-Wagner model. In M. G. Shafto and P. Langley (ed.), *Proceedings of the Nineteenth Annual Conference of the Cognitive Science Society* (pp. 55–60). Hillsdale, NJ: Lawrence Erlbaum Associates.

Burgess, C., Livesay, K., and Lund, K. (1996). Modeling Parsing constraints in high-dimensional semantic space: on the use of proper names. *Proceedings of the Cognitive Science Society,* (pp 737–742). Mahwah, NJ: Erlbaum.

Burnyeat, M. (1983). *The sceptical tradition*. Berkeley: University of California Press.

Byrne, R. M. J. (1989). Suppressing valid inferences with conditionals. *Cognition, 31,* 1–21.

Byrne, R. M. J., Espino, O., and Santamaria, C. (1999). Counterexamples and the suppression of inferences. *Journal of Memory and Language, 40*, 347–373.

Carey, S. (1988). Conceptual differences between children and adults. *Mind and Language, 3*,167–181.

Carnap, R. (1950). *The logical foundations of probability theory*. Chicago: University of Chicago Press.

Ceraso, J. and Provitera, A. (1971). Sources of error in syllogistic reasoning. *Cognitive Psychology, 2*, 400–410.

Chan, D. and Chua, F. (1994). Suppression of valid inferences: syntactic views, mental models, and relative salience. *Cognition, 53*, 217–238.

Chapman, L. J. and Chapman, J. P. (1959). Atmosphere effect re-visited. Journal of *Experimental Psychology, 58*, 220–226.

Charniak, E. and McDermott, D. (1985). *Introduction to artificial intelligence*. Reading, MA: Addison Wesley.

Chater, N. (1993). Mental models and non-monotonic reasoning. *Behavioural and Brain Sciences, 16*, 340–341.

Chater, N. (1996). Reconciling simplicity and likelihood principles in perceptual organization. *Psychological Review, 103*, 566–581.

Chater, N., Crocker, M. J., and Pickering, M. J. (1998). The rational analysis of inquiry: The case of parsing. In M. Oaksford and N. Chater (ed.), *Rational models of cognition* (pp. 441–468). Oxford: Oxford University Press.

Chater, N. and Manning, C. (2006). Probabilistic models of language processing and acquisition. *Trends in Cognitive Sciences, 10*, 287–291.

Chater, N. and Oaksford, M. (1990). Autonomy, implementation and cognitive architecture: a reply to Fodor and Pylyshyn. *Cognition, 34*, 93–107.

Chater, N. and Oaksford, M. (1993). Logicism, mental models and everyday reasoning. *Mind and Language, 8*, 72–89.

Chater, N. and Oaksford, M. (1996). Deontic reasoning, modules and innateness: a second look. *Mind and Language, 11*, 191–202.

Chater, N. and Oaksford, M. (1999a). Information gain and decision-theoretic approaches to data selection. *Psychological Review, 106*, 223–227.

Chater, N. and Oaksford, M. (1999b). The probability heuristics model of syllogistic reasoning. *Cognitive Psychology, 38*, 191–258.

Chater, N. and Oaksford, M. (2001). Human rationality and the psychology of reasoning: where do we go from here? *British Journal of Psychology, 92*, 193–216.

Chater, N. and Vitanyi, P. (2003). Generalizing the universal law of generalization, *47*, 346–369.

Chater, N., Oaksford, M., Nakisa, R., and Redington, M. (2003). Fast, frugal and rational: how rational norms explain behavior. *Organizational Behavior and Human Decision Processes, 90*, 63–86.

Chater, N., Heir, E., and Oaksford, M. (2005). Reasoning. In K. Lambers and R. Goldstone (eds.), *The Handbook of Cognition* (pp. 297–320). London: Sage Publications.

Cheng, P. W. (1997). From covariation to causation: a causal power theory. *Psychological Review, 104*, 367–405.

Cheng, P. W. and Holyoak, K. J. (1985). Pragmatic reasoning schemas. *Cognitive Psychology, 17*, 391–416.

Cheng, P. W. and Novick, L. R. (1991). Causes versus enabling conditions. *Cognition, 40*, 83–120.

Cheng, P. W. and Novick, L. R. (1992). Covariation in natural causal induction. *Psychological Review, 99*, 365–382.

Cheng, P. W., Holyoak, K. J., Nisbett, R. E., and Oliver, L. M. (1986). Pragmatic versus syntactic approaches to training deductive reasoning. *Cognitive Psychology, 18*, 293–328.

Cherniak, C. (1986). *Minimal rationality.* Cambridge, MA: MIT Press.

Chomsky, N. (1957). *Syntactic structures.* The Hague: Mouton.

Chomsky, N. (1965). *Aspects of the theory of syntax.* Cambridge, MA: MIT Press.

Churchland, P. S. (1986). Neurophilosophy: toward a unified science of the mind/brain. Cambridge, MA: MIT Press.

Churchland, P. S., Ramachandran, V. S., and Sejnowski, T. J. (1994). A critique of pure vision. In C. Koch and J. Davis, (ed.), *Large-scale neuronal theories of the brain* (pp. 23–60). Cambridge MA: MIT Press.

Clark, K. L. (1978). Negation as failure. In H. Gallaire and J. Minker (ed.), *Logic and databases* (pp. 293–322). New York: Plenum Press.

Clocksin W. F. and Mellish, C. S. (1984). *Programming in Prolog.* Berlin: Springer–Verlag.

Cohen, L. J. (1981). Can human irrationality be experimentally demonstrated? *Behavioral and Brain Sciences, 4*, 317–370.

Collins, A. M. and Loftus, E. F. (1975). A spreading-activation theory of semantic processing. *Psychological Review, 82*, 407–428.

Collins, A. M. and Quillian, M. R. (1969). Retrieval time from semantic memory. *Journal of Verbal Learning and Verbal Behavior, 8*, 240–247.

Colman, A. M. (2003). Cooperation, psychological game theory, and limitations of rationality in social interaction. *Behavioral and Brain Sciences, 26*, 139–153.

Comrie, B. (1986). Conditionals: a typology. In E. C. Traugott, A. Ter Meulen, J. S. Reilly, and C. A. Ferguson (ed.), *On conditionals* (pp. 77–99). Cambridge: Cambridge University Press.

Coolidge, J. L. (1940). *A history of geometrical methods.* Oxford: Clarendon Press.

Copeland, D. E. and Radvansky, G. A. (2004). Working memory and syllogistic reasoning. *Quarterly Journal of Experimental Psychology, 57A*, 1437–1457.

Corter, J. E. and Gluck, M. A. (1992). Explaining basic categories: feature predictability and information. *Psychological Bulletin, 111*, 291–303.

Cosmides, L. (1989). The logic of social exchange: has natural selection shaped how humans reason? Studies with the Wason selection task. *Cognition, 31*, 187–276.

Cosmides, L. and Tooby, J. (1997). Dissecting the computational architecture of social inference mechanisms. In G. R. Bock and G. Cardew (ed.), *Characterizing human psychological adaptations. (Ciba Foundation symposium,* No. 208. pp. 132–161). Chichester, UK: John Wiley and Sons, Inc.

Cosmides, L. and Tooby, J. (2000). Evolutionary psychology and the emotions. In M. Lewis and J. M. Haviland-Jones (ed.), *Handbook of emotions,* (2nd edn), (pp. 91–115.). New York, NY: Guilford.

Courville, A., Daw, N., and Touretzky, D. (2006). Bayesian theories of conditioning in a changing world. *Trends in Cognitive Sciences, 10*, 294–300.

Cox, R. T. (1946). Probability, frequency, and reasonable expectation. *American Journal of Physics. 14*, 1–13.

Cox, R. T. (1961). *The algebra of probable inference*. Baltimore, MD: Johns Hopkins University Press.

Cristianini, N. and Shawe-Taylor J. (2000). *An introduction to support vector machines and other Kernel-based learning methods*. Cambridge, England: Cambridge University Press.

Cummins, D. D. (1995). Naïve theories and causal deduction. *Memory and Cognition, 23,* 646–658.

Cummins, D. D. (1996). Evidence for the innateness of deontic reasoning. *Mind and Language, 11,*160–190.

Cummins, D. D., Lubart, T., Alksnis, O., and Rist, R. (1991). Conditional reasoning and causation. *Memory and Cognition, 19,* 274–282.

Daston, L (1988). *Classical probability in the enlightenment*. Princeton, NJ: Princeton University Press.

Davidson, D. (1984a). *Inquiries into truth and interpretation*. Oxford: Oxford University Press.

Davidson, D. (1984b). On the very idea of a conceptual scheme. In D. Davidson (ed.), *Inquiries into truth and interpretation* (pp. 183–198). Oxford: Oxford University Press.

Davidson, R. J. (1993). Parsing affective space: perspectives from neuropsychology and psychophysiology. *Neuropsychology, 7,* 464–475.

Dawes, R. M. and Mulford, M. (1996). The false consensus effect and overconfidence: flaws in judgment, or flaws in how we study judgment? *Organizational Behavior and Human Decision Processes, 65,* 201–211.

Dawkins, R. (1977). *The selfish gene*. Oxford, England: Oxford University Press.

DeLong, H. (1970). *A profile of mathematical logic*. Reading, MA: Addison-Wesley.

Dempster. (1967). Upper and lower probabilities induced by a multi-valued mapping. *Annals of Mathematical Statistics, 38,* 325–339.

Dennett, D. (1991). *Consciousness explained*. Boston, MA: Little, Brown and Co.

Dennis, S. (2005). A memory based theory of verbal cognition. *Cognitive Science, 29,* 145–193.

De Finetti, B. (1937). La prévision: ses lois logiques, ses sources subjectives, *Annales de l'Institut Henri Poincaré, 7,* 1–68; translated (1980) Foresight: its logical laws, its subjective ources. In H. E. Kyburg, Jr. and H. E. Smokler (ed.), *Studies in subjective probability*. New York, NY: Robert E. Krieger Publishing Company.

De Finetti, B. (1972). *Probability, induction and statistics*. New York: Wiley.

Dickinson, A., Shanks, D., and Evenden, J. (1984). Judgement of act outcome contingency: the role of selective attribution. *Quarterly Journal of Experimental Psychology, 36A,* 29–50.

Dickstein, L. S. (1978). The effect of figure on syllogistic reasoning. *Memory and Cognition, 6,* 76–83.

Dixon, N. (1976). *On the psychology of military incompetence*. London: Jonathan Cape.

Downs, A. (1957). *An economic theory of democracy*. New York: Harper and Brothers.

Duda, R. O. and Hart, P. (1973). *Pattern classification and scene analysis*. John Wiley and Sons Press, New York.

Duda, R., Hart, P., and Stork, D. (2000). *Pattern classification*, (2nd edn). New York, NY: John Wiley and Sons.

Duhem, P. (1914/1954). *The aim and structure of physical theory*. Princeton, NJ: Princeton University Press.

Earman, J. (1992). *Bayes or bust?* Cambridge, MA: MIT Press

Edgington, D. (1991). The matter of the missing matter of fact. *Proceedings of the Aristotelian society, 65,* 185–209.

Edgington, D. (1995). On conditionals. *Mind, 104,* 235–329.

Eells, E. and Fetzer, J. (2005). *Probability in science*. La Salle, IL: Open Court.

Elman, J. L., Bates, E., Johnson, M., Karmiloff-Smith, A., Parisi. D., and Plunkett, K. (1996). *Rethinking innateness: a connectionist perspective on development*. Cambridge, MA: MIT Press.

Elster, J. (1983). *Sour grapes*. Cambridge: Cambridge University Press.

Elster, J. (ed.), (1986). *Rational choice*. Oxford: Basil Blackwell.

Erev, I., Wallsten, T. S., and Budescu, D. V. (1994). Simultaneous over- and under confidence: the role of error in judgment processes. *Psychological Review, 101,* 519–527.

Espino, O., Santamaria, C., and Garcia-Madruga, J. A. (2000). Activation of end-terms in syllogistic reasoning. *Thinking and Reasoning, 6,* 67–89.

Evans, J. St.B. T. (1972). Reasoning with negatives. *British Journal of Psychology, 63,* 213–219.

Evans, J. St.B. T., and Nearstead, S. E. (1977). Linguistic factors in reasoning. *Quarterly Journal of Experimental Psychology, 29,* 297–306.

Evans, J. St.B. T. (1982). *The psychology of deductive reasoning*. London: Routledge.

Evans, J. St.B. T. (1983). Linguistic determinants of bias in conditional reasoning. *Quarterly Journal of Experimental Psychology: Human Experimental Psychology, 35A,* 635–644.

Evans, J. St.B. T. (1984). Heuristics and analytic processes in reasoning. *British Journal of Psychology, 75,* 541–568.

Evans, J. St.B. T. (1989). *Bias in human reasoning: causes and consequences*. Brighton: Erlbaum.

Evans, J. St.B. T. (1993). The mental model theory of conditional reasoning: critical appraisal and revision. *Cognition, 48,* 1–20.

Evans, J. St.B. T. (1998). Matching bias in conditional reasoning: do we understand it after 25 years? *Thinking and Reasoning, 4,* 45–82.

Evans, J. St.B. T. (1999). Rational analysis of illogical reasoning. *Contemporary Psychology, 44,* 461–463.

Evans, J. St.B. T. and Beck, M. A. (1981). Directionality and temporal factors in conditional reasoning. *Current Psychological Research, 1,* 111–120.

Evans, J. St.B. T. and Handley, S. J. (1999). The role of negation in conditional inference. *Quarterly Journal of Experimental Psychology, 52A,* 739–769.

Evans, J. St.B. T. and Lynch, J. S. (1973). Matching bias in the selection task. *British Journal of Psychology, 64,* 391–397.

Evans, J. St.B. T. and Nearstead, S. E. (1977). Linguistic factors in reasoning. *Quarterly Journal of Experimental Psychology, 29,* 297–306.

Evans, J. St.B. T. and Over, D. E. (1996a). Rationality in the selection task: epistemic utility versus uncertainty reduction. *Psychological Review, 103,* 356–363.

Evans, J. St.B. T. and Over, D. (1996b). *Rationality and reasoning*. Hove, Sussex: Psychology Press.

Evans, J. St.B. T. and Over, D. (1997). Rationality in reasoning: the problem of deductive competence. *Cahiers de Psychologie Cognitive, 16*, 1–35.

Evans, J.St.B. T. and Over, D. E. (2004). *If*. Oxford, England: Oxford University Press.

Evans, J. St.B. T., Clibbens, J., and Rood, B. (1995). Bias in conditional inference: implications for mental models and mental logic. *Quarterly Journal of Experimental Psychology, 48A*, 644–670.

Evans, J.St. B. T., Newstead, S. E., and Byrne, R. M.J. (1993). *Human reasoning*. Hillsdale, NJ: Lawrence Erlbaum Associates.

Evans, J.St.B. T, Handley, S. J., and Buck, E. (1998). Ordering of information in conditional reasoning. *British Journal of Psychology, 89*, 383–404.

Evans, J.St.B. T., Handley., S. J., Harper, C. N. J., and Johnson-Laird, P. N. (1999). Reasoning about necessity and possibility: a test of the mental model theory of deduction. *Journal of Experimental Psychology: Learning, Memory, and Cognition, 25*, 1495–1513.

Evans, J.St.B. T., Handley, S. H., and Over, D. E. (2003). Conditionals and conditional probability. *Journal of Experimental Psychology: Learning, Memory and Cognition, 29*, 321–355.

Fedorov, V. (1972). *Theory of optimal experiments*. New York: Academic Press.

Feeney, A. and Handley, S. J. (2000). The suppression of *q* card selections: Evidence for deductive inference in Wason's selection task. *Quarterly Journal of Experimental Psychology A, 53*, 1224–1242.

Feeney, A., and Handley, S. J., and Kentridge, R. (2003). Deciding between accounts of the selection task: a reply to Oaksford (2002). *Quarterly Journal of Experimental Psychology, 56*, 1079–1088.

Feldman, J. (2001). Bayesian contour integration. *Perception and Psychophysics, 63*, 1171–1182.

Feldman, J. and Ballard, D. (1982). Connectionist models and their properties. *Cognitive Science, 6*, 205–254.

Feldman, J. and Singh, M. (2005). Information along curves and closed contours. *Psychological Review, 112*, 243–252.

Fiddick, L., Cosmides, L., and Tooby, J. (2000). No interpretation without representation: the role of domain-specific representations in the Wason selection task. *Cognition, 77*, 1–79.

Fiedler, K. (2000). Beware of samples! A cognitive-ecological sampling approach to judgment biases. *Psychological Review, 107*, 659–676.

Fiedler, K. and Hertel, G. (1994). Content-related schemata versus verbal-framing effects in deductive reasoning. *Social Cognition, 12*, 129–147.

Fiedler, K. and Juslin. P. (ed.) (2006). *Information sampling and adaptive cognition*. Cambridge: Cambridge University Press.

Fiedler, K., Brinkmann, B., Betsch, T., and Wild, B. (2000). A sampling approach to biases in conditional probability judgments: beyond base rate neglect and statistical format. *Journal of Experimental Psychology: General, 129*, 399–418.

Fitelson, B. (1999).The plurality of Bayesian measures of confirmation and the problem of measure sensitivity. *Philosophy of Science, 66*, S362-S378.

Fodor, J. A. (1975). *The language of thought.* New York: Thomas Y. Crowell.

Fodor, J. A. (1983). *The modularity of mind.* Cambridge, Mass: MIT Press.

Fodor, J. A. (1987). *Psychosemantics.* Cambridge, MA: MIT Press.

Fodor, J. A. and Pylyshyn, Z.W (1981). How direct is visual perception? Some reflection on Gibson's ecological approach. *Cognition, 9,* 139–196.

Fodor, J. A. and Pylyshyn, Z. W. (1988). Connectionism and cognitive architecture: a critical analysis. *Cognition, 28,* 3–71.

Ford, M. (1994). Two modes of representation and problem solution in syllogistic reasoning. *Cognition, 54,* 1–71.

Fox, J. (2003). Probability, logic and the cognitive foundations of rational belief. *Journal of Applied Logic, 1,* 197–224.

Fox, J. and Parsons, S. (1998). Arguing about beliefs and actions: In A. Hunter and S. Parsons (ed.), *Applications of uncertainty formalisms,* (pp.266–302). Lecture Notes in Computer Science (No. 1455). Berlin, Germany: Springer–Verlag.

Frank, R. H. (1988). *Passions within reason: the strategy role of the emotions.* New York: Norton.

Franklin, A. and Howson, C. (1984). Why do scientists prefer to vary their experiments? *Studies in the History and Philosophy of Science, 15,* 51–62.

Frazier, L. (1979). On comprehending sentences: syntactic parsing strategies. Unpublished PhD Thesis. University of Connecticut.

Freeman, W. T. (1994). The generic viewpoint assumption in a framework for visual perception. *Nature, 368,* 542–545.

Frey, B. J. (1998). *Graphical models of machine learning and digital communication.* Cambridge, MA: MIT Press.

Fried, L. S. and Holyoak, K. J. (1984). Induction of category distributions: a framework for classification learning. *Journal of Experimental Psychology: Learning, Memory and Cognition, 10,* 234–257.

Fuhrmann, A. (1998). Nonmonotonic logic. In E. Craig (ed.) *Routledge encyclopedia of philosophy,* Vol. 7 (pp. 30–35). London: Routledge.

Gabbay, D. (1996). *Labelled deductive systems,* Vol. 1. Oxford University Press

Gallistel, C. R. (1990). *The organization of learning.* Cambridge, MA: MIT Press.

Gallistel, C. R. and Gibbon, J. (2000). Time, rate, and conditioning. *Psychological Review, 107,* 289–344.

Galotti, K. M., Baron, J., and Sabini, J. P. (1986). Individual differences in syllogistic reasoning: Deduction rules or mental models. *Journal of Experimental Psychology: General, 115,* 16–25.

Gärdenfors, P. (1986). Belief revisions and the Ramsey test for conditionals. *Philosophical Review, 95,* 81–93.

Garey, M. R. and Johnson, D. S. (1979). *Computers and intractability: a guide to the theory of NP-completeness.* San Francisco: W. H. Freeman.

Garnham, A. (1993). Is logicist cognitive science possible? *Mind and Language, 8,* 49–71.

Gebauer, G. and Laming, D. (1997). Rational choices in Wason's selection task. *Psychological Research, 60,* 284–293.

Geisler, W. S. and Diehl, R. L. (2003). A Bayesian approach to the evolution of perceptual and cognitive systems. *Cognitive Science*, 27, 379–402.

Geisler, W. S. and Kersten, D. (2002). Illusions, perception and Bayes. *Nature Neuroscience*, 5, 508–510.

Geman, S. and Geman, D. (1984). Stochastic relaxation, Gibbs distributions, and the Bayesian restoration of images. *IEEE-PAMI*, 6, 721–741.

George, C. (1997). Reasoning from uncertain premises. *Thinking and Reasoning*, 3, 161–190.

Geurts, B. (2003). Reasoning with quantifiers. *Cognition*, 86, 223–251

Gibson, J. J. (1966). *The senses considered as perceptual systems*. Boston: Houghton Mifflin.

Gibson, J. J. (1979). *The ecological approach to visual perception*. Boston: Houghton Mifflin.

Gigerenzer, G. (2002). *Reckoning with risk: learning to live with uncertainty*. Harmondsworth, England: Penguin Books.

Gigerenzer, G. and Goldstein, D. (1996). Reasoning the fast and frugal way: models of bounded rationality. *Psychological Review*, 103, 650–669.

Gigerenzer, G. and Hoffrage, U. (1995). How to improve Bayesian reasoning without instruction: Frequency formats. *Psychological Review*, 102, 684–704.

Gigerenzer, G. and Hug, K. (1992). Domain-specific reasoning: social contracts, cheating and perspective change. *Cognition*, 42, 127–171.

Gigerenzer, G. and Selten, R. (ed.) (2001). *Bounded rationality: the adaptive toolbox*. Cambridge, MA: MIT Press.

Gigerenzer, G., Swijinck, Z., Porter, T., Daston, L., Beatty, J., and Kruger, L. (1989). *The empire of chance*. Cambridge: Cambridge University Press.

Gigerenzer, G., Todd. P., and the ABC Group (1999). *Simple heuristics that make us smart*. Oxford: Oxford University Press.

Ginsberg, M. (1987). *Readings in nonmonotonic reasoning*. San Mateo, CA: Morgan Kaufmann Publishers.

Girotto, V., Mazzocco, A., and Tasso, A. (1997). The effect of premise order in conditional reasoning: a test of the mental model theory. *Cognition*, 63, 1–28.

Gluck, M. A. and Bower, G. H. (1988). From conditioning to category learning: an adaptive network model. *Journal of Experimental Psychology: General*, 117, 227–247.

Glymour, C. (1980). *Theory and evidence*. Princeton: Princeton University Press

Glymour, C. (1983). On testing and evidence. In J. Earman (ed.), *Minnesota studies in philosophy of science*, Vol. X. Minnesota: University of Minnesota Press.

Glymour, C. and Cooper, G. (ed.) (1999). *Computation, causation and discovery*. Cambridge MA: MIT Press.

Goldman, A. I. (1986). *Epistemology and cognition*. Cambridge: Harvard University Press.

Goldstein, W. M. and Hogarth, R. M. (ed.) (1997). *Judgment and decision making: Currents, connections, and controversies*. Cambridge, UK: Cambridge University Press.

Good, I. J. (1950). *Probability and the weighting of evidence*. London: Griffin.

Good, I. J. (1971). Twenty seven principles of rationality. In V. P. Godambe and D. A. Sprott (ed.), *Foundations of statistical inference*. Toronto: Holt, Rhinehart and Wilson.

Good, I. (1984). The best explicatum for weight of evidence. *Journal of Statistical Computation and Simulation*, 19, 294–299.

Goodman, N. (1951). *The structure of appearance*. Cambridge MA: Harvard University Press.

Goodman, N. (1954). *Fact, fiction, and forecast*. London: The Athlone Press.

Gordon, J. and Shortliffe, E. H. (1985). A method for managing evidential reasoning in a hierarchical hypothesis space. *Artificial Intelligence, 26*, 323–357.

Gorman, M. E. and Gorman, M. E. (1984). A comparison of disconfirmatory, confirmatory and control strategies on Wason's 2–4–6 task. *Quarterly Journal of Experimental Psychology: Human Experimental Psychology, 36A*, 629–648.

Gosselin, F. and Schyns, P. G. (2001). Why do we SLIP to the basic-level? Computational constraints and their implementation. *Psychological Review, 108*, 735–758.

Gosselin, F. and Schyns, P. G. (2004). A picture is worth thousands trials: rendering the use of visual information from spiking neurons to recognition. *Cognitive Science, 28*, 141–146.

Green, D. W. (1995a). Externalisation, counter-examples and the abstract selection task. *Quarterly Journal of Experimental Psychology, 48A*, 424–446.

Green, D. W. (1995b). The abstract selection task: thesis, antithesis and synthesis. In Newstead and J.St.B. T. Evans (ed.), *Perspective on thinking and reasoning* (pp.171–186). Hove, UK: Lawrence Erlbaum Associates Ltd.

Green, D. W. (2000). Review of rationality in an uncertain world: Essays on the cognitive science of human reasoning. *Quarterly Journal of Experimental Psychology, 53*, 281–283.

Green, D. W. and Larking, R, (1995). The locus of facilitation in the abstract selection task. *Thinking and Reasoning, 1*, 183–199.

Green, D. W. and Over, D. E. (1997). Causal inference, contingency tables and the selection task. *Current Psychology of Cognition, 16*, 459–487.

Green, D. W. and Over, D. E. (1998). Reaching a decision: a reply to Oaksford. *Thinking and Reasoning, 4*, 231–248.

Green, D. W. and Over, D. E. (2000). Decision theoretical effects in testing a causal conditional. *Current Psychology of Cognition, 19*, 51–68.

Green, D. P. and Shapiro, I. (1996). Pathologies of rational choice theory: a critique of applications in political science. Yale: Yale University Press.

Green, D. W., Over, D. E., and Pyne, R. A. (1997). Probability and choice in the selection task. *Thinking and Reasoning, 3*, 209–236.

Greene, S. B. (1992). Multiple explanations for multiply quantified sentences: Are multiple models necessary? *Psychological Review, 99*, 184–187.

Grice, H. P. (1975). Logic and conversation. In P. Cole & J. L. Morgan (eds.). *Studies in Syntax* (pp. 41–58). New York: Academic Press.

Griffiths, T. L. and Tenenbaum, J. B. (2005). Structure and strength in causal induction. *Cognitive Psychology, 51*, 354–384.

Griggs, R. A. and Cox, J. R. (1982). The elusive thematic-materials effect in Wason's selection task. *British Journal of Psychology, 73*, 407–420.

Griggs, R. A. and Newstead, S. E. (1982). The role of problem structure in a deductive reasoning task. *Journal of Experimental Psychology, 8*, 297–307.

Grünwald, P. D. (2000). Model selection based on minimum description length. *Journal of Mathematical Psychology, 44*, 133–152.

Grünwald, P. D. (2001). Strong entropy concentration, game theory and algorithmic random-ness. In *Proceedings of the fourteenth annual conference on computational learning theory* (COLT) (pp. 320–336). Amsterdam, the Netherlands.

Grünwald, D., Myung, I. J., and Pitt, I. J. (ed.) (2005). *Advances in minimum description length: theory and applications.* Cambridge, MA: MIT Press.

Guyote, M. J. and Sternberg, R. J. (1981). A transitive-chain theory of syllogistic reasoning. *Cognitive Psychology, 13,* 461–525.

Haack, S. (1974). *Deviant logic: some philosophical issues.* Cambridge: Cambridge University Press.

Haack, S. (1978). *Philosophy of logics.* Cambridge University Press.

Hacking, I. (1975). *The emergence of probability.* Cambridge: Cambridge University Press.

Hacking, I. (1990). *The taming of chance.* Cambridge: Cambridge University Press.

Hahn, U. and Chater, N. (1998). Similarity and rules: distinct? exhaustive? empirically eistin-guishable? *Cognition, 65,* 197–230.

Hahn, U. and Oaksford, M. (2006). A Bayesian approach to informal argument fallacies. *Synthese, 152,* 207–236.

Hailperin, T. (1996). *Sentential probability logic. Origins, development, current status, and technical applications.* Bethlehem: Lehigh University Press.

Handley, S. J., Feeney, A., and Harper, C. (2002). Alternative antecedents, probabilities, and the suppression of inference in Wason's selection task. *Quarterly Journal of Experimental Psychology, 55,* 799–818.

Hardman, D. (1998). Does reasoning occur on the selection task: a comparison of rele-vance-based theories. *Thinking and Reasoning, 4,* 353–376.

Harman, G.(1965). The inference to the best explanation. *Philosophical Review, 74,* 88–95.

Harsanyi, J. C. and Selten R. (1988). *A general theory of equilibrium selection in games.* Cambridge, MA: MIT Press.

Hattori, M. (1999). The effects of probabilistic information in Wason's selection task: an analysis of strategy based on the ODS model. *Procceedings of the 16th Annual Meeting of the Japanese Cognitive Science Society, 16,* 623–626.

Hattori, M. (2002). A quantitative model of optimal data selection in Wason's selection task. *Quarterly Journal of Experimental Psychology, 55A,* 1241–1272.

Hayes, P. (1975). The logic of frames. In D. Metzing (ed.), *Frame conceptions and text understanding* (pp. 46–61). Berlin: Walter de Gruyter and Co.

Hempel, C. G. (1965). *Aspects of scientific explanation.*New York: The Free Press.

Henle, M. (1962). On the relation between logic and thinking. *Psychological Review, 69,* 366–378.

Henle, M. (1978). Foreword to R. Revlin and R. E. Mayer (ed.), *Human reasoning.* Washington: Winston.

Henle, M. and Michael, M. (1956). The influence of attitudes on syllogistic reasoning. *Journal of Social Psychology, 44,* 115–127.

Hertz, J., Krogh, A., and Palmer, R (1991). *Introduction to the theory of neural computation.* Redwood City, CA: Addison-Wesley.

Hochberg, J. E. and McAlister, E. (1953). A quantitative approach to figural goodness. *Journal of Experimental Psychology, 46,* 361–364.

Hodges, W. (1977). *Logic: an introduction to elementary logic*. London: Penguin Books.

Hogarth, R. and Goldstein, W. (1997). *Judgement and decision making: currents, connections, and controversies*. Cambridge, UK: Cambridge University Press.

Holland, J., Holyoak, K., Nisbett, R., and Thagard, P. (1986). *Induction – processes of inference, learning, and discovery*. Cambridge, MA: MIT Press.

Horn, (1989). *A natural history of negation*. Chicago: Chicago University Press.

Horty, J. F., Thomason, R. H., and Touretzky, D. S. (1990). A sceptical theory of inheritance in nonmonotonic semantic networks. *Artificial Intelligence, 42*, 311–348.

Horwich, P. (1982). *Probability and evidence*. New York: Cambridge University Press.

Howson, C. (2003). Probability and logic. *Journal of Applied Logic, 1*, 151–165.

Howson, C. and Urbach, P. (1993). *Scientific reasoning: the Bayesian approach* (2nd edn). La Salle, IL: Open Court.

Hume, D. (1748). *An enquiry concerning human understanding*. Oxford: Clarendon Press.

Inhelder, B. and Piaget, J. (1955). *De la logique de l'enfant à la logique de l'adolescent*. Paris: Presses Universitaires de France. English version, (1958) *The growth of logical thinking from childhood to adolescence*. (trans. A. Parsons and S. Milgram) London: Routledge.

Jackson, F. (1982). Two modes of syllogistic reasoning. *Communication Monographs, 49*, 205–213.

Jaspars, J. M. F., Hewstone, M. R. C., and Fincham, F. D. (1983). Attribution theory and research: Conceptual, developmental and social dimensions. In Jaspars, J. M. F., Hewstone, M. R. C., and Fincham, F. D. (ed.) *Attribution theory: essays and experiments*. London: Academic Press.

Jaynes, E. T. (1978). Where do we stand on maximum entropy: In R. D. Levine and M. Tribus (ed.), *The maximum entropy formalism* (pp. 15–118). Cambridge, MA: MIT Press

Jeffrey, R. (1983). *The logic of decision*, (2nd edn). Chicago: University of Chicago Press.

Jeffrey, R. (1992) *Probability and the art of judgment*. Cambridge: Cambridge University Press.

Jeffreys, H. (1939). *Theory of probability*, (3rd edn). Oxford: Clarendon Press.

Johnson-Laird, P. N. (1983). *Mental models*. Cambridge: Cambridge University Press.

Johnson-Laird, P. N. (1986). Reasoning without logic. In T. Myers, K. Brown, McGonigle and B. O. Mc Gonigle (ed.), *Reasoning and discourse Processes*. London: Academic Press.

Johnson-Laird, P. N. (1994). Mental models and probabilistic thinking. *Cognition, 50*, 189–209.

Johnson-Laird, P. N. and Bara, B. G. (1984). Syllogistic inference. *Cognition, 16*, 1–62.

Johnson-Laird, P. N. and Byrne, R. M. J. (1989). Only reasoning. *Memory and Language, 28*, 313–330.

Johnson-Laird, P. N. and Byrne, R. M.J. (1991). *Deduction*. Hillsdale, NJ: Lawrence Erlbaum Associates.

Johnson-Laird, P. N. and Byrne, R. M. J. (2002). Conditionals: a theory of meaning, pragmatics, and inference. *Psychological Review, 109*, 646–678.

Johnson-Laird, P. N. and Steedman, M. (1978). The psychology of syllogisms. *Cognitive Psychology, 10*, 64–99.

Johnson-Laird, P. N. and Wason, P. C. (1970). Insight into a logical relation. *Quarterly Journal of Experimental Psychology, 22*, 49–61.

Johnson-Laird, P. N., Byrne, R. M. J., and Tabossi, P. (1989). Reasoning by model: the case of multiple quantification. *Psychological Review, 96*, 658–673.

Johnson-Laird, P. N., Legrenzi, P., Girotto, V., Legrenzi, M. S., and Caverni, J. P. (1999). Naive probability: a mental model theory of extensional reasoning. *Psychological Review, 106*, 62–88.

Jordan, M. I. (ed.) (1998).*Learning in graphical models*. Cambridge, MA: MIT Press.

Josephson, J. R. and Josephson, S. G. (ed.) (1994). *Abductive inference: computation, philosophy, technology*. New York: Cambridge University Press.

Juslin, P., Winman, A., and Olsson, H. (2000). Naive empiricism and dogmatism in confidence research: a critical examination of the hard-easy effect. *Psychological Review, 107*, 384–396.

Kacelnik, A. and Bateson M (1997). Risk-sensitivity: cross-roads for theories of decision making. *Trends in Cognitive Sciences, 1*, 304–309.

Kahneman, D. and Tversky, A. (1973). On the psychology of prediction. *Psychological Review, 80*, 237–251.

Kahneman, D. and Tversky, A. (1979). Prospect theory: an analysis of decisions under risk. *Econometrica, 47*, 313–327.

Kahneman, D. and Tversky, A. (ed.) (2000). *Choices, values and frames*. New York: Cambridge University Press and the Russell Sage Foundation.

Kahneman, D., Slovic, P., and Tversky, A. (ed.) (1982). *Judgment under uncertainty: heuristics and biases*. New York: Cambridge University Press.

Kakade, S. and Dayan, P. (2002). Acquisition and extinction in autoshaping. *Psychological Review, 109*, 533–544.

Kamp, H. and Reyle, U. (1993). From discourse to logic. Dordrecht, The Netherlands: Kluwer Academic Publishers.

Kant, E. (1787/1961). *Critique of the pure reason* (trans., N. Kemp Smith). London: Macmillan.

Katz, J. (1990). *The metaphysics of meaning*. Cambridge, MA: MIT Press.

Kemp, C. S. and Tenenbaum, J. B. (2003). Theory-based induction. *Proceedings of the Twenty-Fifth Annual Conference of the Cognitive Science Society*, Hillsdale, NJ: Erlbaum.

Kelley, H. H. (1967). Attribution in social psychology. *Nebraska Symposium on Motivation, 15*, 192–238.

Keynes, J. M. (1921). *A treatise on probability*. London: Macmillan and Co.

Keynes, J. M. (1936/1973). The general theory of employment, interest, and money. General theory of employment, interest and money reprinted. In D. Moggridge (ed.), *The collected writings of John Maynard Keynes*, vol. 7. *The general theory*. London: Macmillan.

Kirby, K. N. (1994). Probabilities and utilities of fictional outcomes in Wason's four card selection task. *Cognition, 51*, 1–28.

Klauer, K. C. (1999). On the normative justification for information gain in Wason's selection task. *Psychological Review, 106*, 215–222.

Klauer, K. C., Musch, J., and Naumer, B. (2000). On belief bias in syllogistic reasoning. *Psychological Review, 107*, 852–884.

Kleindorfer, P. R., Kunreuther, H. C. and Schoemaker, P. J. H. (1993). *Decision sciences: an integrated perspective.* Cambridge: Cambridge University Press.

Knill, D. and Richards, W. (ed.) (1996). *Perception as Bayesian inference.* Cambridge: Cambridge University Press.

Knill, D., Freeman, W., and Geisler, W. (ed.) (2003). Bayesian and statistical approaches to vision. *Special Issue of the Journal of the Optical Society of America A: Optics, Image Science and Vision, 20,* (7).

Kornblith, H. (ed.) (1994). *Naturalizing epistemology,* (2nd edn). Cambridge, MA: MIT Press.

Krebs, J. R. and Davies, N. (ed.) (1996). *Behavioural ecology: an evolutionary approach,* (4th edn). Oxford: Blackwell.

Kreps, D. M. (1992). *A course in microeconomic theory.* New York: Harvester Wheatsheaf.

Kripke, S. A. (1963). Semantical considerations on modal logics. *Acta Philosophica Fennica, 16,* 83–94.

Kugler, P. N. and Turvey, M. T. (1987). *Information, natural law, and the self-assembly of rhythmic movement.* Hillsdale, NJ: Lawrence Erlbaum Associates.

Kuhn, T. (1962). *The structure of scientific revolutions.* Chicago: University of Chicago Press.

Kyburg, H. (1961). *Probability and the logic of rational belief.* Middletown, CT: Wesleyan University Press.

Kyburg, H. (1983). Recent work in inductive logic. In T. Machan and K. Lucey (ed.), *Recent work in philosophy* (pp. 87–150). Lanham: Rowman and Allanheld.

Kyburg Jr., H. E. (2003). Are there degrees of belief? *Journal of Applied Logic, 1,* 139–149.

Lakatos, I. (1970). Falsification and the methodology of scientific research programmes. In I. Lakatos, and A. Musgrave (ed.) *Criticism and the growth of knowledge* (pp. 91–196). Cambridge: Cambridge University Press.

Lakatos, I. (1977). *Philosophical papers,* vol. 1: *The methodology of scientific research programmes.* Cambridge: Cambridge University Press.

Lamberts, K. (2000). Information-accumulation theory of speeded categorization. *Psychological Review, 107,* 227–260.

Lamberts, K. and Chong, S. (1998). Dynamics of dimension weight distribution and flexibility in categorization. In M. Oaksford and N. Chater (ed.), *Rational Models of Cognition* (pp.275–92). Oxford: Oxford University Press.

Laming, D. (1996). On the analysis of irrational data selection. *Psychological Review, 103,* 364–373.

Landauer, T. K., and Dumais, S. T. (1997). A solution to Plato's problem: the Latent semantic analysis theory of acquisition, induction and representation of knowledge. *Psychological Review, 104,* 211–240.

Lauritzen, S. S. and Spiegelhalter. J (1988). Local computations with probabilities on graphical structures and their application to expert systems. *Journal of the Royal Statistical Society, B 50,* 253 -258.

Lea, R. B., O'Brien, D. P., Fisch, S. M., Noveck, I. A., and Braine, M. D. S. (1990). Predicting propositional logic inferences in text comprehension. *Journal of Memory and Language, 29,* 361–387.

Legrenzi, P. (1971). Discovery as a means to understanding. *Quarterly Journal of Experimental Psychology, 23,* 417–422.

Lehrer, K. (1990). *Theory of knowledge.* Routledge and Kegan Paul, London.

Lemmon, E. J. (1965). *Beginning logic.* London: Nelson.

Leeuwenberg, E. (1969). Quantitative specification of information in sequential patterns. *Psychological Review, 76,* 216–220.

Leeuwenberg, E. (1971). A perceptual coding language for perceptual and auditory patterns. *American Journal of Psychology, 84,* 307–349.

Leeuwenberg, E. and Boselie, E (1988). Against the likelihood principle in visual form perception. *Psychological Review, 95,* 485–491.

Levi, I. (1996). *For the sake of the argument: Ramsey test conditionals, inductive inferences, and nonmonotonic reasoning.* Cambridge: Cambridge University Press.

Levinson, S. C. (1983). *Pragmatics.* Cambridge, England: Cambridge University Press.

Lewis, C. I. (1918). *A survey of symbolic logic.* Berkeley, CA: University of California Press.

Lewis, D. (1973). *Counterfactuals.* Harvard University Press

Lewis, D. (1976). Probabilities of conditionals and conditional probabilities. *Philosophical Review, 85,* 297–315.

Li, M. and Vitanyi, P. M.B. (1997). *An introduction to Kolmogorov complexity and its applications,* (2nd edn.). New York: Springer–Verlag.

Lindley, D. V. (1982). Scoring rules and the inevitability of probability. *International Statistical Review, 50,* 11–26.

Liu, I. M. (2003). Conditional reasoning and conditionalisation. *Journal of Experimental Psychology: Learning, Memory and Cognition, 29,* 694–709.

Liu, I. M., Lo, K. C., and Wu, J. T. (1996). A probabilistic interpretation of 'If-Then'. *The Quarterly Journal of Experimental Psychology, 49A,* 828–844.

Lober, K. and Shanks, D. R. (2000). Is causal induction based on causal power? Critique of Cheng (1997). *Psychological Review, 107,* 195–212.

Love, R. E. and Kessler, C. M. (1995). Focusing in Wason's selection task: content and instruction effects. *Thinking and Reasoning, 1,* 153–182.

Lucas, E. J. and Ball, L. J. (2005). Think-aloud protocols and the selection task: evidence for relevance effects and rationalisation processes. *Thinking and Reasoning, 11,* 35–66.

Lucas, J. R. (1970). *The concept of probability.* Oxford University Press, Oxford.

Lucas, J. R. (1972). Expectations on the neutrality of money. *Journal of Economic Theory, 4,* 103–124.

Lund, K. and Burgess, C. (1996). Producing high-dimensional semantic spaces from lexical cooccurrence. *Behavior Research Methods, Instrumentation, and Computers, 28,* 203–208.

Mach, E. (1959). *The analysis of sensations and the relation of the physical to the psychical.* New York: Dover Publications. (Original work published 1914.)

MacKay, D. J.C. (1992). Bayesian interpolation. *Neural Computation, 4,* 415–447.

MacDonald, M. C., Pearlmutter, N. J., and Seidenberg, M. S. (1994). The lexical nature of syntactic ambiguity resolution. *Psychological Review, 101,* 676–703.

Mackie, J. L. (1963). The paradox of confirmation. *British Journal for the Philosophy of Science, 38,* 265–277.

Mackie, J. (1969). The relevance criterion of confirmation. *The British Journal for the Philosophy of Science, 20,* 27–40.

Macnamara, J. (1986). *A border dispute, the place of logic in psychology.* Cambridge, MA: MIT Press.

MacNamara, J. and. Reyes, G. (ed.) (1994). *The logical foundations of cognition.* Oxford University Press: New York.

Manktelow, K. I. and Over, D. (ed.) (1987). *Rationality: psychological and philosophical Perspectives.* London: Routledge

Manktelow, K. I. and Over, D. E. (1991). Social roles and utilities in reasoning with deontic conditionals. *Cognition, 39,* 85–105.

Manktelow, K. I., Sutherland, E. J., and Over, D. E. (1995). Probabilistic factors in deontic reasoning. *Thinking and Reasoning, 1,* 201–220.

Manning C. and Schütze, H. (1999). *Foundations of statistical natural language* processing. Cambridge, MA: MIT Press.

Markovits, H. and Barrouillet, P. (2002). The development of conditional reasoning: a mental model account. *Developmental Review, 22,* 5–36.

Markovits, H., and Quinn, S. (2002). Efficiency of retrieval correlates with logical reasoning from causal conditional premises. *Memory and Cognition, 30,* 696–706.

Markovits, H., Fleury, M. L., Quinn, S., and Venet, M. (1998). The development of conditional reasoning and the structure of semantic memory. *Child Development, 64,* 742–755.

Marr, D. (1982).*Vision.* San Francisco: W. H. Freeman.

McCarthy, J. M. (1980). Circumscription: a form of nonmonotonic reasoning. *Artificial Intelligence, 13,* 27–39.

McCarthy, J. and Hayes, P. J. (1969). Some philosophical problems from the standpoint of artificial intelligence. In B. Meltzer and D. Michie, (ed.), *Machine intelligence 4.* Edinburgh: Edinburgh University Press.

McClelland, J. L. (1998). Connectionist models and Bayesian inference. In M. Oaksford and N. Chater (ed.), *Rational models of cognition* (pp. 21–53). Oxford: Oxford University Press.

McCloskey, D. N. (1985). *The rhetoric of economics.* Madison: University of Wisconsin Press.

McDermott, D. (1982). Non-monotonic logic II: Nonmonotonic model theories'. *Journal of the Association for Computing Machinery, 29,* 33–57.

McDermott, D. (1987). We've been framed: Or why all is innocent of the frame Problem. In Pylyshyn Z. W. (ed.), *The robot's dilemma: the frame problem in artificial intelligence.* Norwood NJ: Ablex.

McDermott, D. and Doyle, J. (1980). Non-monotonic logic I. *Artificial intelligence, 13,* 41–72.

McFarland, D. and Bosser, T. (1993). *Intelligent behavior in animals and robots.* Cambridge, Mass.: MIT Press.

McFarland, D. and Houston, A. (1981). *Quantitative ethology: the state space approach.* London: Pitman.

McKenzie, C. (1994). The accuracy of intuitive judgment strategies: covariation assessment and Bayesian inference. *Cognitive Psychology, 26,* 209–239.

McKenzie, C. R. M. (2000). Examining the rarity assumption and its implications. Unpublished manuscript, Department of Psychology, University of California, San Diego.

McKenzie, C. R. M. (2004). Framing effects in inference tasks and why they are normatively defensible. *Memory and Cognition, 32,* 874–885.

McKenzie, C. R. M. and Mikkelsen, L. A. (2000). The psychological side of Hempel's paradox of confirmation. *Psychonomic Bulletin and Review, 7*, 360–366.

McKenzie, C. R. M., and Mikkelsen, L. A. (In press). A Bayesian view of covariation assessment. *Cognitive Psychology.*

McKenzie, C. R. M., Ferreira, V. S., Mikkelsen, L. A., McDermott, K. J., and Skrable, R. P. (2001). Do conditional statements target rare events? *Organizational Behavior and Human Decision Processes, 85*, 291–309.

McRae, K., Spivey-Knowlton, M. J., and Tanenhaus, M. K. (1998). Modeling the influence of thematic fit (and other constraints) in online sentence comprehension. *Journal of Memory and Language, 38*, 283–31.

Medin, D. L. and Schaffer, M. M. (1978). Context theory of classification learning. *Psychological Review, 85*, 207–238.

Mellor, D. H. (1971). *The matter of chance.* Cambridge: Cambridge University Press.

Michalski, R. S., Carbonell, J. G., and Mitchell, T. M. (ed.) (1983*). Machine learning: an artificial intelligence approach*, vol 2. Los Altos, CA: Morgan Kaufmann.

Milch, B., Marthi, B., Russell, S., Sontag, D., Ong, D., and Kolobov, A. (2005). BLOG: probabilistic models with unknown objects. *Proceedings of the 19th International Joint Conference on Artificial Intelligence (IJCAI)*: 1352–1359.

Milne, P. (1996). Log $[p(h/eb)/p(h/b)]$ is the one true measure of confirmation. *Philosophy of Science, 63*, 21–26.

Mineka, S. and Ohman, A. (2002). Phobias and preparedness: the selective, automatic, and encapsulated nature of fear. *Biological Psychiatry, 52*, 927–937.

Minsky, M. (1974). A framework for representing knowledge. In J. Haugeland (ed.), *Mind design: philosophy, psychology, artificial intelligence* (pp. 95–128). Cambridge, MA: MIT Press.

Minsky, M. (1977). Frame system theory. In P. N. Johnson-Laird and P. C. Wason (ed.), *Thinking: readings in cognitive science* (pp. 355–376). Cambridge: Cambridge University Press.

Morgan, J. I. B. and Morton, J. T. (1944). The distortions of syllogistic reasoning produced by personal connections. *Journal of Social Psychology, 20*, 39–59.

Moshman, D. and Geil, M. (1998). Collaborative reasoning: evidence for collective rationality. *Thinking and Reasoning, 4*, 231–248.

Moxey, L. and Sanford, A. (1987). Quantifiers and focus. *Journal of Semantics,* 5, 189–206.

Moxey, L., and Sanford, A. (1991). *Communicating quantities.* Hove, UK: Erlbaum.

Muth, J. F. (1961). Rational expectations and the theory of price movements. *Econometrica, 29*, 315–335.

Myerson, J. and Miezin, F. M. (1980). The kinetics of choice: an operant systems analysis. *Psychological Review, 87*, 160–174.

Neal, R. M. (1992). Connectionist learning of belief networks. *Artificial Intelligence, 56*, 71–113.

Neal, R. M. (1996). *Bayesian learning for neural networks.* Lecture Notes in Statistics No. 118, New York: Springer–Verlag.

Neapolitan, R. (1990). *Probabilistic reasoning in expert systems: theory and algorithms.* New York: John Wiley and Sons, Inc.

Nelson, J. (2005). Finding useful questions: on Bayesian diagnosticity, probability, impact, and information gain. *Psychological Review, 112*, 979–999.

Nelson, R. and Winter, S. (1982). *An evolutionary theory of economic change.* Cambridge, MA: Harvard University Press.

Newell, A. (1990). *Unified theories of cognition.* Cambridge, MA: Harvard University Press.

Newell, A. and Simon, H. A. (1972). *Human problem solving.* Englewood Cliffs, N.J: Prentice-Hall.

Newell, A. and Simon, H. A. (1976). Computer science as empirical inquiry: symbols and search. *Communications of the Association for Computing Machinery, 19*, 11–26.

Newell, A., Shaw, J. C. and Simon, H. A. (1958). Chess-playing programs and the problem of complexity. *IBM Journal of Research and Development, 2*, 320–25.

Newstead, S. E. (1989). Interpretational errors in syllogistic reasoning. *Journal of Memory and Language, 28*, 78–91.

Newstead, S. E. (1995). Gricean implicatures and syllogistic reasoning. *Journal of Memory and Language, 34*, 644–664.

Newstead, S. E. and Griggs, R. A. (1983). Drawing inferences from quantified statements: a study of the square of opposition. *Journal of Verbal Learning and Verbal Behavior, 22*, 535–546.

Newstead, S. E., Handley, S. J., and Buck, E. (1999). Falsifying mental models: testing the predictions of theories of syllogistic reasoning. *Memory and Cognition, 27*, 344–354.

Nickerson, R. S. (1996). Hempel's paradox and Wason's selection task: logical and psychological puzzles of confirmation. *Thinking and Reasoning, 2*, 1–32.

Niemelä, I. and Rintanen, J. (1994). On the impact of stratification on the complexity of nonmonotonic reasoning. In G. Lakemeyer and B. Nebel (ed.), *Foundations of knowledge representation and reasoning* (pp. 275–295). Berlin: Springer–Verlag.

Nosofsky, R. M. (1984). Choice, similarity, and the context theory of classification. *Journal of Experimental Psychology: Learning, Memory, and Cognition, 10*, 104–114.

Nosofsky, R. M. (1986). Attention, similarity, and the identification-categorization relationship. *Journal of Experimental Psychology: General, 115*, 39–57.

Nosofsky, R. M. (1991). Relation between the rational model and the context model of categorization. *Psychological Science, 2*, 416–421.

Nute, D. (1984). Logical relations. *Philosophical Studies, 46*, 41–56.

Oaksford, M. (1989). *Cognition and inquiry: the pragmatics of conditional reasoning.* Unpublished DPhil thesis. University of Edinburgh.

Oaksford, M. (1993). Mental models and the tractability of everyday reasoning. *Behavioral and Brain Sciences, 16*, 360–361.

Oaksford, M. (1998). Task demands and revising probabilities in the selection task. *Thinking & Reasoning, 4*, 179–186.

Oaksford, M. (2002a). Contrast classes and matching bias as explanations of the effects of negation on conditional reasoning. *Thinking and Reasoning, 8*, 135–151.

Oaksford, M. (2002b). Predicting the results of reasoning experiments: reply to Feeney and Handley. *Quarterly Journal of Experimental Psychology, 55A*, 793–798.

Oaksford, M. (2004). *Conditional inference and constraint satisfaction: reconciling probabilistic and mental models approaches?* Paper presented at the 5th International Conference on Thinking, University of Leuven, Leuven, Belgium.

Oaksford, M. and Chater, N. (1991). Against logicist cognitive science. *Mind and Language, 6*, 1–38.

Oaksford, M. and Chater, N. (1993). Reasoning theories and bounded rationality. In K. I. Manktelow and D. E. Over (eds.), *Rationality* (pp. 136–177). London: Routledge.

Oaksford, M. and Chater, N. (1994a). Another look at eliminative and enumerative behaviour in a conceptual task. *European Journal of Cognitive Psychology, 6*, 149–169.

Oaksford, M. and Chater, N. (1994b). A rational analysis of the selection task as optimal data selection. *Psychological Review, 101*, 608–631.

Oaksford, M. and Chater, N. (1995a). Information gain explains relevance which explains the selection task. *Cognition, 57*, 97–108.

Oaksford, M. and Chater, N. (1995b). Theories of reasoning and the computational explanation of everyday inference. *Thinking and Reasoning, 1*, 121–152.

Oaksford, M. and Chater, N. (1996). Rational explanation of the selection task. *Psychological Review, 103*, 381–391.

Oaksford, M. and Chater, N. (1998a). *Rationality in an uncertain world.* Hove, England: Psychology Press.

Oaksford, M. and Chater, N. (ed.) (1998b). *Rational models of cognition.* Oxford: Oxford University Press.

Oaksford, M. and Chater, N. (2001). The probabilistic approach to human reasoning. *Trends in Cognitive Sciences, 5*, 349–357.

Oaksford, M. and Chater, N. (2002). Commonsense reasoning, logic and human rationality. In R. Elio (ed.), *Commonsense reasoning and rationality.* Oxford: Oxford University Press.

Oaksford, M. and Chater, N. (2003a). Conditional probability and the cognitive science of conditional reasoning. *Mind and Language, 18*, 359–379.

Oaksford, M. and Chater, N. (2003b). Computational levels and conditional reasoning: reply to Schroyens and Schaeken (2003). *Journal of Experimental Psychology: Learning, Memory and Cognition, 29*, 150–156.

Oaksford, M. and Chater, N. (2003c). Modelling probabilistic effects in conditional inference: validating search or conditional probability? *Revista Psychologica, 32*, 217–242.

Oaksford, M. and Chater, N. (2003d). Probabilities and pragmatics in conditional inference: suppression and order effects. In D. Hardman and L. Macchi (ed.), *Thinking: psychological perspectives on reasoning, judgement and decision making.* Chichester, UK: John Wiley and Sons Ltd.

Oaksford, M. and Chater, N. (2003e). Optimal data selection: revision, review and re-evaluation. *Psychonomic Bulletin and Review, 10*, 289–318.

Oaksford, M. and Moussakowski, M. (2004). Negations and natural sampling in data selection: ecological vs. heuristic explanations of matching bias. *Memory and Cognition, 32*, 570–581.

Oaksford, M. and Stenning, K. (1992). Reasoning with conditionals containing negated constituents. *Journal of Experimental Psychology: Learning, Memory and Cognition, 18*, 835–854.

Oaksford, M. and Wakefield, M. (2003). Data selection and natural sampling: probabilities do matter. *Memory and Cognition, 31*, 143–154.

Oaksford, M., Chater, N., Grainger, B., and Larkin, J. (1997). Optimal data selection in the reduced array selection task (RAST). *Journal of Experimental Psychology: Learning, Memory and Cognition, 23*, 441–458.

Oaksford, M., Chater, N., and Grainger, B. (1999). Probabilistic effects in data selection. *Thinking and Reasoning, 5*, 193–244.

Oaksford, M., Chater, N., and Larkin, J. (2000). Probabilities and polarity biases in conditional inference. *Journal of Experimental Psychology: Learning, Memory and Cognition, 26*, 883–889.

Oaksford, M., Roberts, L., and Chater, N. (2002). Relative informativeness of quantifiers used in syllogistic reasoning. *Memory and Cognition, 30*, 138–149.

Oberauer, K. and Wilhelm, O. (2003). The meaning(s) of conditionals: conditional probabilities, mental models and personal utilities. *Journal of Experimental Psychology: Learning, Memory and Cognition, 29*, 680–739.

Oberauer, K., Wilhelm, O., and Dias, R, R. (1999). Bayesian rationality for the Wason selection task? A test of optimal data selection theory. *Thinking and Reasoning, 5*, 115–144.

Oberauer, K., Weidenfeld, A., and Hörnig, R. (2004). Logical reasoning and probabilities: a comprehensive test of Oaksford and Chater (2001). *Psychonomic Bulletin and Review, 11*, 521–527.

O'Brien, D. P., Braine, M. D.S., and Yang, Y. (1994). Propositional reasoning by models? Simple to refute in principle and in practice. *Psychological Review, 101*, 711–724.

Oehman, A. and Mineka, S. (2001). Fears, phobias, and preparedness: Toward an evolved module of fear and fear learning. *Psychological Review, 108*, 483–522.

Osherson, D., Shafir, E., and Smith, E. E. (1993). Ampliative inference: On choosing a probability distribution. *Cognition, 49*, 189–210.

Osherson, D., Smith, E. E., Wilkie, O., and Lopez, A. (1990). Category-based induction. *Psychological Review, 97*, 185–200.

Osman, M. and Laming, D. (2001). Misinterpretation of conditional statements in Wason's selection task. *Psychological Research, 65*, 128–144.

Over, D. E. and Evans, J.St.B.T (1994). Hits and misses: Kirby on the selection task. *Cognition, 52*, 235–243.

Over, D. E. and Jessop, A. (1998). Rational analysis of causal conditionals and the selection task. In M. Oaksford and N. Chater (ed.), *Rational models of cognition* (pp. 399–414). Oxford: Oxford University Press.

Over, D. E., Hadjichristidis, C., Evans, J. St.B. T., Handley, S. J., and Sloman, S., A. (In press). *The probability of ordinary indicative conditionals.* Manuscript submitted for publication.

Paris, J. (1992). The uncertain reasoner's companion, a mathematical perspective. *Cambridge Tracts in Theoretical Computer Science, 39.* Cambridge University Press.

Paterson, K. B., Sanford, A. J., Moxey, L. M. and Dawydiak, E. J. (1998). Quantifier polarity and referential focus during reading. *Journal of Memory and Language, 39*, 290–306.

Pearce, J. M. (1994). Similarity and discrimination: a selective review and a connectionist model. *Psychological Review, 101*, 587–607.

Pearl, J. (1988). *Probabilistic reasoning in intelligent systems.* San Mateo: Morgan Kaufmann.

Pearl, J. (2000). *Causality: models, reasoning and inference.* Cambridge: Cambridge University Press.

Perham, N. and Oaksford, M. (2005). Deontic reasoning with emotional content: evolutionary psychology or decision theory? *Cognitive Science, 29,* 681–718.

Phillips, L. and Edwards, W. (1966). Conservatism in a simple probability inference task. *Journal of Experimental Psychology, 72,* 346–354.

Pickering, M. and Chater, N. (1995). Why cognitive science is not formalized folk psychology. *Minds and Machines, 5,* 309–337.

Pirolli, P. L. and Card, S. K. (1999). Information foraging. *Psychological Review, 106,* 643–675.

Politzer, G. and Braine, M. D. (1991). Responses to inconsistent premises cannot count as suppression of valid inferences. *Cognition, 38,* 103–108.

Polk, T. A. and Newell, A. (1988). Modelling human syllogistic reasoning in Soar. In J. Kruschke (ed.), *Proceedings of the Fourteenth Annual Conference of the Cognitive Science Society* (pp. 181–187). Hillsdale, NJ: Erlbaum.

Polk, T. A. and Newell, A. (1995). Deduction as verbal reasoning. *Psychological Review, 102,* 533–566.

Pollard, P. and Evans, J. St. B. T. (1980). The influence of logic on conditional reasoning performance. *Quarterly Journal of Experimental Psychology, 32,* 605–624.

Pollard, P. and Evans, J. S. B. T. (1983). The effect of experimentally contrived experience on reasoning performance. *Psychological Research, 45,* 287–301.

Pollard, P. and Evans, J. St. B. T. (1987). On the relationship between content and context effects in reasoning. *American Journal of Psychology, 100,* 41–60.

Pollock, J. L. (1986). *Contemporary theories of knowledge.* Rowman and Littlefield, Savage, Maryland.

Pollock, J. L. (2001). Defeasible reasoning with variable degrees of justification. *Artificial intelligence, 133,* 233–282.

Pomerantz, J. R. and Kubovy, M. (1987). Theoretical approaches to perceptual organization'. In K. R. Boff, L. Kaufman and J. P. Thomas (ed.), *Handbook of perception and human performance, Volume II: Cognitive processes and performance* (pp. 36.1–36.46) New York, NY: Wiley.

Popper, K. (1935/1959). *The logic of scientific discovery.* Basic Books, New York

Popper, K. R. (1959). The propensity interpretation of probability. *British Journal for the Philosophy of Science, 10,* 25–42.

Pothos, E. M. and Chater, N. (2002). A simplicity principle in unsupervised human categorization. *Cognitive Science, 26,* 303–343.

Prakken, H. and Vreeswijk, G. A.W. (2002). Logics for defeasible argumentation. In D. M. Gabbay and F. Guenthner (ed.), *Handbook of philosophical logic,* (2nd edn), vol 4, (pp. 219–318). Dordrecht/Boston/London: Kluwer Academic Publishers.

Putnam, H. (1962). The analytic and the synthetic. Scientific explanation, space, and time. In H. Feigl and G. Maxwell (ed.), *Minnesota studies in the philosophy of science,* vol. 3, (pp. 358–397). Minneapolis: University of Minnesota Press.

Putnam, H. (1974). The 'corroboration' of theories. In A. Schilpp (ed.), *The philosophy of Karl Popper,* vol. 2. La Salle, IL: Open Court.

Putnam, H. and Benacerraf, P. (1983). *Philosophy of mathematics: selected readings.* Cambridge: Cambridge University Press.

Pylyshyn, Z. (1973). What the mind's eye tells the mind's brain—a critique of mental imagery. *Psychological Bulletin, 80,* 1–24.

Pylyshyn, Z. (ed.) (1987). *The robot's dilemma: the frame problem in artificial intelligence.* Norwood, NJ: Ablex.

Quine, W. V. O. (1950). *Methods of logic.* Cambridge, MA: Harvard University Press.

Quine, W. V. O. (1953). *From a logical point of view.* Cambridge, MA: Harvard University Press.

Quine, W. V. O. (1960). *Word and object.* Cambridge, MA: Harvard University Press.

Quine, W. V. O., (eds.), (1969). *Ontological relativity and other essays.* New York: Columbia University Press.

Quine, W. V. O. (1990). *Pursuit of truth.* Cambridge, MA: Harvard University Press.

Quinn, S. and Markovits, H. (1998). Conditional reasoning, causality, and the structure of semantic memory: strength of association as a predictive factor for content effects. *Cognition, 68,* B93-B101.

Quinn, S. and Markovits, H. (2002). Conditional reasoning with causal premises: evidence for a retrieval model. *Thinking and Reasoning, 8,* 179–191.

Rabiner, L. and Hwang, L. (1993). *Fundamentals of speech recognition.* New York: Prentice Hall.

Ramsey, F. P. (1931/1990). *The foundations of mathematics and other logical essays.* London: Routledge and Kegan Paul.

Rao, R. P. N., Olshausen, B. A., and Lewicki, M. S. (2002). *Probabilistic models of the brain: perception and neural function.* Cambridge, MA: MIT Press.

Rawls, J. A. (1971). *Theory of justice.* Cambridge, Massachusetts: Belknap Press.

Read, T. R.C. and N. A.C. Cressie. (1988). *Goodness-of-fit statistics for discrete multivariate data.* New York: Springer-Verlag.

Redington, M. and Chater, N. (1998). Connectionist and statistical approaches to language acquisition: a distributional perspective. *Language and Cognitive Processes, 13,* 129–191.

Redington, M., Chater, N., and Finch, S. (1998). Distributional information: a powerful cue for acquiring syntactic categories. *Cognitive Science, 22,* 425–469.

Reichenbach, H. (1944). *Philosophical foundations of quantum mechanics.* Berkley: University of California Press.

Reiner, R (1995). Arguments against the possibility of perfect rationality. *Minds and Machines, 5,* 373–89.

Reiter, R. (1980). A logic for default reasoning. *Artificial Intelligence, 13,* 81–132.

Reiter, R. (1985/1978). On reasoning by default. In R. Brachan and H. Levesque (ed.), *Readings in knowledge representation* (pp. 401–410). Los Altos, CA: Morgan Kaufman.

Rescorla, R. A. and Wagner, A. R. (1972). A theory of Pavlovian conditioning: variations in the effectiveness of reinforcement and nonreinforcement. In A. H. Black and W. F. Prokasy (ed.) *Classical conditioning II: Current research and theory* (pp. 64–99). New York: Appleton-Century-Crofts.

Restle, E. (1970). Theory of serial pattern learning: structural trees. *Psychological Review, 77,* 481–495.

Revlis, R. (1975a). Two models of syllogistic inference: feature selection and conversion. *Journal of Verbal Learning and Verbal Behavior, 14*, 180–195.

Revlis, R. (1975b). Syllogistic reasoning: logical decisions from a complex data base. In R. J. Falmagne (ed.), *Reasoning, representation and process*. New York: John Wiley.

Rieke, F., Warland, D., de Ruyter van Steveninck, R. R., and Bialek, W. (1997). *Spikes: exploring the neural code*, Cambridge, MA: MIT Press.

Rips, L. J. (1983). Cognitive processes in propositional reasoning. *Psychological Review, 90*, 38–71.

Rips, L. J. (1990). Reasoning. *Annual Review of Psychology, 41*, 321–353.

Rips, L. J. (1994). *The Psychology of proof*. Cambridge, MA: MIT Press.

Rips, L. J. (2001). Two kinds of reasoning. *Psychological Science, 12*, 129–134.

Rissanen, J. (1987). Stochastic complexity and the MDL principle. *Econometric Reviews, 6*, 85–102.

Roberge, J. J. (1978). Linguistic and psychometric factors in propositional reasoning. *Quarterly Journal of Experimental Psychology, 30*, 705–716.

Rock, I. (1983). *The logic of perception*. Cambridge, MA: MIT Press.

Rosch, T. (1977). *Principles of categorization in cognition and categorization*. In E. Rosch and B. B. Lloyd (ed.), Hillsdale, NJ: Lawrence Erlbaum Associates.

Rosen, S. E. Shimony., and Santos Jr, E. (2004). Reasoning with BKBs – algorithms and complexity. *Annals of mathematics and artificial intelligence, 40*, 403–425.

Rumelhart, D. E. and McClelland, J. L. (1986). On learning the past tenses of English verbs. In J. L. McClelland and D. E. Rumelhart (ed.), *Parallel distributed processing: Explorations in the microstructures of congnition. Vol. 2: Psychological and biological models* (pp. 216–271). Cambridge, MA: MIT Press.

Rumelhart, D. E., Smonlensky, P., McClelland, J. L., and Hinton, G. E. (1986). Schemata and sequential thought processes in PDP models. In J. L. McClelland and D. E. R. Rumelhart (ed.), *Parallel distributed processing: Explorations in the microstructures of cognition. Vol. 2: Psychological and biological models* (pp. 7–57). Cambridge, MA: MIT Press.

Russel, B. (1946). *A History of western philosophy*, New York: Simon and Schuster; London: George Allen and Unwin.

Russell, B. (1919). *Introduction to mathematical philosophy*. London: George Allen and Unwin; New York: The Macmillan Company.

Ryle, G. (1929). Negation. *Aristotelean society*, (Suppl.), *9*, 80–86.

Ryle, G. (1949). *The concept of mind*. New York: Barnes and Noble.

Sahotra, S. (ed.) (1996a). *Logical empiricism at its peak: Schlick, Carnap, and Neurath*. New York: Garland Publishing.

Sahotra, S. (ed.) (1996b). *Decline and obsolescence of logical empiricism: Carnap vs. Quine and the critics*. New York: Garland Publishing.

Samuelson. P. (1937). A note on the measurement of utility. *Review of Economic Studies, 4*, 155–161.

Sanford, A. J., Moxey, L. M., and Paterson, K. B. (1994). Psychological studies of quantifiers. *Journal of Semantics, 11*, 153 – 171.

Sanford, A. J., Moxey, L. M., and Paterson K. B. (1996). Attentional focusing with quantifiers in production and comprehension. *Memory and Cognition, 24*, 144–155.

Savage, L. J. (1954). *The foundations of statistics*. New York: Wiley.

Schank. R. C. and Abelson, R. P. (1977). *Scripts, plans, goals and understanding*. Hillsdale, NJ: Lawrence Erlbaum Associates.

Schell, E.D, (1960). Samuel Pepys, Isaac Newton, and Probability. *American Statistician, 14,* 27–30.

Schiffer, S. (1987). *Remnants of meaning*. Cambridge, Mass: MIT Press.

Schroyens, W. and Schaeken, W. (2003). A critique of Oaksford, Chater and Larkin's (2000) conditional probability model of conditional reasoning. *Journal of Experimental Psychology: Learning, Memory and Cognition, 29,* 140–149.

Schroyens, W., Schaeken, W., Fias, W., and d'Ydewalle, G. (2000a). Heuristic and analytic processes in conditional reasoning with negatives. *Journal of Experimental Psychology: Learning, Memory and Cognition, 26,* 1713–1734.

Schroyens, W., Verschueren, N., Schaeken, W., and d'Ydewalle, G. (2000b). Conditional reasoning with negations: implicit and explicit affirmation or denial and the role of contrast classes. *Thinking and Reasoning, 6,* 221–251.

Schroyens, W., Schaeken, W., and d'Ydewalle, G. (2001a). The processing of negations in conditional reasoning: a meta-analytic study in mental models and/or mental logic theory. *Thinking and Reasoning, 7,* 121–172.

Schroyens, W., Schaeken, W., and d'Ydewalle, G. (2001b). *A meta-analytic review of conditional reasoning by model and/or rule: mental models theory revised*. Manuscript submitted for publication. (http://www.psy.kuleuven.ac.be/~walters/ cognition.pdf).

Schustack, M. W. and Sternberg, R. J. (1981). Evaluation of evidence in causal inference. *Journal of Experimental Psychology: General, 110,* 101–120.

Scruton, R. (1982). *A short history of modern philosophy: from Descartes to Wittgenstein*. London: Routledge.

Seidenberg, M. S. and MacDonald, M. C. (1999). A probabilistic constraints approach to language acquisition and processing. *Cognitive Science, 23,* 569–588.

Sellars, W. (1956). Empiricism and the philosophy of mind. In H. Feigl and M. Scriven (ed.), *Minnesota studies in the philosophy of science*, vol. 1. (pp. 253–329) Minneapolis: University of Minesota Press.

Sellen, J., Oaksford, M., and Gray, N. (2005). Schizotypy and conditional inference. *Schizophrenia Bulletin, 31,* 1–12.

Sells, S. B. (1936). The atmosphere effect: an experimental study of reasoning. *Archives of Psychology, 200.*

Shafer, G. (1976). *A mathematical theory of evidence*. Princeton, NJ: Princeton University Press.

Shanks, D. R. (1995). *The psychology of associative learning*. Cambridge: Cambridge University Press.

Shanks, D. R. Holyoak, K. J., and Medin, D. L. (ed.) (1996). *The psychology of learning and motivation*, vol. 34: *Causal learning*. San Diego, CA: Academic Press.

Shannon, C. E. and Weaver, W. (1949). *The mathematical theory of communication*. Urbana: University of Illinois Press.

Shaw, V. F. and Johnson-Laird, P. N. (1998). Dispelling the 'atmosphere' effect in reasoning. In A. C. Quelhas and F. Pereira (ed.), *Analise psicologia, special issue on cognition and context* (pp. 169–199).

Shieber, S., Schabes, Y., and Pereira, F. C.N. (1995). Principles and implementation of deductive parsing. *Journal of Logic Programming, 24*, 3–36.

Shepard, R. N. (1992). The perceptual organization of colors: an adaptation to the regularities of the terrestrial world? In J. H. Barkow, L. Cosmides and J. Tooby (ed.), *The adapted mind* (pp.495–532). New York: Oxford University Press.

Sher, S. and McKenzie, C. R. M. (In press). Information leakage from logically equivalent frames. *Cognition.*

Shiffrin, R. M. and Steyvers, M. (1998). The effectiveness of retrieval from memory. In M. Oaksford and N. Chater (ed.), *Rational models of cognition* (pp. 73–95). Oxford, UK: Oxford University Press.

Shortliffe, E. and Buchanan, B. G. (1990). A model of inexact reasoning in medicine. In G. Shafer and J. Pearl (ed.), *Uncertain reasoning* (pp. 259–273). San Mateo, CA: Morgan Kaufman.

Simon, H. A. (1955). A behavioral model of rational choice. *Quarterly Journal of Economics, 69*, 99–118.

Simon, H. A. (1956). Rational choice and the structure of the environment. *Psychological Review, 63*, 129–138.

Simoncelli, E. P. and Olshausen, B. A. (2001). Natural image statistics and neural representation. *Annual Review of Neuroscience, 24*, 1193–1216.

Skyrms, B. (1977). *Choice and chance.* Belmont: Wadsworth.

Slater, H. (2004). Ramsey's tests. *Synthèse, 141*, 431–444.

Sloman, S. A. (1996). The empirical case for two systems of reasoning. *Psychological Review, 119*, 3–22.

Sloman, S. A. (2005). *Causal models: how people think about the world and its alternatives.* New York: Oxford University Press.

Smedslund, J. (1970). Circular relation between understanding and logic. *Scandinavian Journal of Psychology, 2*, 217–219.

Snippe, H. P., Poot, L., and Van Hateren, J. H. (2000). A temporal model for early vision that explains detection thresholds for light pulses on flickering backgrounds. *Visual Neuroscience, 17*, 449–462.

Sobel, J. H. (2004). *Probable modus ponens and modus tollens and updating on uncertain evidence.* Unpublished manuscript, Department of Philosophy, University of Toronto, Scarborough. (www.scar.toronto.ca/~sobel/ConfDisconf.pdf).

Sobel, D., Tenenbaum, J., and Gopnik, A. (2004). Children's causal inferences from indirect evidence: backwards blocking and Bayesian reasoning in preschoolers. *Cognitive Science, 28*, 303–333.

Sober, E. (2002). Intelligent design and probability reasoning. *International Journal for Philosophy of Religion, 52*, 65–80.

Sperber, D., Cara, F., and Girotto, V. (1995). Relevance theory explains the selection task. *Cognition, 57*, 31–95.

Spiegelhalter, D. J. and Lauritzen, S. L. (1990). Sequential updating of conditional probabilities on directed graphical structures. *Networks, 20*, 579–605.

Spirtes, P., Glymour, C., and Scheines, R. (1993). *Causation, prediction and search.* Cambridge, MA: MIT Press.

Stalnaker, R. C. (1968). A theory of conditionals. In N. Rescher (ed.), *Studies in logical theory* (pp. 98–112). *American Philosophical Quarterly Monograph Series, 2*. Oxford: Blackwell.

Stanovich, K. E. and West, R. F. (1998). Cognitive ability and variation in selection task performance. *Thinking and Reasoning, 4*, 193–230.

Stanovich, K. E. and West, R.F (2000). Individual differences in reasoning: implications for the rationality debate? *Behavioral and Brain Sciences, 23*, 645–665.

Stein, E. (1996). *Without good reason: the rationality debate in philosophy and cognitive science*. Oxford: Clarendon Press.

Stenning, K. and Lambalgeln, M. (2004). A little logic goes a long way: basing experiment on semantic theory in the cognitive science of conditional reasoning. *Cognitive Science, 28*, 481–530.

Stenning, K. and Oberlander, J. (1995). A cognitive theory of graphical and linguistic reasoning: Logic and implementation. *Cognitive Science, 19*, 97–140.

Stenning, K. and Yule, P. (1997). Image and language in human reasoning: a syllogistic illustration. *Cognitive Psychology, 34*, 109–15.

Stephens, D. W. and Krebs, J. R. (1986). *Foraging theory*. Princeton University Press, Princeton.

Stevenson, R. J. and Over, D. E. (1995). Deduction from uncertain premises. *The Quarterly Journal of Experimental Psychology, 48A*, 613–643.

Stewart, N., Brown, G. D. A., and Chater, N. (In press). Identification of simple perceptual stimuli: a new model of absolute identification. *Psychological Review, 112*, 881–911

Stewart, N., Chater, N., and Brown, G. D. A. (In press). Decision by sampling. *Cognitive Psychology, 53*, 1–26

Stewart, N., Chater, N., Stott, H. P., and Reimers, S. (2003). Prospect relativity: how choice options influence decision under risk. *Journal of Experimental Psychology: Learning, Memory, and Cognition, 32*, 22 – 46

Steyvers, M., Tenenbaum, J. B., Wagenmakers, J. B., and Blum, B. (2003). Inferring causal networks from observations and interventions. *Cognitive Science, 27*, 453–489.

Stich, S. (1983). *From folk psychology to cognitive science*. Cambridge, MA: MIT Press.

Stich, S. (1985). Could man be an irrational animal? *Synthese, 64*, 115–135.

Stich, S. (1990). *The fragmentation of reason*. Cambridge, Mass.: MIT Press.

Stich, S. and Nisbett, R. (1980). Justification and the psychology of human reasoning. *Philosophy of Science 47*, 188–202.

Sutton, P. and Barto, A. (1981). Towards a modern theory of adaptive networks: expectation and prediction. *Psychological Review, 88*, 135–170.

Tenenbaum, J. B. (1999). A Bayesian framework for concept learning. Ph.D. Thesis, Department of Brain and Cognitive Sciences, MIT.

Tenenbaum, J. B. and Griffiths, T. L. (2001). Generalization, similarity, and Bayesian inference. *Behavioral and Brain Sciences, 24*, 629–641.

Thagard, P. (1988). *Computational philosophy of science*. Cambridge, MA: MIT Press.

Thompson, V. A. (1994). Interpretational factors in conditional reasoning. *Memory and Cognition, 22*, 742–758.

Thompson, V. A. and Mann, J. (1995). Perceived necessity explains the dissociation between logic and meaning: the case of 'only if'. *Journal of Experimental Psychology: Learning, Memory and Cognition, 21*, 1554–1567.

Tirole, J. (1986). Hierarchies and bureaucracies. *Journal of Law, Economics, and Organization, 2*, 181.

Toulmin, S. (1961). *Forecast and understanding*. Bloomington, IN: Indiana University Press.

Turvey, M. T., Shockley, K., and Carello, C. (1999). Affordance, proper function, and the physical basis of perceived heaviness. *Cognition, 17*, B17-B26.

Tversky, A. and Khaneman, D. (1974). Availability: a heuristic for judging frequency and probability. *Cognitive Psychology, 5*, 207–232.

Tversky, A. and Kahneman, D. (1986). Rational choice and the framing of decisions. *Journal of Business, 59*, 251–278.

Tversky, T., Geisler, W. S., and Perry, J. S. (2004). Contour grouping: closure effects are explained by good continuation and proximity. *Vision Research, 44*, 2769–2777.

Ullman, S. (1980). Against direct perception. *Behavioral and Brain Sciences, 3*, 373–415.

Van der Helm, P. A. (2000). Simplicity versus likelihood in visual perception: from surprisals to precisals. *Psychological Bulletin, 126*, 770–800.

Van der Helm, P. A. and Leeuwenberg, P. A. (1996). Goodness of visual regularities: a non–transformational approach. *Psychological Review, 103*, 429 – 496.

Van Frassen, B. C. (1980). *The scientific image*. Oxford: Oxford University Press.

Vapnik, V. (1998). *The nature of statistical learning theory*. New York: Springer–Verlag.

Vapnik, V. N. and Chervonenkis, A. Y. (1971). On the uniform convergence of relative frequencies of events to their probabilities. *Theory of Probability and its Applications, 16*, 264–281.

Veltman, F. (1985). *Logics for Conditionals*. Unpublished PhD. thesis. University of Amsterdam.

Von Helmholtz, H. (1910/1962). *Treatise on physiological optics*, vol. 3 (ed. and trans., J. P. Southall). New York: Dover.

Von Mises, R. (1939). *Probability, statistics, and truth*. New York: Macmillan.

Von Neumann, J. and O. Morgenstern (1944). *Theory of games and economic behavior*. Princeton, NJ: Princeton University Press.

Wagner, C. G. (2004). Modus tollens probabilized. *British Journal for Philosophy of Science, 55*, 747–753.

Waldmann, M. R. and Martignon, L. (1998). A Bayesian network model of causal learning. In M. A. Gernsbacher and S. J. Derry (ed.), *Proceedings of the Twentieth Annual Conference of the Cognitive Science Society* (pp. 1102–1107). Mahwah, NJ: Erlbaum.

Wallis, J. W. and Shortliffe, E. H. (1985). Customized explanations using causal knowledge. In B. G. Buchanan and E. H. Shortliffe (ed.), *Rule based expert systems: the MYCIN experiments of the Stanford Heuristic Programming Project* (pp. 371—390). Reading, MA: Addison Wesley.

Walton, D. (2004). A new dialectical theory of explanation. *Philosophical explorations, 7*, 71– 89.

Wason, P. C. (1960). On the failure to eliminate hypotheses in a conceptual task. *Quarterly Journal of Experimental Psychology, 12*, 129–140.

Wason, P. C. (1968). Reasoning about a rule. *Quarterly Journal of Experimental Psychology, 20*, 273–281.

Wason, P. C. (1972). In real life negatives are false. *Logique et Analyse, XV*, 17–38.

Wason, P. C. and Brooks, P. G. (1979). THOG: the anatomy of a problem. *Psychological Research, 41*, 79–90.

Wason, P. C. and Evans, J. St. B. T. (1975). Dual processes in reasoning? *Cognition, 3*, 141–154.

Wason, P. C. and Green, D. W. (1984). Reasoning and mental representation. *Quarterly Journal of Experimental Psychology, 36A*, 598–611.

Wason, P. C. and Johnson-Laird, P. N. (1970). A theoretical analysis of insight into a reasoning task. *Cognitive Psychology, 1*, 134–148.

Wason, P. C. and Johnson-Laird, P. N. (1972). *Psychology of reasoning: structure and content.* London: Batsford.

Wason, P. C. and Shapiro, D. (1971). Natural and contrived experience in a reasoning problem. *Quarterly Journal of Experimental Psychology, 23*, 63–71.

Wayne, A. (1995). Bayesianism and diverse evidence. *Philosophy of Science, 62*, 111–121.

Weiss, Y. (1997). Interpreting images by propagating Bayesian beliefs. In M. C. Mozer, M. I. Jordan, and T. Petsche (ed.), *Advances in neural information processing systems, 9*, 908–915. Cambridge MA: MIT Press

Wetherick, N. E. (1989). Psychology and syllogistic reasoning. *Philosophical Psychology, 2*, 111–124.

Wetherick, N. E. (1993). Human rationality. In K. I. Manktelow and D. E. Over (ed.), *Rationality* (pp. 83–109). London, UK: Routledge.

Wetherick, N. E. and Gilhooly, K. (1990). Syllogistic reasoning: Effects of premise order. In K. Gilhoody, M.T. G. Keane, R. Logie, and G. Erdos (eds.), *Lines of Thought, Vol. 1.* London, UK: John Wiley.

Wiener, N. (1948). *Cybernetics.* New York: Wiley.

Wildman, T. M. and Fletcher, H. J. (1977). Developmental increases and decreases in solutions of conditional syllogism problems. *Developmental Psychology, 13*, 630–636.

Williamson, O. (1964). *The economics of discretionary behavior: managerial objectives in a theory of the firm.* Englewood Cliffs, NJ: Prentice-Hall.

Williamson, O. (1985). *The economic institutions of capitalism.* New York: Free Press.

Winograd, T. and Flores, F. (1986). *Understanding computers and cognition.* Norwood, NJ: Ablex.

Wobcke, W. (1995). Belief revision, conditional logic and nonmonotonic reasoning. *Notre Dame Journal of Formal Logic, 36*, 55–103.

Wolf, F. M. (1986). *Meta-analysis: quantitative methods for research synthesis.* Newbury Park, CA: Sage.

Woods, W. A. (1975). *What's in a Link: foundations for semantic networks.* Cambridge, MA: Bolt, Beranek and Newman.

Woodworth, R. S. and Sells, S. B. (1935). An atmosphere effect in syllogistic reasoning. *Journal of Experimental Psychology, 18*, 451–460.

Yama, H. (2001). Matching versus optimal data selection in the Wason selection task. *Thinking and Reasoning, 7*, 295–311.

Young, R. (1998). Rational analysis of exploratory choice. In M. Oaksford and N. Chater (ed.), *Rational models of cognition* (pp.469–500). Oxford, UK: Oxford University Press.

Yuille, A. and Kersten, D. (2006). Vision as Bayesian inference: Analysis by synthesis? *Trends in Cognitive Sciences, 10,* 301–308.

Zeelenberg, M., Van Dijk, W. W., Manstead, A. S. R., and Van der Pligt, J. (2000). On bad decisions and disconfirmed expectancies: the psychology of regret and disappointment. *Cognition and Emotion, 14,* 521–541.

Index